CW01369755

TUBE GUITAR AMPLIFIER ESSENTIALS

Kendrick Books
531 Country Road 3300
Kempner, Texas
76539-5755
© 2004 Gerald Weber

All rights reserved.
No part of this book covered by the copyrights hereon may be reproduced or copied in any form or by any means, or stored in a database or retrieval system whatsoever without written permission, except in the case of brief quotations embodied in critical articles and reviews. For information contact the publisher.

ISBN: 0-9641060-2-7

Art Direction and production: R. K. Watkins / Corporate Design and Graphics
Printed in the United States of America

Disclaimer: Tube amplifiers contain high voltages which may be lethal, even if the amplifier has been off for some time. We do not recommend that you open your amplifier or try to perform any repair operations unless you are properly trained in electronic servicing. Gerald Weber and Kendrick Books accept no responsibility for accidents resulting in personal injury or destruction of property. Again, there are large voltages present in your amplifier that can kill, even with your amplifier unplugged from the wall.

Dedication

I dedicate this book to my wife and soulmate, Jill Kendrick Weber.

Acknowledgement

In no particular order:

Jill Kendrick Weber, my devoted wife and soulmate, for her constant unselfish support.

Billy "F" Gibbons, my tone hero, for defining that good "Texas tone" back in 1970 at the Town House in Groves, Texas.

Terry Oubre, the worlds best guitarist, for his support and valuable insight.

Robert and Jeanne Watkins for their support and enthusiasm.

Alan and Cleo Greenwood, for publishing the articles from which this book was compiled, in *Vintage Guitar* magazine.

All of the employees at Kendrick for providing me the freedom to spend time on this project.

Everyone else who participated in this book.

Anyone else I forgot to acknowledge.

Preface

Even though it has been well over a decade since my first book, "A Desktop Reference of Hip Vintage Guitar Amps" and nearly a decade since the release of my second book, "Tube Amp Talk for the Guitarist and Tech," I have never stopped writing about Tube Guitar Amplifiers. For nearly two decades I have written two amp columns each month for *Vintage Guitar* Magazine. From these writings, I have combined relevant articles into chapters and woven the chapters into the book you now hold in your hands. How do I know what to write about? It is simple, I write about what comes up and what people ask me about. I work with guitarists everyday to help them get the tone they desire from their tube amp. My tube amp restoration shop and amplifier factory keep me supplied with plenty of topics and food for thought.

Regardless if you are a technician that makes his living by making tube amps sound spectacular, or a collector that wants his collection to "give it up" sonically as well as cosmetically, or a player that realizes his tone is as important as his chops; there is something in here for you. If you are looking for engineering formulas and a bunch of math, you won't find it here. I write from the vantage point of a guitarist wanting to squeeze every ounce of performance from his tube amp — because that's what drives me.

I know that a guitarist always plays better when he sounds better. And oddly enough, when he sounds better he plays better. And I think inspiration occurs when the amp is performing as good as the performer.

Disclaimer: Tube Amplifiers contain potentially lethal high voltages even after they are unplugged, that may cause personal injury or death. Do not attempt to repair or modify any amplifier unless you are absolutely certain that you know what you are doing.

Foreword

    I love great guitar sounds. Great guitar sounds inspire, elevate great performers and manufacturers to legendary status, and in some cases define the sound of a geographic region. Whether it's "Pearly Gates" or the "Woman Tone," just thinking about it makes you want to pick up your guitar and play. The guitar feels so much more vital when the tone is great. It responds to your every nuance, inspiring you to play things you've never played before. This book, from the world's leading authority on tube amps, Gerald Weber, is an edited compilation of over eight years of two Vintage Guitar columns. It's filled with tips for anybody who loves to work on and play through tube amps as much as I do. Achieving great tone is a never-ending search for perfection, and with this book you will be many steps closer.
    Good Luck
    Joe Bonamassa

SECTION I
GETTING THE MOST FROM YOUR AMP

Tube Amps of our Times — Vintage vs. Modern vs. Boutique	19
Getting the Most from Your Tube Guitar Amp	25
"Playing" Your Tube Amp	31
Fine Tuning Your Amp Setup	37
Fine Tuning Your Amp Tone	45
Adjusting a Tube Amp for Tone	51
Tube Amp Basics	57

SECTION II
TIPS FOR THE NON-TECHNICAL GUITARIST

Making Sense of Tube Amp Talk	65
Amp Tips for the Technically Challenged	85
Tube Amp Tips Every Guitarist Should Know	91
Servicing Tube Amps: Getting Started	97

SECTION III
THE FOUR PARTS OF A GUITAR AMPLIFIER

Basic Preamp Tube Amplification for Guitar Amplifiers	107
Basic Output Tube Amplification for Guitar Amplifiers	113
Basic Power Supplies for Guitar Amplifiers	119
Speakers and How They Affect Tone	125

SECTION IV
BIASING

More on Bias Explained and Defined	133
Fixed Bias vs. Cathode Bias	139

SECTION V
CAPACITORS

Everything You Always Wanted to Know about Capacitors	147
What You Should Know About Coupling Capacitors	153

SECTION VI
RECTIFIERS

Converting a Solid State Rectifier to Tube	161
The Port Arthur Rectifier	167

Section VII
TUBES

The 12AX7 Preamp Tube	173
Tube Substitutions in Guitar Amps	179
Current EL34 Tube Tests	183
Tests of Current and Old Style 6L6 Tubes	187

Section VIII
TRANSFORMERS

Transformer Questions Answered	197

Section IX
SPEAKERS

What Guitar Players Should Know about Speaker Impedance	205
Easy Speaker Fixes	217

Section X
TROUBLESHOOTING

Simple Amp Troubleshooting Techniques You Should Know	223
Simplifying the Electronics Math	227
Guerrilla Troubleshooting	231
Taming the Parasitic Beast	239

Section XI
MODIFICATIONS

Correcting the Vintage Amp Deficiencies	251
Amplifier Bloopers and Their Corrections	257
Getting the Tone you Don't Have	261
Hot Rodding Your Vintage Tubes Guitar Amp for More Gain	267
What To Do "After" the Blackface Mod	273
Tweed Deluxe Tone from a Black or Silverface Amp	279
Harp Amp Secrets and Tips	285
"Beefing Up" Your Tube Guitar Amp for More Headroom	291
Converting Your Normal Channel to British	297
Save that Blackface Deluxe	303
Adjustable Fixed Bias for Small Practice Amps	309
Adjustable Fixed Bias for your Non-adjustable Fixed Bias Amp	315

SECTION XII
AMP BUILDING

Ten Amp Building Tricks	323
Amplifiers Circuit Layouts	329
Tube Guitar Amp Power Supplies	335
Vintage Tube Amp Design Flaws	341
Voicing a Tube Guitar Amplifier	347
Conversations for Tone	361

SECTION XIII
QUESTIONS AND ANSWERS

Fender	379
Gibson	432
Silvertone	441
Other American	446
Marshall	462
Other British	474
Speaker Questions	478
Transformer Questions	488
Miscellaneous	495
Gerald Weber's Next Phase	515
A Final Word From The Author	520
Index	523

Getting the Most From Your Amp

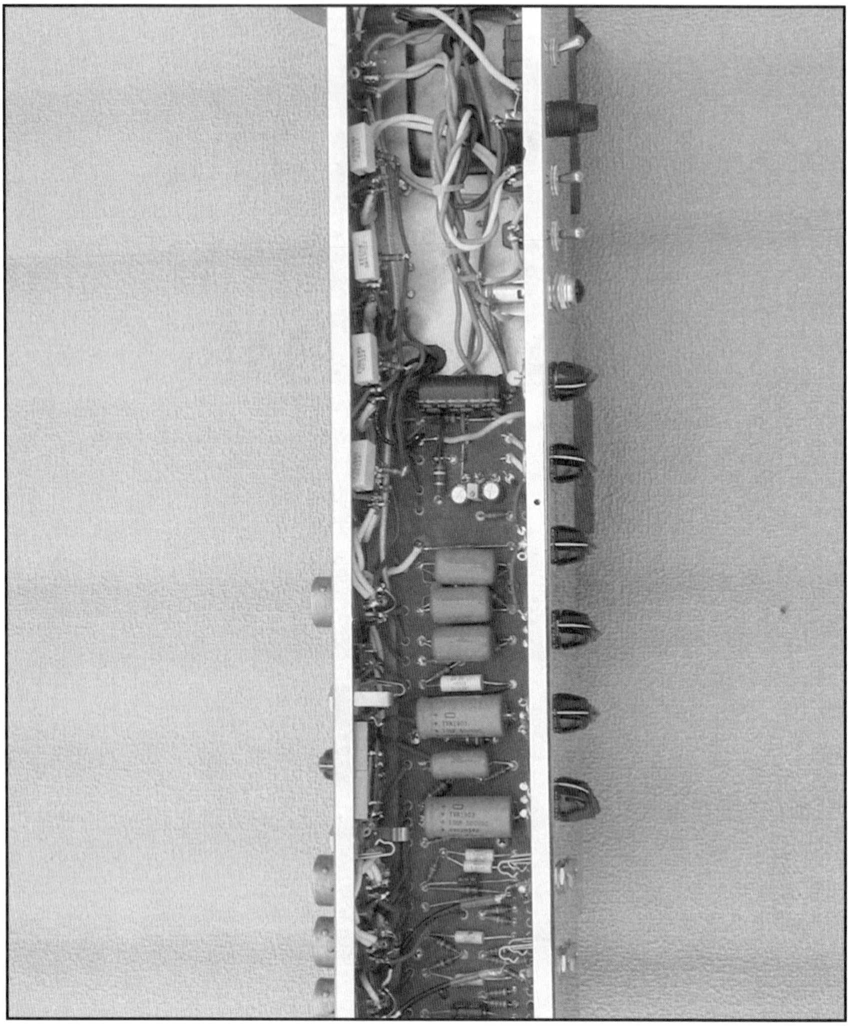

TUBE AMPS OF OUR TIMES—VINTAGE VS. MODERN VS. BOUTIQUE

What makes an electric guitar "electric" is the fact that it is amplified using electricity. For the first 40 years or so, all guitar amplifiers were made using electronic vacuum tubes. Mid twentieth-century vacuum tube companies such as RCA, wanting to create a better market for their tube products, published example tube circuits for use as audio amplifiers, radios, oscillators, preamp gain stages, and many others. Pioneer tube guitar amplifier companies copied the recommended circuits developed and published by the vacuum tube companies. Early Fender, Gibson, Rickenbacker, National, Supro, Danelectro, and Ampeg circuits can be found in suggested tube manual example circuits.

The tube companies developed these example circuits by copying the basics and adding slight modifications. For example, Leo Fender added treble and bass tone controls to his designs. In the later 50s, the oscillator was added to produce vibrato. Sometimes an extra channel was added. Players needed the extra channel, because in the early days there were no PA systems and the bands needed a microphone for the vocals.

Having grown up in the fifties and sixties, I can remember seeing bands that the guitar player plugged his guitar into one channel and his microphone into the other. Everyone used high impedance microphones back then. The volume levels were very low by today's standards.

The essence of these early vintage amps was a modest (and under-filtered) power supply, a small and cheap power and output transformer, and low preamp gain. Since no one played very loud, the power supplies in these early amps did not need a lot of filtering.

Filtering is a function of current and low volume amps don't draw much current. Also, transformers are perhaps the most expensive component in a vacuum tube amplifier. Because the amplifiers were not played very loud, and because transformers are expensive, the early designers used the smallest and cheapest transformers. This kept the cost down and seemed to do the job.

WHICH CAME FIRST THE CHICKEN OR THE EGG?

You might think, how did the early tube amp designers know that the tone of their amps would become classic? Since all early electric guitar recordings were made using vacuum tube amps that were configured in "Western Electric" style circuitry, I propose that after listening to "Western Electric" style, vacuum tube amps for 40 years, "that tone" became the definition of electric guitar tone. It was familiar and it felt good. Perhaps if we had listened to transistor amps for 40 years and then later discovered tubes, we may have thought the tube amps were too "rich" sounding and not "thin" enough!! Yes, the tube amps had too much "character."

TRANSISTORS ARE BETTER!

There was a period from the early 70s to the late 80s when tube amps were not that popular. Transistor amps were cheaper to build. For one thing, they didn't need an output transformer and the transistors themselves only cost only a few pennies. Amplifier manufacturers could earn huge profits if they could get these cheap amps on the market and make them popular. I remember a famous manufacturer of transistor amps telling me that he could sell cheaper and still double his profits on transistor amps and "99% of the players couldn't hear the difference." I remember the magazine ads that ridiculed players that used tube amps.

Rack-mounted systems with rack-mounted effects and transistor power amps became very popular by the 80s. It was starting to look like transistors were here to stay.

Let's "fast forward" to 1989. It was about this time that I built the Kendrick 2410, the first "tube rectified" new guitar amp design in over a decade. Brad Jeters had started the original Bedrock Amplifier Company. His original designs were similar to a Fender 5F8A Tweed

Twin, but with EL34 output tubes and a solid-state rectifier. Andy Marshall of THD fame had designed and built his modern vintage printed circuit board amp and Fender had come out with a reissue printed circuit board Bassman. It was also about this time that Mark Sampson had developed the first Matchless DC30 amplifier. The DC30, inspired by the AC30, was point-to-point wired and had a rectifier tube! Things were about to change back to tubes, however they changed back in two different directions.

THE MODERN TUBE AMP

Modern tube amps consists mostly of printed circuit board designs with hip, modern, features such as: effects loops, channel switching, distortion, reverb, etc. Some of the modern designs use op amps and transistors in combination with tubes. These amps are popular because they are relatively cheap, offer many features, sound OK in most instances, and are very profitable for the dealers that sell them.

Many modern amps are made in foreign or third world countries. The components are bought from the lowest bidder (almost always from a different foreign country). These amps are built using high-volume production techniques. Some of these cheaper techniques might include: surface mounting of components, push-on connectors, snap-in fuse holders, printed circuit boards, PCB mounted potentiometers, wave flow soldering. These production techniques allow manufacturers to make amps very cheaply. The dealers can still mark them up considerably; yet sell for very competitive pricing. Since 99% of the people can't really tell the difference, these products sell in large quantities and make up the bulk of tube amps sold today.

Amps made with the high volume production techniques never last very long or sound very good. Wave flow solder joints are not known for their longevity and the joints sometimes crack at stress points. Snap-in components snap out or otherwise come unsnapped. Circuit boards can warp from heat, or traces can come off the board.

Because these modern amps are not designed to ever service, technicians hate to work on these types of modern amps. If there is a component that needs to be replaced, usually the entire amp must be disassembled to get to the part. So it ends up taking 2 hours to do a 2 minute solder job.

THE BOUTIQUE AMP

The boutique amp can be considered the other path of tube amp design. Boutique amps are built up to a standard and not down to a price. Almost all boutique amps keep semiconductor devices out of the signal path and therefore do not use op amps or transistors. Boutique amps are always point-to-point wired using brass eyelets, turrets, or terminal strip construction. These amps almost always have massive power supplies with oversized transformers. The boutique designers learned long ago that the transformer, though expensive, is the most important factor in an amplifier's tone. Good sounding ones cost money and are necessary if the amp is to sound its best. Even the power transformers are usually rated for much more power than actually needed. This gives punch and responsiveness. These hearty power supplies allow the tubes to have the power they need to do their job most efficiently. Higher valued filter caps for the main B+ supply are the norm on boutique amps. They allow the boutique amps to have more sting in the attack while having less 120 hertz ripple current. Beefy filtering keeps the tones pure and in-tune with themselves.

With boutique amps, there is usually a minimum of circuitry. Less is more. Features that degrade the signal path, such as channel switching, are rarely if ever used.

All boutique amps are either easy to adjust the bias or self-biased. The circuits are basic "Western Electric" style — but tweaked by ear to the designer's taste.

SUMMARY

Although vacuum tube amplifiers dominated the first 40 years of electric guitar amplification, manufacturers still attempted to steer the players away from tube circuits in favor of cheap transistor amps and huge corporate profits. Eventually the players went right back to vacuum tubes. The vintage tube amp, the modern tube amp and the boutique amp have some common ground but are very different just the same.

Vintage amps will need servicing. Just like an old car, there are constant problems with old electronic devices. A vintage amp will need an overhaul and it is best to recap all electrolytic capacitors. The main filter caps should be increased in value to account for the fact that the amplifier will be played harder today than it was in its day. Speakers almost always blow. The paper bobbin voice coil former in almost all vintage speakers can get very brittle after 30 to 50 years. Have you ever seen a piece of 40-year-old paper? If you are going to play a vintage amp, you should replace the speakers before you blow them. That way, you will have the original speakers should you ever want to sell the amp.

The modern amps are fine for those on a limited budget but require many features. The amps won't last long and when they break, will cost dearly to service, but they offer bang for the immediate buck — like a disposable razor.

The boutique amps are the coolest, will sound the best and last the longest. The price of a boutique amp will approach the cost of a vintage amp plus an overhaul. Of course, the boutique amp will be new and have an extra 50 or so years of life.

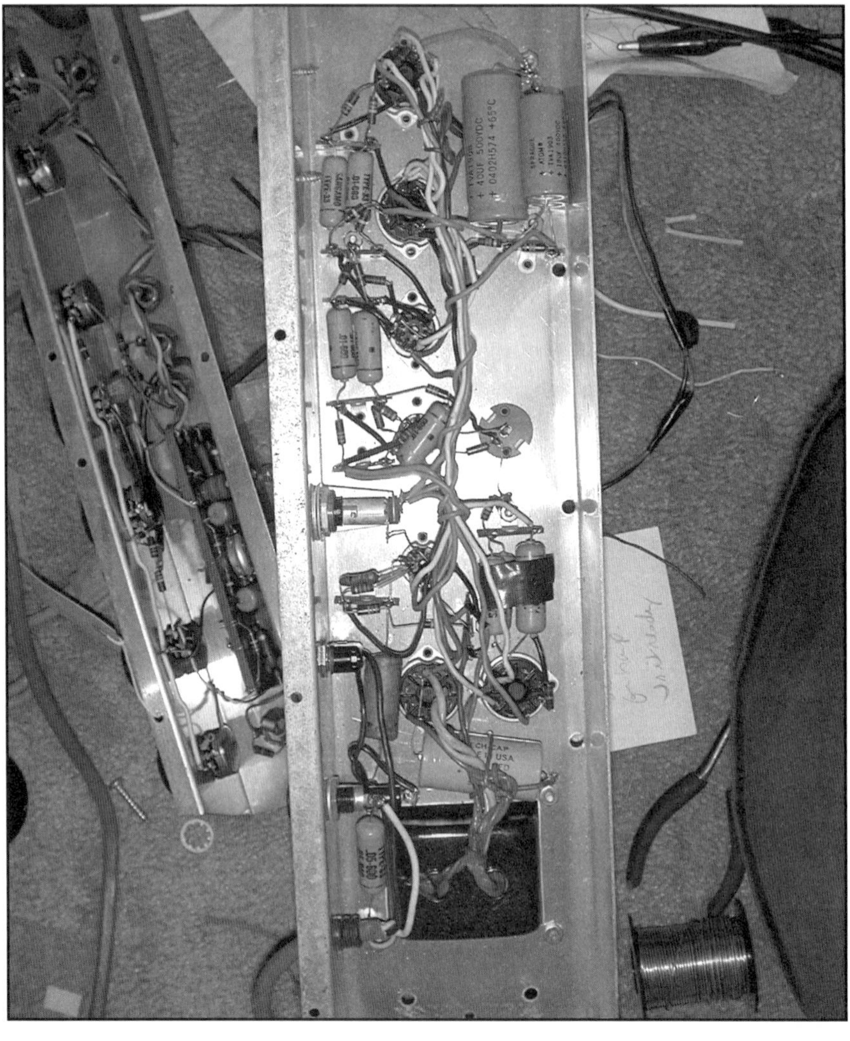

GETTING THE MOST FROM YOUR TUBE GUITAR AMP

When I was growing up in the fifties, almost every family in America owned a black and white vacuum tube television set. Ours was a Silvertone (Sears and Roebuck) with a beautiful korina wood cabinet and a very small round picture tube. When our family T.V. would malfunction, my dad would simply remove the 25 or 30 tubes from the T.V. and bring them (in a paper grocery bag) to the drugstore for testing. There would be a vacuum tube tester at the drugstore and an inventory of tubes for sale. The tubes that tested weak or bad were simply replaced with new tubes and most of the time, this would fix the T.V.

A vacuum tube guitar amp is very similar to our old black and white tube television in that when a vacuum tube guitar amp malfunctions, most of the time, the problem is tube related.

Preamp tubes sometimes become noisy or microphonic. The driver tube (phase inverter), which drives the output tubes can lose output and fail to deliver the full signal to the output tubes. In this case, it doesn't matter how good the output tubes are. If the output tubes are not receiving the full input signal from the driver, the result will be less than optimum.

Output tubes begin to lose power after a while. Worst yet, they can short and take out the associated screen resistor (usually the 470 ohm or 1000 ohm resistor mounted to pin #4 of the tube sockets) or hum balance resistor (these are the 100 ohm or 200 ohm resistors that balance hum from the 6.3 volt filament supply). Sometimes the fuse will blow.

Rectifier tubes can arc which also could blow the fuse. Rectifier tubes can also get weak and deliver less than optimum voltage. Both output tubes and rectifier tubes can "get loose" internally, and resonate to certain low frequencies causing a rattle on top of the note. This sometimes sounds like a speaker problem even though it is tube related.

Unfortunately, there is nothing that any of us can do to prevent the inevitable. The tubes will eventually wear out. Tubes, like tires on a car, will last according to how they are driven. Drive them fast and hard (loud) and they won't last as long. Baby them and drive them soft (read not very loud) and they could last for years. None last forever.

GET YOURSELF SOME GOOD TUBES

Most of us got a tube amp in the first place because we like the sound of tubes. Wouldn't it then follow to re-tube the amp with good sounding tubes? The tonal quality of a vacuum tube deteriorates as hours and abuses are put on the tube. That is to say that new output tubes sound very differently than the same brand that has been played loudly for 1,000 hours. Ok, good tubes cost good money. Get over it; you simply will not get what the amp can give without using good sounding tubes.

BASIC CARE

When choosing a place to store your amp, ask yourself this question, "Self, would I sleep here?" If the answer is "no," don't leave your amp there. Extremes of temperature or humidity are bad for your amp and bad for your speakers. We certainly don't want rust on the transformers. And you don't need the snap, crackle, pop of humidity in the resistors. You don't need speakers with mushy cones. Specifically, don't leave your amp in a damp basement or overnight in the trunk of an automobile or an equipment trailer.

If you are forced to put an amp in a cold environment, which may occur during transit (read trunk of the car in February), do not plug the amp in right away. Let it warm up to room temperature before attempting to plug it in. If the amp is colder than the dew point of the room it is in, moisture (dew) will condense on the internal components. This could cause many awful problems not limited to rusting, noise, and arcing.

HOW'S THE SPEAKER?

The obvious fact is this: the speaker is what is vibrating the air and therefore is responsible for the sound you are hearing. Just as water will not rise above its source, an amp will not sound any better than its speaker. Stated another way, the speaker is the final filter that colors the sound. If it has no liveliness or is dull sounding, your amp cannot sound any better.

In older vintage speakers, sometimes the speaker may not be blown but the gap energy is gone. It's hard to be inspired when playing a lifeless speaker. Do yourself a favor, if you have a vintage tube amp with a crappy sounding speaker, replace the speaker and save the original. (If you ever decide to sell the amp you can offer it with the original speaker.)

CHOOSING THE RIGHT AMPS

There is no one perfect amp. Tube amps have personalities that are appropriate for certain tones. For example, an amp with a spongy power supply and an abundance of compression (read Silvertone amp in a guitar case or Fender Tweed Deluxe) may work great when going for a Ry Cooder slide tone, but would not work at all for doing precision Eric Johnson fast licks. If the licks are fast with precision, a tighter envelope (less sponginess and less compression and quicker response) may work better.

An amp with lots of chime and scooped mids (read blackface Fender) may work better for clean than overdrive. An amp with lots of midrange bark doesn't work well for closely voiced dissonant harmonies. (In this case, the mids fatten the note so much that in close voicing, each note will compete for space and try to crowd each other out; then none of it sounds good. An amp with more space in the mids allows each note a place to live, without being crowded out.

I am somewhat amused when people ask me what is the perfect amp. When selecting a tube amp, one should consider the situation and choose the appropriate amp for the occasion. If you are playing at home and there are others living in the same house, you may want to either use a lower wattage amp or higher wattage amp with a power attenuator. This will allow you to get output tube overdrive without blowing everyone out of the house.

On the other hand, when playing out, you should use an amp that is loud enough to keep the respect of the drummer. Another option is to use a lower wattage amp, but mike it and pump some of the sound through the monitors so that it feels right on stage.

GET AN OVERHAUL

Nothing lasts forever. If you are going to play a vintage amp, get it overhauled. I've heard collectors object to getting an overhaul because they didn't want to change any of the original caps, resistors, etc. I guess that's OK if you never intend to ever use the amp again. If you have caps that are ruptured on the ends and chemicals are bleeding out, your amp has already lost its original caps. I can assure you that these caps were not worn out and ruptured when they left the factory. If a resistor is burnt, cooked or drifted in tolerance—that isn't original either. If you drove a 1959 T bird, would you insist on using the original battery, brake shoes, spark plugs, radiator hose and fan belts even though they were all non-functional? Your amp will not be its best until the bad components are replaced.

PLEASE YOURSELF

Tube amp tone is personal. Your amp has to "feel right" to you, for you to experience your own musicality as inspiration. You may want to personalize the tone by substituting other brands and/or types of compatible rectifier tubes, output tubes and preamp tubes. I have written another chapter on this, but in general; 12AU7, 12AY7, 12AT7 and 12AX7 tubes all have the same pin out and can be substituted for each other. The gain characteristics are different, the 12AU7 having the least gain, ascending to the 12AX7, which has the most gain.

Similarly, many output tubes are interchangeable as well. For example, the KT66, EL37, 5881, 6550 and 7581A all have identical pin outs to the 6L6GC. With only a re-bias, these tubes can be substituted for tonal variations.

BIAS THE OUTPUT STAGE

You wouldn't think of replacing the carburetor or fuel injectors in your car and then not doing an idle adjustment. If the car idled correctly at all, it would be an accident. Biasing the output tubes sets the idle level of the tube. Figure it this way; a tube is an electronic valve. Turn the valve all the way "on" and we have a condition called "saturation." In this condition, the current is flowing as much as possible. We simply cannot let any more current flow. On the other hand, all the way "off" is called "cutoff." Once something is "off," it cannot become any more "off." In this condition, current ceases to flow. Biasing the output tubes simply adjusts the "no signal, just idling current" to somewhere about half way between saturation and cutoff. Your amp will not sound its best if it is under-biased or over-biased. One way causes premature saturation and you lose your clean tone; the bottom end will especially suffer. The other way will sound cold with no sustain and buzziness following the note.

As the amp wears in, it will need to be re-biased. Biasing an amp can be fun and very easy to learn. Complete instructions appear in my second instructional video, "Basic Tube Guitar Amplifier Servicing and Overhaul" and on page 101 of my first book, *A Desktop Reference of Hip Vintage Guitar Amps*.

If you don't care to learn how to bias an amp, find someone close to you that can. Your amp cannot sound its best without proper biasing.

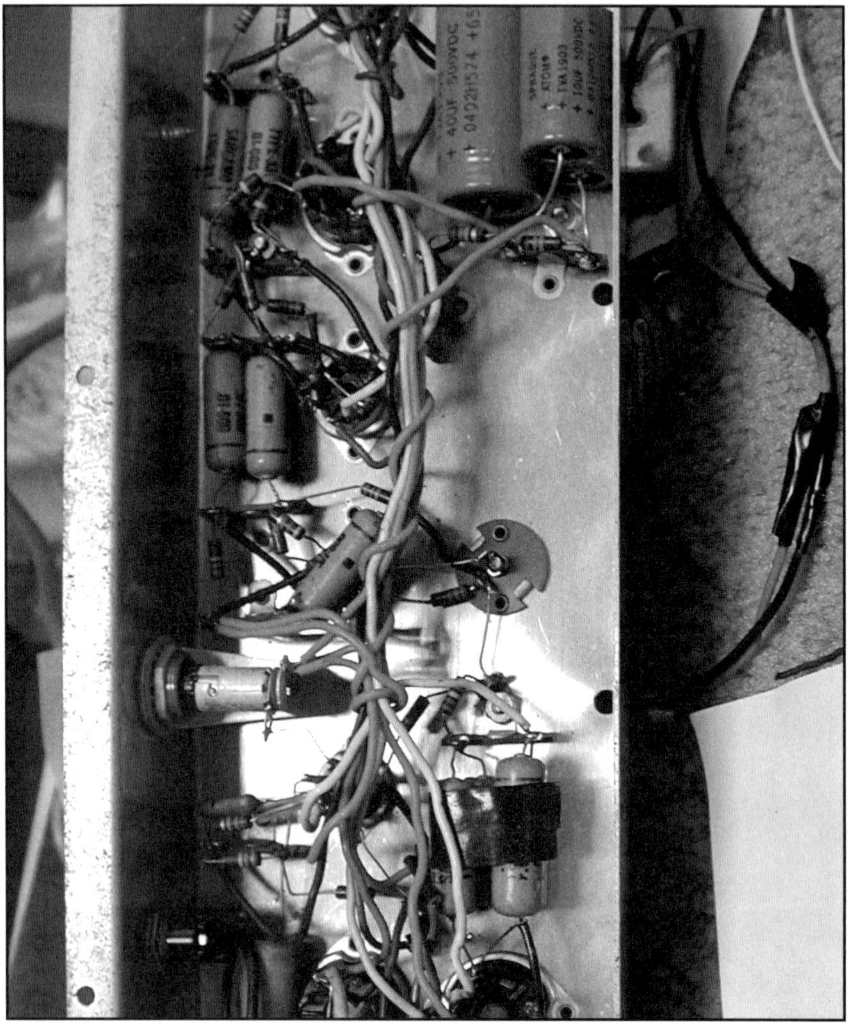

"PLAYING" YOUR TUBE AMP

Many of us plug into our amplifiers and expect to automatically sound good. A tube amplifier is not just something to amplify sound! An amplifier is as much a part of the "musical instrument" called "the electric guitar" as is the other part called "the guitar." Any musical instrument can sound bad or good depending on the skill of the musician.

For example, my old booking agent, Frank Hawthorne, had a very fine quality violin that he carried with him everywhere he went. Frank was a big man that smoked expensive cigars. He would play this violin under his belly (rather than under his chin) and get a tone that sounded very close to angels singing. However, when I picked up his violin, I could not produce such a tone. It wasn't the violin's fault. Like the violin that can sound either bad or good depending on whose "playing" it, your amplifier produces sounds depending on how it is set and played.

SETTING THE AMPLIFIER'S CONTROLS FOR CLEAN

We want to get a round, rich, natural tone but with enough "space" or "air" to hear every note. If the amplifier has more than one input per channel, it is likely that one input will be full gain and the other minus 3dB gain. Listen to each input and determine which sounds better. Usually, the lower gain input gives the better clean sound. The amplifier may have more than one channel. Listen to each channel and determine which channel sounds better for clean. To sum it up, we want to select the correct input that gives us the best clean sound and we want to select the best channel. Once we have gotten this far, it is time to adjust the controls.

As you turn the volume up on the amplifier, there will become a point when the clean sound begins to distort. The actual setting will depend on who is "playing" the amp. We want to turn up the volume to the threshold of distortion and then back it off until the best clean tone is achieved.

Also the actual gain of a channel will be dependent somewhat on the tone settings. Most amplifiers have subtractive tone controls. That is to say, when you turn down the treble, you are just subtracting treble. If you turn down the midrange, you are subtracting midrange. And the same is true with the bass control. If you turn all the tone controls down, you are subtracting treble, midrange and bass! This means you won't have anything left! This is the case on the Blackface Fenders and many others. For this reason, we might get best results by readjusting the volume control after the tone controls have been fine-tuned.

Generally, dropping the mids out somewhat and turning up the treble will get the cleaner sound. Acoustic guitars have chimey, defined high-end with good bass but with enough "air" to hear every note. This will have to be adjusted by ear but the basic idea is to scoop the mid-range enough to get some "air" in the middle. We may even want to adjust the volume on our guitar, perhaps back it off a number or two and then compensate by turning the amp up slightly.

SETTING YOUR AMPLIFIER FOR OVERDRIVE

When setting a tube amp for overdrive, we are probably going to want to use the higher gain input jack. If the amp has more than one channel, we will want to listen to see which channel lends itself better to overdrive. Keep the volume control on the guitar turned up. Turn the volume control on the amp until it starts breaking up. The actual degree of break-up would depend on how far you turn the amp's volume, and what kind of overdriven sound you are going for.

Turning up the mids makes the amp overdrive better. Sometimes rolling off the tone control on the guitar will smooth out the overdrive tone by reducing high frequencies. We don't want a lot of high-end on an overdrive sound unless we are going for "brittle." In summary: to get it smooth, you may need to roll some high-end off your guitar as well as turn the mid-range up on the amp.

A bass control on a guitar amp is used to compensate for lack of bottom end when the volume is turned down. It is just like on a loudness control on your stereo. As the volume comes down, then the bass should come up. Conversely, when the volume comes up, the bass should come down. Therefore, for an overdrive setting where you are obviously turning the volume up, you should turn the bass control down. Maybe so far down, it is almost off. If you don't drop the bass control when the volume comes up, the bass notes will turn to mush. Ironically, you will actually have more bass by turning the bass control down! Keep your mids turned up and adjust the treble for taste.

SPEAKER PLACEMENT

Proper speaker placement will affect the sound. The high-end is coming out of the center of the speaker. The dispersion angle of the high-end is going to be more acute of an angle, therefore the people standing in front of the amp are going to hear most of the high-end, the people standing on the sides won't hear as much high-end.

Perhaps in a club situation, leaning the cabinet back somewhat so that the high-end bounces off the ceiling may produce a better tone. There is a blues player from east Austin that has his amplifier actually tilted back but facing the back of the band so that it bounces off the back wall. Depending on the room that you are playing in, you may elect to even turn the amp sideways so that the sound is bouncing off a wall.

Although I wouldn't recommend this because of heat dissipation problems, Stevie Ray Vaughan would on occasion, lay his Fender Twin on its back, facing straight up to the ceiling. A mike was placed on top for the soundman, but Stevie's tone was bouncing off the ceiling!

Elevating the amp so that the sound travels over peoples' heads can help throw the sound out there; however, you will get more bottom-end with the amp on a solid floor. This is where you have to look at the situation and do what works.

Here's a trick I learned from a working blues player on 6th Street in Austin. The guy is known for the tone he gets out of his Silverface Deluxe (that I changed to Blackface specs.) The amp has an original JBL 12" speaker. He places his amp slightly tilted back on a chair. The chair is placed facing his back. The amp is aimed directly at his back. This makes the sound bounce off his back, thus dispersing the high-end. When it is time to take a lead, he simply steps away from the front of the amp and the sound goes straight into his vocal mike, thus bumping his solo up through the P.A. Also, the sound is aimed at such an angle, that it goes up over people's heads.

PUTTING IT ALL TOGETHER

Certainly there is plenty to be said about "playing" an amplifier. Certain amplifiers have interactive volume controls, in which case adjusting the volume control that you are NOT USING affects the tone of the channel you are using! If your amp has interactive volume controls, by all means, adjust the other volume control.

Many other amps have certain settings that sound bad. For instance, you would not want to crank the presence and the treble on a Plexi-Marshall because that setting will likely induce a parasitic oscillation that sounds like a mosquito on top of the note. Blackface Fenders can produce a "raspy" high-end when using the bright switch and cranking the treble and volume. Use common sense. If you find a bad setting that the amp just doesn't like, quit using that setting!

Remember that humbucking pick-ups will have much more output than a single coil. Generally the bridge humbucker will give you the most harmonically dense overdrive lead sound. A single coil neck pick-up will give the classic Hendrix/Stevie Ray/Jimmy/Billy clean tone.

I like putting a compensating cap across the volume control of my guitar. I'm using a 500 pf. It goes from the hot side to the wiper, just like a bright cap. When I turn down the volume control to get a clean tone, the high end is boosted slightly which gives me a chimey and somewhat jangley high-end. This works especially great when using the neck humbucker clean tone.

TRUST YOURSELF

If you like the tone you are hearing, it is right. If it doesn't sound good, don't kid yourself. You know what sounds good and what doesn't. I know it is hard to trust yourself on this. You will want another opinion. Don't be afraid to experiment. If you want to have great tone, sure you need a great tube amp, but you still must be able to "play" your instrument, "the Electric (as in amplifier!) Guitar."

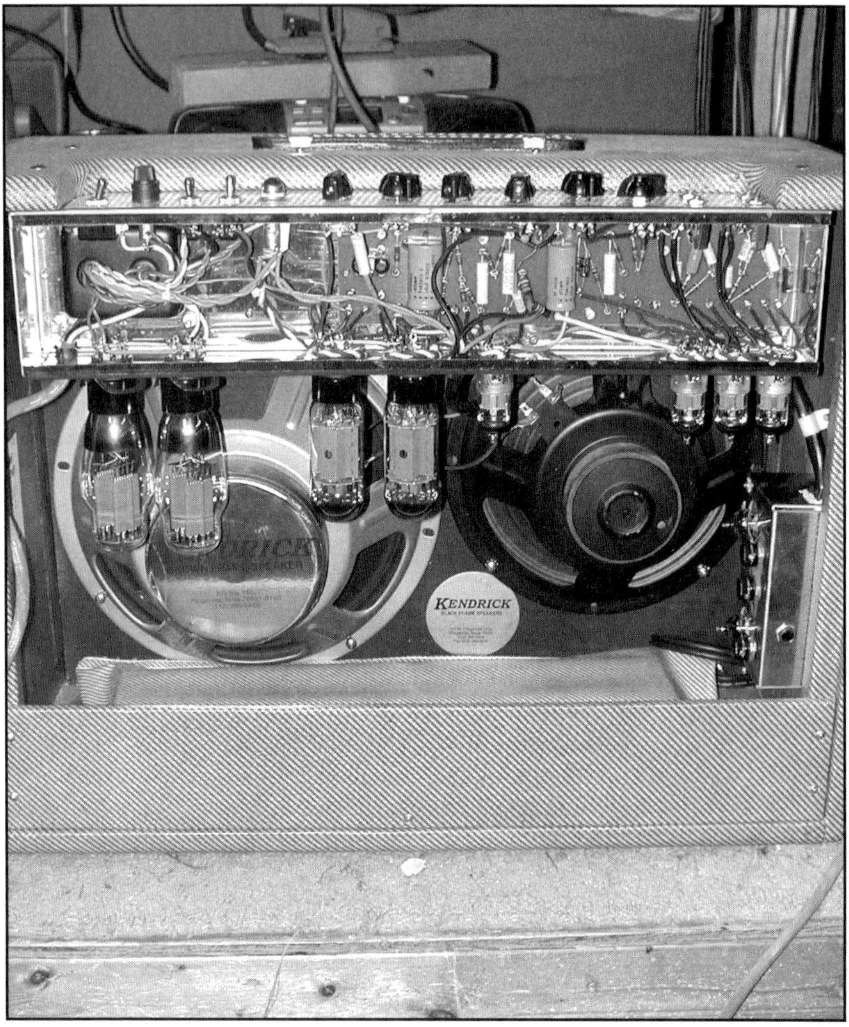
KENDRICK

FINE TUNING YOUR AMP SETUP

Living in central Texas near Austin, the music capital of the world, affords me the opportunity to hear many live bands and see many great guitar players. It is rare to come across a guitarist with his amp setup sounding its best. In most cases, I will see a player that has mastery of his instrument, yet his overall sound is lacking. I can only imagine what a huge difference it would make if a player's amp setup did him justice.

It is nice to play well, but there is more going on than depressing a string on a fret. An electric guitar must have an amplifier for it to sound good. Even if the amplifier in question is a quality tube amplifier, one must set it up right to "get the tone." You could have five amps, all of the same brand, and yet have five completely different sounding amps — depending on the quality of the tubes, the quality of the speakers, the biasing of the output tubes, the condition of the filter caps, bypass caps and coupling caps.

For the guitarist, fine-tuning the amp may seem to be the job of the tech. But if you don't have a tech, or want to DIY, here's some basic guidelines about how to fine-tune your amp setup.

The four parts to any tube amplifier are the power supply, the preamp, the power amp, and the speaker. We will take a look at each part and fine tune each part. When this is done, the entire system will be functioning on a new level.

POWER SUPPLY —The most obvious part of the amplifier is the power supply. It consists of the power cord, power transformer, rectifier, filter caps and dropping resistors. It could be said that a guitar amplifier is simply a modulated power supply that drives a speaker. That being the case, the power supply is the core of your sound.

The choice of rectifier — whether tube or solid-state — will affect the blossoming quality of the amp. If you need more "meow," you could use a softer rectifier. If you need more "front edge" of a note, a more efficient rectifier such as a 5AR4 or a solid-state rectifier may be the ticket. If you are a fast player, you will not like a soft rectifier because by the time the rectifier recovers from the initial attach of the note, you are already playing another different note. It is as if the amplifier can't keep up with you! Faster players need less "sag" or "meow" and more punch.

Consequently, a bluesier player might prefer a softer rectifier to add some character to his sound. This is where it gets tricky. What sounds good to you alone in a room make not work with a pounding drummer. If you drummer plays loud, you will need more "front edge" of the note so that your sound will punch through and not become buried by the drums.

If your power transformer is rusted, there is a possibility that it is being bogged down with eddy currents. If this is the case, the transformer should be replaced. I don't care if it still makes sound, it will not sound its best if eddy currents are dragging it down.

The filter caps need to be fresh and of good quality. I change mine every six years in every amp I own whether they need it or not. It is like changing oil in your car every 4,000 miles just because. Old filter caps may function yet not perform. We are not talking about "just getting by" here. We are talking about getting superior tone. Good filter caps keep the note you are playing in tune! They pull everything together so you don't get that ugly, out-of-tune subtone that is caused by weak filter caps. They also supply power to the other tubes and when you are bearing down, you need caps that will continually deliver the power your tubes demand and not "wash out" tonally. The filter caps need to be of good quality because even new ones can sound bad if they are poor quality. Stay away from the Illinois brand (which is made in Taiwan) and the LCR brand. These imported filter caps sound bad even when they are new. If you have a new Marshall with LCR caps or a new Fender with Illinois caps, change them at once. You cannot afford to screw up your sound by having ugly and out-of-tune subtones underneath your fundamental tone. Use Sprague or Tech Cap or any other quality American-made capacitor.

PREAMP — This is the section of your amp that amplifies the weak signal from the guitar pickups so that the signal is strong enough to drive your power amp. It consists of preamp tubes (usually 12AX7) and a few components to make the preamp tubes work. These components are basically resistors, coupling capacitors, and bypass capacitors. Unless you are getting excessive hiss or noise, the resistors are probably just fine.

Bypass caps, which are found in the cathode circuit of each preamp tube, can go bad and need replacing. Typical values are 25 uf at 25 volts or 10 uf at 16 volts. These should be replaced with good quality, American-made capacitors. I always replace these when replacing filter caps because they are electrolytic type capacitors and don't last forever.

Coupling caps rarely need replacing. When they die, they still function, but pass a minute amount of D.C. electricity. This tiny voltage could be as little as .25 volts, yet it is enough to throw the biasing scheme off on the downline preamp tubes and make the amp sound choked and ratty. These caps can be checked easily enough by unsoldering one end (not the end connected to the plate of the preamp tube, but the other end), and checking between the lifted lead and ground with a voltmeter set for D.C. volts. You should get zero volts. If you get more than .25 volts, the coupling cap must be changed. Notice that on some amps (mid 60s Fender, for example), the tone caps are sometimes arranged as coupling caps. The same holds true for these caps as any other coupling cap. If it leaks D.C. voltage, change it.

The preamp is where the amp gets its gain. It is also where the tone controls are usually located. The exact gain characteristics can be fine tuned by substituting other lower gain preamp tubes. For example, if you had an amp that used a 12AX7 preamp tube and you wanted to get a cleaner sound, you may want to substitute a 12AT7 or a 12AY7 for the 12AX7 in order to reduce the gain and consequently clean everything up some.

Preamp tubes generally last longer than power tubes, but replacing worn ones with unworn ones can improve your tone. Also the actual quality of the preamp tube is important to achieve good quality tone. For example, a 12AX7WA Sovtek, though very quiet, still lacks fullness. This tube would work fine as a vibrato oscillator, but you would not want to use it in a socket that was directly in the signal path. You want to use good sounding brands of tubes that are relatively unworn for best tone.

POWER AMP — The power amp section of the amplifier would include the phase inverter, the output tubes, and the output transformer. The phase inverter, though part of the output stage, still uses a preamp tube. The preamp tube that works the hardest and wears out the quickest is the phase inverter tube. These are usually run at higher voltages than any other preamp tube, and they have a larger input and output than the other preamp tubes. I like to change the phase inverter tube at the same time as the output tubes.

To get your output tubes sounding their best, you need new, good sounding output tubes. Output tubes are like tires on a car. They can last a long time if you don't drive them hard, and if you drive them hard, you will be amazed at how quickly they wear out. If you are playing the amp really hard, you should change tubes at least once a year. It goes without saying that you should reset the bias setting of the output tubes every time the output tubes are changed. The output tubes simply will not sound their best unless the bias is readjusted. The actual bias setting can be varied slightly to make the amp perform more like you desire. If you are going for a squeaky clean tone, you may want to adjust the bias so that the output tubes only draw about .025 A (same as 25 milliamps) of current per tube. On the other hand, if you are going for a quicker breakup, you will want to idle the output tube hotter (as much as 45 milliamps per side.). When you idle them hotter, you simply start them out running so fast that it just doesn't take much to kick them into overdrive.

The output transformer is critical to your sound. If you have a transformer that is multi-tap with various impedances, the highest impedance setting will sound the best (provided that you have the appropriate speaker load impedance.) There are two reasons for this. First, higher impedance settings have a lower turns ratio which means less coupling loss. And secondly, when a tapped transformer is wound, the highest impedance setting is the whole transformer. All other taps are a percentage of the transformer being used. A 16-ohm transformer with a 4 ohm tap is only using half of the transformer when the 4 ohm tap is selected. A whole transformer performs better than a half transformer.

SPEAKER — Sound is made from vibrating air. Sometimes overlooked, we must remember the speaker and speaker enclosure is what is actually vibrating air. The speakers are your amp's final filter. If your speaker is inefficient, then the amp will not have the sports car feel.

The speaker is mounted in an enclosure that affects the sound. There are different types of cabinets. A closed back cabinet is highly directional and the sound is coming out of the front in a rather acute angle. People near the side of the amp won't get any sound sent their way. Perhaps aiming an amp like this at a back wall would help disperse the sound. The sound would hit the wall at an acute angle, yet bounce back at complimentary angles, thus increasing dispersion.

The other type of cabinet design, the open back, has a large dispersion angle in the front and sound comes out of the back too. This type design will get the best stage sound. Miking the amp and putting it in the house mix will help give you a bigger sound. You will simply move more air by using the PA speakers too.

Choose speakers that have enough brightness to define the note, yet not enough to cause brittle breakup when overdriven. You want the speakers to have enough clear bottom-end to be satisfying, yet you don't want boominess.

MULTI-AMP SETUP — Many players are using more than one amp in their setup. This is fine as long as all the speakers are moving the same direction at the same time. I once heard a player with mastery of his instrument but he sounded thin and weak because he was using a multi-amp setup that was done incorrectly. He could have improved his sound by turning one of his amps off!

It starts with making sure all the speakers in one amp are moving together. This can be checked with a simple 9 volt battery. Hook the + of the battery to the + of the speaker cabinet and minus of the battery to minus of the cabinet. All the speakers should move forward. Any speaker that does not move forward should have its individual leads reversed. These are the wires going to the individual speaker. You would reverse them at the speaker lead end.

Once you get the speakers in a particular amp all moving together, you would then need to have the amps synchronized. It doesn't matter that the speakers in each amp are hooked up correctly; you need to make sure the amps are working together. On some amps, when a positive signal is applied to the input, a positive signal comes out of the speaker. On other amps, when a positive signal is applied to the input, a negative signal comes out of the speaker. You want to make sure the amps are working together.

Here's the easy way. Place both amps (or speaker cabinets) facing you and play a little. Now turn one amp facing backwards and play a little. One configuration will sound great and the other way will sound horrible. If it sounded great by having both face you, you needn't do anything. If they sounded great with one (speaker cabinet) facing backwards, you would need to reverse the leads on one of the speaker cabinets. That way, both amps will sound great when facing you.

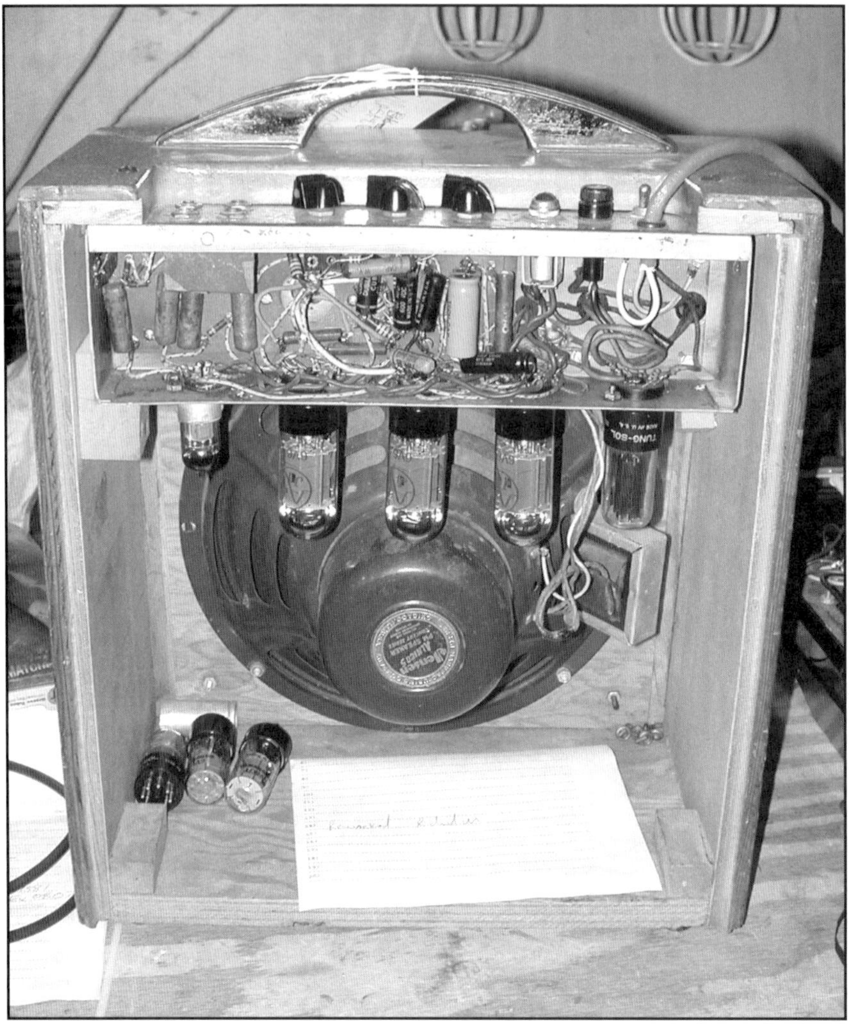
TUNG-SOL

FINE TUNING YOUR AMP TONE

Most of us began playing guitar for fun and without the notion of having to learn anything technical. We assumed there would be no math. As our playing improved, we wanted better tone, and began discovering technical basics that make a huge difference in the way we actually sound.

Three things instantly come to mind: speaker placement, proper grounding, and proper phase relationships.

SPEAKER PLACEMENT — Where you put your amplifier greatly affects your overall tone! All high-end comes from the center of the speaker and comes out in an extreme acute angle! The bottom-end comes from the sides of the speaker in an obtuse dispersion angle! When setting up your rig, it is sometimes best to bounce the sound off of something in order to diffuse the highs before they reach the audience. Stevie Ray used Plexiglass to bounce his sound around before it got to his audience. I saw a legendary Austin blues player, W. C. Clark, with an amp on tilt-back legs, but the amp was turned around backwards facing the back wall! At the Armadillo World Headquarters in the 70s, Stevie Ray sometimes laid his Twin on the floor facing the ceiling. Tilt-back legs work great because the sound bounces to the ceiling and then back to the listener. This really spreads the highs out while allowing the guitarist to hear himself well. Back in the 60s, I remember putting my amp in a chair and tilting it back to point at the ceiling.

Look at the room you are in. Ask yourself: Where can I place my amp so the highs are diffused? You do not want your amp pointing at the bar. The waitresses and bartender will hate you, as all your highs are pinpoint focused directly in their face! In a long room with a narrow stage, I have set my amp almost completely sideways, with the side of the amp facing the audience so the sound will bounce off the walls a few times before it hits the listener. This fattens the tone by adding ambience, natural delay and diffusing high-end. Who needs reverb? You could even angle it facing the wall slightly and bounce those highs. Remember every time the highs bounce on a hard surface, the dispersion angle becomes wider.

PROPER GROUNDING — Most vintage amps use a two-prong A.C. plug. Such a plug connects to the A.C. wall supply; however, it is not directly earth grounded. On amps that use this type of two-conductor plug, there is usually a switch on the amplifier labeled "ground." This switch normally would connect a .05 uf capacitor from the chassis of the amp to one side of the A.C. line. When the ground switch is tripped, the capacitor connection is switched to the other side of the A.C. line. The correct setting would be whichever one produces the least hum. It is interesting to note that neither position of the ground switch actually grounds the amplifier chassis!

THE THREE-PRONG A.C. CONNECTOR — Sometime during the 70s and thereafter, amplifiers began coming with a different type of A.C. plug. The plug had the regular two flat prongs like earlier plugs, except there was an extra round pin added. This extra pin was connected directly to the chassis of the amp. When plugged into the wall, the extra pin was designed to connect to an actual "earth" ground. The theory was that if everything is earth grounded, it would be impossible to get shocked. To a certain degree, that is true, however, for this idea to work, the wall socket had to be wired correctly. Club owners are notorious for overspending to make sure all the electrical outlets in their club are wired to highest standard electrical code. Not!

When three-prong plugs came into existence, the .05 uf capacitor and ground switch was becoming obsolete, but some manufacturers still included the "ground" switch just in case the wall plug had a two prong female receptacle and a three-prong-to-two-prong adapter was used.

GROUND LOOPS — Around the late sixties, players such as Eric Clapton, Billy Gibbons and Jimi Hendrix began using multiple amplifiers. These amplifiers were made in England where the A.C. line voltage is 240 volts balanced. (That means they used a three prong A.C. wall connector and one of the prongs was earth grounded). This introduced a new guitar amp problem – the ground loop.

A ground loop is a huge loop (of mostly wire) that acts as an antenna and picks up 60 cycle hum (50 cycle hum in Euro town) that is present everywhere. To understand ground loops, one must understand that one conductor of the guitar cable, the shielded conductor, is actually connected to the chassis of the amplifier. You can look closely at an input jack on an amplifier and see that the sleeve of the guitar plug connects to both the shielded conductor of the guitar cable and ultimately to the chassis of the amp.

When interconnecting two or more amplifiers, their chassis are connected together via this shielding on the patch cord.

Now consider that the third prong of a three-prong A.C. plug also connects to the chassis of an amplifier. Let's follow the entire loop, so you can see it.

Starting at the third prong of a three-prong A.C. cord, which leaves the wall outlet, and follows the A.C. cord up to the first amp chassis. Since the chassis is connected to the shielding of your guitar patch cord, you would then follow the shielding on the patch cord to whatever device is being used to connect the two amplifiers together. The shielding attaches to the chassis of the device, which attaches to another patch cord. From there, follow the shielding of the patch cord going from the device to the second amplifier. Now the circuit continues through the chassis of that amplifier and down the third wire of the A.C. cord (of the second amp) back to the wall. Then it proceeds through the wall wiring to the point where it started on the first three-prong A.C. plug. You end up with a huge loop antenna that picks up loads of hum.

There are ways to interrupt the ground loop and thus stop the hum. The easiest way is to use three-prong-to-two-prong A.C. adapters on every amplifier in the setup except one. When you have one device earth grounded, and all the chassis are connected together via the patch cords, then ALL are ultimately earth grounded. These three-prong-to-two-prong adapters are sold at all hardware stores and most grocery stores. To avoid electrical shock during setup, hook all the patch cords up first and then hook up all the A.C. supplies. When taking everything down, unhook the A.C. supplies first and then disconnect the patch cords.

Ground loops do not occur using a two-prong A.C. wall plug. They only occur when using a three-prong A.C. plug.

UNDERSTANDING PHASE — When a guitar sound is produced, there is a sound wave. Most of us have seen a picture of a sound wave on an oscilloscope. It looks like a hill and a valley, then a hill and a valley, etc.

PHASE RELATIONSHIP — It is important to have all waves, whether sound waves or electrical representations of the same, moving with each other and not against each other. In other words, you would not want to have a hill occurring and a valley occurring simultaneously. They would cancel each other and your tone would have no bottom-end and very little volume.

PROPER ELECTRICAL CHANNEL PHASE — When a signal goes into a tube, it comes out with the phase inverted. In other words, if it goes in positive, it comes out negative. That is to say that when a guitar signal goes into a preamp section of an amplifier, the phase inverts every time the signal goes through another preamp tube section (triode).

Certain preamps have an even number of stages and others have an odd number of stages. For example on a Blackface Twin Reverb, the normal channel has two stages of gain, which means the signal coming out of the preamp is in phase with the input. (Positive in = Positive out.) The Vibrato channel has three stages of gain (an extra stage for the reverb mix). This means the signal coming out of the vibrato preamp is 180 degrees out of phase with the input. (Positive in = Negative out)

In such an amp, you would not want to bridge both channels at the same time, as the signal from one channel would cancel the signal from the other.

PROPER PHASE BETWEEN AMPLIFIERS — When a positive signal is placed on the input of certain amplifiers, a positive signal comes out of the output jack. In such a case, the amplifier is said to play "forward." With certain other amplifiers, when a positive signal is applied to the input, a negative signal comes out of the output jack. In such a case, the amp is said to play "backwards." This is important to know when hooking up multiple amplifiers. To make two dissimilar amplifiers work together, the polarity of the speaker load (of one of the amps) must be reversed. This will correct the phase relationship of both amps. More on this later.

PROPER SPEAKER LOAD PHASE — By changing the polarity of the speaker load wiring, one can reverse the phase of the speaker load. In every speaker cabinet, there are two wires that connect to the speaker input jack. If you reverse the wires connecting to the jack, you have reversed the polarity (or phase) of the speaker cabinet.

PROPER SPEAKER PHASE — Besides the phase relationship of the channel, the amplifier, and the speaker load, the individual speakers within a speaker load must work together and not against each other. If a speaker cabinet (speaker load) is wired correctly, all the speakers will move the same way at the same time. When a positive signal is applied to the cabinet, all the speakers should move forward.

This can be checked with an ordinary 9 volt battery. You would simply hook the battery up to the speaker cabinet (the positive goes to the tip and the negative goes to the sleeve of the plug). When a connection is made, all the speakers should move forward. If one of the speakers moves backwards, that speaker's polarity is wrong and should be reversed. Reversing the wires going to the leads of the offending speaker will correct this problem.

CORRECTING THE PHASE BY EAR — Let's say you have an amplifier and you are plugging in an extra speaker cabinet. Or you may have two amps you are hooking together. Once you determine (per the battery test) that all the speakers within a particular cabinet are wired in phase with each other, you would need to know that the amplifiers (or speaker cabinets) are in phase with each other, as well. Here's the easiest way to determine that: Place both speaker cabinets facing you and play guitar through them. Listen to them. Now take one of the speaker cabinets and turn it around facing backwards with respect to the first one. Play guitar and listen. Whichever position had rich bottom-end and was thick sounding, is phase correct. Whichever way sounded thin, with no bottom-end and weak volume was out of phase. If they were in phase with each other when they were both facing you, you need do nothing. But, if they were in phase when one of the speakers was facing backwards, you need only reverse the wires that connect to the jack of the speaker cabinet. Do this on only one of the speaker cabinets and then you may set both speakers facing the same direction and have great tone.

Fine Tuning Your Amp Tone

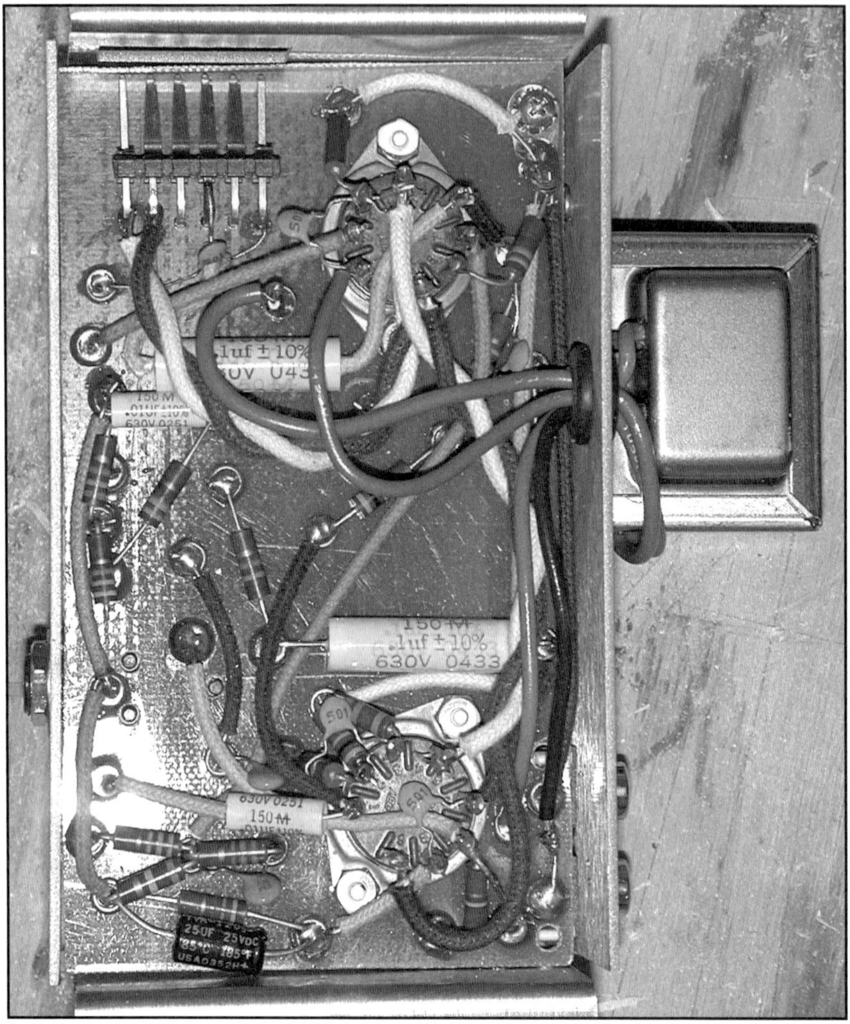
.1uf ± 10%
630V 0433

ADJUSTING A TUBE AMP FOR TONE

If you are not sure exactly how to set your amplifier for best tone, you are not alone. Many exceptionally gifted guitarists, producers, and even recording engineers have little clue about how to adjust their tube guitar amp to its sweetest setting. Let's get this out in the open once and for all.

WHAT'S THE DIFFERENCE?

Let's make a distinction right now between a tube guitar amp and virtually all other audio equipment. With the exception of effects devices and signal processors, all other audio equipment is designed to be as transparent as possible. In other words, audio equipment is not intended to color the sound. Let's take a mixing console as an example. The perfect mixing console would have a flat frequency response from 20 to 20,000 Hertz when the EQ was set flat. The same is true for a power amp or studio monitor, or tape deck. Even recording tape or patch cords are more desirable when they do not color the sound.

A tube guitar amplifier is meant to color the sound. Maybe I should say that again; A TUBE GUITAR AMP IS MEANT TO COLOR THE SOUND! In other words, the amp is actually a part of the instrument. It is the part that makes the sound. Now you know what makes a guitar amp different from virtually all other audio devices.

Let's compare the tube guitar amp to a studio monitor power amp. The studio power amp is designed to take whatever signal it is given and amplify it exactly. That is to say, the amp should not have an envelope of its own, it should not fatten up the sound, it should not compress, and it should not introduce any distortion whatsoever. It should have no sound of it's own.

A well-designed tube amp is deliberately coloring tone from input jack to speaker. It is designed to have an envelope, natural compression, sustain, harmonic richness, fatness, meatiness, etc. In short, it is an instrument and like all other instruments, has a sound of its own.

I once had a conversation with a very knowledgeable recording engineer that asked me if the tone controls on a Kendrick amplifier were passive or active. I asked him why did he want to know. He retorted, "If they are passive, the frequency response is flat when they are set all the way up and if they are active, the frequency response is flat half way up."

The truth is that whether they are active or passive, the frequency response of a tube guitar amp is never flat. The tone was already colored after the first gain stage, not to mention all the stages after the tone controls, the tubes, speakers, cabinet, and the room it is in!

This brings me to another point. While metalized film resistors and special coupling caps are useful in high-end audio gear (because of their transparency), they are not useful in creating an instrument such as a tube guitar amp. Different types, values, and brands of capacitors and resistors will color the sound in their own unique way.

EVERY TUBE GUITAR AMP IS UNIQUE

GUITAR AMP TONE AXIOM #1 STATES: Since no two-tube guitar amps are exactly the same, duplicating settings on two or more amps will not achieve the same tone. How many times have we all seen a player who is familiar with one particular amp, plug his guitar into a different amp and immediately adjust the tone controls to the same settings he would normally use with the first amp? Even with identical brand amps, the numbered control settings are not the same. Why? Among other reasons, component values are not exactly the same — because of normal component tolerances including individual preamp tube gain. There is even mechanical variance of the exact positioning of the knob on the pot's shaft.

Several years ago, a well-known, young Austin guitar slinger that had recently been featured in *Guitar Player* magazine stopped by my shop to test a Kendrick amplifier. Before ever listening to the amp, he set the midrange tone control to "2" and boldly informed me that he "never uses mids." I didn't doubt that with his guitar, his cabling (this also colors the tone), his amplifier, his speaker, and his speaker cabinet; he felt HIS entire rig sounded best with his middle control set to "2." This brings us to...

HOW DO I MAKE THE ADJUSTMENTS?

GUITAR AMP TONE AXIOM #2 STATES: Every component of your guitar/amp rig colors the tone — from your fingers to the actual room you are listening in; therefore, tone controls are used to compensate for everything else. Yes, to get the best tone, you must forget about numbers on dials and do something extremely daring: TRUST YOUR EARS! Get bold and don't look at the numbers on the controls. Turn knobs and listen.

YOU HAVE TO CRITICALLY LISTEN TO YOUR TONE

I cannot overstate the importance of listening to your guitar tone. Later we will talk about what to actually listen for, but for now, I'd like to share a story that parallels what I wanted to say about critical listening.

A couple of years ago, my band, RED HOT BLUE, began working on the bands first CD. Knowing how much difference good drum tone makes, we thought it would be a good idea to change drum heads. Wanting the absolute best tone, my drummer hired a "drum tuning expert" to help him tune his drums. The guy spent a whole day in our studio tuning, playing, stretching and re-tuning, then fine tuning. This turned out to be quite successful and the drums definitely sounded their best.

Hoping to learn enough about "drum tuning" so that I could spare my drummer's checkbook for next time; I made it a point to be in the studio while this drum tuning was going on. This gave me the opportunity to quiz the "drum tuning expert." When I asked him what was his technique, he told me that every drum has a personality. You simply listen to the drum, listening for how it wants to sound and then make it sound that way! Of course there are physical considerations such as getting even tension all the way around the rim, but the essence is to listen to the drum and it will tell you where it wants to be tuned.

I think the same philosophy would work well to adjust an amp. To begin, you start by trusting your own ears. You simply listen and trust what you are hearing. If it sounds bad, you'll know it and if it sounds good, you'll know.

Every amp also has its more soni-genic settings. Its tonal personality manifests itself in many different ways. This personality will change as the volume and other controls are adjusted. Here's a partial list with some ideas of:

WHAT TO LISTEN FOR AND WHAT TO ADJUST

1. THE ATTACK OF THE NOTE. When a string is first plucked, a different sound is made than when the string is simply sustaining. Almost any control adjustment will affect the initial attack sound. For instance, as the volume of a tube amp is turned louder, you will likely notice more compression and a softening of the attack. Turning the volume down will generally result in a more "pingy" and less compressed attack.

Adjusting treble or presence higher will put more "pick attack sound" on the front of the note. Subtracting treble and presence will result in less "pick attack sound." Adding more bass with the volume setting up will mush-out the initial attack, whereas subtracting bass will gain "headroom" ON THE FRONT OF THE NOTE.

2. THE BLOSSOMING OF THE NOTE. After the initial attack sound is heard, the note will unfold as a sustaining sound that has an envelope of loudness and tone. This blossoming is affected by how loud the volume control is set, what kind of rectifier tube, your tone controls and your guitar settings. Turn the volume control and listen for the blossoming after the initial attack. Set it where the envelope, or blossoming, feels right.

3. THE OVERALL CLARITY OF THE NOTE. Are you going for clean or dirty? Increasing mids will make the amp distort more easily. Cutting mids will help your clean tone. Rolling your guitars volume control down a little will help your clean tone. If the amp has a bright switch, try turning it "on" for clean. Let your ears decide. Of course turning the volume "up" will help your distorted tone. Here's where biasing the amp and selecting the output tubes makes a difference as well. For instance, I once had the "strange pleasure" of setting up an amp for a well known Texas guitar icon that was known for his clean sound and understated hot licks. With trial and error listening tests, I ended up replacing the 5881 output tubes in both 80 watt amps with 7581A tubes and biasing them on the cold side (idle plate current at 25 mA

per tube). I changed his first 12AX7 preamp tube on each amp to a 12AY7. This allowed him to crank both amps so that they stayed clean when turned to 75% full volume. Most players would not have liked this sound, and yet I talked to people all over the country that had heard him play this rig in concert and remarked about what a wonderful tone he had. This player trusted his ears and went with what he thought sounded good to him.

4. THE EQ OF THE NOTE. What kind of sound are you going for? Scooping out mids — but not too much — will help your clean sound. Listen to the note. If the bass is too mushy, try turning it down some. Is the treble too piercing? This can be adjusted on the amp as well as turning down the tone control on your guitar. Your pick attack can also affect the EQ; for instance, if you pick closer to the bridge, you will get more highs in the sound. Treble can be adjusted by listening to the bite of the note. If you get too much, the tone will be unpleasant. If not enough, the note will lack enough edge to "cut through the mix." Listen and use your ears. Is the tone pleasing to your ears?

5. OVERALL RESPONSE. How does the amp feel? It should feel like it is an extension of the player. Any knob will affect how it feels. Placing the amp at chest level so that its sound will vibrate your guitar will certainly contribute to controlled feedback and sustain. For a pretty clean sound, perhaps adding a little reverb will improve the feel; but not too much. Effects usually sound best when they are not very noticeable. Less can be more. Does the amp have enough punch? If it doesn't perform to your liking, it might be time for some better sounding speakers, new tubes, or a cap job. I once had a Blackface Twin brought to my shop that was formerly owned by Eric Johnson. It was tubed with old Chinese 6L6's and when turned up, sounded very wimpy. Retubing it with NOS RCA 6L6GC's was truly dramatic. The amp became so loud and fat sounding, that you just couldn't turn it up past "4" and remain in the same room with it!

PUTTING YOUR BEST TONAL FOOT FORWARD

Don't be afraid to critically listen to various amps and play with the controls. Experiment with the tone controls on your guitar. In short, trust your own ears.

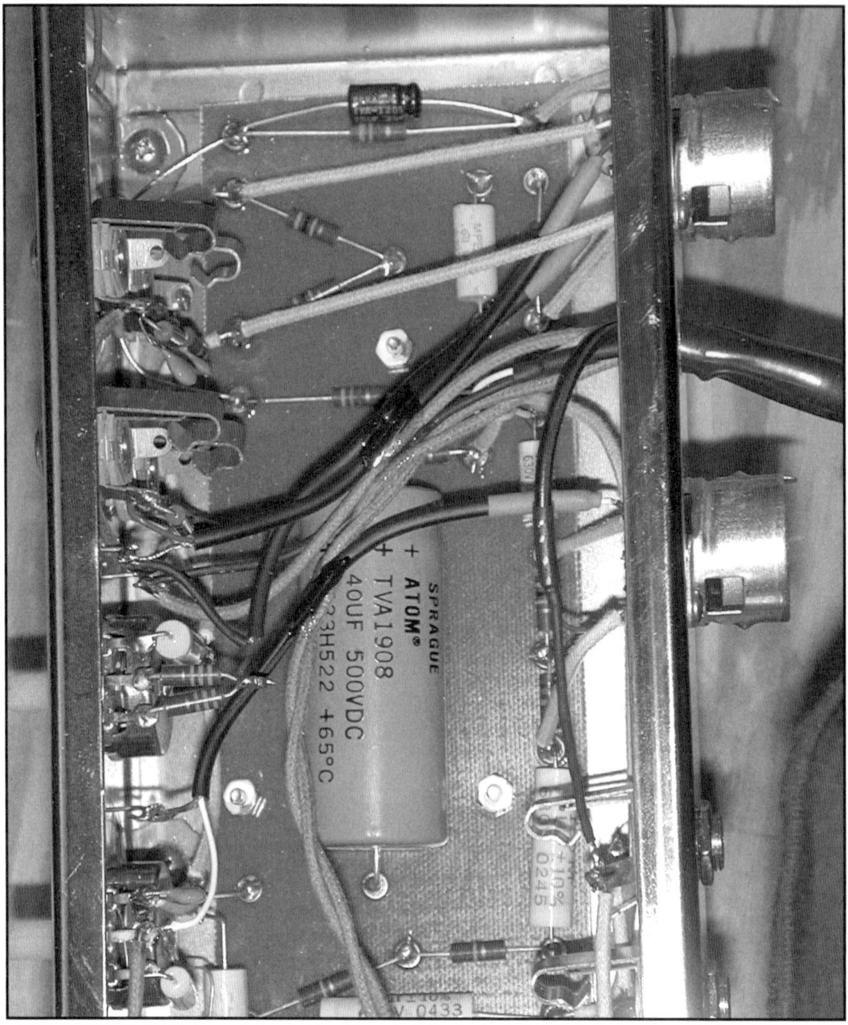
SPRAGUE
ATOM®
TVA1908
40UF 500VDC
+65°C

TUBE AMP BASICS

When is it best to change tubes? Do I change all tubes at the same time? Must I bias? How often between cap jobs? In short, what maintenance or preventive maintenance must I take with my vacuum tube guitar amplifier? What extra parts and tools should I "not leave home without"? Have you ever asked yourself any of these questions? Read On!

Maintenance—Like any other piece of equipment, your tube amp will need attention from time to time—just like your car. Here are the basics.

1. OUTPUT TUBE REPLACEMENT BASICS—A set of output tubes is like a set of automobile tires. They wear out gradually over a period of time, last according to how they're driven, and last longer when not used as much. Also, they are best changed in sets.

Output tubes can last almost forever if they are played at extremely low volume. On the other hand, crank it up daily and you may need new tubes every 6 months. Tube life depends on how often you play and how hard you play. If you are an average weekend warrior, change your output tubes perhaps once a year or every other year. Figure yourself about average if you get 1,000 hours out of a set of output tubes. If you do better, consider it a bonus.

Your amp may function yet not perform! Tubes wear so gradually, that you never notice the difference from one day to the next. Worn tubes may still pass signal, but lack liveliness and punch. When you change from an old set of output tubes to a new set, you will most likely be amazed at the difference in tone and the way the amp "feels."

Always remember to have the amp biased when changing output tubes. It will make the tubes sound better and in some cases could make them last longer.

You do not need to bias a cathode-biased amp. It is self-biasing and will adjust automatically according to the particular tube.

2. PREAMP TUBE BASICS—Some preamp tubes last forever and some should be changed frequently. For instance, the phase inverter tube is usually worked pretty hard and should be replaced when replacing the output tubes. Another hard-worked tube is the 12AT7 reverb driver in all Blackface reverb amps. A fresh one can make a world of difference in the quality and quantity of the reverb effect.

The earlier stage preamps tubes generally last the longest and usually don't need replacing unless they become noisy or microphonic.

Here's a tip when replacing preamp tubes on a Blackface Fender. A used tube (hereinafter referred to as "pull") can be used for the vibrato tube (usually the preamp tube next to the phase inverter tube). It doesn't matter if the tube is microphonic or not. The signal doesn't actually pass through the vibrato tube. As long as this tube has enough gain to oscillate, it has done its job, therefore; a good "pull" works perfectly and saves the cost of a new tube.

3. CAP JOBS—Like it or not, electrolytic capacitors do not last forever. Let's compare the electrolytic caps to the battery in your car. They are quite similar. Both depend on an electro-chemical process in order to store D.C. electricity. Both have a positive and a negative electrode. Both are constantly being charged by something else. And the chemical process that occurs inside eventually malfunctions. When caps are worn out, symptoms could include a slight loss in power or loss of gain, mushiness in the bottom-end, dissonant sub-harmonics that follow the note unnaturally, abnormal hum, or all of the above. Check your caps if you notice any of these symptoms. Be aware of these symptoms—especially if the electrolytic capacitors are known to be 6 or more years old.

If you check the caps and see any bubbling or rupture on the positive end, the cap needs replacing. If you have a vintage amp and a couple of the caps are bubbled, you might as well just change them all. If they are all the same age, and one or two are bad, the rest are not going to last much longer. Save yourself the aggravation. Get a complete cap job and change every electrolytic in the amp. If you are certain the caps are older than 10 years, you will probably want to change them anyway unless, of course, none of the caps are bubbling on the positive end. Preventive maintenance—an ounce of prevention is worth a pound of cure.

1. STANDBY SWITCH BASICS—Get in the habit of always using your standby switch. Keep it in the standby mode for at least a minute or two before switching to the "play" mode. Inside every tube is a cathode that must be heated before it can be safely subjected to high voltage; otherwise, the cathode chemical coating will become stripped as a consequence. The purpose of the standby switch is to disconnect the high voltage supply from the tubes and allow the tubes to heat without high voltage present. Nothing wears out tubes faster than ignoring the standby switch.

2. ENVIRONMENTAL CONSIDERATIONS—Store your amp only where you would be willing to sleep. No leaving it in the trunk overnight after the gig. Keep it away from dampness, extreme heat or cold. The resistors in your amp can pick up humidity, which manifest itself later as noise.

Another consideration when transporting the amp from a cold environment to a warm environment: look for condensation and do not turn on the amp until all condensation has had a chance to dissipate. This is especially a problem in colder climate areas.

YOUR TUBE AMP FIRST AID KIT—If you play a guitar, you most surely bring extra strings to a performance. A string could break for no apparent reason and so could your amp. Here are the bare basics.

1. FUSES—Keep a box or more of the correct type, size, amp rating and voltage rating (For example: Slo-Blo, Littlefuse, 3 amp, 125 volt fuse). If you need more than one kind, get a box or two of each.

2. OUTPUT TUBES—I like to keep at least one set that is matched to the set in my amp. This way, if a tube malfunctions, I can replace the set without having to bias. This is really convenient in a gig situation.

3. PREAMP TUBE—One or two extra preamp tubes just in case one goes noisy or microphonic.

4. RECTIFIER TUBE—If your amp uses a rectifier tube such as a 5AR4, bring an extra as a backup.

5. PHILLIPS SCREWDRIVER—Many minor repairs can be made with this device.

6. EXTRA 9-VOLT BATTERIES—For when that wah wah finally slows down.

7. NEEDLE NOSE PLIERS—Many minor repairs can be made with these also.

8. MULTIMETER—This can be used for simple troubleshooting, biasing, or testing.

9. GROUND LIFT ADAPTERS—These are used to stop ground loop induced hum.

10. ADDITIONAL PATCH CORDS—If a patch cord malfunctions, you don't have time to fix it. It is best to have several extras—just in case.

11. FLASHLIGHT—Stages are dark. The inside back of an amp is also very dark.

12. ANYTHING ELSE—that you feel you must have that I have not included in this list. I know people that would not go to a gig without all of this and an extra amplifier!

Tips for the Non-Technical Guitarist

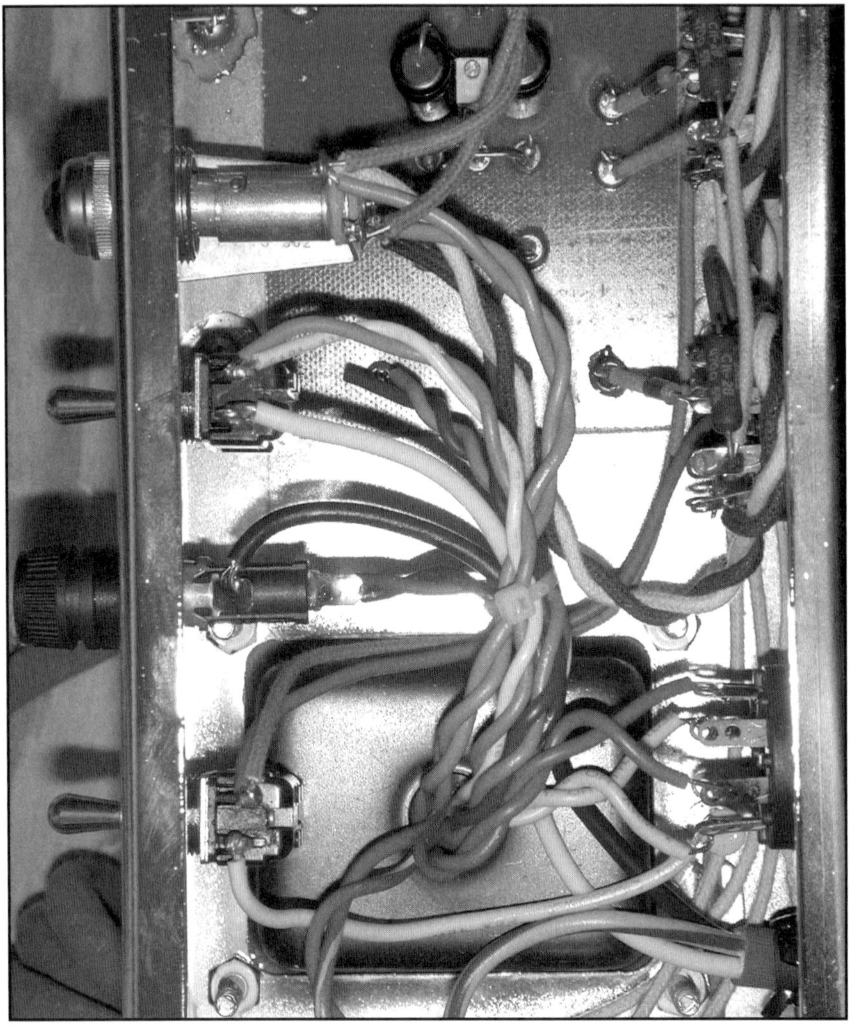

MAKING SENSE OF TUBE AMP TALK

So you play guitar but want to learn more about your tube guitar amp? Whether you are an inexperienced tech or a guitarist wanting to know more about your tone, you are bound to hear terms such as voltage, current, resistance, inductance, capacitance, wattage, power, A.C., D.C., voltage drop, bias, etc. These terms are not as confusing as they seem. Let's look at some of these terms and simplify the meanings and make them easily understood. Here are the practical definitions.

VOLTAGE is electrical pressure. The measurement for voltage is volts. For an analogy, think of a high-pressure car wash, which is like high voltage. If you picture a leaky faucet, that is like low voltage. For example, a 1½ volt battery would have low pressure, err, voltage — while the 120 volt wall outlet has much higher electrical pressure.

In a guitar amplifier, there are different voltages to operate different circuits. Low voltages, usually 6.3 volts, operate the heaters (a.k.a. filaments or filament heaters) in the tubes. This is the part of the tube that lights up like a light bulb. The function of the heater is to warm the inside of the tube hot enough so that it will operate properly. There are also high voltages on the plate circuits of all the tubes. Some tubes are run at higher voltages than other tubes depending on the actual type of tube.

CURRENT is the quantity of electrons flowing past a certain point. The measurement for current is amperes or amps for short. If electricity were water, current would be gallons. For example, the volume of water flowing through a drinking straw can be seen as low current, whereas the volume of water flowing from the mouth of the Mississippi River can be seen as high current. A hole in the dam is low current, but if the dam collapsed, there would be high current.

WATTAGE OR POWER is the combined effect of current and voltage. The power of an electrical circuit is the product of voltage times current. The voltage is expressed in volts, while the current is expressed in amps and power is expressed in watts. If you have 1 volt of electricity at 1 amp of current, you would have 1 watt of power. If either the voltage or the current goes up, so does the power. For example 2 volts at 1 amp is 2 watts of power. Or 2 volts at 4 amps would be 8 watts. Remember, Power = Voltage times Current.

A.C. AND D.C. ELECTRICITY — Electrical current can consist of two types: Direct current (D.C.) and Alternating current (A.C.). Direct current is where the electricity flows in one direction and the direction does not change. Alternating current is where the electricity flows one direction and then changes to go in the opposite direction.

Your wall outlet is an example of A.C. The electricity from a wall outlet changes directions 60 times per second. Another good example of A.C. is your actual guitar signal. For example, the "A" note of a guitar will change directions 440 times per second.

All amplifiers work on D.C. electricity, but the wall outlet only puts out A.C. electricity, so every amplifier has a power supply section that takes the wall A.C. and converts, or "rectifies," it into D.C. Usually the D.C. needs to be much higher than the 120 volts coming from the wall, so the electricity from the wall is first run into a step-up transformer (called a power transformer) that brings the voltage up to a higher level. The electricity is then put through a rectifier circuit to change it to D.C. A rectifier circuit can be made either with diodes or a tube, but it is basically an electrical check-valve that only lets the electricity flow one direction instead of both directions. This is how it takes A.C. (both directions) current and rectifies it to D.C. (all going the same direction) current.

RESISTANCE is any opposition to the flow of electrical current. This is somewhat like friction, because resistance generates heat. With the water example above, resistance would be analogous to a "bottleneck" in a pipeline or a kink in a garden hose. In a guitar amplifier, resistors are used to create resistance in various parts of the circuit. Resistors have a property that can be very useful. When you run an electrical current through a resistor, then a voltage develops across that resistance. If you increase the current, that voltage will increase. If you decrease the current, the voltage will decrease. This is an extremely useful quality that can be used for a number of functions.

Think of an analogy of trying to quickly force a gallon of water through a drinking straw. There would be more pressure on the input side of the straw than on the output side. This build up of "pressure" would be similar to the build up of voltage that occurs when current is passed through a resistor.

Resistors are used in many different circuits throughout an amplifier, but the essence of a resistor is the fact that a voltage will develop across it when electrical current passes through it. The exact amount of voltage that develops or "drops" across a resistor is known as voltage drop. A mathematical formula called Ohm's law is useful to determine exact voltage drop.

OHM'S LAW — Is a basic tool of circuit analysis that states the relationship of current, voltage and resistance. The current flowing in a circuit is directly proportional to the applied voltage and inversely proportional to the resistance. Simply stated, the more current that is flowing (through the resistance), the more voltage drop (across that resistance); the less current, the less voltage drop. As resistance goes up, less current flows. It can be expressed mathematically as: I (amperes) = E (volts) / R (ohms). This equation solves for the amount of current when the voltage and resistance is known. You can transpose the equation if you need to solve for voltage. E (volts) = I (amperes) times R (ohms). Or, if you knew only the voltage and the current, you could find the resistance by this form of the equation. R (ohms) = E (volts) / I (amperes).

INDUCTANCE — Inductance is the ability for a coil of wire to store energy and oppose changes in current. Sometimes an inductor, called a "choke," is used in the D.C. power supply of a guitar amp. It is used to oppose any changes in current. It works great for smoothing out the ripples in the current that occur when A.C. is rectified into D.C.

CAPACITANCE — Capacitance can be defined as how well a capacitor stores electrical charge. A capacitor is a device that stores electrical charge on conducting plates through the action of an electrostatic field between the plates. In reality, a capacitor is simply two conductors separated by a non-conductor.

Think about combing your dry hair on a winter night. Your comb will build up a static electrical charge on it. You can even use the comb to pick up small pieces of paper. The comb is an example of capacitance. The comb has an electrical charge stored on it. When I was a young child, I played with a plastic army rifle that made the hairs on my arm stand up when my arm was close to it. I was seeing the effects of capacitance.

Capacitance is measured in farads, which happens to be a great deal of capacitance, so to simplify everything; the farad is divided by a million and called a microfarad. Most of the capacitors inside an amp are rated in microfarads. If you divide a microfarad by a million you get a picofarad. A picofarad is a very small amount of capacitance. It is so small, that you could have a few picofarads of capacitance just by having two wires lay side by side! Even your shielded guitar cable has several hundred picofarads of capacitance between the center conductor and the shielding! For example, a 1000 picofarad (pf) capacitor and a .001 microfarad are the same value. To go from microfarad to picofarad you would move the decimal 6 places to the right.

In a guitar amplifier, the capacitor is used in many different ways. For example, it is useful for removing the A.C. signal component from a D.C. circuit. Sometimes a circuit has both D.C. (electrons moving the same direction) and A.C. (electrons moving in both directions.) A capacitor can be used to separate the A.C. signal voltage from the D.C. power supply voltage because it will pass A.C. signal voltage while blocking D.C. power supply voltage. Remember a capacitor is two conductors separated by a non-conductor, so A.C. cannot really pass through a capacitor; but it appears to. Actually, as a positive charge builds up on one conductor, an opposite charge will appear on the other conductor simultaneously, so the illusion is that the A.C. is passing. The capacitors in an amp used to separate A.C. from D.C. are called coupling capacitors or blocking capacitors. A typical value would be anywhere from 500 picofarads to .1 microfarads.

Capacitors are also used in tone shaping circuits. Although the capacitor can pass A.C., it does not pass all A.C. frequencies equally. The faster the frequency of the A.C. (think high-end), the easier it gets through a capacitor. The slower the frequency (think bottom-end), the harder it is for the A.C. signal to pass. Also, the more capacitance a capacitor has, the easier it is for a given frequency to get through. So as the frequency goes up or as the capacitance goes up, the capacitor passes A.C. more easily. By selecting certain value capacitors, a circuit can pass more or less of certain frequencies making possible tone shaping.

Obviously, tone shaping is done in the tone controls. But tone shaping is also achieved by placing a capacitor across the resistor that feeds the cathode (place where electricity enters) of a preamp tube. These capacitors are called bypass caps because they allow A.C. to bypass the cathode resistor of a preamp tube, thus improving the amplification of those frequencies. The D.C. current (think of this as idling current) passes through the resistor and creates a small voltage drop across the resistor while the A.C. signal current goes through the capacitor instead. If we want lower frequencies to bypass the resistor, we simply use a larger cap. Typical values for a bypass cap range anywhere from .1 microfarads to 350 microfarads. The 25 microfarad value is the most common because when used in conjunction with a 1.5K cathode resistor, it bypasses all the frequencies that a guitar is capable of producing. A smaller value would not bypass all the lows and you would hear this as less bottom end.

Capacitors oppose a change in voltage, so large value capacitors are used to smooth out the ripples that occur when A.C. wall voltage is rectified into D.C. power. We want the ripples smoothed out so there is no hum present in the power supply. Typical filter cap values range from 8 microfarad to 220 microfarad with the 20 microfarad being the most common. These filter capacitors are also used to isolate or "decouple" one amplifier gain stage from the next stage. We don't want the A.C. voltage from one stage to superimpose itself on another stage. This could cause oscillations!

BIAS — A tube is a type of electrical valve. Current comes in the cathode of the tube and leaves through the plate. The electrical charge of the grid with respect to the cathode controls how much current can flow through the tube. This "grid to cathode" relationship is called "bias"(noun). On a preamp tube, the bias of the tube is such that when the tube is idling, it is idling at half way up. Preamp tubes are self-biased. In self-biasing, a resistor is used on the cathode of the tube. When current passes through the resistor, a voltage drop occurs across the resistor. Since the cathode is connected to the resistor, the cathode has the same voltage on it. The grid has no voltage on it and the cathode has a positive voltage on it, so the grid is negative with respect to the cathode.

On output tubes, a different type of biasing scheme is sometimes used. A negative voltage supply is constantly injected onto the grids of the output tubes and the cathode of each output tube is grounded. This makes the grid negative with respect to the cathode. This is called fixed biased because a fixed amount of negative voltage is always present on the grids of the tubes. Some amps have a trim adjustment for the negative voltage supply. When one adjusts the trim adjustment of this negative voltage supply, then one is said to "bias" (verb) the amp.

SERIES CIRCUIT — When two or more electronic components are connected in a linear fashion such that all the electrical current must pass through one component before it can go through the other component; then that type of connection is called a series circuit. For example, if you had two speakers and you connect the plus lead of one speaker to the minus lead of the other speaker and then used the free lead on each speaker to apply electrical current, then those speakers are said to be wired in series. In order for the current to flow, all of it must go through one speaker before it can go through the other.

With a series connection of resistive components such as speakers, or resistors, the overall resistance of the circuit is the sum of each resistance in that circuit. If you had two 8 ohm speakers that were series connected, then the total ohms would be 16 ohm.

With a series connection, all of the current must go through each component, so the current is always the same for each component. However the voltage will drop across each component in accordance with Ohm's law.

PARALLEL CIRCUIT — When two or more electronic components are connected across each other such that the electrical current has two or more possible paths it can go, then those components are said to be connected in parallel. In a parallel circuit, the voltages are the same across each component, but the current is split up among the various components in the parallel connection.

For example, if we took two 8 ohm speakers and connected the plus leads together, then connected the minus leads together and then applied signal between the plus and minus leads, those speakers are said to be wired in parallel. When parallel wiring speakers of the same impedance, the total ohm value is found by dividing the ohms of one speaker by the number of speakers. With parallel connections, it is easier for the current to pass because there are multiple paths (like having an hour glass with two ways for the sand to pass instead of only one). Two 8 ohm speakers connected in parallel become 4 ohms. If you used three 8 ohm speakers wired in parallel, you would get 2⅔ ohms. Of course four in parallel would give 2 ohms. Every time you add another, there is another path the current can go and the resistance is lowered.

SERIES/PARALLEL OR PARALLEL/SERIES CIRCUIT Sometimes an electronic circuit will have some of the components in parallel and other components in series. When both parallel circuits and series circuits are combined we know that:

1. The sum of current flowing through each component in a parallel circuit equals the applied current.
2. Parallel connected components will have the same voltage across them.
3. The sum of voltage drops across each component in a series circuit equals the applied voltage.
4. Series connected components will have the same current flowing through them.

Using the speaker example, if you had four 8 ohm speakers and wired them such that there were two pairs — the two speakers of each pair wired in parallel (this would make each set 4 ohms) and then wired the two sets in series (you would add the 4 ohms from each set to get 8 ohms); then those speakers are said to be wired in Parallel/Series.

Alternately, one could wire four speakers such that there were two pairs with two speakers in each pair wired in series with each other (this would make 16 ohms per pair) and then wire those two sets in parallel with each other (this would bring it back to 8 ohms total). Then those speakers are said to be wired in Series/Parallel.

VOLTAGE DIVIDER — If you take ten 1 ohm resistors and connect them in series — that is one lead of one resistor connected to the next, then the other end of that one connected to the next, etc such that you would end up with a long string of 1 ohm resistors with two ends. There are a couple of things we know about that.

1. Since they are all in series, you would add the sum of the resistances to get the total resistance. If you used 10 of them, the resistance would be 10 ohms.
2. If you applied 20 volts to one end and you connected the other end to a point of zero volts (a.k.a. ground), then each 1 ohm resistor would have 2 volts of electricity across it. That is to say, if we measured from ground, to the fifth resistor; then we would get exactly 10 volts.
3. Also with the scenario above, if you measured across any single resistor by connecting the two leads of your voltmeter to the ends of any single resistor, then the meter will read 2 volts.

To sum it up, the voltage drops evenly across an even resistance. This principle is exploited in many different ways to achieve particular results in a guitar amplifier.

For example, the volume control is basically a long carbon trace that has the property of resistance. When you turn the shaft, there is an element (called a wiper and connected to the shaft) that can be adjusted to any point on the resistive carbon trace. This will vary the resistance from the wiper to either end. Let's say we are feeding the volume control with a 10 volts signal. That 10 volt signal is connected to one end of the resistive carbon trace inside the potentiometer, the other end of the trace is connected to ground (zero volts), and the wiper can be adjusted anywhere from zero to 10 volts — depending on where the wiper is physically touching the carbon trace. When the wiper is closest to zero volts, then it too will be zero volts. If the wiper is place half way up the trace, then the voltage on the wiper will be 5 volts.

One could take this same voltage divider (volume control) idea and combine it with frequency sensitive circuitry to get tone controls. Your treble, middle and bass controls are designed by arranging various capacitors and resistors that select certain ranges of frequencies and sending those signals to a voltage divider.

Besides almost every potentiometer on the amp operating as a voltage divider, the voltage divider concept is also used in many other circuits in the amplifier. For example the number 2 input on a Fender Blackface or Silverface amp is configured as a voltage divider. When you plug into the number 2 input, a switch is opened that puts two 68K resistors in series. One free end is connected to your guitar pickup and the other end goes to ground. The output signal is taken off the junction of these two resistors, thus the signal is actually cut in half. This configuration actually cuts the voltage from your pickup in half, thus reducing the overall gain by 3 dB.

There are two 220K resistors on the main filter totem pole stack in the power supply of almost all Blackface and Silverface Fenders. By putting these resistors in series with each other, but in parallel with the two 70 uf 350 volt filter caps, the voltage is divided exactly in half across each filter cap. This insures that there are equal voltages across each 70 uf filter capacitor.

The voltage divider concept regulates how much negative voltage the bias supply is putting out to the grids of the output tubes. Negative voltage bias supply circuits will always have two or more resistors and possibly an adjustment pot, configured as a voltage divider, to divide off just the right amount of voltage.

Sometimes, the voltage divider is used to drop the gain of a particular stage. In the 6G15 Fender reverb, for example, the 12AT7 between the input jack and dwell control uses a voltage divider on the actual plate load resistor. Two resistors are put in series such that only $\frac{1}{11}$th of the signal is divided off to go to the dwell control.

POLARITY — Probably the most simple example of polarity is the battery. One end is plus or positive and the other end is minus or negative. The battery is a D.C. electrical source. All of the electrons flow in one direction only, from negative to positive.

Some components in guitar amps must be mounted in a particular polarity. For example, all filter capacitors in a guitar amp are mounted with the minus lead going to ground with only one exception. In a negative voltage supply, the positive of the filter cap goes to ground and the negative goes to the circuit.

SINGLE-ENDED — When a single tube is used in a circuit to amplify an audio signal, then that tube is said to be operated as single-ended. All preamp tubes are single-ended. Since all preamp tubes are operated single ended, when someone speaks of single-ended, they are usually referring to the output stage and not the preamp stage.

With amplifiers using only one output tube, the output stage is always configured as single-ended. Single-ended audio amplifiers must always be operated in class A. That means all single-ended

Making Sense of Tube Amp Talk

amplifiers are class A, but that does not necessarily mean that all Class A amplifiers are single-ended.

VOLTAGE AMPLIFIER — Tube amplifiers circuits may be classified in a number of ways according to use, bias, frequency response or resonant quality. When classified according to use or type of service, amplifiers fall into two general groups — voltage amplifiers and power amplifiers. Voltage amplifiers are so designed so that signals of relatively small amplitude (small voltage) applied between the grid and cathode of the tube will produce large values of amplified signal voltage across the load in the plate circuit. The preamp tubes in an amp are almost always configured as a voltage amplifier, but not always. Output tubes are not considered voltage amplifiers.

POWER AMPLIFIER — When a tube delivers a large amount of power to the load in the plate circuit, it is said to be a power amplifier. Since power, in general, is equal to the voltage times the current, a power amplifier must develop across its load sufficient voltage to cause rated current to flow; however with a power amplifier, the primary focus is on power and that is what distinguishes it from a voltage amplifier such as a 12AX7. The output tubes in a guitar amplifier are the power amplifiers. Their main purpose is to add current to the signal. This is different from a preamp tube (voltage amplifier) whose main purpose is to increase signal voltage.

GAIN — In a voltage amplifier, such as a 12AX7 or other voltage amplifier device, gain is the ratio of A.C. output voltage to A.C. input voltage. Certain preamp tubes have more gain than others. For example, with a 12AX7, if there is a change in grid voltage of 1 volt, it will produce a change in plate voltage by 100 volts. In a 12AT7, a change of 1 volt on the grid will produce a change of 60 voltages on the plate. Similarly, a 12AY7 will have a 44 volt change when the grid voltage is changed by 1 volt.

POWER AMPLIFICATION — In a power amplifier, power amplification is the ratio of output power to the input grid driving power. This is a concept similar to gain, but gain is increase in A.C. signal voltage whereas power amplification is increase in power. You could think of it as power gain.

CATHODE FOLLOWER — The cathode follower is a single-ended class A degenerative amplifier, the output of which appears across the unbypassed cathode resistor. This circuit is used in the preamp section of some guitar amps. Though rare, an output tube could be configured as a cathode follower. The gain of a cathode follower is always less than unity. That means the voltage output is always slightly less than the voltage input however the circuit is capable of producing power gain.

So why would anyone use this type of circuit if it slightly loses gain? It is used to match a high impedance to a low impedance. Think of it as a buffer circuit that separates two other circuits. It gets its name because the output voltage FOLLOWS the input voltage. The output not only has the same waveform, but it has the same instantaneous polarity. The output is almost the same as the input, except is has more current (power). Also, this circuit sounds very rich and detailed. It improves the stability of the amp because it is a degenerative amplifier. You will see it as the third stage in all early Marshalls, Fender Tweed Bassmans, most Kendrick amplifiers and many others. You can also find it in "dry signal" circuit of the 6G15 Fender standalone Reverb unit. Originally, Fender used it to buffer the tone circuits from the rest of the amp, but it really had great tone. I suspect that Marshall used it because they were trying to copy Fender!

PUSH-PULL — There are two popular ways that the output tubes in an amp can be configured as power amplifiers. The first way, is single-ended. In single-ended, a single tube (or two tubes in parallel) connect to ONE END of an output transformer. Hence the name: single-ended. The other end of the output transformer goes to a high voltage (B+) supply. This type of configuration is always operated in Class A.

There is another way of configuring two or more tubes in an output stage and it is called PUSH-PULL. In push pull, a center-tapped primary is used on the output transformer.

The plate of one tube connects to one end of the transformer primary, the plate of the other tube connects to the other end of the primary and the high voltage supply connects to the center-tap. For this to work, the signal voltage driving these two tubes must be 180 degrees out of phase with each other. You've probably seen a picture of a sound wave where it has a hill and a valley. The top of the hill is 180 degrees out of phase with the bottom of the valley. Out of phase, simply put, means one tube is getting positive signal while the other is getting negative signal and vice versa.

What makes this work is the fact that the power tubes are driven out of phase, but the transformer "flips phase" to reinvert the signal coming off the secondary of the transformer back "in phase." How does it do this? Picture a bar of iron with a coil of wire wound around it. For example, if you situate the bar such that it is vertical and you are looking directly on top of the bar, you might notice that the turns of wire on that bar appear clockwise. Keeping the bar vertical, but changing your viewing perspective to directly underneath the bar, the turns now appear counterclockwise. So when plate current from one tube feeds the beginning of the transformer winding and moving "down" towards the center-tap, it will produce current in the secondary of the transformer that is 180 degrees out of phase with the signal produced when current is introduced from the end of the winding and flowing "up" towards the center-tap. That is why we want to drive the two tubes with out of phase signal — because the transformer will "reinvert" the signals so that they become "in phase" with each other when they appear on the secondary. Interestingly, the secondary develops signal that is the average of what the two tubes are putting out. This is why push-pull overdrive rules. When one of the tubes is pushed to cut-off (no current), the other tube is pushed to saturation. The average of those two will give a smooth overdriven waveform both at the hill and the valley of the wave.

Sometimes, to achieve greater power and more headroom, four tubes are used such that two tubes are connected in parallel to one end of the output transformer primary with the other two tubes connected in parallel to the other end. You've seen this in all high-powered amps such as the Marshall 100 watt or the Kendrick Spindletop.

There are many advantages to be gained by using the push-pull power amplifier configuration. Second harmonics and all even numbered harmonics, as well as even-order combinations of frequencies will be effectively eliminated if the tubes are balanced and if the harmonics are introduced within the output tubes themselves. Hum from B+ power supply, a big problem in single-ended designs, is substantially reduced because ripple components which are present in both halves of the primary on the output transformer, phase cancel each other. Also, filament hum which inevitably leaks from the 6.3 volt heaters to the plate circuit, will also phase cancel in the primary of the output transformer. So you end up with a quieter, more hum-free design.

Besides all that, a push-pull design can be operated in class AB which is more efficient than a single-ended Class A design. The result is greater than the sum of the parts. For example, a single-ended 6L6 might produce only 10 watts of power, so if you used two 6L6's in parallel with a single-ended design, you may end up with 20 watts. However, take two 6L6's with a push-pull configuration and you could end up with 50 watts or so. This is why you almost always see amps with two or more output tubes configured as push-pull.

Push-pull doesn't have to always be Class AB. It can also be operated in Class A. To do so, all you have to do is bias the tube where the idle plate current is half way between cutoff and saturation and limit the drive signal such that the tube never gets driven in to cutoff. This gives you class A push-pull, ala Vox AC30.

PHASE INVERTER — This is a circuit, the purpose of which, is to create two signals that are 180 degrees out of phase with each other. The phase inverter is used in a push-pull amplifier to drive the power tubes out of phase with one another. One phase inverter output supplies signal to the grid of one output tube and the other phase inverter output, which is 180 degrees out of phase with the first output, feeds the grid of the other output tube. There are several ways to achieve phase inversion. It could be done with a phase inversion transformer or with tubes. If done with tubes, it is usually done with a single triode or with two triodes.

Besides being used in push-pull power amps, you are likely to see this circuit in the preamp vibrato circuit of certain early 60s Fender amps. In these types of vibrato, an oscillator signal drives a phase inverter which modulates different frequencies. It is like having two oscillators that are exactly synchronized to modulate different frequencies in a pin-ponging effect.

TRANSFORMER PHASE INVERTER — Perhaps the simplest way to achieve phase inversion is through the use of a center-tapped interstage coupling transformer. The transformer style phase inverter was used on many Gibson amps. The transformer has a centertap on the secondary that is either grounded or attached to a negative bias voltage supply — depending on whether the output stage is cathode biased or fixed biased. The two ends of the secondary each feed an output tube in the push-pull output stage. Of course, the transformer secondary must be tapped at the exact electrical center; otherwise the signals on the secondary will not be symmetrical.

This type of phase inversion has limited application because of losses and distortion inherent in transformers. For example, the loss in voltage (through leakage reactance) is greater for high frequencies than it is for lower frequencies. Also the shunting capacitance effect also increases with frequency. A really great sounding phase inversion transformer is cost prohibitive, which can explain why all the transformer phase inverters used on guitar amps lack detail and sound dull.

PARAPHASE INVERTER — The paraphase inverter uses two triodes or two sections of the same tube. We have all seen this circuit used on all "B" and "C" series tweed Fender push-pull amps. The first triode is configured as a regular amplifier. The output of this tube feeds one of the output tubes and a voltage divider. The voltage divider feeds another triode. When the signal goes through the second triode, the phase is flipped 180 degrees and the output feeds the other output tube. To keep the gain balanced, the voltage divider is used to bump the gain down slightly before the signal hits the second triode.

The inherent flaw in this design is the fact that the inverted signal will have distortion present that the uninverted signal lacks. Because of this, it is impossible to get a very clean tone. Also, because every triode is slightly different, it is nearly impossible for this circuit to ever have perfect balance.

SELF-BALANCED PARAPHASE INVERTER — This circuit is nearly identical to the regular paraphase inverter, except for way the voltage divider in between the two triode sections is configured. We have all seen this circuit on "D" series tweed Fenders. The voltage divider is configured such that the second triode section's output is also put back through the same load resistor. If the second section has too much gain, it will slightly phase cancel some of the input signal coming from the first triode section and correct itself.

Although this circuit might be more balanced than the paraphase inverter, it still has the same inherent flaw of having distortion present in one side that is not present in the other. Again, a quality clean tone is impossible with this setup.

DISTRIBUTIVE LOAD PHASE INVERTER — We've all seen this circuit on "E" series tweed Fender amps. In this type of circuit, a single tube is used to achieve phase inversion. This circuit exploits the fact that the cathode of a tube is 180 degrees out of phase with its plate. A signal is introduced to the grid of the distributive load phase inverter tube. The output of the phase inverter is taken from two different places - the cathode and the plate. These two components are 180 degrees out of phase with each other, so one output drives one power tube and the other output drives the other power tube. Because two out of phase signals are taken from the same tube, sometimes this circuit is called a phase splitter.

The quality of the distributive load phase inverter is much better than the other types covered thus far. This type of inverter uses only one triode section and that makes it different from the others. Also, with the distributive load inverter, there is always a slight loss in gain. The other types of tube phase inverters produce gain.

We've also seen the distributive load phase inverter used on most Ampegs — including the SVT and the V4.

LONG-TAILED PAIR PHASE INVERTER — Perhaps the most commonly used phase inverter today is the long-tailed pair. We have seen this circuit on "F" series tweed Fenders; Brownface, Blackface and Silverface Fenders; almost all Marshalls, all Boogies, almost all Kendricks, all Vox AC30s and many others. It has other names such as the Schmitt Phase Inverter, Common Cathode Impedance Self-balancing Inverter, Grounded Grid inverter, or Long-tailed Pair. With this type of circuit, two triode sections are used and an exact balance may be obtained by suitable proportioning of the two load resistors.

In this type of circuit, there is no bypass capacitor on the cathode resistor and the entire cathode circuit stands on a "long-tail" resistor. The larger the value of the "long-tail" resistor, the more balance but less gain the circuit will produce. The grid of the second triode section is connected to both a grid resistor and a coupling capacitor. The capacitor is in parallel with the entire cathode circuit/long tail resistor. Any out of balance voltage across the long-tail resistor excites the grid of the second triode through the coupling capacitor.

TONE STACKS — A tone stack is a variable filter circuit in which the frequency response of an amplifier is adjustable to suit one's own taste. There are many different ways to achieve this because one can boost treble, boost bass, attenuate treble, or attenuate bass. To further complicate matters, one can have the tone stack directly in the signal path, or in a feedback path. Even though there are dozens of circuit possibilities, there are five circuits that are most common.

SINGLE-KNOB TONE STACK — Certainly the most simple, a single-knob tone stack is a capacitor in series with a potentiometer. It is almost always configured as a treble attenuation circuit. For example, we see this circuit as the single knob tone control on most guitars. A capacitor is placed in series with a pot. The cap/pot series assembly is connected between the hot lead of the circuit and ground. As the pot is turned to have less resistance, more of the highs are grounded out. Remember high frequencies go through a capacitor very easily but low frequencies do not. When the knob is turned to its least resistance, the capacitor allows high frequencies to ground out, but not lows. When the knob is turned to its highest resistance, very little of the high frequency signal can pass to ground.

There are other ways of configuring such a circuit. For example, instead of grounding the circuit, it could be connected across the grids of a push-pull output stage. As the pot's resistance is decreased, the highs would phase cancel each other. We have seen this circuit as the high-cut of a Vox AC30.

COMPOUND SINGLE-KNOB TONE STACK — We can take this treble attenuation circuit to another level by configuring it such that as the knob is turned one way the highs are attenuated, but as it is turned the other way the highs are boosted. We see this circuit across the instrument channel of a 5E3 Tweed Deluxe. When the tone control is turned up, the circuit actually bypasses highs around the volume control to boost treble, yet grounds highs out when the knob is turned down. It is interesting to note that the microphone channel is not configured this way. It is configured only as a treble attenuation circuit, yet both channels use the same knob!

AMPEG TONE STACK — Almost all Ampeg amps use a high fidelity tone stack that is also called the Baxandall tone stack. This circuit first appeared in Audio Engineering magazine in the 50s and was touted as a low-loss "active" tone control. By "active," we mean when the tone control is half way up the circuit is "normal." Turning the control either up or down will either boost or attenuate certain frequencies. This is a clever arrangement of capacitors and pots such that there are two controls: a bass and treble. When the bass is turned up, the bass frequencies are boosted. When it is turned down, the bass frequencies are attenuated. Likewise, when the treble control is turned up, the treble frequencies are boosted. If the treble control is turned down, the treble frequencies are attenuated. Because of less loss than other types of tone circuits, this circuit was very popular for Hi Fi amplifier circuits in the 50s and 60s. It has a different sound than other types of tone circuits because there is no midrange boost or attenuation.

FENDER/MARSHALL TONE STACK — Although Fender experimented with different types of tone controls in the 40s, 50s and early 60s, the tone stack used on the 5F6A Bassman eventually emerged as their favorite. It was used on all Blackface and Silverface amps. It is basically a passive crossover that divides the frequencies into ranges. The pots allow one to select more or less of these frequencies. All Marshall amps 50 watts and over used this same tone stack. This type of stack has a characteristic tone that is unique. We've seen the same tone stack on all Vox amps 30 watts and up.

It is interesting to note that where the tone stack occurs in the circuit makes a huge difference on how well it performs. For example, a Blackface Super Reverb has the tone circuit immediately after the first gain stage where signal voltages are relatively small. Any change produced by the tone circuit has a big impact on the overall sound. Contrast this with a plexi-glass Marshall, whose similar tone stack occurs after the third stage where signal voltage is fairly high. Notice how turning the knobs on the Marshall will have little effect on the overall tone of the amp. It is because the signal voltage is so high, that the tone controls have less relative effect on the signal.

NEGATIVE FEEDBACK DRIVEN TONE STACK — We see this circuit over and over again on the presence circuits for Fender and Marshall amps. To understand how it works, we must first understand negative feedback. The negative feedback circuit takes a very small signal from the output of the amp and injects it back into a previous section of the amp. Care is taken to inject it into a section of the amp that is out of phase with the output. This causes slight phase cancellation. The amount of negative feedback is limited because we only want a little phase cancellation. This is done so that the amp will play more evenly at all frequencies. If a particular frequency wants to amplify more than normal, more of that frequency will be fed back, thus, phase canceling that frequency a little more than normal and correcting it to be the same level as the other frequencies. The presence control basically limits the amount of high-end that is fed back. If less highs are fed back, then there will be less phase cancellation to those frequencies and thus the highs will seem to be boosted. In the presence circuit, the frequencies controlled are above 5K. There are no notes on a guitar this high. So why would we want to boost signals above 5K? Because there are overtones and harmonics in this range and those are the frequencies give that jangly, acoustic guitar-like quality.

Tube Guitar Amplifier Essentials

AMP TIPS FOR THE TECHNICALLY CHALLENGED

When I look at a vintage tube amplifier, I love to check out the actual circuit layout, how components are grounded, the lead dress, and some of the clever little tricks that builders have used to "help" their designs. You may ask, "Why does it matter how a circuit is laid out in an amp chassis?" A capacitor is simply "two conductors separated by a non-conductor." Since every wire in the amp is a conductor, and each wire has non-conductors between it and all the other wires: doesn't that qualify as the definition of a capacitor? Stray capacitance could occur between any two wires in the amp! Of course, the closer the two wires are together, the more capacitance they will have and the easier it is for the signal from one wire to appear on the other one! One can actually measure the capacitance on two adjacent wires with a capacitance meter.

Regardless if you make your living playing guitar, play as a weekend warrior, or pick a few licks just for personal satisfaction, there are some electronic basics that are important for you to know. Although I have heard it said that "Ignorance is bliss," in this case "Ignorance" can mean a blown up amp or premature tube failure, which is not bliss. If you are an electric guitar player, but not very technical-minded, don't worry. There is hope for you.

BASIC #1 — GUITAR CABLES (PATCH CORDS) AND SPEAKER CABLES ARE NOT INTERCHANGEABLE. If you use a guitar cable as a speaker cable, you could likely damage your amp. If you use a speaker cable as a guitar patch cord, you will have major-league, industrial-strength hum.

Guitar cables are used for very low-level signals. A guitar pickup puts out ¼ volt or less at almost no current. The wire inside a guitar cable has a very small diameter because that is what is needed for this miniscule signal. Also, the guitar cable is shielded to keep from picking up hum.

The output of an amp puts out as much as 40 volts at perhaps as much as 9 amps of current. That is why speaker cable is extremely thick. It is used to carry large current at relatively higher voltages to the speakers. If you use a guitar cord for a speaker cable, it is likely that the current will not be able to get through the wire. Think of it as though you are trying to squeeze a fast flowing river through a garden hose. Something has to give. It could cause arcing and subsequent destruction in your output transformer, tubes or tube sockets. You may have been getting away with the wrong cable while at low volume playing, but medium to high volume invites disaster.

BASIC #2 — A TUBE AMPLIFIER MUST HAVE PROPER LOAD AT ALL TIMES. This means if the amp has an output jack, you are not to turn the amp on unless there is a speaker cord going from the output jack to the speakers. It is best to use the correct speaker load, although certain parameters of mismatch are acceptable.

If you run a tube amp without a speaker load connected, it could result in arcing across the output tube sockets; and it could possibly arc the output transformer, thus ruining it. Once a transformer or a socket arcs, it will leave a carbonized spot that will promote arcing in the future. Simply put: arc it once and it is history.

If you have a bad speaker cable that has an open circuit, the harm will be the same as if you ran the amp with no load. That is why you should always use quality and proper cabling to your speakers.

If you ever turn on a tube amp and start playing and there is no sound coming out, stop playing at once! You do not want to chance the damage that a lack of speaker load can cause. Check your cables, speaker, etc, before playing the amp again.

Never operate an amp at an impedance mismatch of more than 100%. If you mismatch with a smaller speaker load than is normally required, it will work, but the output tubes wear twice as fast.

For example, if you have a 4 ohm amp and you use a 2 ohm speaker load, it will definitely wear the tubes out much faster.

On the other hand, if you mismatch the impedance with a higher load than what is normally required (let's use a 16 ohm cabinet on an

8 ohm amp), you will have more compression, less volume, and the tubes will last much longer than they normally would.

BASIC #3 — USE THE STANDBY SWITCH. Vacuum tubes are meant to be hot before high voltages are present. If high voltage is placed on the tube before it is warmed up, then the chemical coatings on the cathode of the tube will begin to be stripped off and the tube will not sound good any more.

There is a reason why there is a standby switch on a tube amp. The idea is to turn the power on and let the tubes warm up for at least a minute or two and then turn the standby switch into the play position. It is not necessary to turn the standby switch any particular way when turning the amp off. Just make sure you have the switch in the standby mode when powering up.

What about tube amps that don't have standby switches? Some of those amps don't need a standby switch if they use a controlled warm-up time rectifier tube, such as a GZ34 or a 5V4. The rectifier tube is the tube that makes high voltage DC. If it takes longer for this tube to warm up than all the other tubes, then you don't need a standby switch. The controlled warm-up time rectifier tube will provide high voltage only after the other tubes have warmed up.

On the other hand, some of those "standby switchless" amps are mistakes. For example, the Orange amps were solid-state rectified with no standby switch. This would wear the tubes out very quickly and therefore is a design flaw. Another example of bad design is the fabled Tweed Champ, which has a 5Y3 rectifier and no standby switch. (The 5Y3 tube has a directly heated cathode and provides high voltage almost immediately). This design flaw can be corrected by simply using a 5AR4/GZ34 (controlled warm-up time) rectifier tube.

BASIC #4 — TUBE AMPS MUST BE FIRED UP AT LEAST TWICE A YEAR. If you have many amps in your collection, you must turn them on and play them at least twice a year. Just as you must drive your car occasionally to keep it in good working order, your amp must be played for it to sound its best. When you turn it on and play it, you are charging the electrolytic capacitors and helping those capacitors keep their functionality. If you neglect to use them, you will need a cap job sooner rather than later.

This explains why some of the cleanest examples of vintage amps are the absolute worst sounding and some of the vintage amps that look "beat to death" are the best sounding. Use it or lose it.

BASIC # 5 — TURN OFF YOUR AMP BETWEEN SETS. Tube amps get very hot when they are in use. A Dual Showman will burn your finger if you touch either the standby switch or the power switch after the amp had been on for an hour. Many Blackface amps and tweed amps get hot enough to fry an egg after an hour of usage. Heat is not good for non-tube electronic components such as diodes, capacitors, and resistors. Turning the amp "off" will give these non-tube components a chance to cool down before the amp starts cooking again.

BASIC #6 — THERE IS A HUGE TONALITY AND RESPONSE DIFFERENCE BETWEEN PREAMP TUBE OVERDRIVE AND OUTPUT TUBE OVERDRIVE. When a tube is overdriven, how it is configured will determine how it sounds. For example, all preamp tubes are configured as single-ended. Almost all output tubes are configured as push-pull.

Most of us have seen a picture of a sound wave, with its hill and valley. When we say a preamp tube is single-ended, what we mean is that the single tube amplifies both the hill and valley portion of the sound wave. The single-ended tube amplifies the hill by drawing more current and amplifies the valley by drawing less current. When a single-ended tube is overdriven, there comes a point when the hill cannot get any bigger and the tube saturates. This sounds full and rich. The top of the wave gets rounded and smooth. At the same time this happens, the valley is drawing less and less current until it gets to the point where it is cut off. There are not different degrees of "off"! When something is "off," it is simply "off." So when a preamp tube is overdriven, the hill portion of the wave is rounded and smooth while the valley portion is whacked off flat. This results in a buzzy, over-compressed distortion that produces listener fatigue after a few minutes or so. Preamp overdrive is not very responsive to picking nuance. Pick hard — it is buzzy, pick soft — it is still buzzy. Preamp tube overdrive will not cut through a mix because it is too compressed to stand out.

When an output stage is configured as push-pull what we mean is that one tube amplifies the hill portion of the wave while the other output tube amplifies the valley portion. The one output tube that amplifies the hill does so by drawing more current; and the other output tube that amplifies the valley also does so by drawing more current. When the tubes are overdriven the one tube amplifying the hill saturates and produces a rounded and smooth hilltop. While this is occurring, the other tube is amplifying the valley by drawing more and more current until it also saturates at the same time. We end up with both a rounded hilltop and a rounded valley resulting in an organic sounding overdrive that does not produce listener fatigue.

Output stage overdrive is touch sensitive as one can pick lightly and not overdrive, then pick hard and cause overdrive. Output stage overdrive has dynamics and although compressed, is not over-compressed.

BASIC #7 — FIND A GOOD TECH OR LEARN HOW TO BIAS YOUR OWN AMP. Tube amps need to have the output tubes biased to sound their best. Just as a high-performance car needs certain adjustments (timing, valve, fuel injection), your amp will do its best when the output tubes' operating level is adjusted properly.

If you have a good tech and you don't care to learn to bias, that is fine. But, if you don't have a tech you trust or you just want to learn to do it yourself; complete instructions on amp biasing can be found starting on page 101 of my first book, *A Desktop Reference of Hip Vintage Guitar Amps.* You will need only a simple digital multimeter.

After you have performed the biasing procedure a few times, you will find yourself biasing your amps more frequently. You can change output tubes anytime you want and then set the bias on that particular set so that your amp always sounds its best. There is no one perfect biasing point. Biasing involves a range of parameters that can make your amp break up faster or slower, depending on how you like it. When you know how to bias your own amp, you can take the time to listen to these different settings and determine which setting works best with your playing style. Once you know that, you can duplicate that setting every time with a particular amp. Your amp will always sound its best and when it sounds its best, you will be inspired to play your best. When you are playing your best and the amp is sounding its best, the experience of making music gets elevated to a higher level.

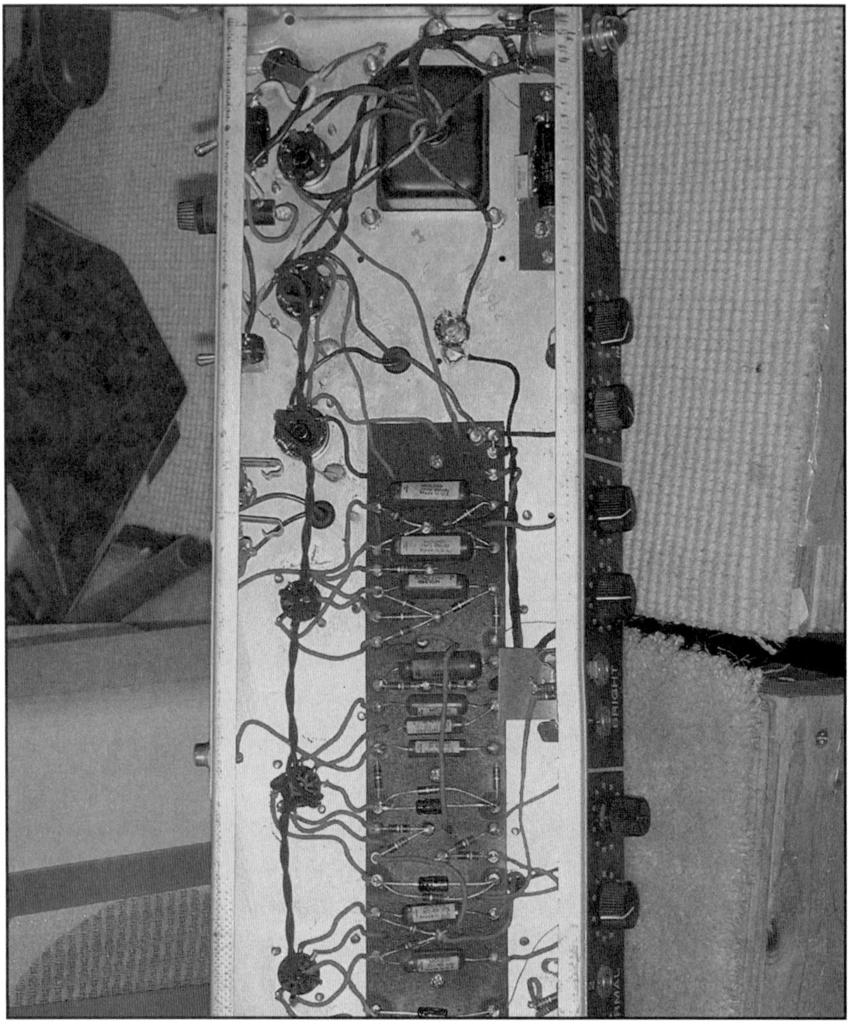
Deluxe Amp
BRIGHT

TUBE AMP TIPS EVERY GUITARIST SHOULD KNOW

Nothing works perfectly all the time. There will be times when your tube amp malfunctions. Why? Well, for one thing, tube amps operate at high voltages and high heat. Also, there are many components and connections. If any one of these components or connections fails, there will be trouble with the amp. Just as a driver of an automobile needs to know what to do if the car does not start, here are some tips for troubleshooting and repairing common malfunctions with tube amps.

THE FUSE BLOWS — You are playing a gig and your amp stops playing. A fuse has just blown. What do you do? I hope that you have several extra fuses with you. Fuses generally come in a small box that holds about five fuses. I keep a box of these in the bottom of my amp cabinet. That way, if I blow a fuse, I have several handy. (Make sure and use the correct type and amperage rating. Most amps use Slo-Blo fuses.)

It is important to know that when a fuse blows in an amp that has otherwise been working fine, in almost every case, **either a power tube went bad or there is a problem with the rectifier.** (The rectifier may be a tube, but in some amps, it will be a diode.) When a fuse blows, it is NEVER a bad fuse!

Here is the quick way to troubleshoot.
1. Remove both (or four depending on the design) output tubes
2. Replace the fuse with the correct value and type
3. Turn on the amp
A. **If the fuse does not blow at this point,** one of the output tubes is probably bad. To find out which one, simply replace only one of them in the amp. Turn on the amp. If the fuse blows, that tube was bad. On the other hand, if the fuse does not blow, it is probably the other tube. (You could verify this by replacing the other tube and see if the fuse blows.) We removed the output tubes and replaced

them one at a time to see which one caused the fuse to blow.

B. **If the fuse blows with both (or four depending on the design) output tubes removed from the amp, most likely your rectifier tube or rectifier diode is bad.** If you have a rectifier tube, remove it from the amp, install a new fuse and turn on the amp again. If the fuse still blows without a rectifier tube and without output tubes, it is almost a sure bet your power transformer is bad. Of course, if removing the rectifier stopped the fuse-blowing problem, then replace the rectifier tube with a fresh tube and you should be good to go.

C. **If there is no rectifier tube and the fuse blew after removing both output tubes, then there is a great chance that one or more of the rectifier diodes are shorted.** Although it would be difficult to change diodes at a gig, that would be the next step. If you are troubleshooting and you do not have any diodes handy for replacement, you could simply remove the rectifier diodes from the amp and replace the fuse. Turn on the amp. If the fuse blows, there is a 99.99% chance that your power transformer is bad. If the fuse does not blow, replace the diodes with new ones and that should fix the problem. When replacing diodes, I like to use better ones than stock. Most manufacturers use 1N4007 diodes that are rated at 1 amp and 1000 PIV (peak inverse voltage). I like to use either a 1N5399, RL207, RL257, or 1N5408. These are the 1.5 amp, 2 amp, 2.5 amp and 3 amp versions respectively of the 1N4007. Remember, diodes are heat sensitive, so using one rated for more amperage will be more dependable — especially when the amp is heated up hot enough to barbecue some beef ribs.

No Sound — You turn on your amp with the cabling correct, and there is no sound! You know there is power, because the pilot lamp is shining brightly. Knowing what to do at this point could possibly save you an output transformer! Here is what to do.

1. **Stop Playing.** Serious damage can occur to a tube amp if the amp is played with a disconnected speaker. If you operate the amp without a speaker correctly hooked up, then it is likely that arcing will occur — possibly in the output transformer and possibly across the output tube socket. Never play through an amp that is not producing sound, unless you want to run up a huge repair bill.

2. **Check all connections, especially the speaker.** Naturally, the "no sound" problem could be with the guitar or cabling, so we want to check this. Also, make sure the speaker is connected properly. This includes looking at the lead on the speaker itself to make sure BOTH wires are connected to the speaker. This also includes checking that the speaker is plugged into the speaker output jack and not the external speaker jack. (Note: Many amps have the main speaker output jack shorted with a switch to protect from accidentally running the amp without a load. That is why on Fender Blackface amps, for example, the speaker jack must be used. This prevents the shorting jack from shorting the output.)
3. **Look at the tubes.** Are they all in the socket? Sometimes a tube will fall out of the socket during transit to a gig. Do a visual check to make sure all tubes are securely in the socket.
4. **Check to make sure the speaker is responding.** You could touch a 9 volt battery to the speaker plug (or speaker leads as the case may be) to see if the speaker is responding. If there is a ¼" plug that plugs the speaker into the amp, try unplugging this and touch the batterys + and - terminals to both the tip and sleeve of the plug. You should hear a "pop" sound coming from the speaker when the battery is connected. If there is no sound; then the plug, the speaker cable or the speaker is bad.

If there is no "pop" when the battery touches the tip and sleeve, try putting the battery directly on the speaker leads. (There are two leads on the speaker and two on the battery. In this case, polarity makes no difference. We are just checking to see if the speaker is responding.) From this test, you should be able to determine if the speaker or the plug is the offending problem.

A NOISE DEVELOPS — You are playing along then unexpectedly… snap crackle pop. You think it is a tube but which one?

1. **If the noise occurs when you are not running a guitar through the amp,** you can troubleshoot (using the omission technique) to find which tube is noisy. Start with the amp "on" and in the "play" mode. Begin removing preamp tubes — one at a time — starting at the preamp tube closest to the input jack. When you remove the first tube, notice if the noise was affected. If not, try removing the next tube. Continue removing and listening until the noise stops.

Tube Amp Tips Every Guitarist Should Know

A. **If the noise is still there after removing all the preamp tubes**, the noise is not coming from the preamp stage. It is coming from the output stage.
B. **When a preamp tube is removed and the noise disappears**, then either that tube is responsible for the noise, or the noise is coming from the circuitry — in the circuit before that particular preamp tube.
2. **If the noise occurs only when you are running the guitar through the amp**, you can troubleshoot (using the substitution technique) to find which tube is noisy. To do this, take a known good preamp tube and substitute it with another preamp tube in the amp. Hopefully, the preamp tubes will be the same type, in which case you could take the one pulled and use it to substitute in the next socket until the offending tube is found.

FIRST AID KIT FOR THE GUITARIST — What we know is this: Any tube guitar amp that is used continuously and played hard will eventually malfunction. What we don't know is: When will it malfunction? Be prepared for the unexpected by carrying a **Tube Amp First Aid Kit** to every gig. It could be a small case loaded with items you may need, such as:

1. Set of output tubes
2. Rectifier Tube
3. Extra Preamp tubes
4. Box of fuses
5. Extra patch cords
6. Flashlight
7. 9 volt battery
8. Ohmmeter (for checking continuity in cabling or speakers)
9. Phillips screwdriver
10. Needle nose pliers

CONCLUSION — Driving a car does not require you to rebuild an engine, although every driver should know the basics of how to check oil level, change a tire or add water. If you are playing a tube amp, there will be times when knowing these simple basics could help save you time and frustration with simple malfunctions.

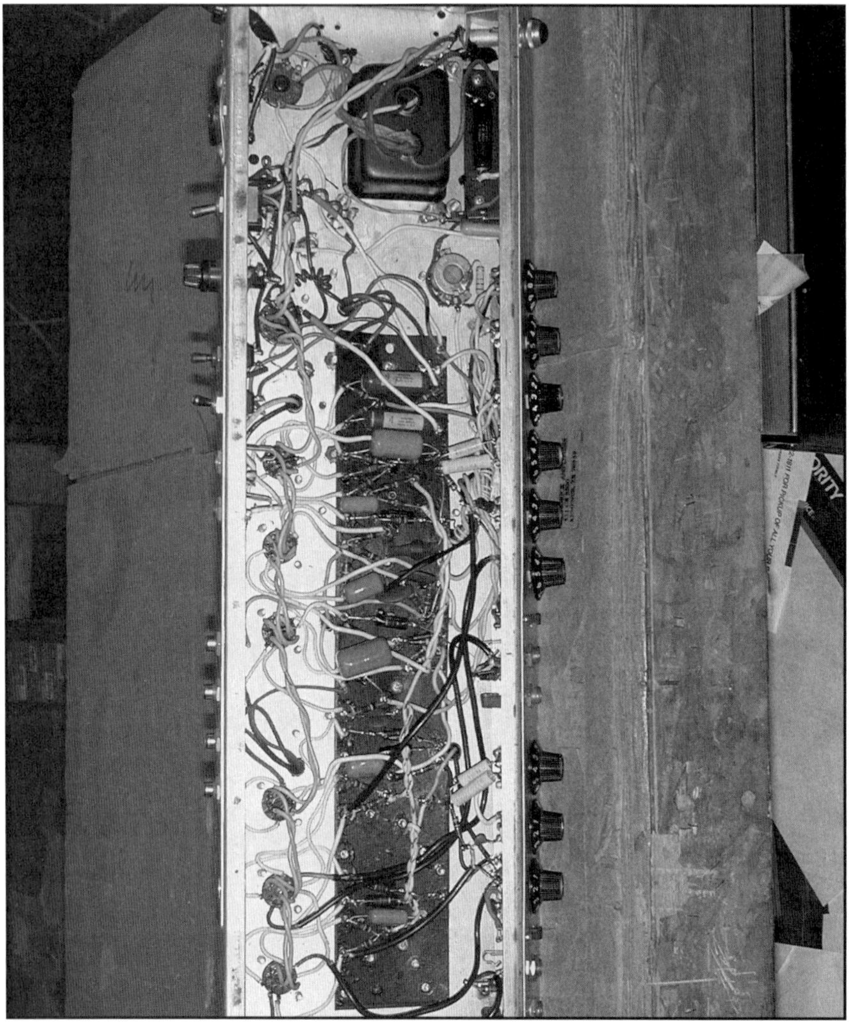

SERVICING TUBE AMPS: GETTING STARTED

In the last ten years, more and more guitarists, smitten by the tube amp bug, have become obsessed with their amp sounding its absolute best. In the same spirit that a sports car enthusiast wants to do his own valve adjustments, oil changes, and tune-ups; many guitarists are wanting to perform minor service, maintenance and biasing adjustments on their own tube guitar amplifiers.

If you want to get under the hood, yet you feel like an electronics illiterate, there's hope for you. Here are some simple basics of getting started.

HOW TO DETERMINE PINOUT ON A TUBE SOCKET

Almost all tubes, whether preamp tubes or output tubes, have a "key." On the larger 8 pin tube socket, there is a guide-pin hole in the center of the tube socket. This guide-pin hole has a notch in the hole so that the tube can only go in one way. The notch is referred to as the "key." If the amp chassis is removed from the cabinet and you are looking at the underside of the socket and looking at the key, the first pin clockwise from the key is pin #1. Going clockwise from there, the next pin is pin #2. Continuing clockwise you would have pin #3, pin #4, etc.

On a 9 pin miniature socket there is no guide-pin hole in the center. Instead, the pins are are evenly spaced as if for 10 pins except only 9 pins are used. This leaves a space where the tenth pin could have gone and yet is not included. That space is the "key." With the chassis removed from the cabinet and looking at the bottom of the socket, pin #1 is the first pin clockwise from the key. Going clockwise from there, the next pin is pin #2. Continuing clockwise you would have pin #3, pin #4, etc.

If your chassis is mounted in the cabinet and you are looking at the socket from the top, then pin #1 is the first pin counter-clockwise from the "key." Pin #1 is clockwise (from the key) looking at the bottom of the socket but counter-clockwise looking from the top.

HOW TO SAFELY DRAIN THE HIGH VOLTAGE POWER SUPPLY

On some amps, high voltage remains in the amplifier long after the A.C. cord is unplugged from the wall. If you are doing service inside the amp, it is better to drain the high voltage from the power supply to avoid the possibility of a shocking experience.

Certain amps have bleeder circuits built into the power supply of the amp. All Fender amps built after 1964 (except for those using multi-can capacitors), all Kendrick amps over 25 watts, all Orange amps, and many others, have these built-in bleeder circuits. To drain an amp that has the bleeder circuit, simply unplug the amp from the A.C. wall outlet and put the standby switch in the "play" mode. Wait about 30 seconds and the power supply will be drained of stored electricity.

If your amp doesn't have a bleeder circuit, you can drain the power supply by this simple sequence.
1. Unplug the amp's A.C. cord from the wall outlet.
2. Turn the standby switch to the "play" mode if the amp has a "standby" switch.
3. Connect a jumper from the metal amplifier chassis to the plate of any preamp tube. (With a 12AX7, 12AY7, 12AT7 or 12AY7, pin #1 or pin #6 are plates. Either pin shorted to ground will drain the power supply.) It will take about 30 seconds for all of the stored electricity to be completely dissipated.

Here's how it works. All guitar amps use resistor/capacitor coupling in the preamp stages. That means the plate of the tube is connected to the power supply via a plate resistor. When you short the plate to ground, the electricity from the power supply goes through the plate resistor. The plate resistor limits the current so the power supply discharges slowly, and not all at once. This is easy on the power filters.

WHAT SPECIAL TOOLS ARE REQUIRED?

Just as you would need an oil filter wrench, a spark plug tool and a timing light to keep your sports car tuned up; there are certain tools necessary for servicing your tube amp. We are going to assume you already own a couple of Phillips and flathead screwdrivers and a set of nutdrivers. All of the following tools can be had for $100 or less.

1. AN AMERICAN MADE DIGITAL MULTIMETER — Don't kid yourself into thinking you are saving money by buying a Taiwanese-made meter. I would recommend getting a Fluke. I use the 8060A Fluke, which is top of the line and very expensive; but Home Depot and Builder's Square sell a Model 10 Fluke for under $60. The Model 10 Fluke is auto-ranging. The good meters have two fuses—one that can be changed easily (usually a 200 mA) and a 600 volt fuse that the meter must be disassembled to change. A cheap meter is not able to measure an inductive load, so when you attempt to set output tube bias using the shunt method (page 105 of *A Desktop Reference of Hip Vintage Guitar Amps* by Gerald Weber), the cheap meter will burn up.

2. A CURRENT LIMITER — This can be made with less than $20 worth of parts. Complete instructions and a diagram are on page 328 of *Tube Amp Talk for the Guitarist and Tech* by Gerald Weber. This device allows you to safely work on an amp that would otherwise be blowing fuses. With a current limiter, a light bulb shines brightly if the amp is drawing too much current. One can troubleshoot the amp without fear of burning anything up and when the short circuit is found, the light bulb no longer shines brightly. Current limiters are helpful when forming electrolytic capacitors after performing a cap job. A safety device anytime major service work has been performed, the current limiter allows you to make sure there are no shorts in the amps BEFORE anything burns up.

3. JUMPER WIRES — These are short wires with alligator clips on each end. They are handy for bleeding the electrical charge from a power supply and many other things. I use them for troubleshooting noise. You can turn off a tube by either grounding the grid or shorting across its plate resistor. Jumper wires are also great for troubleshooting grounds or even jumping parts into the circuit (for voicing and/or troubleshooting).

4. A WOODEN CHOPSTICK — Other than the jumper wire, this is probably the most used tool in the shop. I use it to troubleshoot noise, microphonic tubes, solder joints and a variety of other things. They are great for adjusting lead dress while the amp has live voltages. Make sure to use a wooden (non-conductive) one.

5. A SOLDERING IRON — Since all of the components are soldered in an amp, you must have a soldering iron to replace any components other than tubes. More on this later.

6. DESOLDERING WICK OR SOLDER SUCKER — When changing components, one must desolder the old part before soldering in the new part. Desoldering wick looks like braided copper shielding. When you put it between the joint to be desoldered and your soldering iron, the solder is "wicked" onto the copper braid—thus cleaning the old joint of old solder. Some people prefer a solder sucker to soldering wick. The solder sucker is "cocked" and when the solder has been melted, a button is pushed on the solder sucker that causes a fast vacuuming of air over the work. I have used both and generally prefer the solder sucker when there is a lot of solder to remove. The wick seems to work best when there is a very small quantity of solder to remove.

7. SOLDER TOOL — Get the kind with a pick on one end and a slotted tip on the other. This is helpful when placing leads for soldering and desoldering.

8. NEEDLE NOSE PLIERS — Get the smaller 3" size. These work great for crimping components and getting into tight places.

9. WIRE CUTTERS/STRIPPERS — When you are cutting wires and stripping insulation, you will certainly appreciate a good set of wire cutters and wire strippers. You will want to adjust your wire strippers so that they can strip the wire of insulation without causing any scoring on the actual wire. If the wire gets scored, it may break later. Just be careful not to score it in the first place.

SOLDERING HINTS

You may regularly make your own patch cords, which would qualify you as an experienced solderer; however, here are hints to help you solder better.

1. USE A GOOD SOLDERING IRON. I would recommend using a Weller 35 watt soldering iron (Model WP35) with an ST-1 tip. This works great for everything except chassis grounds. For chassis grounds, I recommend using a Weller 175 watt soldering iron (Model SP-175). Do not use the soldering gun type. Although the soldering guns come in high wattages, the tips do not have the surface area required to transfer enough heat to do chassis grounds. You need the type that looks like a large steel cylinder. These 175 watt irons are sold by places that sell plumbing supplies.

2. KEEP A CLEAN SOLDERING TIP. Take a sponge and moisten it with tap water. Rub the hot tip of the soldering iron on this wet sponge and it will clean the tip. Solder joints are better if the soldering tip is clean.

3. TIN THE SOLDER TIP. Put a modest amount of solder (rosin core solder only) on the tip of your soldering iron so that heat transfer will be good (this is called tinning the tip). To make sure you are not putting too much solder, shake the soldering iron slightly and the excess solder will fall off. Heat up the joint to be soldered before applying any solder to the actual work being soldered. I like to apply the heat from one side and apply the solder from the other side of the joint being soldered. This assures me that the work is hot enough for the solder to melt completely and flow evenly. Never apply the solder directly to the tip of the soldering iron to make a joint. It will result in a joint with questionable integrity. The solder will melt, but the work may not have gotten hot enough to adhere properly to the solder!

4. DON'T MOVE! After the joint is soldered, keep the work still. If anything moves before the solder cools, the integrity of the joint is lost.

5. USE ONLY AS MUCH SOLDER AS IS NECESSARY. Try to avoid globbing it on.

6. INSPECT THE FINISHED SOLDER WORK. A good solder joint will be shiny. Make sure the solder has flowed to all leads.

7. USE HEAT SINKS WHEN SOLDERING HEAT-SENSITIVE COMPONENTS. If you don't have a heat sink, an alligator clip works great. Capacitors and resistors can take lots of heat, but when you are dealing with plastic-based components (certain switches, relays, etc.), diodes, LED's or other semiconductor devices; use a heat sink to keep that heat off the component being soldered. The heat sink goes between the work and the component so that when heat from the work spreads towards the component, the heat is absorbed by the heat sink.

HEADS UP TO AVOID ELECTRICAL SHOCK

There are potentially lethal voltages present in tube amplifiers. There are times when you must have the amp "plugged in and turned on" while you are working on it. For example, troubleshooting blown fuses and setting output tube bias requires you working on "a live" amp. We want to make sure you stay "alive" too.

1. **BE AWARE OF WHERE YOU ARE STANDING** — For example don't be standing barefoot on concrete! Likewise, I would not recommend working on an amp while standing on a damp floor. Make safety a priority.

2. **KEEP ONE HAND BEHIND YOUR BACK (OR IN YOUR POCKET)** — You are less likely to get shocked if you are only using one hand. When you use two hands, you can touch two points simultaneously, which may not be at the same electrical potential. In this case, the current will flow through your body (similar to a condemned man that has been sentenced to death in the electric chair except with slightly less voltage).

3. **KEEP YOUR ARM FROM RELAXING ACROSS AN OPEN, LIVE CHASSIS** — When working on an amp for extended periods of time, you will be tempted to inadvertently rest your arm on the chassis. If you relax your arm on the chassis and forget the chassis has "live" voltages, it will remind you—EVERY TIME!

FAMILIARIZE YOURSELF WITH TUBE CIRCUITS

Experience is the best teacher. If you are just starting out, why not purchase an old tube phonograph or amp and use it to familiarize yourself with tube circuits. One could be purchased at a garage sale for a few dollars. Draw out the schematic and study it. Check voltages. Study the voltage supply circuit and the signal circuit. Learn why each part is there. Start with simple ones and study other schematics to see how they compare.

Brush up on Ohm's law. Ohm's law can be stated many ways. $I = E/R$, $E = RI$, $R = E/I$.

Just become familiar with how changing the value of one will affect the other.

For example, if you raise the resistance in a circuit, and keep the current constant, then the voltage will go up in order for the equation to be balanced. Or if the voltage was constant, the current would decrease.

If you increase the current and keep the resistance constant, the voltage will increase. Keep the voltage constant while increasing the current and the resistance will decrease.

Visit the library. If you go to a college engineering library, there will be many books on tube technology that were written in the 40s, 50s and 60s. At the University of Texas library, I found a complete collection of Audio Engineering magazines from around 1948 to 1960, or so. I even found the article written in 1953 where Tung Sol announced the creation of a brand new tube type, the 5881! All of the Western Electric reference writings on tube circuits were available too. There is a wealth of tube knowledge available, you just have to know where to look.

The Four Parts of a Guitar Amplifier

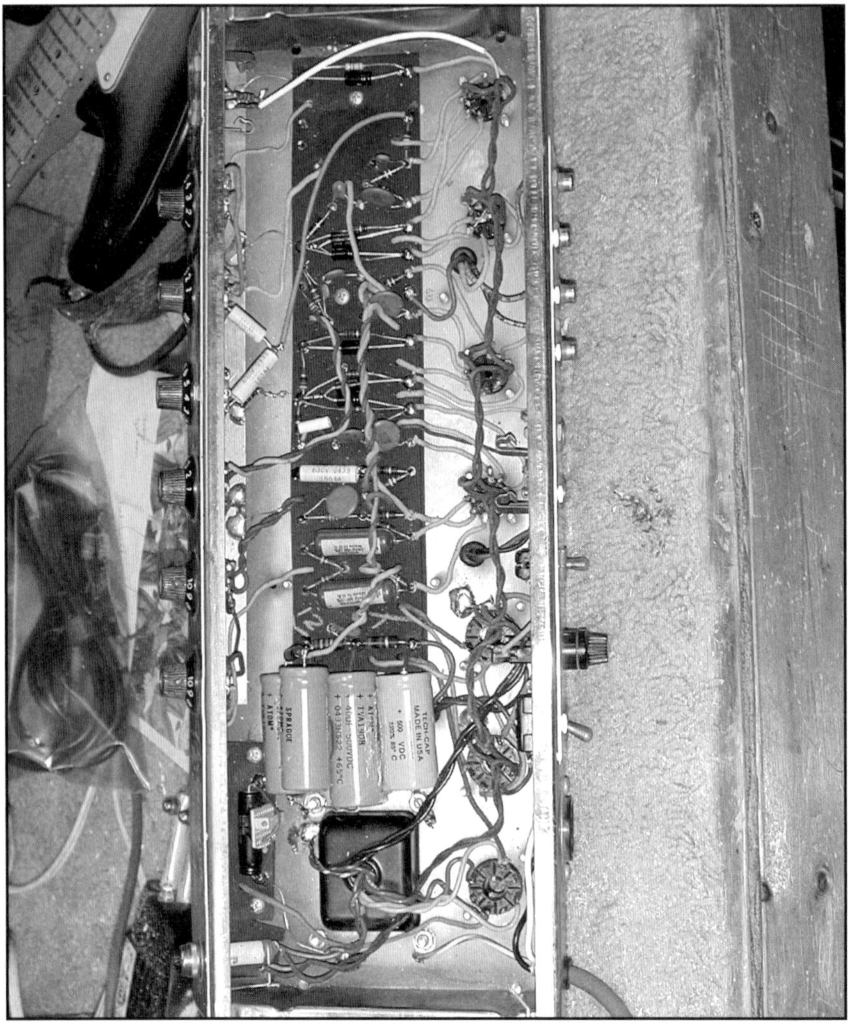

BASIC PREAMP TUBE AMPLIFICATION FOR GUITAR AMPLIFIERS

All tube guitar amplifiers have four parts, namely: the preamp, the output stage, the speakers and the power supply. The preamp takes the guitar signal and amplifies the voltage (same as gain or amplitude). This higher voltage signal then goes to the output stage where current is added. With higher voltage and higher current, we end up with more power. (Remember that power is voltage times current). We need enough power to drive the speaker, which vibrates the air to reproduce the audio wave. Of course for the tubes to operate, there are many power requirements, so the amp must have a power supply to supply the many voltages necessary to make the tubes work.

For example, the rectifier tube may need a 5 volt A.C. supply for its filament while the other tubes need a 6.3 volt filament supply. Perhaps the high voltage supply needed is around 450 volts D.C. and yet there is perhaps another negative voltage bias supply needed of −48 volts. LED or switching circuits require yet other operating voltages. It is the power transformer and its associated rectifiers, dropping power resistors, choke, and filter capacitors that make up the power supply. The power supply satisfies all of the voltage and current requirements for the various simultaneous circuits.

LET'S LOOK AT THE PREAMP

Most preamp stages use a 12AX7-style preamp tube, which is by far the most popular preamp tube among guitar amplifiers. The 12AX7 is actually two triodes in one miniature 9 pin tube. With space requirements small, power requirements low and gain high; the

12AX7 is ideal for guitar amplifier applications.

In a preamp, a small A.C. signal voltage of about 100 millivolts (a tenth of a volt) coming from your guitar is connected to the grid of a 12AX7. Since the amplification factor of the 12AX7 is 100, for every volt change on the grid, there is 100 volts change on the plate. We are talking serious amplification here.

The preamp consists of stages of gain interspersed with volume control, tone controls, reverb send, reverb recovery, FX loop send, FX loop recovery, etc. Depending on the particular 12AX7, the actual operating voltages and everything considered, typical dB gain is generally in the 32 - 35 dB ranges. A typical tone control loses somewhere around 30 dB. Therefore, we would amplify the signal but when the tone circuit was added, the signal voltage would be back down to almost no signal left, so we would amplify the signal again through yet another section of a 12AX7. The same would hold true for the volume control, reverb circuitry, etc. For example, we may send a nicely amplified signal to the reverb pan, but the signal coming back from the pan is almost nothing, so we have to use another stage to "bring the signal back up."

Inside the 12AX7, there are seven parts. (That is what the "7" is for at the end of its name, 12AX7.) It consists of a 12.6 volt center-tapped filament heater, and two triodes (each triode consisting of a cathode, grid and plate).

There are a few resistors and capacitors needed for the tube to even work. For each triode section, there must be a grid return resistor, a cathode resistor and a plate load resistor. There must also be either a coupling capacitor (usually) or a coupling transformer (almost never). Sometimes a cathode bypass capacitor is used in parallel with the cathode resistor—more on this later.

TONE SHAPING CAN BE DONE IN MANY WAYS. AMONG THOSE WAYS:

CHANGING PLATE VOLTAGE — When we change the plate voltage, we are changing the headroom of the stage and the frequency response. The supply voltage comes from a filter cap and connects to the plate load resistor (usually 100K). This load resistor connects to the plate (pin #1 or pin #6 on a 12AX7, depending on which triode section we are talking about) of the tube. The 12AX7 idles at roughly 1 milliamp. All of this current is passing through the plate load resistor (usually 100K). By Ohms Law and using the 100K plate load resistor for calculations, there will be approximately a 100 volt difference between the supply voltage (coming from the filter cap) and the plate voltage (either pin #1 or pin #6 on the 12AX7). Plate voltage dictates the amount of clean headroom for that particular stage. Typical voltages may range from 100 - 300 volts with the higher voltages being the cleanest and the lower voltages breaking up sooner. When I designed the Kendrick Texas Crude Harmonica amp, I wanted both channels to break-up very easily. Through experimentation, I ended up with 100 volts on the plate of one channel (grind) and 80 volts on the other channel (extra grind).

In a 60s Fender design, 220 volts on the plate is typical. In a 60s Marshall, a 150 volt plate voltage is typical. Some modern amps use plate voltages in the 280 to 300 volt range. When the voltage goes up, so does the frequency response. Lower voltages tend to filter off high-end, thus making the tone "browner." I've seen many designs that run a small signal through a low plate voltage 12AX7 purely as a tone-shaping device.

BIASING THE PREAMP TUBE — If all components in a preamp circuit remain the same and the only thing we change is the supply voltage, the idle current of the tube will go up as the supply voltage goes up, and the idle current will go down as the supply voltage goes down.

Choosing the proper cathode resistor value biases a 12AX7. Typical cathode resistor values could range from 820 ohms to 10K. Most Fender circuits used a 1.5K cathode resistor. Occasionally you will see the cathodes of both triode sections tied together with only one cathode resistor used. Since this design has two cathodes sharing the same cathode resistor, we now have twice as much current going through the cathode resistor. In this case, we select a resistor value equal to half of what we would normally use for only one tube.

A small value cathode resistor idles the tube hotter and therefore the tube will break up easier. (It is interesting to note that idling the tubes hotter will actually reduce the plate voltage because all the current must pass through the plate load resistor. A larger voltage drop will appear across this resistor, thus leaving less voltage on the plate.)

Basic Preamp Tube Amplification for Guitar Amplifiers

Larger value cathode resistors such as the 2.7K, 4.7K, and 10K can take bigger input voltages without distorting. In the Kendrick 2410, for example, there is an extra gain stage between the preamp and the output stage. I use a 4.7K cathode resistor for this circuit because I do not want this stage to distort. Larger value cathode resistors are helpful when we are going for clean such as a bass amp or a tube mic preamp.

SELECTING COUPLING CAPACITOR VALUE — The coupling capacitor connects the A.C. output signal from the plate to the next stage in the circuit. We use a capacitor for this because the capacitor will pass the A.C. signal but will block the D.C. voltage. Typical capacitor value could range from 500 pf to .1 mfd. Remember that bottom-end has a hard time going through small capacitors. In fact, the smaller the capacitor, the harder it is for bottom-end to pass. We use a smaller value capacitor to lose some bottom or get rid of "boominess." For example, the bright channel of the early Marshall used a .002 mfd. coupling cap whereas the dark channel used a .02 mfd.

SELECTING CATHODE BYPASS CAPACITOR VALUE — If we put a capacitor in parallel with the cathode resistor, then certain frequencies will easily go through the capacitor instead of the cathode resistor. These frequencies will bypass the resistor and the tube will amplify those frequencies more. The actual effect of this capacitor will go up as the cathode resistor value goes up. That is to say that the effect of putting 5 mfd cap across the cathode resistor will be more noticeable using a 4.7K cathode resistor value than if we used a 1.5K.

In general, the 25 mfd. value generally increases all frequencies evenly. As this value is made smaller, less of the lower frequencies get through. For example, the Plexi Marshall that uses a .68 mfd bypass cap is boosting the highs and upper mids.

USE OF HIGH PASS OR LOW PASS FILTERS — Most of us are familiar with the bright cap across the volume pot of most amps. This is a simple high-pass filter. It is a voltage divider with a cap across it. The highs see the cap as an almost direct short, but the lows do not. Therefore, more highs pass than lows, hence the name—high-pass filter.

You do not need a potentiometer to make a filter. You could use two resistors in series to ground as a voltage divider and simply place the capacitor across the first resistor. This would increase highs. The output in this circuit is taken from the junction of the two resistors.

Using the same two resistors in series as a voltage divider, we could achieve an opposite effect by putting the capacitor across the second resistor. This would short the highs to ground thus creating a low pass filter. Again, the output is taken from the junction of the two resistors.

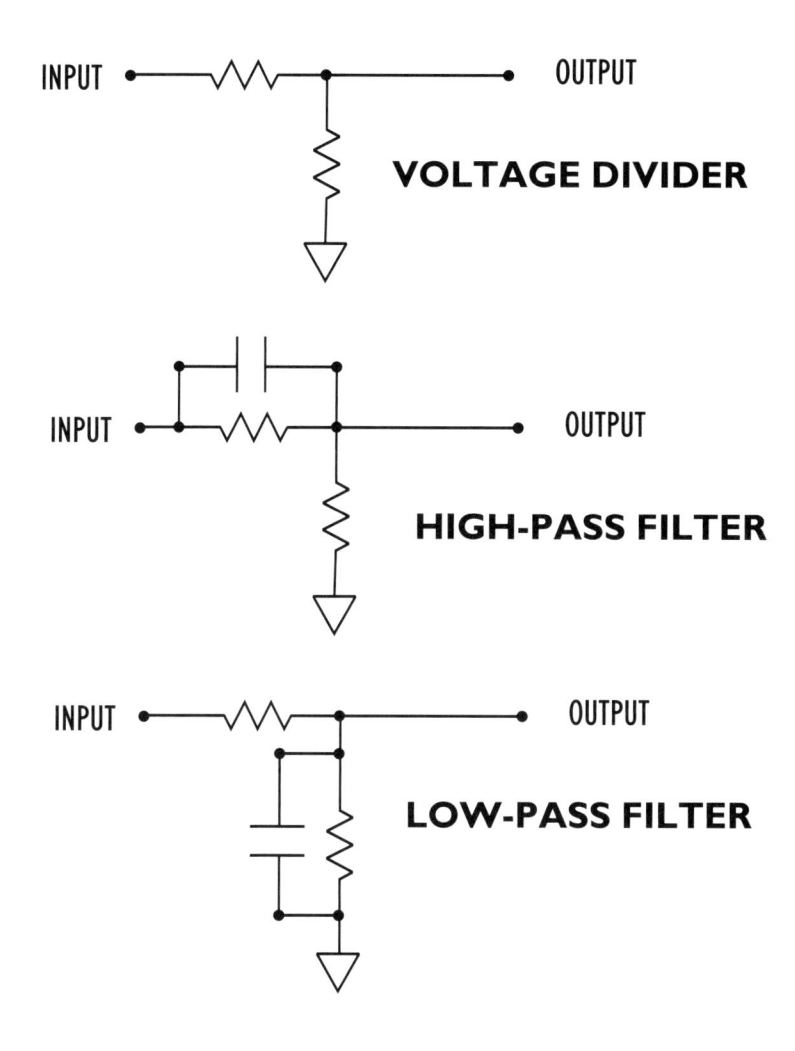

VOLTAGE DIVIDER

HIGH-PASS FILTER

LOW-PASS FILTER

Basic Preamp Tube Amplification for Guitar Amplifiers   111

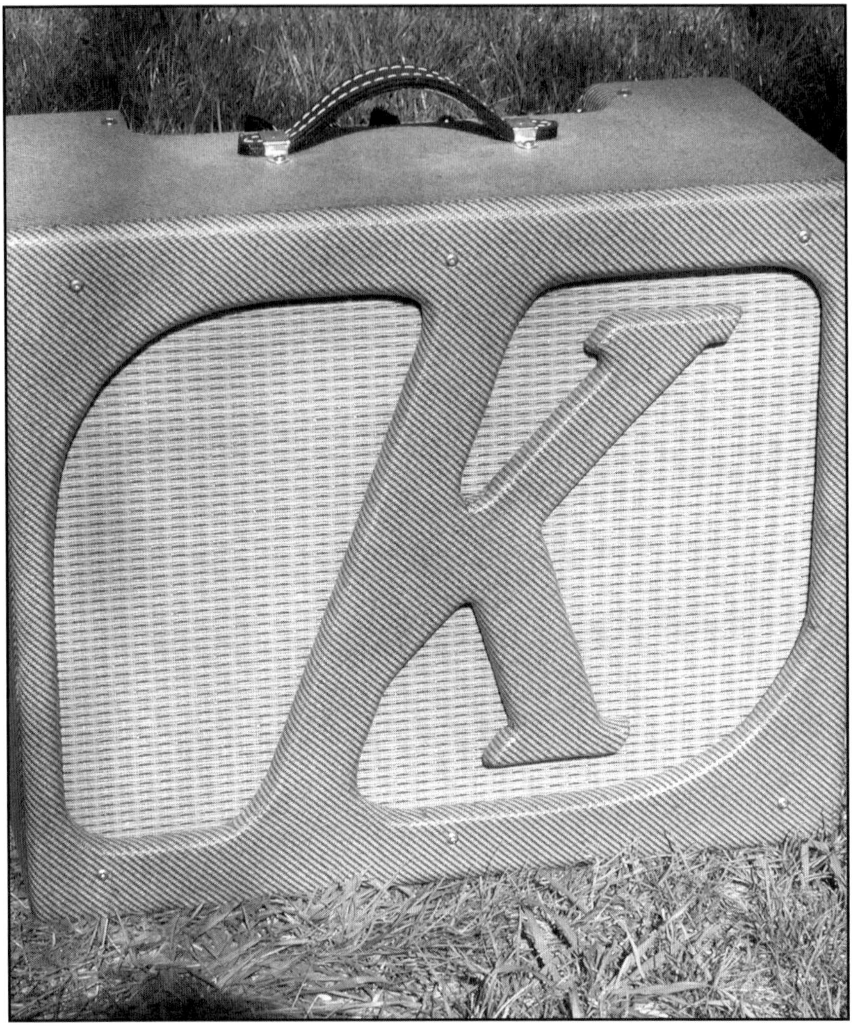

BASIC OUTPUT TUBE AMPLIFICATION FOR GUITAR AMPLIFIERS

The output stage is the part of the amp that adds power to the amplified signal it receives from the preamp. The output stage includes the output tubes, output transformer; and when using a push-pull configuration, a phase inverter.

DISTINCTIONS OF THE OUTPUT STAGE
All tube guitar amps are designed to operate either in Class A or Class AB. In order to explain class of operation; let us look at the output tube, which is a valve that lets more or less current pass, depending on the input signal. If the valve is wide open and maximum current is passing through, then the tube is said to be "in saturation." On the other extreme, if the tube is turned "off" such that zero current is allowed to flow through it, then that tube is said to be in "cutoff."

AN AMP IS OPERATING IN "CLASS A" IF THE OUTPUT TUBE (OR TUBES) NEVER GO INTO CUTOFF.
A Class AB output stage uses two tubes connected in push-pull, but with a higher negative grid bias than would be used for Class A. Because of this increased negative bias, the plate and screen voltage can be raised to higher voltage than if operating in Class A. This is because the extra negative bias keeps the tubes within the limit of plate dissipation. Because of the higher voltages, more power can be obtained.

In order for a tube to be pushed into Class AB, there has to be sufficient input signal to drive the tube into "cutoff." In other words, an amp designed as a Class AB amp, may sometimes operate in Class

A—particularly at a low volume. A case in point would be most Blackface Fenders. If you take one of the output tubes out of a Princeton Reverb and turn the volume down low, the amp will sound normal. This is because the one remaining output tube is always "on" and never in "cutoff" and therefore operating in Class A. If you advance the volume while playing, you will find a point on the volume control where the amp begins to sound like a blown output transformer. This is the point where the preamp volume is enough to drive the one output tube into "cutoff" for a small portion of the input cycle. Now put the other output tube back into the amp and your amp will be operating in Class AB. Should you turn the volume down, you will not drive the output tubes hard enough to go into "cutoff," and therefore will actually be operating in Class A.

PUSH-PULL OR SINGLE-ENDED?

Single-ended refers to the way the output transformer is connected. On a single-ended design, the output tube connects to one end, hence the name single-ended. The tube is always "on" but is never given enough preamp signal to drive it into "cutoff." If more than one tube is used, the tubes are simply paralleled and connected to the same one end of the output transformer. Of course, the other end of the output transformer primary connects to the power supply.

In a simple "push-pull" design, two output tubes are used. Each tube is attached to opposite ends of a transformer primary winding which is center-tapped. The center-tap goes to the high voltage power supply. A phase inverter (driver circuit) is used so that one output tube is driven normally and the other is driven 180 degrees out of phase with respect to the first output tube. The reason this works so well is that the transformer primary configuration causes phase reversal on one of the tubes. This brings it back in phase with the first tube. The transformers output becomes the average performance of both tubes. You can see how it gets its name. Since the tubes are operating out of phase with each other, one is "pushing" while the other is "pulling"—so to speak.

All class AB amps are push-pull, but not all push-pull amps are Class AB. For example, the Vox AC30 would be an example of a Class A push-pull amp.

METHOD OF BIASING

There are two different biasing scenarios used with output tubes, "fixed biased" and "cathode biased." In "fixed biasing," a negative D.C. voltage supply is used to inject a fixed negative voltage on the grid of the output tube (or tubes). This keeps the grid negative with respect to the cathode and therefore tames the idle current of the tube to the appropriate level. When an amp is "fixed biased," it may have an adjustment pot to adjust the exact amount of negative voltage. Sometimes it does not have an adjustment and can therefore be adjusted by substituting a different value resistor in the negative voltage power supply.

Some players think it is "fixed bias" if it lacks an adjustment pot! It does not matter if it has an adjustment or not, if it injects a fixed negative voltage on the input (grid) of the output tube (or tubes), it is said to be a "fixed bias" output stage.

The other type of biasing method used for output tubes is called "cathode biasing" or "self biasing." In this arrangement, a resistor is placed between the tubes cathode and ground. All of the current that goes through the tube must go through the resistor first. As current passes through the resistor, a positive voltage develops on the cathode of the output tube. With the cathode more positive than the grid, the tube "sees" this the same as the grid being more negative than the cathode, and thus bias is achieved.

If the tube tries to draw too much current, more voltage will develop on the cathode. This increases bias and therefore reduces idle plate current. The tube quickly reaches a state of equilibrium, and this is why "cathode biasing" is sometimes also referred to as "self-biasing."

Cathode biased amps sometimes have a bypass cap across the cathode resistor so that alternating current of the amplified signal "bypasses" the resistor. This keeps the bias voltage more stable. A value of capacitor is chosen whose capacitive reactance (at the lowest possible signal frequency) equals one tenth of the cathode resistor's value. This assures that the alternating current goes through the capacitor instead of the resistor.

Cathode bias amps have a singing quality about them that is most desirable. Even with the bypass capacitor, the bias voltage does fluctuate slightly as the strings on the guitar ring. When the strings are initially plucked, a surge of voltage passes through the cathode resistor, thus slightly dropping the current of the tube. As the strings begin to die, less current passes through the cathode resistor and therefore the bias voltage goes down slightly, thus increasing the power of the tube. This has a compressing effect and a spongy feel.

Some examples of cathode biasing would include the Tweed Deluxe, Vox AC30, and Fender Champ. It is interesting to note the Tweed Deluxe is cathode biased Class AB push-pull; the Vox AC30 is cathode biased Class A push-pull and the Champ is cathode biased single-ended Class A.

WHAT IS ULTRA-LINEAR?

An ultra-linear output stage refers to a specific type of transformer, which uses a tap on the output transformer for the screen supply of the output tube. Although these are usually push-pull design, it is possible to configure a single-ended transformer as ultra-linear.

This type of output configuration is used when loud and clean is wanted. That is why you see this circuit mostly on bass and keyboard amps. It was used on the Fender 135 watt Twin.

PLATE VOLTAGE

Plate voltage affects the performance of the output tubes. Higher plate voltage means more headroom (less breakup), tighter bottom-end, crisper highs and more power.

Changing plate voltage for an output stage is not an easy task because plate voltage is a function of the power transformer that is being used in the amp. However, if the amp has a rectifier tube, using a different type can alter the plate voltage by 10 to 30 volts.

Lower voltages tend to de-emphasize high-end, thus making the tone "browner."

BIASING OF THE TUBES

It is interesting to note that idling the tubes hotter will actually reduce the plate voltage. As more current passes through the power supply and output transformer, a larger voltage drop will occur across the internal resistance f the transformers, thus leaving less voltage on the plate.

Biasing affects how hard a tube can be driven before it starts to break up. Think about it. If a tube is a valve and all the way "on" is saturation, wouldn't it make perfect sense that the hotter the tube is biased (more idle current), the less it will have to be pushed in order to saturate? Conversely, if it is biased with low idle current, it will have much further to go before it reaches saturation.

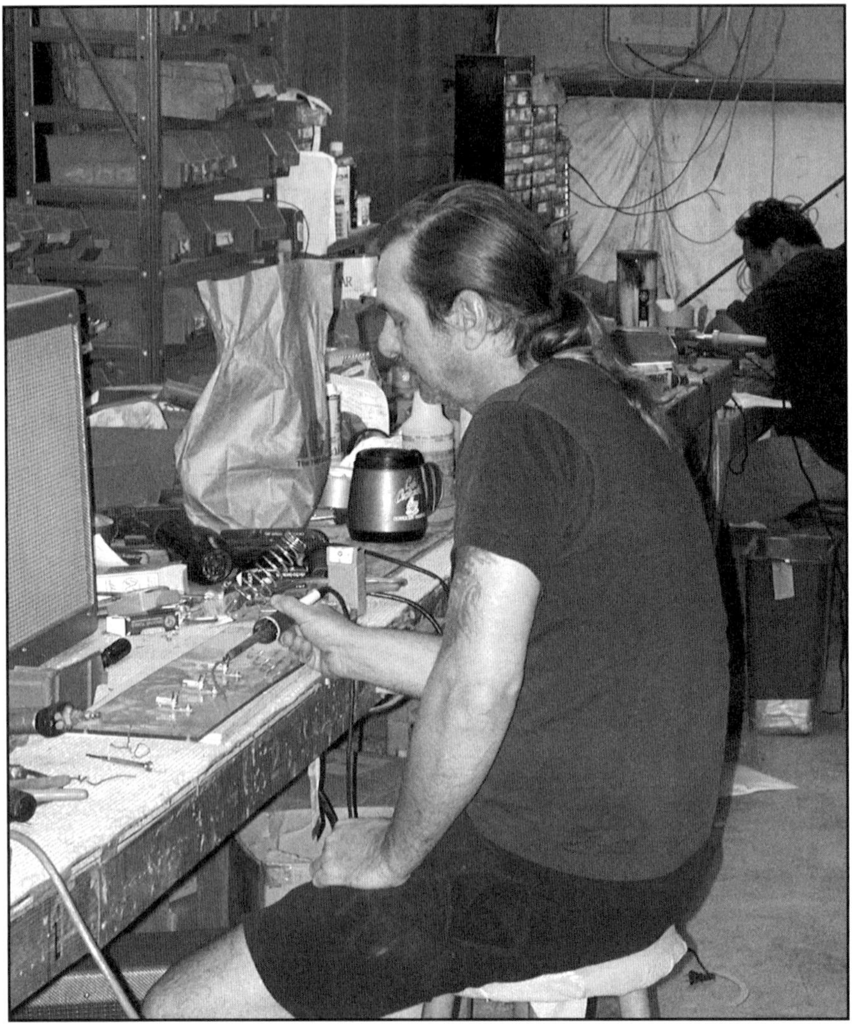

BASIC POWER SUPPLIES FOR GUITAR AMPLIFIERS

Vacuum tube amplifiers have many different voltage requirements. For example, the plates of the preamp and power tubes require high voltage D.C. At the same time, tubes also require other voltages. For example, a lower filament voltage—usually 6.3 volts A.C. for preamp and power tubes and 5 volts for most popular rectifiers is common. In addition to this, some tubes are pentodes and therefore require a high voltage screen supply. Some output stages are fixed biased and therefore require a negative D.C. voltage supply. Your wall outlet provides only 120 volts A.C. current. The power supply is designed to take the 120 volts A.C. from your wall outlet and transform it to provide all of these different voltage requirements.

THE POWER TRANSFORMER

The heart of the power supply is the power transformer. The power transformer consists of several coils of wire around an iron core. The first coil of wire hooks up to the 120 volts A.C. wall current and is called the primary. The other coils of wire are called secondaries. We can make them different voltages depending on the ratio of primary turns to secondary turns. For example, if we wanted a secondary with 240 volts A.C. and our primary is connected to the wall outlet (120 volts A.C.), we would simply make the secondary have twice as many turns as the primary. If we needed only 60 volts, we could wind a secondary with half as many turns as the primary. In other words, the ratio of turns between primary and secondary determines the secondary's A.C. voltage.

THE FILAMENT SUPPLY OR A+ VOLTAGE

Before electric guitar amplifiers, in the early days of tubes, batteries were used to provide power in tube circuits. The filament voltage was called the "A+" supply; the plate supply used another battery with higher voltage and was called the "B+" supply. With fixed biased amps, a third battery was used, but since it was hooked up reverse polarity, it was called the "C-" supply.

A tube guitar amp may need more than one filament supply. For example, if it has a 5AR4 rectifier tube, it will need a 5 volt filament supply to heat it. If it has 6V6 output tubes, it will need 6.3 volts to heat them. In this case, there would be two separate secondaries to supply the 5 volts and the 6.3 volts respectively. Most filament supplies are run A.C., so they do not need to be rectified to D.C. You could run the filament supplies with D.C. if you wanted to, but almost all amps use A.C. filament supplies.

The difference in A.C. voltage and D.C. voltage is that the A.C. goes both ways back and forth and D.C. only goes one direction.

THE PLATE SUPPLY OR B+ VOLTAGE

On the other hand, all plate supply voltage must be D.C. Therefore, rectification is necessary. We could rectify the A.C. voltage with either a tube rectifier or a diode.

These devices are like check valves that only allow the electricity to move in one direction, thus creating D.C. from A.C. There are several different circuits to rectify D.C. from A.C.:

HALF-WAVE RECTIFIER

In a half-wave rectifier, one end of a B+ secondary winding is attached to the anode of a diode (or rectifier tube). The other end of the secondary winding is grounded. Since the diode (or tube) only lets electricity move in one direction, we end up with a pulsating D.C. on the cathode of the diode (or tube). The D.C. is all going in the same direction, but it will pulse at 60 cycles. This is why we use filter caps. They will charge as the voltage peaks and discharge as the voltage falls, thus smoothing the pulsating D.C. to a more constant level.

FULL-WAVE RECTIFIER

With a full-wave rectifier, each end of the secondary winding goes to the anode of a separate diode (or separate anodes in a full wave rectifier tube). The secondary winding is center-tapped with the center-tap grounded. The secondary is wound for twice the voltage of the half-wave rectifier, because we will never use but half of it at one time! If you look at this long enough, you begin to see that it is nothing more than two half-wave rectifiers operating simultaneously with reverse polarity from each other. The cathodes of both diodes are connected together and connected to the main filter cap. This arrangement produces pulsating D.C., but it will pulse at 120 cycles — exactly twice the frequency of the half-wave rectifier.

FULL-WAVE BRIDGE RECTIFIER

The full-wave bridge rectifier is similar to the full-wave rectifier because it will pulse at 120 cycles, however the secondary is wound for half as much voltage and the secondary is not center-tapped. Instead, we will use the entire winding for each half-cycle of the input voltage. We connect each end of the secondary to the anode of a diode. The cathodes of these two diodes are attached to a filter cap and become the B+ supply. We also connect each end of the secondary winding to the cathode of a separate diode. The anode of these two diodes connects to ground. This provides a path to ground just like the center-tap did with the full-wave rectifier. The difference is either end of the winding can "see" a path to ground, depending on which way the current happens to be flowing at the time.

ECONOMY FULL-WAVE BRIDGE

A variation of the full-wave bridge is the full-wave bridge economy supply. This circuit was used in some early Marshall amplifiers and late 70s Fenders. It is the same as a full-wave bridge, except a center-tap is used on the secondary winding. For the main filter caps, a totem-pole stack of two filters in series is used. The center-tap for the secondary winding connects to the junction formed by the two filter caps in series.

DIFFERENT B+ VOLTAGES WITHIN THE AMP

The power tubes may need 450 volts while the preamp tubes may need 200 volts. We do not use a separate rectifier for each because the preamp tubes draw very little current. Instead, the rectified D.C. plate supply (or B+) has dropping resistors coupled to a filter cap to provide

Basic Power Supplies for Guitar Amplifiers

various D.C. voltages for different tubes within the amp.

Here is a typical example. Let us say the power tubes need 450 volts for the plate, 400 volts for the screen, and the oscillator tube for the tremolo needs 350 volts, the phase inverter needs 300 volts, and the other preamp tubes need 200 volts. We would have a power supply designed to provide the 450 volts D.C.. We would then have a resistor connected to that to bump it down to 400 volts. We would then add yet another resistor to the first resistor to obtain the 350 volts for the oscillator tube. Adding yet another resistor to that, we get the 300 volts for the phase inverter and adding one more resistor to that gets us the 200 volts for the preamp tube. Each junction of dropping resistors would have a filter cap that stabilizes the voltage there and decouples it from the adjacent stages. If you did not have a filter cap, the circuits would "think" the dropping resistor was part of the plate load resistor. This would cause various stages to interact and possibly oscillate.

BIAS SUPPLY VOLTAGE OR C – VOLTAGE

All bias supplies provide negative D.C. Although any type of D.C. rectification can be used, almost all bias supply circuits use a half-wave rectifier. Since the bias voltage supply uses very little current, the half-wave is the design of choice. It has fewer parts and costs less to build.

To make a negative D.C. supply, the diode (or tube) and the filter caps are hooked up in reverse polarity. That is to say, the cathode of the diode goes to the transformer winding and the anode goes to the filter cap and circuit. The filter cap is connected with the positive lead to ground and the negative lead to the anode of the diode.

There are three ways to obtain voltage for the C- supply. You could have a separate secondary winding solely for C- bias voltage. You might have a voltage tap on the B+ winding. Alternatively, you might have a large resistor connecting from the end of the B+ winding to the bias supply rectifier circuit.

NEED HELP ON
YOUR TUBE GUITAR
AMP PROJECTS?
(512) 990 5486
KENDRICK
KENDRICK

SPEAKERS AND HOW THEY AFFECT TONE

In previous chapters, we identified the four parts of a tube guitar amplifier, namely: the preamp, the output stage, the power supply, and the speakers. We have already looked at the first three of these separately. Now we will look at speakers.

THE SPEAKER MAKES THE SOUND
When we look at sound as vibrating air, then it becomes apparent that the speaker makes the actual sound. Of course, if it were possible to make a speaker with a perfectly flat frequency response, we would find it less than desirable for guitar. A good guitar speaker will color the sound, which actually enhances the overall guitar tone. Picking a speaker for a particular amp requires choosing a speaker that compliments the signal coming from the amp. For instance, if you have an amp that sounds too bright, perhaps choosing a speaker that is somewhat dark will compensate so the high-end gets smoothed out. Conversely, a darker sounding amp may sound better with a speaker that has crisper highs. The obvious fact is this: the speaker is what is vibrating the air and therefore is responsible for the sound you are hearing. Just as water will not rise above its source, an amp will not sound any better than its speaker. Stated another way, the speaker is the final filter that colors the sound. If it has no liveliness or is dull sounding, your amp cannot sound any better.

SPEAKER SIZE
I am often asked, "What is the difference in tone between a 12" and a 10" speaker?" Certainly the 12" speaker moves more air than a 10" speaker and can generally take more wattage too. Nevertheless, tonally, I think the sustaining portion of the note is where most of the

difference lies. I am talking about the part of the note that we hear immediately after the initial attack. With a 10" speaker, the sustaining part of the note sounds like a long "e" vowel sound, whereas the 12" speaker has the sustaining part of the note sound more like an "ahh." I am talking in general terms here; there are exceptions to every rule.

SPEAKER CABINET STYLE

Although there are many different styles of speaker cabinet design, two styles are mainly used in guitar amplifiers: open back and closed back. Each has its own set of advantages/disadvantages.

An open back design allows sound to come out of the front and the back of the speaker cabinet at the same time. This wider dispersion allows for a fuller tone on stage. The disadvantage is that the open back cabinet will not have as much bottom end as a closed back cabinet.

The closed back design allows sound to come only from the front. In a closed back design, the dispersion angle in the front is also a sharper angle than if the cabinet were open back. If you are standing to the side of the cabinet, you may have a hard time hearing it, even though the sound pressure may be killing anyone standing directly in front. It does, however, offer more bottom end.

In a closed back design, batting (or fiberglass insulation) is used on three inside sides and the inside bottom. This keeps the waves from bouncing around ad infinitum. It makes the cabinet respond as if it was much larger.

SPEAKER TYPE

In the early days of tube guitar amps, technology did not exist to make a magnet strong enough to operate a dynamic loudspeaker. At that time, the only type of speaker that was available was the field-coil speaker. In this design, an electromagnet (field coil) was mounted to the speaker frame and provided the magnetism necessary to make the speaker work. The electromagnet (field coil) doubled as a filter choke and was connected to the power supply of the amp in the same way as a filter choke would connect.

The field coil was not the ideal arrangement. For one thing, the field coil speakers were not very efficient. Any hum, from ripple current when rectifying A.C. to D.C., would appear in the magnet, causing audible hum. Some of these field coil speakers actually had an extra voice coil that was hookup up to the power supply in reverse polarity so that the hum would get phase cancelled as this hum repelled itself.

With the discovery of an alloy called Alnico, it finally became possible to design a speaker with a permanent magnet. The field coil was now obsolete. Later, ceramic magnets were developed. Over the years, other magnet materials (neodymium for example) have been developed for other loudspeaker application, but only ceramic and Alnico magnets are commonly used for guitar amps.

One difference between Alnico and ceramic magnets is the fact than Alnico is a metal (an alloy consisting of Aluminum, Nickel, and Cobalt) and ceramic is a nonmetal. Because of this, the Alnico magnet speaker, everything else being equal, will have more inductance. This usually translates to better bottom-end. Alnico magnets are more powerful, ounce for ounce, than ceramic. For example, it takes about 6 oz. of Alnico to have the same amount of magnetism as 20 ounces of ceramic.

Alnico speakers are generally louder than ceramic speakers. Because Alnico has a half-life of roughly 80 years (this is how long it takes to lose half its magnetism), new Alnico does not sound like old Alnico. Ceramic speakers are generally warmer sounding.

WHAT IS THE BEST WAY TO CONNECT TWO SPEAKERS?

There are two ways in which two speakers can connect to each other. They can either connect in parallel, or series. To connect in parallel, the positive of each speaker connects to the positive from the amp and the negative from each speaker connects to the negative from the amp. Assuming the two speakers are of identical impedance, in a parallel connection, half of the current goes through each speaker.

In a series connection, the positive of one speaker connects to the negative of the other speaker. The remaining lead of each speaker then connects to the amp. With series, all of the current goes through both speakers, so it seems like this would be the best way to wire speakers. Why not just run all speakers in series? The reason is inductance. A coil of wire, such as a speaker voice coil, has inductance. When speakers are in series, the inductance is additive. Without going into an explanation of inductance, let's just say that if you get too much, it has the effect of blocking high frequencies. If you run several speakers in series, the result will be a garbled, muddy sound with no sparkle or high-end note definition.

WHAT IS THE BEST WAY TO CONNECT FOUR SPEAKERS?

Let's say you have a 4x10 speaker cabinet and your amplifier has a 2 ohm, 4 ohm and 8 ohm impedance selector. How should you wire the 4x10 cabinet? We are going to wire this cabinet using 8 ohm speakers and there will be three possibilities. We could wire all four speakers in parallel. This way, we would have 2 ohms. We could wire them in series/parallel and get 8 ohms; or we could wire them in parallel/series and get 8 ohms. All three ways are valid options. The difference in sound of the three possible wiring schemes is related to inductance. The 2 ohm wiring (all four speakers in parallel) would give the least inductance and therefore would have the most high-end sparkle. The 8 ohm parallel/series and the series/parallel both have the same total impedance, but will sound differently because the series/parallel has more branch inductance than the parallel/series. Actually, the parallel/series will be a little cleaner with crisper highs, while the series/parallel will be less clean with a softer high end.

It is interesting to note that Fender always wired their speakers in parallel to get the least inductance and therefore the cleanest, crispest tone while British companies like Vox and Marshall used series or series parallel to get less clean and more grind.

A WORD ON SPEAKER POLARITY/ PHASE

It is important to have all of the speakers moving the same direction at the same time. If the polarity of a speaker is reversed in a multiple speaker configuration, the air that is being pushed by one speaker will be sucked in by the vacuum created by the other and vice versa. Considerable loss of volume and loss of bottom end will occur as these speakers phase cancel each other.

A few weeks ago, I saw a live band with a very impressive guitarist. The only problem was that he was using a multi-amp setup where the speakers were not moving in the same direction at the same time. He had lots of equipment, good technique, excellent mastery of his instrument, but his tone was awful. His sound would have improved if he had turned off one of the amps. I did not feel it was my place to tell him, but it was obvious what was going on.

BIASING

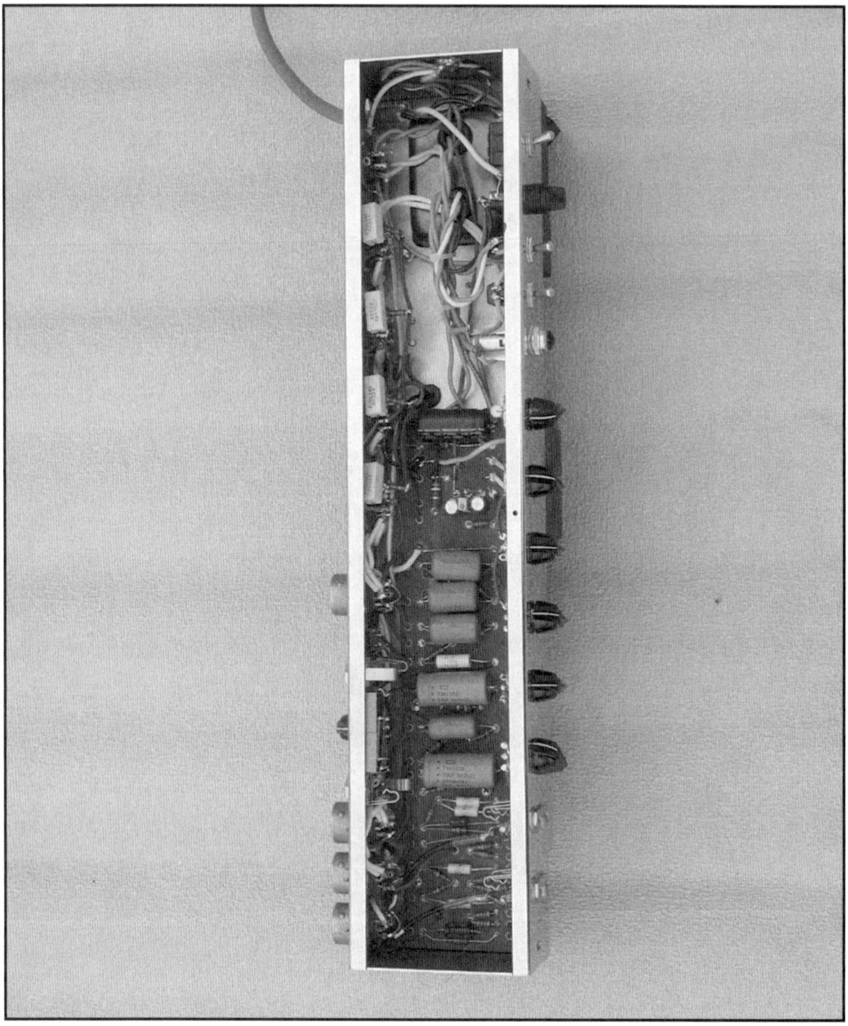

MORE ON BIAS, EXPLAINED AND DEFINED

Output tubes will "wear in" and need a bias adjustment frequently in order to achieve the optimum tone. This is something that many players neglect. Keeping the amp in tune is just as important as keeping the guitar in tune. No one would think of putting strings on a guitar and not tuning it, but players will change output tubes and expect the new tubes to sound good without a bias adjustment. And just like your new strings will go out of tune after they have been on the guitar a while, you output tubes will drift also.

Many guitarists are not sure what biasing a tube guitar amp is all about. Why do we bias an amplifier, and why is it important? And more importantly, what is bias in the first place?

WHY BIAS?

Let's look at a vacuum tube, or "valve" as the British like to call them. The vacuum tube is a valve that can allow a controlled amount of current to flow, just like our kitchen faucet can be adjusted so that a controlled volume of water can flow. Adjusting the electrical charge relationship of the grid (with respect to the cathode) controls our electronic "valve." Basically, the more negative the grid, the less current will flow.

Your kitchen faucet can be turned up all the way such that it would be impossible for any more water to flow. When our electron "valve" is turned up to where maximum current is flowing, it is said to be "saturated." This occurs when the grid is positive electrically, with respect to the cathode. Just as we can "turn down the flow" on our kitchen faucet, we can do the same thing on our electron valve. If we make the grid more negative (with respect to the cathode), then less current will flow. In fact, we can make less and less current flow by making the grid more and more negative.

If we keep making the grid more negative, we will eventually reach a point where current stops flowing completely. This is what is known as "cutoff." Making the grid any more negative (with respect to the cathode) will accomplish nothing, because when something is already "off," you simply can't get more "off."

From the above comparison of an electron valve to your kitchen faucet, one could easily deduce that the usable range of a faucet or an electron valve ranges from "off" (cutoff), to "completely on" (saturation) and "all points in between!" The "point in between," where the tube idles when no signal is applied, is the bias point.

For an amp to sound its best, the tubes bias point or operating center must be selected for optimum tone. If we select a point that is too close to "saturation," then even a smaller signal can result in a saturated distortion tone. If we select a point too close to "cutoff," we will cutoff the bottom of the waveform and get a buzzy unmusical distortion.

WHAT IS "CATHODE BIAS" OR "SELF BIAS"?

There are basically two types of biasing designs. One type is called the "self biasing" or "cathode biased" circuit. In this design, you would rarely, if ever, need any type of adjustment. Preamp tubes all use this design and therefore never need biasing. Sometimes output stages use this design (more on this later.)

In this design, a resistor (cathode resistor) is placed between the cathode and ground. The grid is operated at ground potential using only a high impedance load resistor. Since the cathode is pulling current through the cathode resistor, a positive voltage develops on the cathode. The tube "sees" this the same as the grid being negative with respect to the cathode (even though you and I know that the grid was really neutral and the cathode was positive.) This arrangement is sometimes referred to as "self bias" because if a tube wants to idle at too much current, the extra current would cause a larger positive voltage to appear on the cathode. The tube would see this the same as the grid getting more negative. A more negative grid would cut the flow of current down, thus causing equilibrium in terms of the operating level of the tube.

Conversely, if the tube tries to idle too low, not much positive voltage develops on the cathode and the tube "sees" this as the grid being not very negative. This makes more current flow, again achieving equilibrium.

With "cathode biased" circuits, a capacitor is placed in parallel with the cathode resistor. This allows A.C. signal current to bypass the resistor thus stabilizing the D.C. positive voltage on the cathode.

Some amps are designed with the output stage "self biased." Such amps possess a singing quality that is loved by guitarists and harmonica players alike. Some examples of the "self biased" or "cathode biased" designs would include most all Fender Champs, Kendrick Roughneck, tweed Deluxe, Gibson GA30, and Vox AC30.

WHAT IS "FIXED BIAS"?

The other type circuit design, called "fixed bias," does not use a cathode resistor. Instead, a fixed negative voltage is imposed on the grids of the output tubes. The cathode is grounded, so the tube "sees" the grid as being negative with respect to the cathode. This causes the tube to idle somewhere between "cutoff" and "saturation," and is the bias point or operating center. When an A.C. signal is imposed on the grids of the output tube it will make more or less current flow. Some examples of fixed biased amps would include the Fender Super Reverb, Fender Twin, most all Marshalls, and Kendrick 2410. Usually but not always, higher-powered amps are designed as "fixed bias" and lower powered amps are "cathode biased."

CAN WE USE A COMBINATION "FIXED" AND "CATHODE BIAS"?

When CBS redesigned the Blackface Fender into a Silverface, they tried using a combination of "fixed" and "cathode biased" styles on the output stage. It seemed like a good idea at the time. The "fixed bias" would allow better efficiency and the cathode resistor would help the amp to "self bias."

The result was bad tone. These Silverface amps are the ones that gave the Silverfaces the bad name. Should you have one of these amps, any competent technician could convert this to "fixed bias." It would involve removing the cathode resistor (and cathode capacitor), ground the cathodes and modify the negative voltage bias supply to achieve proper biasing. In fact, if I owned such an amp, I

More On Bias, Explained and Defined

would do a complete Blackface conversion!

WHAT IS CLASS "A"?

When the signal voltage never gets negative enough (with respect to the cathode) to put the tube into "cutoff," then the amp is said to be operating as a Class "A" amplifier. On Class "A" amplifiers; the output tube or tubes are biased so they operate exactly—halfway between "cutoff" and "saturation". Some people think that all "cathode biased" amps are Class "A"—not necessarily so. All single output tube "cathode biased" amplifiers are Class "A." Some two and four output tube "cathode biased" amps are Class "A" and some are Class "AB."

WHAT IS CLASS "AB"?

When an amplifier is designed such that the output tubes are "cutoff" during a short portion of the input cycle (less than 180 degrees of the input cycle), then the amp is said to be operating in Class AB. This arrangement is used with two tubes whose inputs are driven 180 degrees out of phase, so that the amplifying devices conduct on opposite half cycles of the input signal. The outputs of the tubes are similarly coupled out of phase (usually with a transformer) to reproduce the input signal faithfully. These type of amps are called "push-pull" and are not biased exactly halfway between "cutoff" and "saturation." Instead, a bias point is adjusted for the desired compromise among efficiency, power gain and linearity. The main advantage of this design is efficiency.

All guitar amps operate either in Class "A" or Class "AB." There are other classes of operation such as Class "B," "C," etc.; however all of these are too distorted for use in guitar amps.

BIAS—NOUN, VERB, OR ADJECTIVE

When we speak of "bias," (pronunciation: buy us) when dealing with tube guitar amps, we generally mean one of three things. Either we are using the term as a:

Noun, in which case the term bias means "the relationship (electrically) between grid and cathode." For example, one would speak of setting the "bias" of an amplifier. The translation would be, "the fixed negative D.C. voltage that is always present on the control grids that determines the best operational center of my output tubes."

Verb, in which case the term "bias" generally means "the act of adjusting the relationship (electrically) between grid and cathode. i.e. I love to "bias" my output tubes.

Adjective, in which case the term "bias" could be used to describe circuits or circuit components. I.e. the bias circuit of an amp, the bias diode, bias resistor, bias capacitor, bias pot, bias setting, etc.

What about plate current?

Occasionally, I hear someone say that they biased an amp for 35 milliamps. What they mean is they adjusted the "fixed bias" negative voltage grid supply, so that the tubes would allow 35 milliamps of plate current to flow.

ADJUSTABLE OR NON ADJUSTABLE FIXED BIAS

Some manufacturers such as Fender, Marshall, and Kendrick design their amplifiers so that a technician can easily adjust the bias voltage. These amps use a potentiometer that can easily be set to provide an exact negative voltage bias supply. Other amps do not have a variable resistor but use a dropping resistor and a load resistor without an adjustable potentiometer. For example most Ampegs, Boogies, and 50s Fenders have no adjustment. These amps can still be adjusted by substituting a decade box or potentiometer for the load resistor to determine the exact value resistor needed.

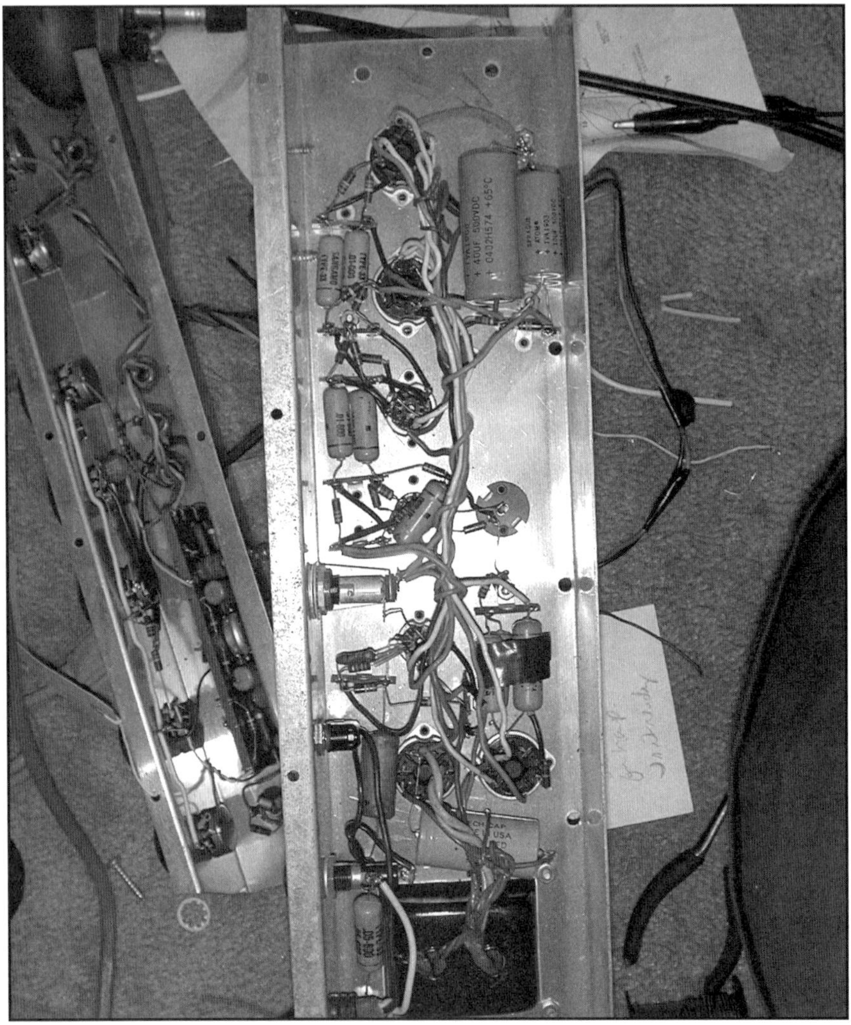

FIXED BIAS VS. CATHODE BIAS

The output tubes in a tube guitar amp must be configured to achieve proper operating level. There are two ways in which this can be done, namely: Fixed bias or cathode bias. There is much confusion among guitarist about what this actually means.

WHY BIAS AT ALL? Consider that a tube is a valve. If a valve is turned full open, then the most possible current that can flow is flowing. This condition is called saturation. (Think of a faucet that is wide open.) On the other hand, if a valve is closed, then no current can flow. This condition is called cut-off. (Think of a faucet turned off). It is the voltage relationship between the grid and cathode that determines how much current can flow. As the grid becomes more negative, with respect to the cathode, the valve tends to turn off. When the grid becomes less negative, with respect to the cathode, then more current flows. When we set bias of the output tubes, we are simply adjusting the grid/cathode relationship so that the tubes idle somewhere near the midway point. In other words, the tubes (valves) are set to idle between cut-off (no current flowing) and saturation (the most possible current flowing). This way, when signal is applied, it is possible for the tube to amplify the waveform properly.

FIXED BIAS — In a fixed bias amp, there is a fixed negative voltage that is applied to the grid (pin #5 on 6V6, 6L6, KT66, 5881, 7581A) of the output tubes via the grid return resistors R1 and R2. These resistors are almost always 220K. The cathodes of the output tubes (pin #8 on 6V6, 6L6, KT66, 5881, 7581A) are grounded. The actual amount of fixed negative voltage on the grids is adjusted so that the tubes are idling about halfway between cut-off and saturation. Fixed biased amps sometimes have a trim pot in the negative bias supply to adjust the actual amount of negative voltage. The act of adjusting this negative voltage is referred to as "biasing" the amp. Because of variances in output tubes, even with the same type and brand, one should readjust bias any time output tubes are replaced. Some examples of fixed biased amps with trim pot adjustments would include the Blackface Super Reverb, Blackface Twin, Plexi Marshall, and the Kendrick 2410.

Some fixed biased amps lack a trim pot to adjust the actual amount of negative bias voltage. These can still be adjusted, however one must adjust negative bias voltage with a decade box (also called a resistor substitution box) or by patching in a trim pot. Examples of fixed biased amps that lack a trim pot would include all 50 and 100 watt Boogies, 5F6A Bassman, 5F8A Twin, and all other fixed bias tweed Fenders.

How Can Non-Adjustable Fixed Bias Be Adjusted? In the negative voltage supply of a fixed biased amp, there are usually two resistors: namely a dropping resistor and a load resistor. When the load resistor increases (this is the one that goes to ground), the negative voltage goes up and the tube tends to cut off. When the dropping resistor increases (this is the one between the diode and the load resistor), the negative voltage goes down and the tube draws more current. The decade box replaces one of these resistors, depending on whether you need more current or less current at idle, and the bias is set by changing values until the proper bias is achieved.

Another way that fixed bias can be configured is without a trim adjustment, but with a balancing pot. Of course, the negative voltage supply is designed so that the amount of negative voltage would approximate what would be needed to bias the average tube.

Manufacturers that do not care about using matched tubes use this method. In a push-pull amp, the filament hum induced in the output tubes is hum canceling. By adjusting a bias balancing pot for the least amount of audible hum at idle, one can surmise that the idle current will be close to matched, even though the output tubes themselves are not necessarily matched. This way two tubes that are not necessarily matched can be made to have their idle current matched. An example of this design would include all Silverface Fenders 25 watts and up.

Cathode Bias — The other way to achieve proper output tube bias is to configure the output tubes as cathode biased. In a cathode bias configuration, there is not a fixed negative voltage on the grids. The grid return resistors (R1 and R2, usually 220 K) are grounded.

Instead of the cathodes of the output tubes being grounded, the cathodes are attached to a resistor (R3). When current flows through the resistor (R3), a positive voltage develops on the cathode of the output tubes. This makes the grid (pin #5 on most output tubes) negative with respect to the cathode, because the grid is at ground potential via R1 and R2 grid resistors. Remember, it is the voltage relationship between grid and cathode that causes the tubes to achieve proper bias. A tube cannot tell the difference between a grid that is negative in relationship to a grounded cathode and a grid that is grounded with the cathode positive. In either case, the grid would be negative with respect to the cathode.

To stabilize the positive voltage on the cathode resistor, a capacitor (C1) is placed across the cathode resistor. This is called a bypass capacitor. Since A.C. current sees a capacitor as very low impedance, the A.C. goes through the capacitor, thus bypassing the cathode resistor (R3). D.C. (idle current) cannot pass through a capacitor, so the D.C. goes through the cathode resistor.

Examples of cathode biased amps would include the Vox AC30, all Fender Champs, almost all amps with EL84 output tubes, the Kendrick 118, most low wattage vintage amps, and Leslie tone cabinets.

Cathode biasing is generally used on low wattage amps because these amps are lower cost and the cathode biasing only takes a resistor and a capacitor to make. Fixed bias amps need a negative voltage supply that would include a tapped B+ on the transformer, a diode, a couple of filter caps, one or two resistors and possibly a trim pot.

EL84 tubes need very little bias voltage, so they are almost always cathode biased. Actually because of the very small bias voltage needed for an EL84, one would be hard pressed to tell the difference tonally between a fixed bias and cathode bias configuration of the EL84.

A cool feature with cathode-biased amps is that they don't need a bias adjustment when output tubes are replaced. As the tube draws more current through the cathode resistor, more voltage is developed on the cathode. As more voltage is developed, the tube tends to draw less current. It will quickly reach a state of equilibrium. That is why cathode biased amps are sometimes referred to as "self biased."

WHAT'S THE TONAL DIFFERENCE? Although the cathode biased amps have the bypass capacitor, not 100% of the A.C. goes through the bypass cap. Some of the A.C. goes through the resistor, which affects the biasing of the tube. It makes the tube tend to cut off slightly, as the tube is pushed harder. As the strings begin to die out and less signal is applied, the tube tends to increase in current (and volume) as the bias voltage on the cathode recovers. This results in a singing quality and compression not found in fixed biased amps. Cathode biased amps are great for playing Ry Cooder slide licks or blues. Think sustain del maximo. Cathode biased amps have a spongy envelope and can be made to "meow" easily. They work great in small rooms or lower volumes where compression is needed.

Also, with a cathode biased amp, the tubes actually "see" less voltage than the same amp fixed biased. Let say an amp has 400 volts on the plate. If it is fixed biased and the cathodes are grounded (zero voltage), the output tube would see 400 volts (the difference between the plate and cathode). Take the same amp and cathode bias it and let's say the cathode voltage develops to 45 volts. The output tubes would only see the difference between the plate (400 volts) and the cathode (45 volts), which is 355 volts. The tubes perform differently at lower voltage. For example, they will have less power, break up quicker and have less high-end response.

Fixed biased amps are generally very punchy. They are less compressed and more dynamic than cathode biased amps. Since the fixed negative voltage is unwavering, the amp will punch harder and not compress off the front edge of the note. If you are playing with a pounding drummer, fixed bias is the only way to go.

THE KENDRICK SWITCHABLE FIXED/CATHODE BIAS In the summer of 1993, Kendrick introduced the Texas Crude amps that featured a switch to change between fixed bias and cathode bias. Depending on the circumstance, one type of biasing would be preferred. If you were playing a small club with a bitchy club owner and the sound police at the door holding a dB meter and a can of mace, you could switch into the cathode bias mode. This would make the amp have slightly less volume, more compression (sounds fuller at a lower volume), more sustain, and quicker breakup. On the other hand, if you were doing an outdoor gig with a pounding drummer, you could still punch through by going to fixed bias mode.

Using a negative voltage bias supply, a Double-Pole Double-Throw switch, a cathode resistor and a bypass capacitor made this switchable configuration possible. I used a 300 ohm 20 watt cathode resistor (R3), and a 100 uf 100 volt electrolytic bypass capacitor (C1). As with any bypass capacitor, the minus lead went to ground and the plus lead went towards the cathode. The physical placement of the bypass capacitor was away from the heat of the output tubes and the cathode resistor, because electrolytic capacitors are affected by heat.

WHICH IS BETTER? Neither is better, they are just different. Just as an artist would want to have several colors on his palette, serious players should own several amps with both cathode and fixed bias types. Each type has uniqueness of tone worth owning.

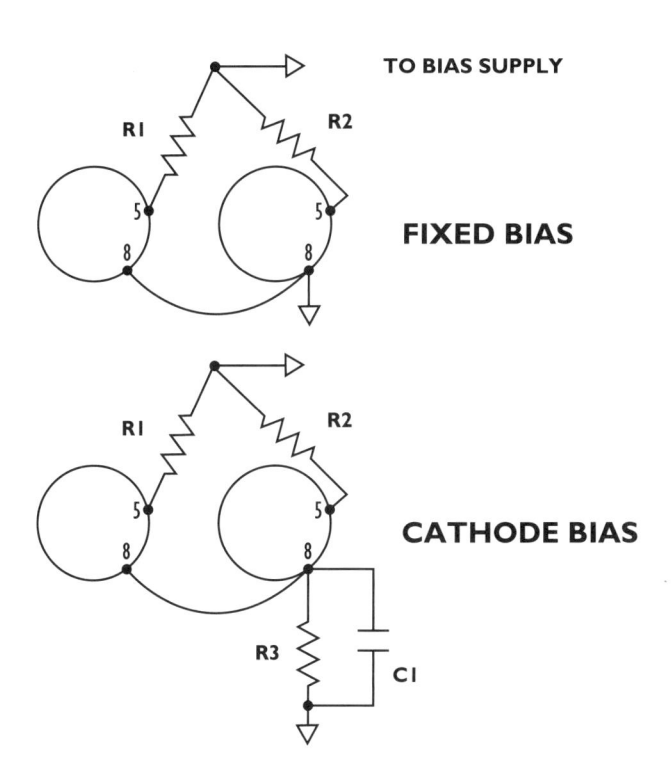

Fixed Bias vs. Cathode Bias

CAPACITORS

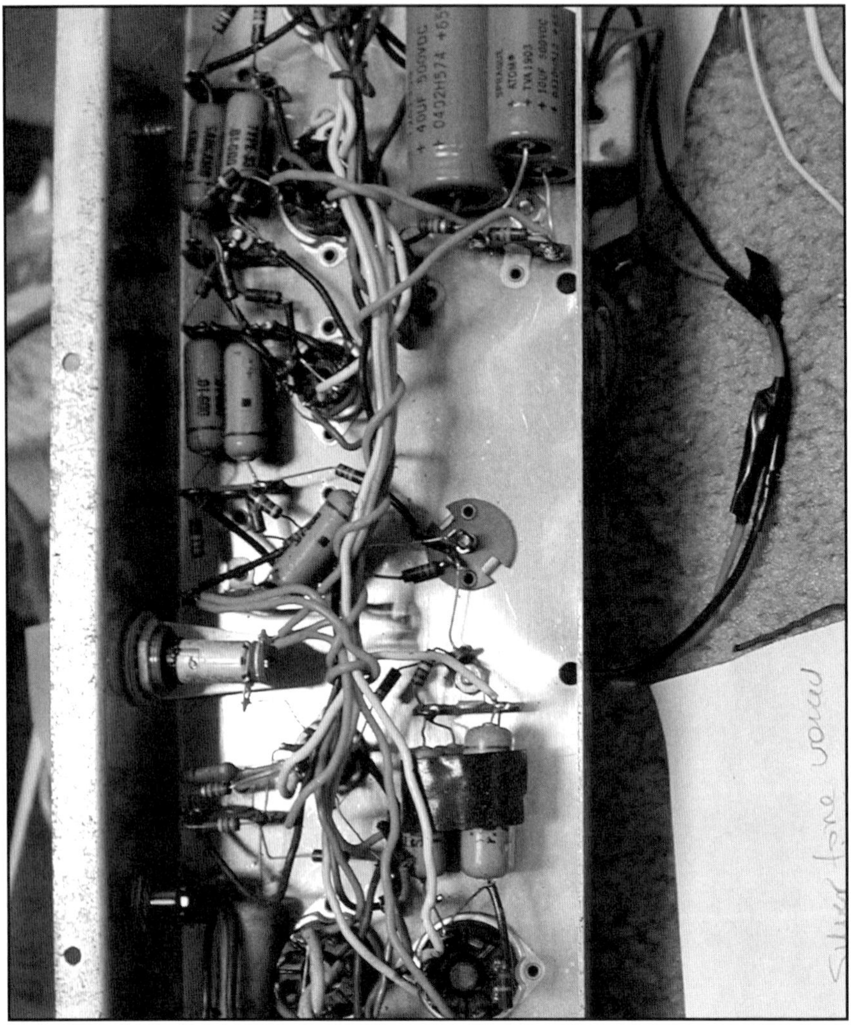

EVERYTHING YOU ALWAYS WANTED TO KNOW ABOUT CAPACITORS

If you are servicing amplifiers or building project amplifiers, you may have wondered what different types of capacitors are available and what they sound like. You may also have wondered if different brands are better sounding or more reliable than others. Why do they have different kinds of capacitors in the same amp? Tubular foil, ceramic, electrolytic, silver mica, polypropylene and polyester capacitors are some of the types used in tube guitar amps.

WHAT IS A CAPACITOR?

Two conductors separated by a non-conductor exhibit the property called capacitance. This combination can store electrical energy. Since the two conductors are separated by a non-conductor, capacitors cannot pass D.C. electrical current, although they will allow A.C. signal to pass. The non-conductor in between the conductors is called a dielectric. All sorts of non-conductors can be used and each different dielectric will sound different.

Capacitors, also called condensers, oppose any change in voltage. Because of the many electrical properties found in capacitors, they can be used for a variety of different functions in guitar amplifiers.

Capacitors are microphonic. That is right, you can talk into one and hear it coming out of the speaker in a guitar amp. Some capacitors are more microphonic than others. In fact, some of the best microphones in the world are condenser microphones, which are simply a capacitor that is intentionally made to be extremely microphonic.

FILTER CAPACITORS

Every tube guitar amplifier has filter capacitors in the power supply. These are always large value electrolytic capacitors. All tube circuits need a high voltage D.C. power source. The wall electricity is A.C. power, so the amplifier will have a rectifier circuit to change wall A.C. to high voltage D.C. This is done with a step-up transformer to get the wall voltage up, and a rectifier — either tube or solid-state — to change the electricity from A.C. (electrons go both ways) to D.C. (electrons all go only one way). When the A.C. gets rectified to D.C., it actually becomes pulsating D.C., and it's not very smooth. Filter capacitors are used in the power supply to smooth out pulsating D.C. current and make it pure D.C. This requires a lot of capacitance. Remember, capacitance opposes any change in voltage.

Electrolytic capacitors are used where large values of capacitance are required. Electrolytic capacitors deliver the most capacitance in a given physical size than any other type of capacitor. They are also the least expensive price-per-microfarad than any other type of capacitor. These capacitors are made with an electrolyte paste placed between two plates. The plates are rolled up and placed in a cylindrical aluminum container, with one of the plates connected to the aluminum container, which acts as the negative terminal. Sometimes these are made with several capacitors in one container and these are called multisection type electrolytic capacitors or simply: can caps. The multisection types are used to conserve space. These resemble a metal tube.

American-made electrolytics are the best. Most foreign–made electrolytic capacitors are inferior to American-made electrolytic capacitors. Although they may read good on a meter, they allow too much ripple current, resulting in out-of-tune sub notes. Stay away from anything made in Taiwan. Cornell Dublier, Illinois Capacitor, and many other former American-made capacitors are now made in Taiwan and sound nothing like the earlier American versions.

Even the LCR British caps should be avoided, unless you desire an ugly, out-of-tune sub note that is not in tune with the note you are playing. Certain electrolytic capacitors made in Germany perform with excellence and are as good as American made.

Avoid smaller size electrolytic capacitors. If you have two electrolytic capacitors of the same value and one is twice the physical size of the other, the larger one will always sound better.

BYPASS CAPACITORS

Almost all preamp tubes are cathode biased. In order to prevent degenerative feedback and to get the best gain characteristics, the cathode resistor is bypassed with an electrolytic capacitor. These capacitors are typically 10 uf to 50 uf, at very low voltage — usually 25 volts or less. The D.C. quiescent current, coming into the cathode of the tube, travels from ground through the cathode resistor into the cathode of the tube. Remember, D.C. can't pass through a capacitor. A.C. sees a capacitor as a short circuit, or very low resistance path. So, the A.C. component of the signal will travel through the bypass capacitor (and not the cathode resistor) because it is the path of least resistance for A.C. This is why it is called a bypass capacitor, because the A.C. signal current bypasses the cathode resistor and goes through the capacitor instead.

Likewise, the American-made electrolytic capacitors are best for use as a bypass capacitor.

Sometimes, a bypass capacitor can become very microphonic. On a bypass capacitor with axial leads, if the leads are tight, the capacitor can vibrate and resonate on certain notes and this resonance can come through the speaker. I've seen this occur where the amp would sound like a rattle in the speaker and upon further troubleshooting, a resonant bypass cap was the source of the noise!

COUPLING CAPACITORS

When a preamp tube amplifies, there is both a D.C. component and A.C. component on the plate of the preamp tube. Generally, a coupling capacitor (also called a blocking capacitor) is used to block the D.C. voltage and to pass the A.C. signal voltage.

The Fender tweed amps used an Astron brand cap. Later amps used other brands. I like Mallory 150 series caps for preamp coupling capacitors. These are made by taking two strips of foil, which are coated with polyester (used as the dielectric); and then everything is rolled up like a cigarette. They are bright yellow in color. There is also a Mallory 152 series, which is the 600 volt version, that I like equally as well. These are physically larger and work great.

For the phase inverter section of the amplifier, I like to use the Mallory Orange Drop coupling caps. These are called Orange Drop because they are dipped in Orange Epoxy and look like an orange blob, however they are made similar to the Mallory 150's.

In the old days, there were coupling caps made from two sheets of foil separated by a sheet of paper as the dielectric. The foil/paper/foil would then be rolled up like a cigarette and dipped in wax to keep it together. These are true paper capacitors.

Silver mica caps work great and sound wonderful as coupling caps. Typical coupling capacitor values may range from 500 pf to .05 uf.

TONE CAPACITORS

Not always, but in most amps with tone circuits, the tone capacitors are sometimes configured where they are both the tone stack and the coupling cap. In this case, I like the Mallory 150 series polyester tubular foil caps the best. For the treble cap, which is generally a much smaller value than is available in a Mallory 150, I like either a silver mica or a ceramic disc cap. In the silver mica, small mica sheets are used as the dielectric whereas in the ceramic disc, ceramic is used. The Mica sounds smoother while the ceramic is clear and trebly.

GROUND CAPACITORS

On amplifiers with a ground switch, there is a 600 volt .05 uf capacitor going from the 120 volt A.C. power line to ground. These caps are not in the signal path and do not affect tone. Any type cap will work in this circuit. There is a reason why a 600 volt or better value is used. The capacitors are rated in D.C. working voltage. When a cap is connected to an A.C. power source, its D.C. rating should be approximately 5 times the A.C. voltage. So don't replace that 600 volt cap with a lesser voltage. It will blow up.

When I first started shipping Kendrick amplifiers to Europe in 1989, after thoroughly testing an amp, I converted it to 230 volts without removing the ground capacitor. When a conversion to Euro voltage is done, the ground cap (.05 uf at 600 volts) should be removed. Europe uses a balanced A.C. line, so you don't need the ground cap; but since the voltage there is 230 volts, if you were going to use a ground cap, you would need a 1200 volt rated capacitor. After the customer played the amp for about 10 minutes, the ground cap burnt up with a nice little cloud of smoke. It was hard to convince the customer that the amp was fine and there was no problem to fix — especially after the fireworks show.

Tube Guitar Amplifier Essentials

WHAT YOU SHOULD KNOW ABOUT COUPLING CAPACITORS

A coupling capacitor is a device used for coupling one stage of gain to another in a vacuum tube guitar amp. Although there are other ways of coupling one stage to the next, such as direct coupling or transformer coupling, the coupling capacitor is almost always used. It passes A.C. (current going both directions) while blocking D.C. (current going the same direction) and is relatively inexpensive.

A coupling cap, like other capacitors, consists of two metal conductors separated by a non-conductor, or dielectric as it is sometimes called. Any non-conductor can be used as the dielectric. Capacitors are produced in a variety of forms. Mica, paper, oil, polypropylene and polyesters can be used as dielectrics.

When one conductor is charged with positive electricity, the other becomes negative and vice versa. In this way, A.C. signal is passed by the capacitor, however; since the dielectric is a non-conductor, D.C. current cannot pass through it.

Here is another analogy to illustrate how the capacitor passes A.C. yet blocks D.C. Think of a pipe with a membrane stretched across its internal path. We are using this membrane to simulate the dielectric in a capacitor. If we try to pass water through the pipe, the membrane would prevent water from flowing through the pipe, just as the dielectric in a capacitors stops D.C. current from flowing.

However, if water pressure were applied to one end of the pipe, the membrane allows the pressure to be passed on to the other end even though the water cannot pass directly through. If the pressure changed on one end, the change could be noticed on the other end.

HOW DOES THIS AFFECT TONE?

When coupling capacitors go bad, they sometimes will allow a small amount of D.C. voltage to leak through. When D.C. voltage leaks, it will appear on the grid circuit of the following stage and that stage will not perform correctly. Most preamp circuits use 12AX7 tubes or similar that bias at about one or two volts (grid to cathode relationship). If a volt of D.C. leaks through the capacitor, it could throw the bias of the next stage off drastically — although the plate voltages may check out fine!

I like to measure the D.C. leakage in a coupling capacitor. If there is more than two tenths of a volt D.C. leakage, I change the capacitor. If the capacitor is feeding the output tubes, two tenths of a volt does not really make much difference; however, when we are feeding another preamp stage such as a 12AX7, two tenths of a volt is substantial.

HOW DO WE CHECK COUPLING CAPACITORS?

Typical coupling capacitor values range from 500 pf to .1 mfd with .02 mfd as the most common. For example, every plate in the preamp circuit will likely have a coupling capacitor linking it to the grid of the next stage. If you check voltage on each end of the capacitor, the end connecting to the plate will have high voltage D.C. on it and the other end should have no D.C.. Because of other shunts in the circuitry, it is best to unsolder the side that is not supposed to have voltage on it and check it with a meter. Set the meter to D.C. One end of the meter goes to ground and the other end goes to the end of the coupling capacitor opposite the plate voltage. If there is no D.C., the cap is good. If there is .2 volt D.C. or more, the cap is bad. If you measure less than .2 volts, the cap is good. Typical measurement may be .003 volts on a good capacitor.

DUAL PURPOSE COUPLING/TONE CAPACITORS

Certain amps use the coupling cap both as a tone shaping cap and a coupling cap. For example, the Blackface Fenders used three different value caps to couple the first stage with the second stage. The different value caps were used because frequency response is a function of capacitor value. By putting potentiometers between these coupling caps, tone controls were created. The same D.C. leakage problems that occur with other coupling caps can also occur with these coupling/tone caps. If there is very much D.C. leaking through any of these caps, one or more of the tone controls (or volume control) will usually be scratchy. You can clean the pot or even replace it and the scratchiness will not go away because it is caused by D.C. voltage appearing on the pot and not from the pot being dirty or bad.

CORRECTING THE POLARITY OF THE COUPLING CAPACITORS

A capacitor is two conductors separated by a non-conductor. To get enough capacitance in a small component, two strips of metal foil are cut in very long strips with a non-conductor separating them. They are rolled up — each foil with its own lead — one lead on each end. The whole thing is then encased in epoxy. Only one of the foil strips will be nearest the outermost edge of the cap. The lead that goes to this outermost foil should go to the most grounded (least positive) side of the circuit. Why is that necessary? When you connect the outermost lead to the most grounded part of the circuit, it is as if the component itself is shielded by this more grounded connection. This helps to have less noise and hum.

My experience is that early amp builders paid no attention to which way was the best way to install a cap. In fact, in my experience, more caps are mounted backwards. How do you know which lead is the outermost? A simple test with a capacitance meter will tell the story. Take a piece of tin foil and wrap it around the capacitor. Connect one lead from the capacitance meter to the foil and the other meter lead to one of the cap leads. Take a reading. Now test from the foil to the other cap lead. The lead with the highest capacitance to the foil is the outermost lead. Most current manufactured caps have the outermost lead on the "right" side when reading the writing on the cap from "left to right." Older manufactured caps sometimes had a black line around the end of the cap indicating the end with the outermost foil.

This would apply to tone caps as well as coupling caps. For instance, the outermost lead on a tone cap always goes towards the tone controls, and the innermost lead goes to the plate circuit. Likewise, on the coupling cap, the outermost lead goes to the grid circuit of the next stage while the innermost lead goes to the plate circuit (high voltage).

In other words, if the cap has a black line around it, the side opposite this black line goes to the high voltage on the plate circuit.

CONCLUSION

Checking coupling capacitors for D.C. leakage and correct polarity can dramatically improve the tone and the noise and hum level of your vintage tube guitar amplifier.

RECTIFIERS

160 Tube Guitar Amplifier Essentials

CONVERTING A SOLID STATE RECTIFIER TO TUBE

Many of the so-called re-issue amplifiers are made with solid-state rectifiers. One question that comes up: Can I install a tube rectifier in my solid-state re-issue amp? And if so, How? Can it be done without having to replace the Power transformer? And if so, How?

CAN IT BE DONE?
We are going to use the existing power transformer and simply add a 5 volt auxiliary filament transformer. This 5 volt transformer needs to be rated at 3 to 6 amps so that we will have a built in safety factor.

First, we need to look at the amp. Is there space for another tube socket and another small filament transformer? The tube socket for a rectifier tube should be located near the power transformer because there is high voltage A.C. going to the tube and therefore it must be physically located away from the preamp circuit. Locating the rectifier tube near the preamp circuit will result in loud hum! The auxiliary rectifier filament transformer must also be located near the power transformer for the same reason.

Certain amps do not lend themselves to a rectifier tube conversion — either because of lack of space or because the amp draws more current than one rectifier tube can safely handle. For instance, in a Twin Reverb, you probably will not want to install a rectifier tube because one rectifier tube would not be able to handle the current and there is no room for another socket anyway.

WHAT TUBE SHOULD I USE?
Most amps work fine with a 5 volt type rectifier such as a 5Y3,

5V4, 5AR4/GZ34, or 5U4. If the amp uses 6L6's, you will want to stay with a 5AR4 or a 5U4. With smaller tubes such as 6V6, or 6BQ5, 7189A, etc. use a 5V4 or a 5Y3.

WHAT RECTIFIER TYPE DO I HAVE?

Although there are several styles of rectifier circuits, the two most common that are found in guitar amps are the full wave and the full wave bridge. You almost never see a half wave rectifier circuit, except in the case of the 6G15 Fender Reverb and the Kendrick Pipeline Reverberator. A few Marshalls had a full wave bridge economy power supply, which is the only instance I can think of where you have a center-tap on a full wave bridge rectifier. (However, in this case, the center-tap does not go to ground but to the junction point of the main filter totem pole stack.) Almost every guitar amp uses a full wave or a full wave bridge. The easy way to tell these apart is that the full wave (as used on all vintage Fender amps) has a center tapped transformer (on the B+ secondary winding) and the full wave bridge does not.

This is important to know what circuit your amp is using because the existing transformer secondary will be wound for only one style circuit and you must use the same style rectification circuit when using the same power transformer. Another way to tell is to measure the A.C. voltage across the entire B+ secondary. On a full wave bridge, the end-to-end measurement will generally be somewhere around 300 to 350 volts. On the full wave rectifier the end-to-end measurement will be twice that amount. Also on the full wave rectifier, the center-tap to either end will be around 300 to 350 volts. In other words, the full wave rectifier uses twice the B+ secondary voltage of an equivalent full wave bridge and the bridge is not center-tapped.

Don't assume you already know if your amp uses a full wave (not bridge) or a full wave bridge rectifier. You will have to look at how it is wired. Remember the idiot rule, if it has a grounded center-tap, it is full wave (not bridge).

PARTS NEEDED
You are going to need:
1. An octal socket
2. A 5 volt, 4 to 6 amp filament transformer

3. A rectifier tube
4. Hook-up wire
5. Two or four 1N4007 diodes if your amp currently uses full wave bridge rectification (in other words, the B+ does not have a center tap).

HOOKING IT ALL UP

Mount the tube socket in the chassis. The two wires from your existing power transformer B+ winding (usually both red) go to the socket. One goes to pin #4 and one goes to pin #6.

Mount the 5 volt rectifier filament auxiliary transformer. The primary (120 volts) is hooked up in parallel with the existing power transformer primary and the secondary (usually yellow) wires go to the tube socket. One goes to pin #8 and one goes to pin #2.

NOTE: On certain Fender amps there is a pan that covers the capacitors. I have mounted the auxiliary filament transformer on this pan and it worked perfectly.

Locate the existing rectifier circuit. Notice that the diodes in the existing supply have a D.C. output. Look for where the D.C. output terminates — possibly to the hot side of the standby switch, or the main filter caps or to the output transformer. Disconnect the solid-state rectifier circuit and connect a wire from pin #8 of the new rectifier socket to wherever the D.C. termination side of the existing solid-state rectifier was connected. If there was a wire already connected to the solid state rectifier, you could simply disconnect the D.C. output side of the existing solid state rectifier and move it to pin #8 of the rectifier tube socket.

If your amp was a full wave rectifier circuit, you are done. You may need to re-bias the amp because by changing to a tube rectifier, you have dropped the plate voltage 20 to 80 volts and this will dramatically affect your idling plate current.

However, if it was a full wave bridge circuit, you will need to put a 1N4007 diode from pin #4 to ground and another 1N4007 diode from pin #6 to ground. The bands on the diodes should face the tube socket. If you want to go the heavy duty approach, use two 1N4007 diodes in series for pin #4 to ground and two more for pin #6 to ground. The bands still face the socket. The advantage of using two diodes for each is this: If one of the diodes shorts on either side, the amp still works and the roadworthiness is thus improved. Also, using two diodes in series doubles the peak inverse voltage, thus increasing reliability.

The diodes mentioned above for the full wave bridge circuit will not affect the tone or envelope of the tone. Since the bridge is not center-tapped, the diodes simply create the necessary path to ground. All of the current must still go through the rectifier tube — exactly the same as in the full wave rectifier.

166　　　　　　　　　　　　　　　　　　　　　　　Tube Guitar Amplifier Essentials

THE PORT ARTHUR RECTIFIER

When Leo Fender put four output tubes into the 5F8 Twin to produce an unheard of (pun intended) 80 watts, a breakthrough in guitar amps was made. Although it was the first high wattage guitar amplifier in history, there were still design deficiencies that would reveal themselves in due time. These deficiencies were mainly in the power supply. For one thing, the rectifier used was a GZ34 (or 5AR4 as the Americans sometimes called it.) The GZ34/5AR4, rated for 250 ma of current, was being used in an amp that could pull as much as 300 to 400 ma of current when dimed. Of course, back then, players were not playing as loudly and Fender was testing the amp with Fender guitars, which had the lower output single-coil pickups and therefore would not cause the output stage to draw as much current. In addition, no one was using tube screamers, fuzz boxes or linear boosters at that time.

When I began experimenting with this circuit, I noticed that the Tweed Twin circuit would eat most rectifier tubes for breakfast. If you were playing through humbucking pickups or used a tube screamer, only a Mullard GZ34 would hold up in that circuit. Mullard GZ34 tubes were almost impossible to find in the early 90s, and there were no viable rectifier tubes currently being made. The Russian 5V4 was being relabeled and marketed in the US as a GZ34, but the 5V4 is only rated for 175 ma. Not only that, the Tweed Twin circuit would not be fooled by mislabeled rectifiers!

WHAT IS A "PORT ARTHUR RECTIFIER"?

It was about this time that I was facing the same dilemma that Leo Fender and Jim Marshall had faced thirty years earlier. In 1960, Leo Fender scratched the tube rectifier design and opted for the solid-state rectifier on all new four-output tube amps. There would never be another Fender Twin with a rectifier tube. Jim Marshall made the same choice with his four-output tube design.

Actually, many two output tube EL34 style amps draw more current than the GZ34 rectifier tube can handle safely. If you ever tried putting a tube rectifier in even a 50 watt Marshall, you would know that two EL34s, driven with sufficient gain, could easily cause rectifier tube failure.

I did not want to go solid state, so I invented what my friends and employees affectionately refer to as the "Port Arthur Rectifier" (so named because I was born and raised in Port Arthur).

My idea was to use a GZ34 style rectifier tube, but with a slight modification. I experimented with a solid-state rectifier circuit in series with a couple of high wattage wire-wound resistors until I ended up with a circuit that sounded like a tube rectifier. I would place this in parallel with the tube rectifier as a bypass circuit. My logic was this: If a small percentage of current was bypassed through a solid-state device designed to sound like a tube rectifier and the other current went through the tube rectifier; then I could still have the tube sound, but without the fear of constant rectifier tube failure. The solid-state device would take away enough of the current to allow the rectifier to operate within its design limitations!

HOW IT'S MADE

Although a GZ34 fits an 8 pin socket, only four of the pins are actually used (namely pins #2, #4, #6, #8). Pins #2 and #8 go to the 5 volt filament heater (usually yellow wires from the transformer) and pins #4 and #6 go to the B+ winding (usually red wires from the transformer). Pin #8 also connects to the standby switch.

For starters, we wire the rectifier socket the same way it would normally be wired for use with a GZ34 tube. We are going to add some parts to the socket wiring. We will use pins #1, #3, #5, and #7 as mounting terminals because as I said before, these pins are not used on a GZ34 tube socket. You will need these parts:

Four - 1N5399 solid state rectifiers
Two - 250 ohm 25 watt Wire Wound resistors

THEY ARE TO BE WIRED AS FOLLOWS:

One 1N5399 goes from pin #4 to pin #1, the cathode faces pin #1.

One 1N5399 goes from pin #6 to pin #7, the cathode faces pin #7.
One 1N5399 goes from pin #1 to pin #3, the cathode faces pin #3.
One 1N5399 goes from pin #7 to pin #5, the cathode faces pin #5.
One 250 ohm 25 watt resistor goes from pin # 8 to pin #3.
One 250 ohm 25 watt resistor goes from pin # 8 to pin #5.

I like to put spaghetti insulation on all 250 ohm 25 watt resistor leads. Although the resistors are mounted directly on the tube socket, the resistors are quite large and if you fail to insulate them, you will have exposed leads with high voltage on them. If one of those leads shorted to ground, you could easily fry the power transformer!

LET'S TEST IT

When you are done, put a GZ34 rectifier in the socket and you are good to go. If you do ever happen to blow the rectifier tube and do not have a spare GZ34 handy, you may remove the failed rectifier tube from the amp (replace the fuse you just blew) and the amp will function perfectly without a rectifier tube! This could really be of benefit in a pinch situation!

As another side benefit, you could use a 5U4 or a 5U4GB in the rectifier socket. These tubes are less expensive and easier to find than the GZ34. Ordinarily, I do not like the over-compression that the 5U4 style tube gives in a high powered amp circuit, however when used with "The Port Arthur Rectifier" circuit, it will have less sag and sound very similar to the popular GZ34.

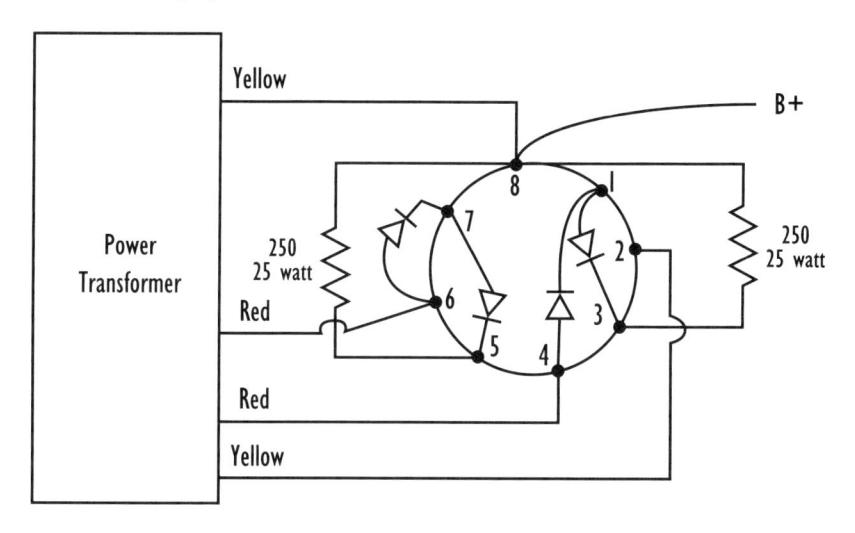

The Port Arthur Rectifier

TUBES

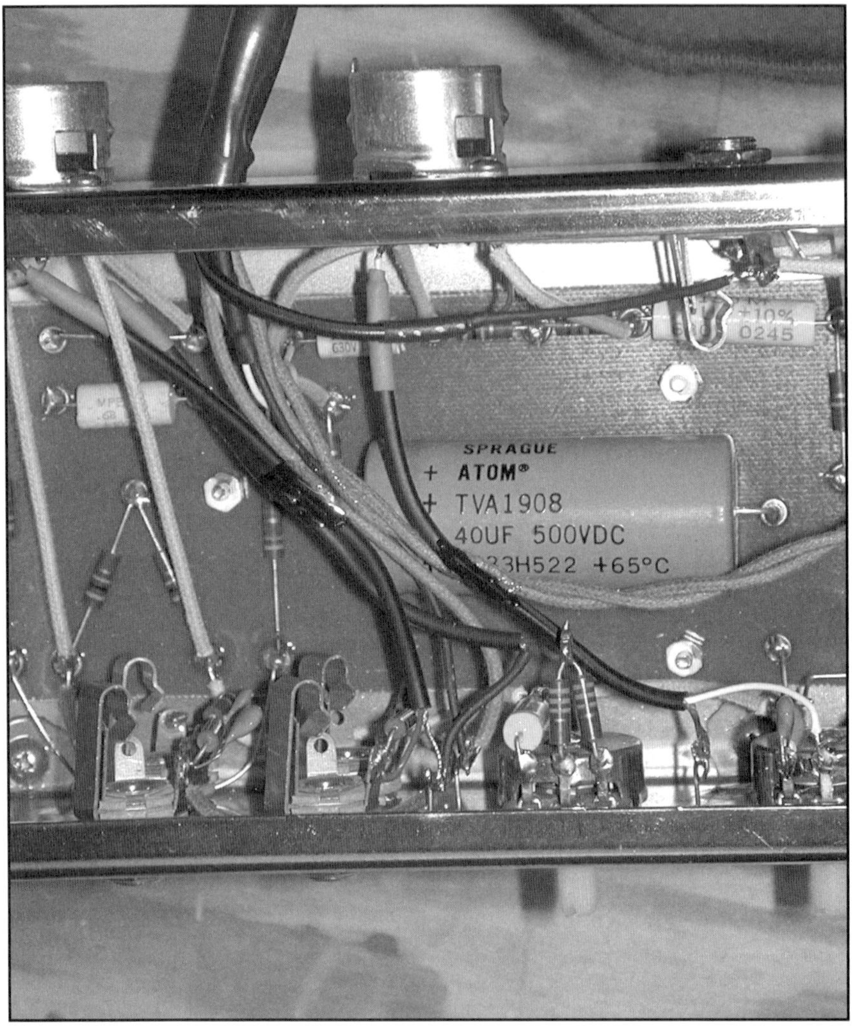
SPRAGUE
+ ATOM®
+ TVA1908
40UF 500VDC

THE 12AX7 PREAMP TUBE

The most common of all tubes used in guitar amplifiers, the 12AX7 can be found in almost every guitar amp. It is a fairly high gain preamp tube that is actually two (clap), two (clap, clap), two tubes in one! Its popularity among designers is primarily because:
1. It has good tone
2. It is small and has two triodes within one miniature envelope
3. It has good gain
4. Its filament can be wired humbucking, for zero hum

Let's talk about the tube itself. It is a nine-pin miniature twin triode tube. Pins #1, #2 and #3 are the plate, grid and cathode, respectively, of one triode section. Pins #6, #7, and #8 are the plate, grid and cathode, respectively, of the other triode section.

FILAMENT HEATER CONFIGURATION Pins #4 and #5 are the two ends of the filament and Pin #9 is the center-tap of the filament. This is a clever filament set up. Although the tube is designed to use a 12.6 volt filament heater by applying voltage to pins #4 and #5 (and simply ignoring Pin #9), the tube can also be wired for 6.3 volts humbucking. It is almost always wired 6.3 volts humbucking. The way to do this is to tie the ends of the filament (Pins #4 and #5) together and count that as one lead of the filament circuit. Use the center-tap (Pin #9) as the other lead of the filament. You now have a 6.3 volt humbucking connection. Since the filaments are wound all in the same direction, when you connect the tube humbucking, any hum induced by the first section of filament (Pin #4 to the center-tap at Pin #9), will be hum-cancelled by the second section (Pin #5 to the center-tap at Pin #9).

Here's an analogy to show how that humbucking connection works. Let's say you have a coil of wire that is wound in a clock-wise direction. If you are looking from the start of the coil toward the finish of the coil, then it looks like the coil is wound clockwise. On the other hand, if you are standing at the finish of the coil looking back at the start, then the

coil appears to be wound counter-clockwise. When the tube is connected humbucking, and the ends (Pins #4 and #5) are connected together and counted as one lead while the centertap (Pin #9) is used as the other lead, then the other coil will cancel any hum induced by one coil. Pretty clever!
TYPICAL TRIODE CONFIGURATION — The two triodes within the 12AX7 can be configured as two entirely separate triodes, or they can share circuitries.

Typical peripheral component values:
PLATE — 100K to 250K plate resistor (with 100K being the most common) When both plates are tied together, the plate resistor value should be cut in half because two plates draw twice the current of one.
GRID — 150K to 2 meg grid return resistor (with 1 meg being the most common.)
CATHODE — 1K to 10K (with 1500 being the most common). When both cathodes are tied together, the cathode resistor value must be cut in half because two cathodes draw twice the current of one.
CATHODE RESISTOR BYPASS CAPACITOR — .1 uf to 350 uf with 25 uf being the most common.
COUPLING CAPACITOR — .001 uf to .1 uf with .02 being the most common.
SPECIAL TRIODE CONFIGURATIONS Sometimes the two sections of the 12AX7 are connected together in parallel to make one triode. If both plates are tied together and counted as one plate, both cathodes tied together and counted as one cathode and both grids tied together and counted as one grid; then it is as if you have one 12AX7 with a huge plate, huge grid and huge cathode. This would give a cleaner tone with more substance. Also the output impedance would be cut in half, thus providing more stable source impedance for the next stage. With this configuration, only one cathode resistor, one grid resistor and one plate resistor is used. The exact value of the plate resistor and cathode resistor should be cut in half (of the values normally used for one triode section) since there will be twice the cathode and plate current. The grid resistor does not have to be changed, because there is negligible current in the grid circuit.
CATHODE BYPASS CAPACITORS In all self-bias preamp tubes, such as the 12AX7, cathode bypass capacitors can be used to achieve maximum

gain. With a typical 1500 ohm cathode resistor, a 25 uf capacitor is placed across the cathode resistor. This will achieve a flat response for guitar frequencies. A 50 uf bypass capacitor is used with the 1500 ohm cathode resistor to achieve a flat response for bass guitar.

When a bypass capacitor is used, the D.C. quiescent voltage goes through the cathode resistor and any A.C. signal voltage will pass through the bypass capacitor. That is why it is called the bypass capacitor — because the A.C. signal bypasses the cathode resistor and goes through the capacitor instead. To A.C., the capacitor looks like a short and since electricity likes the path of least resistance, the A.C. takes the capacitor path. On the other hand, D.C. cannot pass through a capacitor so the D.C. goes through the resistor and actually develops a small positive voltage on the cathode (which biases the tube.)

DEGENERATIVE FEEDBACK When the cathode resistor lacks a bypass capacitor, it is said to be unbypassed. The unbypassed configuration is actually a type of degenerative feedback. Because this type of circuit is very hard to clip, you will see this circuit used on circuits that have hot input signals on the grid.

If a bypass capacitor is not used, then both D.C. and A.C. signal voltage must travel through the cathode resistor. This makes the bias voltage unstable — in a good way. As more signal is applied to the tube, the extra A.C. signal current travels through the cathode resistor thus increasing the bias of the tube and actually cutting down the gain of the tube. This configuration sounds much more compressed, much less gain and much cleaner in general. Usually cathodes are unbypassed in the later stages of the amp — perhaps the phase inverter or the stage before the phase inverter. This is where the signal voltage is getting fairly large and the unbypassed configuration allows little clipping and more compression. Sometimes bass guitar tube amps use this circuit. It is perfect for bass because it is compressed and relatively clean.

The downside of the unbypassed cathode circuit is the loss of gain. The bypassed version has much more gain.

TYPICAL PLATE VOLTAGE AND GAIN With a typical 12AX7, plate voltages from 120 volts to 220 volts are common. With 200 volts on the plate, a 1500 cathode resistor bypassed with a 25 uf capacitor and a 100K plate resistor, the gain will be around 35 dB. The actual gain can vary slightly with the particular tube used. Even tubes of the same brand will perform slightly differently. In fact, the two triodes within the same tube may have slightly different gains.

I built a preamp tube tester that interfaces with a db meter and a signal generator. With this device, I could check decibels gain of each side of the 12AX7.

The higher voltages in general give more headroom, more chimey highs and more gain. Although the design maximum is listed in the R.C.A. tube manual as 300 volts and in the General Electric tube manual as 330 volts, I have found that these high voltages yield a brittle high-end and too much headroom for guitar amplification. For best guitar tone, I like plate voltages ranging from 150 to 240 volts.

Sometimes 12AX7's are run with very low plate voltage. For example, in my harp amp designs, I use 80 volts on the plate of the first gain 12AX7. The lower voltage rounds out the highs, distorts easier and grinds the bottom. Sometimes 12AX7's are used in "tube screamer" pedals in a similar fashion. I have actually seen plate voltages as small as 12 volts! This configuration has little gain, maximum distortion and practically no high-end. In the typical "tube screamer," an OP amp is overdriven and then the signal is run through a low-voltage 12AX7 (using the 12AX7 as a high-end filter.)

OTHER SIMILAR 12AX7 TUBE SUBSTITUTIONS The 12AX7 can be found with other names. The British name for the 12AX7 is the ECC83. The 6681, the 7025, and the 7729 are all industrial versions of the 12AX7. General Electric made a special 12AX7 with slightly less gain called a 5751.

WHERE TO FIND MORE INFORMATION I am frequently asked where to find information about vacuum tubes. In my hometown of Austin, Texas; there is the University of Texas. It has nine libraries, one of which is an engineering library. That particular library has rows and rows of books from the 30s, 40s, 50s, and 60s. If you are near a university or college that has been around a while, it will have at least one library with engineering books. Provided the establishment is 50 years old or older, it will be loaded with writings on tubes and tube circuitry. I would highly recommend your local university as a resource for tube knowledge. If you are not a student, most colleges and universities will sell you a non-student library card.

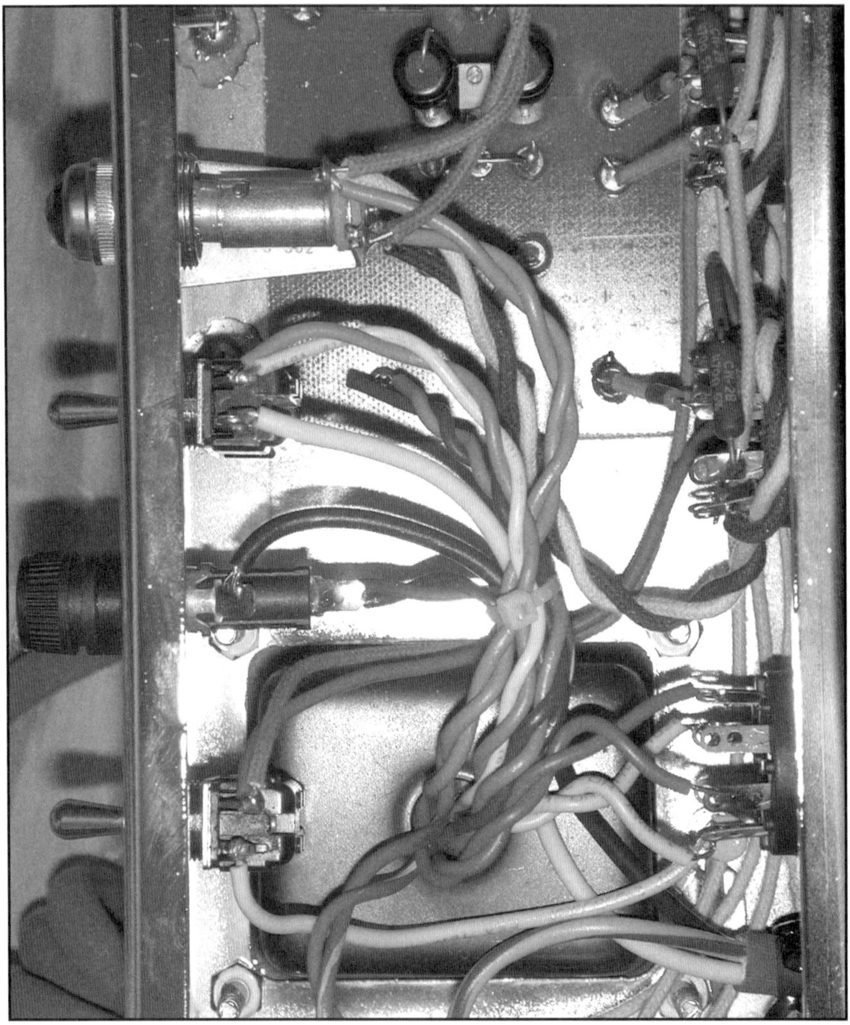

TUBE SUBSTITUTIONS IN GUITAR AMPS

With new old stock tubes becoming more and more scarce, and with most newly manufactured tubes lacking in tone, we begin looking at which tubes can be substituted in our tube amps.

PREAMP TUBES

Nine pin miniature tubes such as the 12AX7 are very popular in guitar amps. Here are some tubes that have the exact same pin out and therefore are interchangeable. There are also gain and power supply considerations. Most of these nine pin tubes are interchangeable. For instance, a 6072 is a replacement for a 12AY7 with about the same gain. If you wanted more gain, for example, you could replace the 12AY7 with a 6201.

TUBE TYPE	AMPLIFICATION FACTOR
12AT7	60
12AX7	100
12AY7	44
12AZ7	60
12BH7	16.5 this one draws twice the filament current
12BZ7	100 this one draws twice the filament current
12DM7	100
12DW7	100/17
12DT7	100
12AU7	17
12AV7	41
5751	70 Special five star G.E. design
5814	17 Special five star G.E. design
5963	21

5965	47
6072	44 (special 12AY7)
6189	17 Special five star G.E. design
6201	60 Special five star G.E. design
6679	60 Special five star G.E. design
6680	17 (special 12AU7)
6681	100 (special 12AX7)
6829	47 Special five star G.E. design
6913	18
6955	16.5
7025	100
7247	100/17 (special 12DW7)
7318	16.5
7728	60
7729	100
7730	17

RECTIFIER TUBES

The most popular rectifier tubes are the 5 volt octal style tubes such as the 5Y3 and 5AR4. The following tubes all have the same pin out and therefore are interchangeable. The filament current and the plate current should both be considered. If you have an amp that uses a rectifier tube that uses 2 amps of filament current, you would not want to substitute one that uses 4 amps of current because the power transformer is probably not designed to deliver that much current. If the tube you are currently using is rated for 250 mA of plate current, you would not want to substitute another tube that can only handle 125 mA of plate current, because if the amp draws more than the rated amount, the tube will arc—thus permanently damaging the tube and possibly blowing a fuse. In other words, you can safely substitute a rectifier that draws the same or less filament current and with the same or more plate current rating. With this in mind, here are the specs.

Tube Type	Filament Current Amps	Plate Current Rating mA
5AT4	5.5	800
5CG4	2	125
5V4	2	175

5Z4	2	125
6087	2	125
6106	1.7	125
5AS4	3	275
5AU4	3.75	325
5AW4	3.7	250
5AX4	2.5	175
5AZ4	2	125
5R4	2	250
5T4	2	225
5U4	3	225
5U4GA	3	250
5U4GB	3	275
5V3	3.8	350
5W4	1.5	100
5Y3	2	125
5931	3	300
5AR4	1.9	250
GZ34	1.9	250

POWER TUBES

Perhaps the most common output tubes are the 6L6 and 6V6 octal style tube. Fortunately, there are many tubes with this same pin out. Always re-bias when substituting power tubes. Re-biasing adjusts the idle plate current flow of the tube to an optimum level. All of the tubes listed here are direct drop-ins with only a re-bias necessary.

6V6 TYPE SUBSTITUTES	**6L6 TYPE SUBSTITUTES**
6EY6	6L6
6EZ5	5881
6V6	5932
5992	5992
7408	7581A
	EL37

Tube Substitutions in Guitar Amps

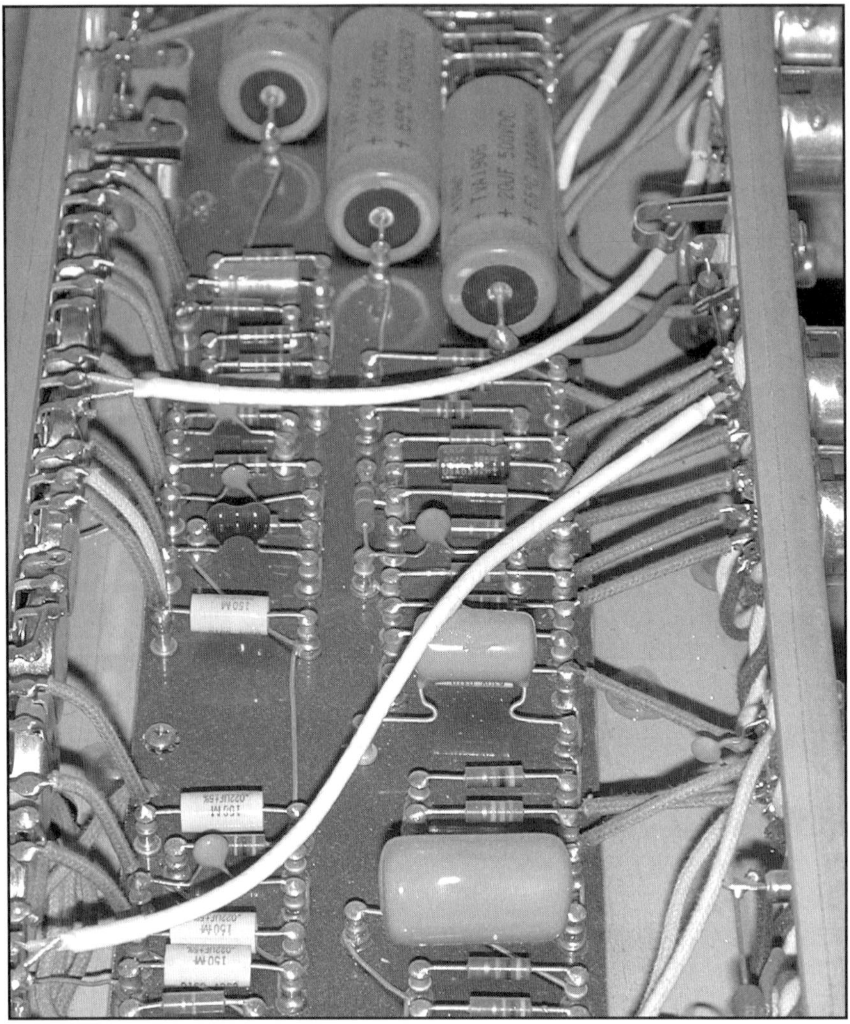

CURRENT EL34 TUBE TESTS

Recently I had the good fortune to test all of the current production EL34 style output tubes. I tested these through a Climax amplifier with both clean and overdriven settings. There are many different brands currently being manufactured and this is what I found:

THE SOVTEK EL34WXT — This is easily one of the best sounding EL34 style tubes around. It had good output, as much or more than most any other EL34. The clean sound was chimey and rich with plenty of note definition. Think of the clean sound as a full bodied clean with good clear bottom and punchy clear lower mids.

When pushed to distortion, the Sovtek tube actually sounded very Mullardesque, but with not quite as much power as an actual Mullard. The overdriven sound was smooth and creamy — like it is supposed to be. The tube has plenty of bottom and loads of tone. Highly recommended.

THE TESLA EL34 — Tesla makes three different versions of this tube. This one is the commercial version. They also make a higher quality military version called an E34L and the E34LS.

It's interesting to note that the British designate military grade by moving the last alpha character to the end to make E34L rather than EL34. The Americans (and apparently the Russians as well), on the other hand, use a W designation (as in 6L6WGB) or change to a military name.

The commercial grade EL34 was stronger than either Russian tube tested. The clean sounds lacked high-end and note definition. It just wasn't as chimey as the others.

When pushed to distortion, the lead sound creamed out — maybe even a little too creamy — almost to the point of losing some note definition when playing chords. The front end of the note compressed nicely and would have been good for recording.

THE TESLA E34L — This is the military version of the tube above. It would probably also be wonderful for high-end audio.

I would describe the clean sound as having more top end with extra clarity — like a 6L6. Think Fendery black face clean with lots of high-end sizzle. These tubes had the highest fidelity of any tubes tested. The E34L Tesla also had more edge than other tubes except for its big brother, the E34LS.

THE GROOVE TUBE TESLA E34LS — This was my favorite of everything tested. Aspen Pittman, of Groove Tubes, has worked with the Tesla factory to improve the regular EL34's. This tube produces more power, because of its specially modified grid design. The grid is gold plated wire and the pitch of the winding is changed to produce more output at the plate. The new heat sink wings attached to the seams of the plates actually improve high power operation. Although Groove Tubes literature suggested not to use current draw method biasing, I did it anyway. This biasing method worked perfectly and is an on-board built-in feature of the Climax amplifier that I was using to test the EL34's.

The E34LS was easily the most powerful tube tested. It's clean sound reminded me of that curly Blackface clean tone — not unlike what you would expect to hear coming out of a pair of matched black-plate RCA 6L6's.

The overdrive sound of the E34LS was creamy, but with good note definition. I cannot imagine anyone not liking this tube — it simply has too much going for it. The dynamic range was wider than other tubes tested.

THE SVETLANA EL34 — This EL34 seem to possess a rather thin clean sound. Maybe it wasn't thin, but just lacked clear bottom and lower midrange.

When pushed to distortion, the tone became creamy — much like the commercial grade Tesla EL34.

CONCLUSION

I felt like the Groove Tubes Tesla E34LS and the Sovtek EL34WXT were special and seemed to be a cut above everything else. I compared both of these tubes to some NOS Seimens EL34's and the E34LS was as good or better. The Sovtek was as good tonally, but once again is not a powerful as either the E34LS or the Seimens.

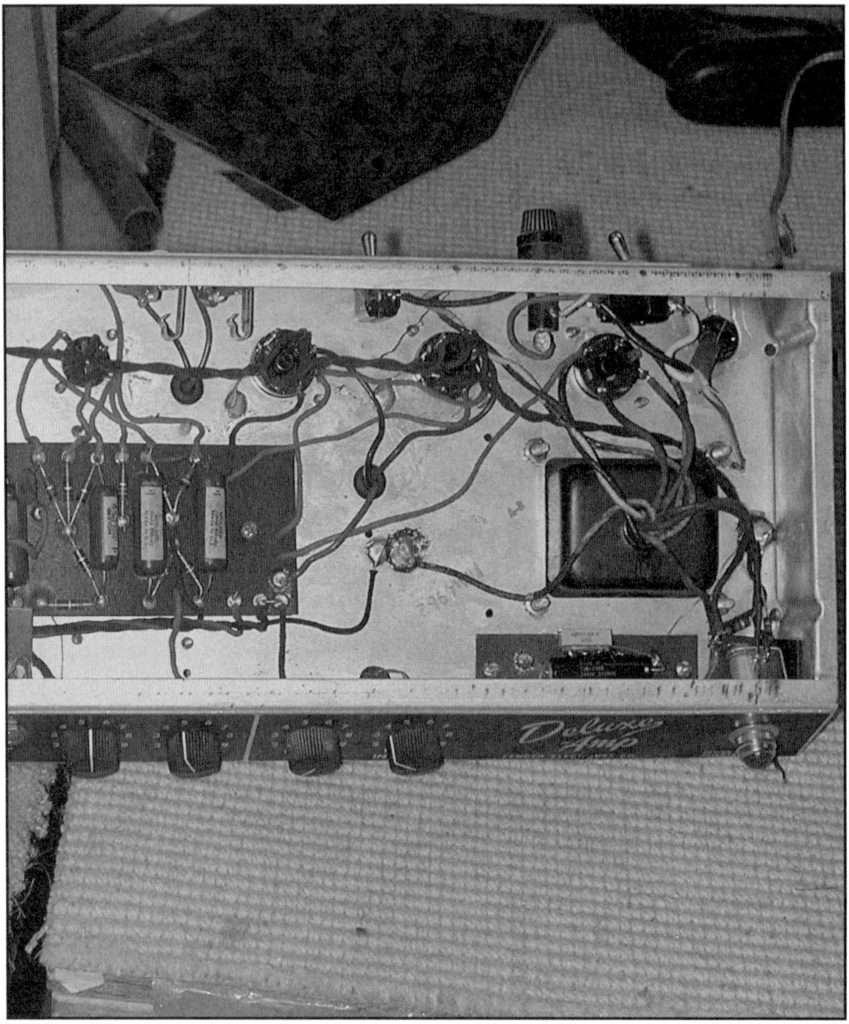
Deluxe
Amp

TESTS OF CURRENT AND OLD STYLE 6L6 TUBES

An acoustic guitar is complete by itself. An electric guitar, on the other hand, is only complete with an amplifier and speaker. Since the inception of the electric guitar and the invention of the guitar pickup by Adolph Rickenbacker in the 1920s, the vacuum tube amplifier has been the industry standard. It is this voice that we have come to know as the electric guitar. But what is the voice of the amplifier? Although there are many factors that affect the voice of the amplifier, one of the most important is the output tube. After all, the output tubes are coupled via output transformer to the speaker we hear. I like to think of the output tubes as a filter that colors the sound.

Every tube amplifier will eventually need output tubes, so the question comes up: How do current production tubes compare tonally with New Old Stock tubes and each other? Which tube should I use for "my sound," and, which tube will compliment my amplifier?

HOW WAS THE TEST CONDUCTED?

Since there were so many tubes to listen to, I decided to go the scientific approach and record each tube. I set up a Kendrick Black Gold 35 watt amp in my 16-track recording studio. I chose this particular amp, because it has an extremely simplistic circuit and I wanted to hear more tubes and less circuit! The Black Gold 35 doesn't have a tone stack like most amps, but a single tone control instead. This control basically just rolls off highs; so with it all the way "up," it is like not having a tone circuit at all. Also, the BG 35 has the added convenience of Quick Bias pin jacks and external trim adjustment which allowed me to adjust bias on any tube in less than 1 minute without moving the amp or taking anything apart. The output transformer is a 7 winding interleaved 1959 Bassman style, but wound for 4 ohms (slightly less coupling loss than original Triad but tonally identical); and the speaker configuration was 2x10 Kendrick Blackframe speakers. These are made with original Donal-Kapi 3KSP paper cones on original Jensen dyes. So the point I am making is that everything was a really pure vintage setup. Also, I used a Shure 57 microphone into a Kendrick Six-Shooter tube mic preamp that went directly into a synced pair of Alesis ADAT 8 track tape recorders. The mike was placed slightly off-axis about 3 or 4 inches in front of the center of the speaker. Again, I didn't want to hear a lot of "room sound," just output tube sound.

All tubes were biased at 35 ma of plate current, the plate voltage on a Black Gold 35 being around 470 volts.

Once setup was complete, everything was left alone. The settings on the amp or tube Mic preamp were never touched. The same guitar was used, by the same player, to play the same licks. Each tube was recorded with a clean example, a percussive clean example and an overdriven sound. To get these different sounds, the patch cord was switched into different channels on the Black Gold 35 amp and the controls were never touched. Even the same channel of the mic preamp was used on every example; the patch cord was simply moved to another input jack on the recorder.

As a matter of fact, the only adjustment made during the entire recording process was adjusting the bias of each pair of tubes, so that quiescent (idle) plate current adjusted to 35 mA.

I originally wanted to record bias voltages of different brands and present this information, however in order to get any real idea of which brands did what, a larger sampling would have been required. In most cases, we only had a pair of tubes to test — especially the KT66 Genelex and most NOS tubes. Using only one pair could give inaccurate conclusions because of wide variations in grid bias from one set to another. I would have liked to have gotten at least a dozen of each tube, determined grid bias for each, and averaged them to get a nominal grid bias for that particular brand. Data from too small a sampling can be misleading.

LET THE TEST BEGIN

I had a little help from my friends on this test. Terry Oubre, the best guitarist I know, helped me extensively with the recording and critical listening in these tests. Terry even took the tapes home and listened to them in his studio on his monitors and took notes on his A/B comparisons there. We then collaborated back in my studio for more listening and comparing. Special thanks to Mr. Oubre. Terry can hear things that few others hear until he points it out, then it becomes so obvious.

We wanted to reference listening to both current production tubes and classic NOS tubes. Sixteen tubes were tested, namely:

NEW OLD STOCK — The Mullard EL37, RCA 6L6GC (roundtops and black plates), Phillips/Sylvania 5881, GE 6L6GC, GE 7581A, Tung Sol 5881, and Genelex KT66.

NEW STOCK CHINESE — Groove Tubes 6L6C, Ruby 6L6GCSTR, and Valve Art 6L6GC, Ruby KT66

NEW STOCK RUSSIAN — Groove Tubes KT66, Sovtek 5881, Sovtek 6L6GCWXT, Svetlana 6L6GC

NEW STOCK SLOVAKIAN — Groove Tubes 6L6S, Ruby 6L6GCCZ (Both of these are made by the former Tesla factory)

Bear in mind, there are no good and bad sounding tubes, only different. For instance, the Sovtek 5881 had the least amount of bottom-end of any 6L6 style tube. Is this good or bad? It depends on what amplifier you are using and what kind of sound you are going for. For example, you may want to use the Sovtek 5881 in an amp that has boomy low end. Its lack of bottom will actually "help" such an amp.

NEW OLD STOCK FIRST

Since the NOS was the foundation of what we've all been listening to for the last half a century, I thought it well to start with the classic sounds of the NOS tubes and here's what was found:

Mullard EL37 — Ultra Mellow tone, but with strength and power. It makes the strings sound like polished round wound. Extremely buttery and smooth. Voiced with a low mid richness.

GE7581A — Very Plinky. More upper mids than the GE6L6GC, but very similar. Middle range fullness not as good as GE6L6GC. Not as compressed as other tubes. Extremely fast attack and pingy.

Phillips/Sylvania 5881 — Classic 6L6. Toothy attack. Strong and clear. Well defined, not harsh. Solid and focused. Firm. More ping on clean.

GE 6L6GC — Chunky clean sound. Smooth throaty sound when overdriven. Makes the guitar sound like it is tuned down or like bigger gauge strings were used. A lower voicing. More meat. Firm.

RCA 6L6GC — Slightly more highs than GE 6L6GC, but similar. Good bottom. Firm, focused and warm. Fast attack. Brighter than Sylvania 5881. Curly highs.

Tung Sol 5881 — Classic 50s tubey, hi-fi tone. Soft focus. Airy highs. Much more mellow than Sovtek 5881.

Genelex KT66 — Rich strong, Warm, Firm. Chunky mids. Fat. Similar to Phillips/Sylvania 5881 but lower voicing. Good note separation. More pure focus than Sylvania. Tighter, mucho headroom.

TAKE A TRIP TO CHINA

Let's focus on the first new production group, which are Chinese made, and compare them.

The Groove Tubes 6L6C — Warmer than the Sovtek 5881. Chunky and smooth. Mellow top. Sounds like a low voltage transformer. Not glassy. Sounds like an overwound single-coil pickup. Good growl when driven hard. More upper mids. Good note definition in chords. Compressed attack. Lower register than Ruby 6L6GCSTR.

Valve Art 6L6GC — More mids than Sovtek 5881. Rounder. Real good clang and chime. Not thin like Sovtek. Plunky not Plinky. More low mids. Not quite as thick as Slovakian 6L6 but similar.

Ruby 6L6GCSTR — Not as full bodied as original NOS Phillips/Sylvania 5881. More compressed attack than Phillips. Stronger and fatter than Sovtek 5881. Not as much upper mid definition. Sounds filtered.

THE KT66

NOS Genelex KT66's could easily be considered as the Holy Grail of 6L6's. The set that I own and used for this comparison are used but still sounded rich, strong, and warm. They had a solid bottom that held together well with chunky mids similar to Phillips/Sylvania 5881; but lower voicing. Good note separation. More pure focus than Sylvania.

How did the current Russian KT66 Compare?

These tubes have the unique octal base similar to a NOS Genelex. The glass envelope is shaped like the Genelex however doesn't have the smoky gray substance on the inside of the glass.

Very similar in tone to the original but with a higher voicing. Voiced more in the midrange with more texture around the note than the Genelex. Slightly less focused and with more headroom than its 6L6 cousin.

RUSSIAN 6L6'S

All Russian 6L6's in general have that softer European focus with the exception of the Sovtek 5881 that sounds nothing like the Sovtek 6L6WXT. In fact, the 5881 almost sounds Chinese when compared — due to its lack of bottom end and diffused upper mids and treble.

When compared to American NOS, the NOS had a much sharper focus than the Russians.

Sovtek 6L6WXT — Similar to the Svetlana 6L6GC. Nice and round with good upper register detail. Softer focus than the Phillips/Sylvania, but overall very balanced tonally. More air and chime than the Phillips.

Svetlana 6L6GC — Voiced slightly lower than the Sovtek 6L6WXT. Exhibits less high end detail than the Sovtek. Less prone to high-end graininess due to it's darker voicing.

Sovtek 5881 — Kinda crunchy with EL34-like breakup when lightly driven. Dry high-end. Grainy midrange lacking bottom-end. Splatty attack when overdriven.

Groove Tubes 6L6B — same tube as Sovtek 5881 but with 6L6WXT octal base. It sounds identical and has the same guts as the 5881. If it looks like a duck and quacks like a duck…

SLOVAKIAN 6L6'S

These tubes are made in the former Tesla factory and are marketed as the Ruby 6L6GC-CZ and the Groove Tubes 6L6S. This tube sounded clear and warm. Presence without airiness. Fat attack — no splat. Rich mid fullness with an "AWH" vowel sound after the initial attack. Big bottom.

CONCLUSION

While the new old stock American and European 6L6 and all its variants (i.e. EL37, KT66, 7581A, 5881) are still superior to any currently made 6L6, there are many very good sounding current production 6L6's. The good news is that they are available. Although they are marketed under many different brand names, it is up to the reader to familiarize himself with the tube and its country of origin and to not be fooled by designer labels. I'm not against designer tubes, these companies do provide the service of matching, but more importantly these designer tube companies seek out the overseas factories and make them hip to what us guitar players want. Special thanks to Aspen Pittman of Groove Tubes, Mike Matthews of New Sensor (Sovtek), Tom McNeil of Magic Parts (Ruby Tubes), and Jay Bertrand of Bertrand Audio Imports (Valve Art). These are the people that are traveling abroad and actually motivating the third world factories to put out quality tubes to push for better tubes. All of these movers and shakers supplied the new samples used in these listening test.

HOW DO THE NEW TUBES RATE?

Our faves were narrowed down to four — namely: the Valve Art 6L6GC, the Slovakian 6L6 (Groove tubes 6L6S and Ruby Tubes 6L6GC-CZ), the Sovtek 6L6WXT, and the Svetlana 6L6GC. Every amp will sound a little different depending on the amp itself and the speaker configuration. Based on this, the Slovakian 6L6 and the Svetlana 6L6GC are recommended for 10" speaker configurations. The Valve Art 6L6GC and the Sovtek 6L6WXT are recommended for 12" speaker configurations.

TRANSFORMERS

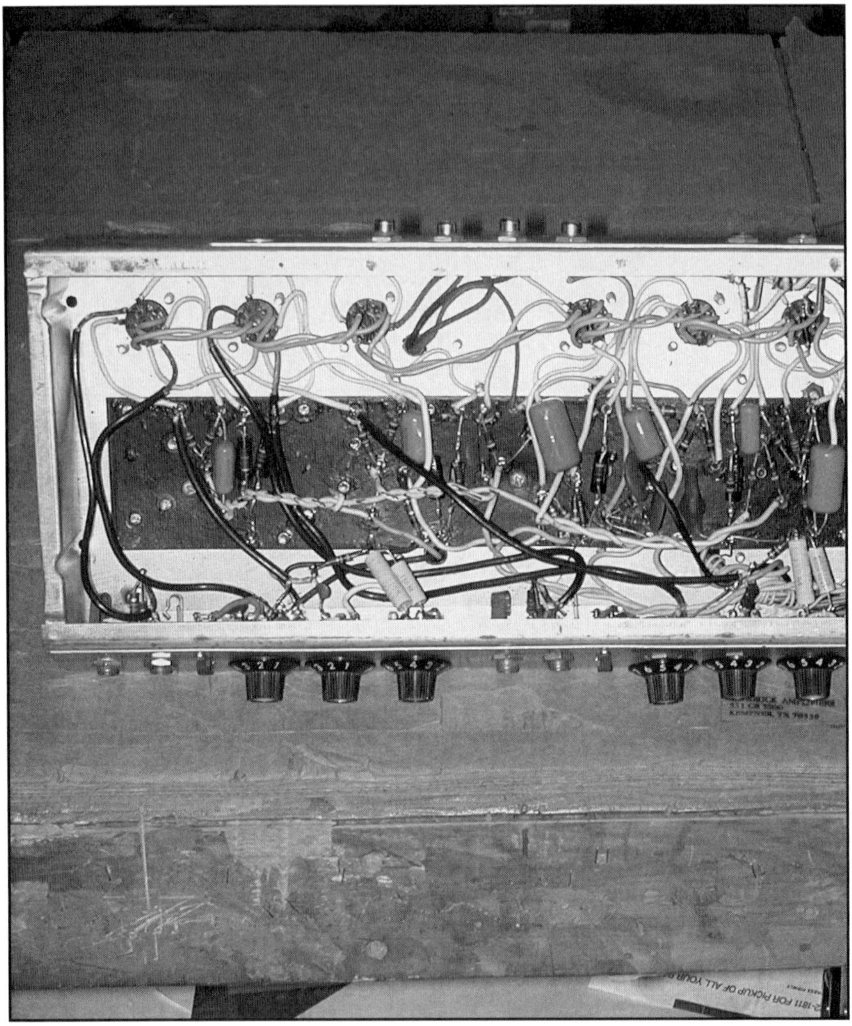

TRANSFORMER QUESTIONS ANSWERED

Let's start off with a little True or False quiz! There are no trick questions. You even get to grade yourself when done!

1. True or False _____ When determining the output impedance of an output transformer, one simply measures the resistance of the output transformer's secondary and multiplies by 2.82.

2. True or False _____ When checking a push-pull output transformer primary, the resistance from the center-tap to one end should equal the resistance from the center-tap to the other end.

3. True or False _____ To determine output wattage, simply multiply the A.C. voltage swing across the primary times the primary current coming off the center-tap.

4. True or False _____ When replacing an output transformer in a guitar amp, almost any transformer that is approximately the same size and has the same impedance will work nicely.

5. True or False _____ When using a tube amp with a multiple impedance transformer such as one that has a 16, 8, 4 ohm output; you should use speakers that allow using the 4 ohm setting — in order to get the greatest power output.

Okay, let's set how you did! Give yourself 20 points for every "False" response.

100 points — You know your transformers.

80 points — You are fairly hip when it comes to transformers.

60 points — You are hipper than most when it comes to transformers.

40 points — You are much hipper than other guitarists are when it comes to transformers.

20 points — You are much hipper than an average drummer, when it comes to transformers.

10 points — Few lead vocalists approach your expertise when it comes to transformers.

0 points — It looks like we got to you just in time!

QUESTION #1 FALSE. Actually, one cannot determine the output impedance of an output transformer by measuring resistance. Resistance and impedance are two different topics. Resistance is simply D.C. resistance. Impedance, on the other hand, is the sum of everything that impedes the flow of electricity. This would include resistance, capacitive reactance, and inductive reactance.

There are some complicated formulas for figuring output impedance so I'll give you a cheater chart that works with most vintage guitar amplifier output transformers. This will spare you the algebra. Disconnect the output transformer from the circuit. Put 10 volts A.C. across the primary. (A variac works best, but a 10 volt A.C. wall wart will do the trick as well.) Do not connect the center-tap to anything. Use a good A.C. voltmeter and measure the voltage across the secondary. Compare it to the chart below to find the transformer's output impedance. For example, if the secondary voltage was .22 volts, you would need to look at the transformer and see if it looks big enough to run a pair of 6L6's. If so, you could run a pair into an 2 ohm speaker load. If you are getting the same .22 volts, but the transformer is smaller; it might be a safe bet that the transformer was intended for 6V6 operation.

	Pair of 6L6's	Pair of 6V6's	Pair of EL34's	Single 6V6
2 ohm	.22 volts	—	.24 volts	—
4 ohm	.31 volts	.22 volts	.35 volts	.20 volts
8 ohm	.44 volts	.31 volts	.49 volts	.28 volts
16 ohm	.62 volts	—	.69 volts	—

QUESTION #2 FALSE. Transformers are not wound to a specific resistance; they are wound to specific turns. The resistance you measure, when you measure the resistance from the center-tap to one end is simply the resistance of the wire. Here's an experiment for you to try. Wind 100 turns of wire onto a spool and then marked the wire with some tape. Now wind 100 more turns (on top of the first 100 turns) and cut the wire. Unwind the whole mess and measure the distance from the start to the tape marking. Next, compare it to the distance from the tape marking to the end. I'll bet the tape marking to the end is longer. Why? Because each of the last 100 turns were wrapped around a larger diameter than the first 100 turns. What does this mean? Longer wire will have more resistance. Conclusion: The resistance from center-tap to start and center-tap to end is not supposed to match. In some cases, it could reveal malfunction as in the case of two ohms on one side and 200 ohms on the other, but for the most part, D.C. resistance of the primary only shows that the wire is not broken internally.

QUESTION #3 FALSE. A.C. voltage swing across the primary has nothing to do with output wattage. There are certain losses that occur in the transformer itself. To measure wattage, simply put a 1000 Hz sine wave of 100 millivolts or so on the input of the amp. With a scope hooked up to the speaker, turn up the volume until clipping is observed. Now back the volume down until the clipping goes away. Using a true RMS meter, measure the A.C. voltage across the speaker. Take this number, square it and divide the product by the speaker impedance in ohms. (Do not use the speaker's actual D.C. resistance, but the impedance rating. For instance 4 ohm for a Fender Twin.) This will give you the RMS wattage that the amp is putting out at the onset of clipping. Although the text books will tell you to use a dummy load, I am more interested in what the amp puts out with a speaker load, because I will be using a speaker when I play the amp and I will not be using a dummy load.

QUESTION #4 FALSE. Output transformers are simple devices, however there are many different types of steel that could be used. The type of steel, as well as the thickness of the laminates dramatically affects tones. In addition, the style of transformer in terms of interleaved or non-interleaved and wire gauges also dramatically affect the tone. Bobbin material also affects tone.

QUESTION #5 FALSE. When a transformer is wound, it is wound for the highest impedance output. That is to say that a multiple output transformer is wound for the 16 ohms and then the 8 ohm tap is put in by dividing the number of turns (on the 16 ohm winding) by the square root of two (1.4142135). To get the 4 ohm tap, the 16 ohm winding is center-tapped. (This is actually the same as taking the number of turns for the 8 ohm tap and dividing by the square root of two.) This being the case, the winding with the lowest turns ratio will be the 16 ohm tap and subject to the least amount of coupling loss.

Had this question been in reference to an output-transformer-less solid state amplifier, the 4 ohm load would provide the most power. In such a design, the speaker load is the load of the transistors. Less impedance means more current can flow. When more current flows, it is easy to get more wattage. Wattage equals current times voltage.

SPEAKERS

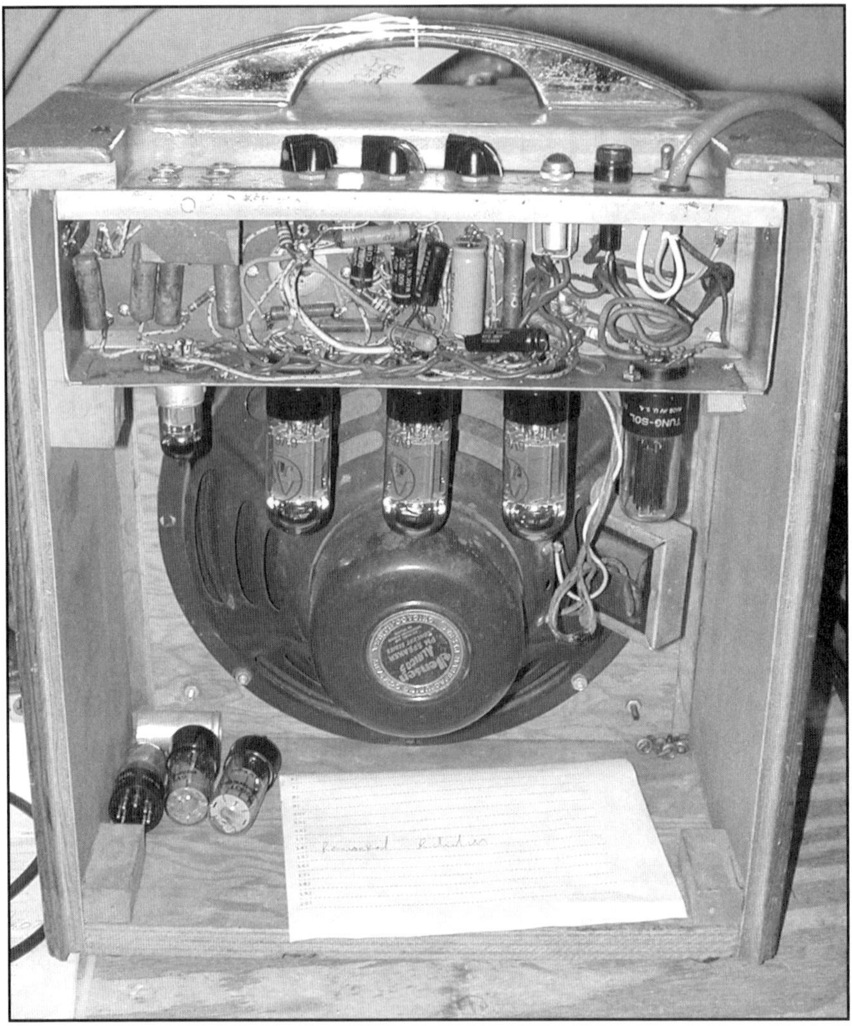
TUNG-SOL

WHAT GUITARS PLAYERS SHOULD KNOW ABOUT SPEAKER IMPEDANCE

There seems to be an awful lot of confusion going on out there about speaker impedance and how to connect what with what. Will a 16 ohm cabinet and an 8 ohm cabinet work together? How do I hook up the speakers inside the cabinet, itself? Is there a difference between series/parallel and parallel/series, even though the impedance is the same? What is series? What is parallel?

WHAT IS IMPEDANCE?
When a circuit contains reactance and resistance, the combined effect of the two is called impedance. Look at the word impedance. Do you see the root word, impede? A speaker impedes the flow of electrons. In a speaker, impedance would be the resistance of the voice coil combined with the inductive reactance of the voice coil. When checking speakers with an ohmmeter, the D.C. resistance will always be less than the rated speaker impedance. Why? Because the meter is only measuring the resistance and is not measuring and adding the reactance. For example, an 8 ohm speaker will measure anywhere from 5 to 7 ohms D.C. resistance, even though it may have a total impedance of 8 ohms. This means the reactance is 1 to 3 ohms, however the ohmmeter doesn't measure reactance.

A speaker resists or impedes the flow of electrons, like a bottleneck in the circuit. For the purpose of hooking up speakers to an amplifier, think of impedance and resistance as synonymous. For the remainder of this chapter, I will use the terms interchangeably.

Speakers are designed to have particular impedance. Most speakers are 4 ohm, 8 ohm, or 16 ohm. The 8 ohm speaker impedes the flow of electrons twice as much as the 4 ohm speaker, but only half as much as the 16 ohm. This should be obvious.

Here's an easy analogy. If electricity were water:

Volts would be water pressure,

Current (measured in amperes and called amps for short) would be the flow of gallons, or the volume of gallons.

Impedance would be anything that impedes the flow of gallons — such as a kink in the hose or a bottleneck in the pipe, or just the actual diameter of the pipe.

A very large pipe would allow more gallons to flow and therefore have little resistance to the flow of gallons (current). A small diameter pipe would resist or impede the flow and therefore have more resistance than a large pipe.

Here's another impedance analogy. If electricity were sand in an hourglass, the impedance would be related to the tiny hole that connects both sides of the hourglass and impedes the flow of sand.

Now that you have a concept of speaker impedance, the rest gets easier.

With guitar amps, we use a speaker cable to connect the amplifier's output to a speaker. This speaker cable is usually made from copper and has very little resistance. It is like having a huge diameter pipe. When the electricity gets to the speaker, the speaker impedes the flow of current much like having a restriction or kink in the pipe would resist or impede gallons of water getting through.

OTHER CONSIDERATIONS

Remember that zero ohms (a condition of no impedance) is a short circuit. 2 ohms is almost a short circuit and there is a larger amount of current flowing than in a 4 ohm circuit. Since the 4 ohm circuit is twice the impedance of the 2 ohm circuit, then only half as much current (think gallons) can flow. Can you see that the less the circuit is impeded the easier that current can flow?

HOOKING SPEAKERS IN PARALLEL

Let's look at a common scenario such as a speaker cabinet containing two 8 ohm speakers connected in parallel. In a parallel connection of two speakers, the positive lead of each speaker and the positive of the speaker jack are connected, while the minus terminals of each speaker and the ground of the speaker jack are connected. The amplifier is connected to the speaker jack. From the amplifier's point-of-view, once the electricity has passed the speaker jack, it now has the luxury of two different paths that it can now take! It can go through either 8 ohm speaker that it chooses! It is now twice as easy to get through. (In the hourglass analogy, it would be like having two holes for the sand to pass through.) In other words twice as easy is another way of saying half as much impedance. What is half the impedance of 8 ohms? 4 ohms! This is why when two 8 ohm speakers are connected in parallel; the total speaker impedance (that the amp sees) will be 4 ohms.

UNEQUAL SPEAKER IMPEDANCE

The question comes up: What happens if you hook up an 8 ohm speaker with a 16 ohm speaker? If you are hooking an 8 ohm speaker in parallel, with a 16 ohm speaker, the 8 ohm speaker will get twice the power of the 16 ohm speaker. In other words, if you are hooking this to a 30 watt amp, the 8 ohm speaker will dissipate 20 watts and the 16 ohm speaker will dissipate only 10 watts. Why? Simple. It is twice as easy (or half as hard, or half as impeding, or half the impedance, etc.) for the electrical current (think gallons) to go through the 8 ohm speaker. It simply doesn't impede the flow like the 16 ohm speaker. Wattage is current times voltage. Both speakers have the same voltage, but the current is twice as much in the 8 ohm speaker. Therefore, in this example, the 8 ohm speaker dissipates twice as much power as the 16 ohm.

With an 8 ohm speaker parallel connected to a 16 ohm speaker, what would be the total impedance? Let's think about this. You know that it will be less than 8 ohms, because in addition to having the 8 ohm path, there is another path, so we know it will have less impedance than 8 ohms. It is actually $5\frac{1}{3}$ ohms.

There is a formula for finding the total resistance of two resistors connected in parallel. This same formula can be used in determining total impedance of two speakers parallel connected. You multiply the two resistance values (example 16 x 8 = 128), and then divide this product by the sum of the two resistances. The sum of the two resistances will be (16 + 8 = 24). So, in other words you divide 128 by 24 and get 5 ⅓ ohms. Remember, when two speakers of unequal impedances are wired in parallel, multiplying the impedances and then dividing by the sum of impedances will determine the total impedance.

MULTIPLE SPEAKERS IN PARALLEL

Let's look at hooking four 8 ohm speakers in parallel ala Super Reverb or Tweed Bassman. From the amplifier's point of view, the electricity has the unheard of luxury of four different paths that it could take. It doesn't look like this arrangement is going to impede very many electrons! It is going to be four times easier (¼ as much impedance) for the electricity to get through those speakers. Now you can easily see that ¼, as much of 8 ohms is 2 ohms, which is the impedance that is used in the Super Reverb and the Tweed 4x10 Bassman. Using the hourglass analogy, it would be like having four holes or one hole four times bigger, thus impeding only ¼ as much.

HOOKING SPEAKERS IN SERIES

Lets look at another common scenario of a speaker cabinet containing two 8 ohm speakers connected in series. In a series connection, the positive of the speaker jack goes to the positive of the first speaker. The minus of the first speaker connects to the positive of the second speaker, and the minus of the second speaker connects to the minus of the speaker jack. In this arrangement, all of the current must go through both speakers, one speaker at a time. There is still only one path but two speakers to impede the flow of current. In short, it is twice as hard to get through. After the electricity has gone through one speaker, it must be subjected to the additional resistance/impedance of yet another 8 ohms of impedance to complete the circuit! Two 8 ohm speakers in series will become 16 ohms total. Can you see that since there is only one path leading through both speakers that it becomes twice as hard for the electricity to get through? If there were two kinks in a hose instead of one, wouldn't it impede the flow of gallons twice as much?

Now what if you hooked a 16 ohm and an 8 ohm speaker in series? Well, the total impedance would be 24 ohms. This should be obvious, because the electricity must first pass through the 16 ohms and then it is required to pass through the additional 8 ohms in order to complete the circuit. It has been impeded 24 ohms worth! The 16 ohm speaker would dissipate twice the power of the 8 ohm speaker. Why? Because ⅔ of the voltage drop would occur across the 16 ohm speaker and ⅓ would occur across the 8 ohm speaker. Both speakers will have the same amount of current because all current that is going through one speaker will also go through the other speaker. Wattage is current times voltage. Since the 16 ohm speaker will get ¹⁶/₂₄ or ⅔ of the voltage drop, it will also take ⅔ of the power, which is twice as much power as the 8 ohm speaker. Note that this result is opposite the result of the parallel-connected 16 and 8 ohm speaker mentioned in an earlier section.

SERIES/PARALLEL AND PARALLEL/SERIES

With series, all of the current goes through every speaker, so it seems like this would be the best way to wire speakers. Why don't we just run all speakers in series? The reason is inductance. A coil of wire, such as a speaker voice coil, has inductance. Without going into an explanation of inductance, let's just say that if you get too much, it has the effect of blocking high frequencies. If you run several speakers in series, the result will be a garbled, muddy sound with no sparkle or high-end note definition.

When using four speakers in a cabinet, the speakers are usually wired series/parallel or parallel/series. In parallel/series, you would wire two speakers in parallel, wire the other two speakers in parallel and then wire the two sets together in series. With series/parallel, you would wire two speakers in series, wire the other two in series and then wire the two sets together in parallel. Either way you will end up with the same impedance. If you are using identical impedance speakers, the resulting impedance of four speakers in series/parallel or parallel/series will be the same as a single speaker. You could easily have figured that out because two 8 ohm speakers in parallel will be 4 ohms. If you wired that in series with another 4 ohm pair, you would get 8 ohms — exactly the same as one speaker by itself. On the other hand, if you wired two 8 ohm speakers in series you would get 16 ohms. Wire that in parallel with another 16 ohm set and you are back to 8 ohms.

WHICH IS BETTER 2 OHM OR 8 OHM?

Let's say you have a 4x10 speaker cabinet and your amplifier has a 2 ohm, 4 ohm and 8 ohm impedance selector. How should you wire the 4x10 cabinet? Since we are going to wire this cabinet using 8 ohm speakers, there will be three possibilities. We could wire all four speakers in parallel. This way, we would have 2 ohms. We could wire them in series/parallel and get 8 ohms; or we could wire them in parallel/series and get 8 ohms. All three ways are valid options.

One thing to consider is this: The output tubes in your amp operate at very high impedances (high pressure but not many gallons). Speakers are much lower impedance than the tubes (low pressure but el mucho gallons). In fact, we must use an output transformer to actually transform the impedance so that the speakers and tubes can work together. A transformer could be considered as two coils of wire, wound to a specific ratio. The ratio of turns is based on the tube-to-speaker impedance. To match to a smaller speaker impedance requires a larger turns ratio. As the turns ratio gets higher, so do the coupling losses. In other words the transformer is more efficient at 8 ohms than it is at 2 ohms. Running the cabinet and amplifier at 8 ohms will sound more aggressive because of less loss in the output transformer, but wait! Using our water analogy, 2 ohms is like millions of gallons at not much pressure, 8 ohms is not as many gallons but at higher pressure. So when running at 2 ohms, hook-up wire becomes an issue. If you had only one pair of wires coming from the amp to the speaker, then the resistance of the hookup wire itself could become a problem. It is like trying to run millions of gallons quickly through a soda straw. This is why Fender used four separate pairs of speaker cables on the 5F6A Bassman. There are four RCA connectors on the bottom of the 5F6A Bassman, one for each speaker. This cuts down on the resistance because there are now four pipes trying to move those millions of gallons instead of one pipe. Many of you know that I built a 2 ohm 4x10 Combo (Kendrick 2410) for many years. I didn't even use a speaker jack, opting to run the transformer wires directly to the speakers instead of back into the chassis to speaker jacks. This design eliminated any extra wire, resistance or resistance from an output jack. In fact, the negative feedback wires came directly off the speaker leads, which explained the question I was always asked, "Why are there two pairs of wires going to the speakers?"

The difference in sound of the three possible wiring schemes is related to inductance. The 2 ohm wiring (all four speakers in parallel) would give the least inductance and therefore would have the most high-end sparkle. The 8 ohm parallel/series and the series/parallel both have the same total inductance, but will sound differently because the series/parallel has more branch inductance than the parallel/series. Actually the parallel/series will be a little cleaner with crisper highs, while the series/parallel will be less clean with a softer high end. It is interesting to note that Fender always wired their speakers in parallel to get the least inductance and therefore the cleanest, crispest tone while companies like Vox and Marshall used series or series/parallel to get less clean and more grind.

HOW DOES THE OUTPUT TRANSFORMER AFFECT IMPEDANCE?

All tube amps use an output transformer to couple the speakers to the output tubes. All transformers transform impedance, voltage and current to some degree. When designing a transformer, certain aspects are emphasized over others, depending on the task that the transformer is to perform. For instance, with a power transformer, the emphasis is placed on voltage because that is the task of the power transformer. With an output transformer, the emphasis is placed on impedance because we want to match the impedance of the tubes with the impedance of the speakers.

Remember the analogy of electricity and water. If water was electricity, then current (or amperes) would be the flow of gallons; pressure would be voltage, and the size of the pipe would represent impedance (or resistance). We have been using resistance and impedance as interchangeable terms. An output tube is high impedance, which means it is low current and high voltage (Think high pressure hose at the car wash.) A speaker is low impedance, which means it is high current and low voltage (Think slow moving river.)

When we wind an output transformer for emphasis on impedance transformation, we figure the ratio of the primary to secondary winding by taking the square root of the primary impedance divided by the secondary impedance. For example, if we wanted to match a 100 ohm source (primary) with a 25 ohm load (secondary), the turns ratio would be 2: 1. How do I know that? I took the primary impedance and divided by the secondary impedance and got 4 - (100 divided by 25 = 4). The square root of 4 equals 2. Therefore the ratio is 2: 1. For every two turns of primary, there should be one turn of secondary.

While this transforms impedance, it will also step down voltage. That is to say that if we had a 10 volt A.C. signal on the primary at 100 ohms, we would end up with a 5 volt A.C. signal on the secondary at 25 ohms. How did I know that? Because the volts per turn of the primary will be the same on the secondary. Since the secondary has half as many turns, the voltage will also be half. This would double the current of the secondary, assuming no other losses. Using the water analogy, we now have twice as many gallons at half as much pressure when we transform 100 ohms to 25 ohms. Now we see that every transformer transforms impedance, voltage and current, but how does this relate to tone? First we will need to know about reflected impedance.

WHAT IS REFLECTED IMPEDANCE?

A transformer doesn't know anything about impedances; it only knows turns ratio. So if you were to hook a larger impedance load to the secondary, because of the turns ratio, the primary impedance would become larger. That is to say that if we hooked a 50 ohm load up to the 25 ohm secondary in the above example, the 100 ohm primary would "think" it is 200 ohms! This could be proved algebraically. For now we will skip the math, but if you used the same formula just presented with a 2:1 turns ratio and a 50 ohm secondary and solved for the primary impedance, you would get 200 ohms.

The above example is like hooking a 16 ohm speaker cabinet to an 8 ohm amp. The tubes "think" they are operating into a primary that is twice as much as when the amp is hooked to an 8 ohm speaker. This "new primary impedance" is called "reflected impedance" because it is reflected back from the secondary to the primary.

This may not be bad for tone. You will lose some power, but the current limiting effect of this larger "reflected impedance" will give a spongier envelope, a smoothing of high-end (browner tone), and the tubes will last longer because the higher reflected impedance of the primary will limit how much current can go through the tubes.

I remember spending an entire Saturday with harmonica/vocalist Kim Wilson of the Fabulous Thunderbirds. We were performing various listening tests to see what speakers and tube impedances worked best for blues harmonica. This research was a prelude to my designing the Kendrick Texas Crude Harmonica amp. All of these tests were done completely blind. That is to say, Kim didn't know what speaker or what impedance he was listening to. All he knew was what he heard. I was amazed that he consistently preferred the sound of a speaker whose impedance was twice the rated transformer secondary impedance. This would cause a "reflected impedance" of twice the primary to be seen by the tubes. What little wattage was lost by the mismatch did not matter because a harp mike can only be turned up to the threshold of feedback anyway. Kim liked the browner tone and spongier attack of higher "reflected impedance" on the tubes.

REFLECTED IMPEDANCES CAN WORK FOR YOU IN OTHER WAYS

Most of you already know the trick of removing two output tubes from a four-output tube amp in order to reduce the volume and headroom. A four-output tube amp uses half the primary impedance of its two-output tube amp counterpart. Said another way, the two-output tube amp needs twice the primary impedance of its four-output tube amp counterpart. When you remove two of the output tubes, the primary must be doubled to accommodate the two remaining output tubes. An easy way to do this is to use a speaker load that is twice of what you would normally use when running all four-output tubes. For instance, let's say you have a Twin Reverb amp, which normally runs at 4 ohms, and you remove two of the output tubes. You could disconnect one of the Twin's speakers to change the secondary load to 8 ohms. This would cause reflected impedance that would correct the primary impedance for the two remaining tubes. If you had an amp with an impedance selector, you would set it for half of the real speaker load. In the case of a 100 watt Marshall that two output tubes were removed, you would set the impedance selector at 8 ohms if you were using a 16 ohm cabinet. This would make the two remaining tubes 'think' they were seeing the correct impedance.

HOW DOES FREQUENCY AFFECT IMPEDANCE?

Up until now we have used impedance and resistance as interchangeable terms. Actually the term "impedance" would include all things that would impede current flow. Inductive reactance would be included. Speakers and transformers are inductive loads. As an inductive load, they will have inductive reactance. Inductive reactance is like a resistance except it changes with frequency; so the higher the frequency, the more inductive reactance (think higher resistance). Conversely, lower frequencies have less reactance. What does this all mean?

Well for one thing there is no such thing as an 8 ohm speaker, except under ideal conditions. The impedance is constantly changing with different frequencies. Depending on the inductance of the speaker (a higher inductance speaker will have more inductive reactance) and the frequency of the signal to drive the speaker, the speaker could end up being 16 ohms in an actual circuit condition. Remember, everything else being equal, that an Alnico magnet speaker is going to have more inductance than a ceramic magnet speaker. Alnico is a metal and ceramic is not, therefore the voice coil in an Alnico speaker will have more inductance. (This is like an iron core inductor vs. an air core inductor. The metal core will have more inductance.) The impedance will go even higher when higher frequency signals pass through it.

For another thing, you might now see why some amps are so tolerant of impedance mismatches. Take a Fender Blackface Bassman that normally uses a 2x12, 4 ohm cabinet. Add an extra speaker cabinet and you are now at 2 ohms. In an actual playing situation, because of changing reactance with frequency, you would not be operating the amp at exactly 2 ohms. In fact, the ohms would be changing all the time and the amp could tolerate this very well.

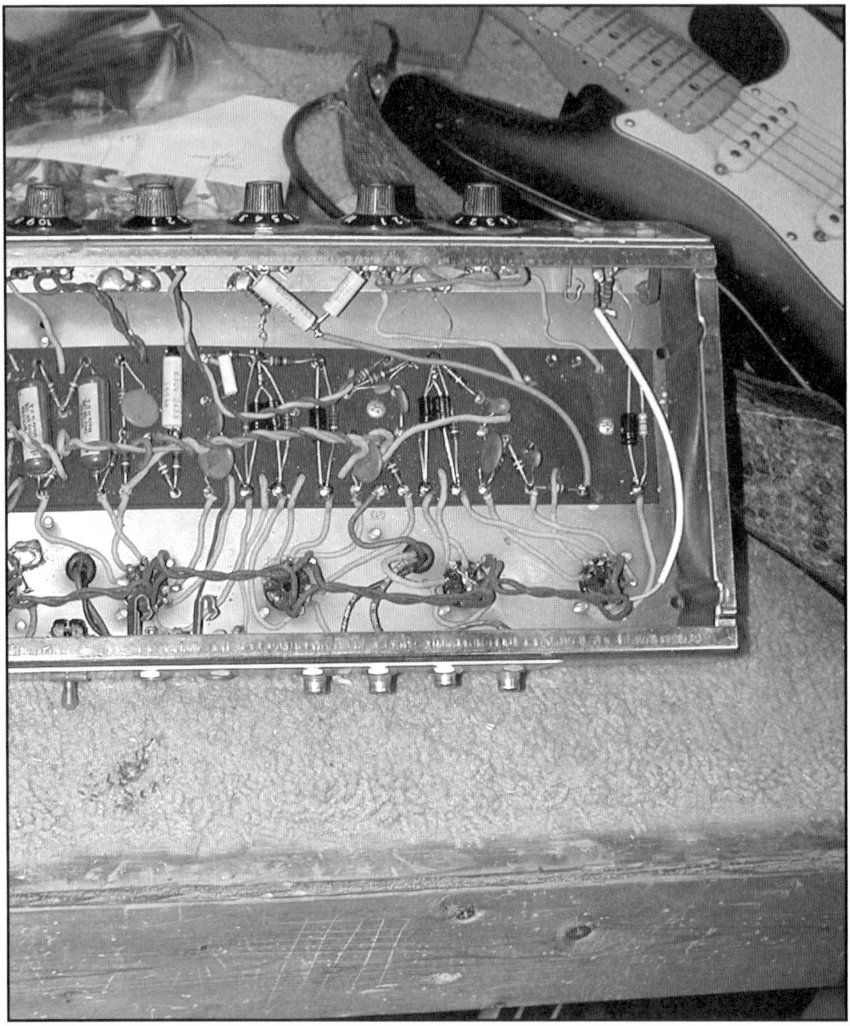

EASY SPEAKER FIXES

With all the work we've done to get our amp re-tubed, overhauled, re-biased and a killer cap job, all is for naught if our speaker and speaker cabinet are adding aberrant sounds/noises of their own. There are a variety of speaker problems that are both simple and easy to repair. Here are a few.

BAFFLEBOARD BUZZ AND/OR RATTLE FIX

Have you ever had a speaker cabinet that usually sounds wonderful—I mean "Full of Wonder!," but on certain notes and/or at certain volume levels, you can hear a buzz on top of the note? Don't let it drive you crazy; this problem is usually either something loose in the cabinet, or bad baffleboard seating. Simply tightening everything; namely the speakers, backpanels, and other cabinet components, can repair the former. Pay particular attention to logos or nameplates.

Once you are convinced there is nothing loose, it's time to check the baffleboard seating. Weber's Baffleboard Theorem 457 clearly states: IF THERE IS A SMALL AIR-GAP BETWEEN THE BAFFLEBOARD AND THE SURFACE IT MOUNTS AGAINST, THERE WILL BE A RATTLE IN THE CABINET. This might be a little tricky to check, because the gap is usually obscured from line-of-sight vision. For instance, on a Blackface Fender Combo amp, the baffleboard mounts against two battenboards (³/4" by ³/4" vertical molding) on either side. Two Phillips wood screws are used on each side. Sometimes the wood (that the screws are fastened into) can get chewed up and the baffleboard seating will be compromised. One way to fix this is to move the mounting hole about an inch or so. You must remove the baffleboard to access the battenboard. Drill a mounting hole in the battenboard that is slightly larger in diameter than your baffleboard mounting screw. It is only possible to drill this from the front and therefore the baffleboard must be removed to allow access to the front of the battenboard. Note:

If the hole is not drilled larger than the screw, the screw will bind and there will be an air gap caused when the screw finally penetrates the baffleboard. Refer to Weber's Baffleboard Theorem 457 above.

SPEAKER RATTLE/DISTORTION FIX

Sometimes a speaker will rattle or have out of tune harmonics and other distortion because it is about to blow, in which case no simple fix is possible; but sometimes a speaker rattles because the frame geometry is slightly off axis with respect to the cone. When the frame geometry is off, the distortion sometimes occurs as just a slight fuzzy sound that is only apparent when the note is dying out. Believe it or not, when this problem occurs with stamped frame speakers, it can sometimes be corrected.

Notice that your speaker has four or more mounting screws. The speaker has a gasket around its mounting face perimeter, which will give slightly when compressed. Notice that the mounting screws can be loosened or tightened like a drummer adjusts the head of a drum. Varying the mounting screw pressure will vary the tension ever so slightly on the stamped frame and shift the speaker axis with respect to the cone. You might need to use a little trial and error testing on this fix. This fix doesn't always work, but it has worked and saved original speakers from being re-coned. It costs nothing to try.

CONE FIX

Here's a common problem: A speaker with a $^3/_8$" hole in the surround. How did it happen? Someone tried to mount a speaker to a baffleboard, and not paying attention, stabbed the surround with an adjacent mounting screw. There are also other types of cone wounds, whether self-inflicted, lack-of-grill-cloth induced or otherwise.

Here's a fix that works and cost almost nothing. You will need some scissors, a 2-ply paper towel, some Elmer's glue, and some flat black spray paint. Begin by preparing the cone itself. Smooth the paper around the puncture to get it as back to normal as possible. Next, separate the 2-ply paper towel into 2 separate plies. Cut a single ply to make a patch that is slightly larger than the tear. Now make another patch exactly like the first. Using an abundance of glue, saturate each patch. Place a patch on the front hole. Work the excess glue out with your finger. When the glue is worked out, the paper will fray slightly on the edges in small fibers. Now in a like manner, apply the other patch to the backside. Work the fibers in well. Allow this to set until dry. When completely dry, spray-paint the patch on each side with a very light coat of flat black paint. Use only enough to make the patch look black.

I'll tell you a little story. Almost a decade ago, a customer shipped a British vintage amplifier to my shop for restoration. This had a 12" Goodman Alnico Magnet speaker. The cone on the speaker was rotted away with about 40% of the cone missing, but the voice coil was still intact. The speaker had an unusual, bell shaped cone that really looked like the bell of a trombone. The customer didn't want to ship back such a heavy speaker and had no intentions of re-coning the speaker. I had no use for the speaker so I trashed it. A technician that worked for me asked if he could remove the speaker from the dumpster. He repaired it, using my paper towel technique, and the speaker out-performed a Vox Bulldog Speaker in his dramatic A/B comparison! Not only that, but the flat black spray paint allowed the speaker to look normal when mounted in a cabinet.

CONNECTOR FIX

Most speakers use a terminal strip type of speaker lead. The two tinsel wires from each side of the voice coil are soldered to this strip. I have seen speakers that have a bad connection at the tinsel wire, terminal strip solder joint. The speaker would check as an open circuit on a meter, which would normally indicate a blown voice coil.

Simply re-solder the tinsel wire, taking care to leave the length slightly more than enough to allow for cone excursion.

Another variation of this problem is when the tinsel wire becomes disconnected with the voice coil itself. This can be repaired, but is very tricky. I have actually been able to dig out a small piece of the voice coil and re-solder to the tinsel. You must be careful to use a long enough tinsel wire so that the cone excursion doesn't cause the cone to rip. You have to use tinsel because nothing else will tolerate the constant movement. If you have to poke a hole in the cone to install a tinsel wire, use an ice pick and seal the hole with a tiny dot of black silicone glue. Be careful not to use too much lest the mass of the glue will affect the speaker's performance.

TROUBLESHOOTING

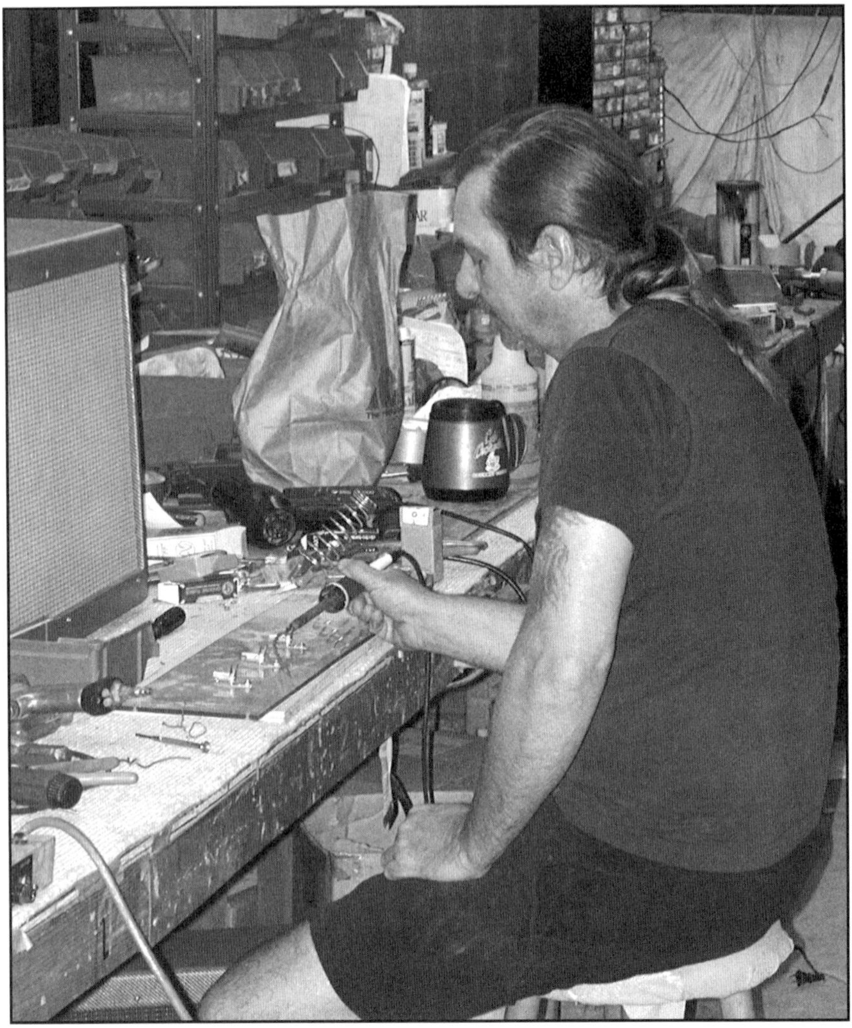

SIMPLE AMP TROUBLESHOOTING TECHNIQUES YOU SHOULD KNOW

You don't have to hold a doctorate in electronics engineering to troubleshoot an amp. In fact, there are three techniques that require no tools (accept maybe a screwdriver), no soldering, and no electronics knowledge. If you never intend to service an amp in your life and you play guitar, you need to know about these techniques.

INSPECTION

Look at everything in the amp. Are there any arced spots? Burnt spots? Look at the solder joints. Take your time. Use a flashlight if needed. Look at the input jacks. Are they grounded properly? Look at each component. Are the electrolytic capacitors bubbling at the positive end? Look at the grounds, the sockets. In short, Look at everything very carefully and completely. Are any wires broken?

My company used to manufacture an add-on three knob reverb module for vintage tube amps without reverb. These were extremely difficult to assemble, because there were about 100 components wired point-to-point in a 3"x5" metal chassis. In fact, big tweezers were used to assemble these. We once had a production run of about 25 with only half of them working on first try. No one was excited about troubleshooting these units. In fact, my technician was having trouble with them and asked for help. I repaired all defective units in a couple of hours without ever having to plug one up. How? I simply looked at each one very carefully and compared it to a known working unit. I would find something wired wrong or an incorrect value or a missing ground.

SUBSTITUTION

Another easy and effective technique is the "Substitution Technique." The idea here is to locate the problem by substituting a known good component in place of the suspected bad component. One day you notice a funny noise coming from your amp. You suspect it's the speaker. You disconnect the speaker and hook the amp to another speaker and see if the problem is cured. If cured, the first speaker was the problem. If not cured, we have ruled out the speaker as a problem.

Next we think, " Maybe it's the reverb pan." And we substitute a known good reverb pan. We can quickly determine what is bad by substituting something that we know is good. If the pan cures the problem and has its own connecting cables, then the cables need to be substituted and ruled out.

Here's another for instance, let's say you notice a loud hum in your amp. You look at the output tubes and see that one tubes' plate is glowing cherry red and the other tubes' plate looks perfectly normal. You quickly turn "off" the amp. Exchange the output tubes with each other. Turn the amp "on" to see if the problem stays with the tube or with the socket. If it stays with the tube, then your tube was definitely bad and should be replaced. If the problem stays with the socket, then there is a malfunction in the amp and there is not a problem with the tube.

I use the substitution technique on amps that I do not have readily available parts — such as the Music Man Amplifier. Music Man amps have two channels that use the same kinds of transistors with a tube output stage. When one channel is not working, I substitute the transistors for the known working channel with the transistors for the defective channel. These simply plug into small sockets, so you really don't need to solder anything. One can quickly find out if it is a transistor problem and which transistor — very quickly.

OMISSION

This is an easy way to trouble shoot a blown fuse. Every guitar player needs to know what to do when a fuse blows. You do carry extra fuses in your guitar case with your extra strings, don't you? Do you carry extra strings? Get some extra fuses! They come in a five fuse package. Just be sure to get the correct type and amperage rating. When a fuse blows, the first thing to suspect is a power tube. Why? Because out of every 10 times a fuse blows, 9 of those times will occur after an output tube malfunction.

Here's what to do:
1. Turn the amp "off."
2. Remove the power tubes.
3. Replace the fuse with the correct replacement.
4. Turn the amp "on," leaving the tubes out.

If the fuse does not blow, then we know that one of the output tubes was bad. We could take a chance and put one tube back into the amp. If after the tube warms the fuse doesn't blow, we try the next power tube. If at any point a fuse blows after we have replaced a suspected defective part, we suspect the last component replaced before the fuse blew.

But let's say the amp is still blowing fuses with the output tubes removed. Then what? REMOVE THE RECTIFIER TUBE!! Earlier we said 9 out of ten times the output tubes caused the fuse to blow. The tenth time will be power supply related and most of the time, power supplies malfunction because of the rectifier. The rectifier tube is removed. The fuse gets replaced. Turn it "on," leaving the rectifier tube out. If the amp is still blowing fuses, you probably have a bad power transformer or a short in the actual wiring. If it doesn't blow a fuse with the rectifier removed, try substituting a known good rectifier tube.

Here are some more Omission tricks: Let's say you have a noise in your amp and suspect it is coming from a preamp tube. Start taking preamp tubes out (starting with the one closest to the input.) In other words, you simply take the first gain preamp tube out. If the noise doesn't stop, you take the next tube, etc. until you pull a tube that stops the noise. Just to verify that this last tube is the culprit, put it back in and see if the noise returns. If the noise returns, try substituting a known good preamp tube in the offending tube's socket. If the noise stops, the problem was obviously the tube. If the noise problem doesn't go away when a known good tube is placed in the socket, then the problem is probably in that same stage but not a problem with the tube itself.

Simple Amp Troubleshooting Techniques

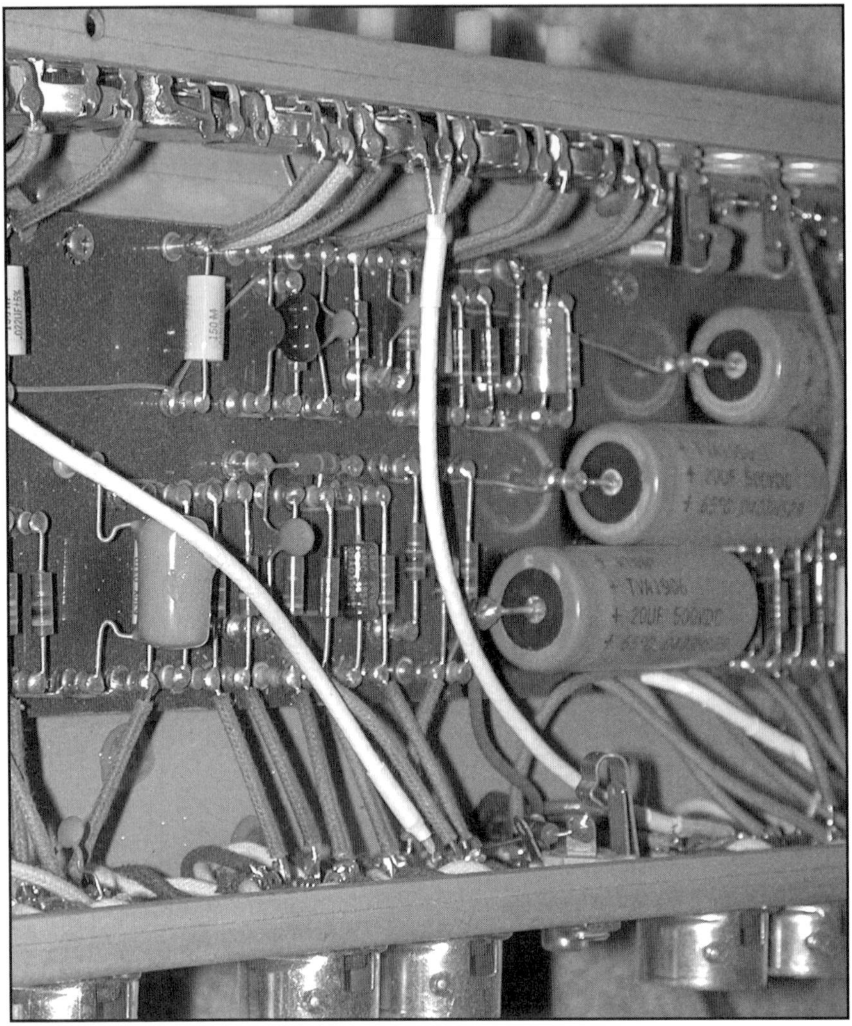
150 M
TVA1906
+ 20UF 500VDC

SIMPLIFYING THE ELECTRONICS MATH

Here's a little chart for you to copy and hang on your workbench wall. No need to clutter your mind with remembering these kinds of things, but better to focus remaining brain cells on guitar tone.

Whether repairing, restoring, modifying or designing amps, there are times when electronics math will be needed. Most of us at are at least somewhat familiar with Ohm's law. From Ohm's law we have the relationships between current, voltage and resistance. Current equals voltage divided by resistance. From this basic equation, the equation can be manipulated, using basic algebra, to express voltage as current times resistance and resistance as voltage divided by current. Now when you consider that power equals voltage times current, one could substitute formulas to end up with twelve equations.

HOW DO I USE THE OHM'S LAW CHART?

Remember that "I" is current, "R" is resistance, "E" is voltage, and "W" is power. In these equations, current is represented in amps. This means 35 milliamps is represented as .035 amps. Resistance is represented in ohms. Voltage is represented as volts and power is wattage.

The center of the chart has four quadrants marked "W," "I," "R," "E." Each quadrant has three formulas expressing that item in relationship to any two "knowns" of the other three. For instance, if you are looking for voltage, you have three options:

1. If you know the wattage and resistance
2. If you know the current and resistance
3. If you know the wattage and the current

What are some examples of using the Ohm's Law Chart?

Here's the scenario, you have just changed a power resistor in an amp to a different value. Stock value was 4.7K and you changed to a

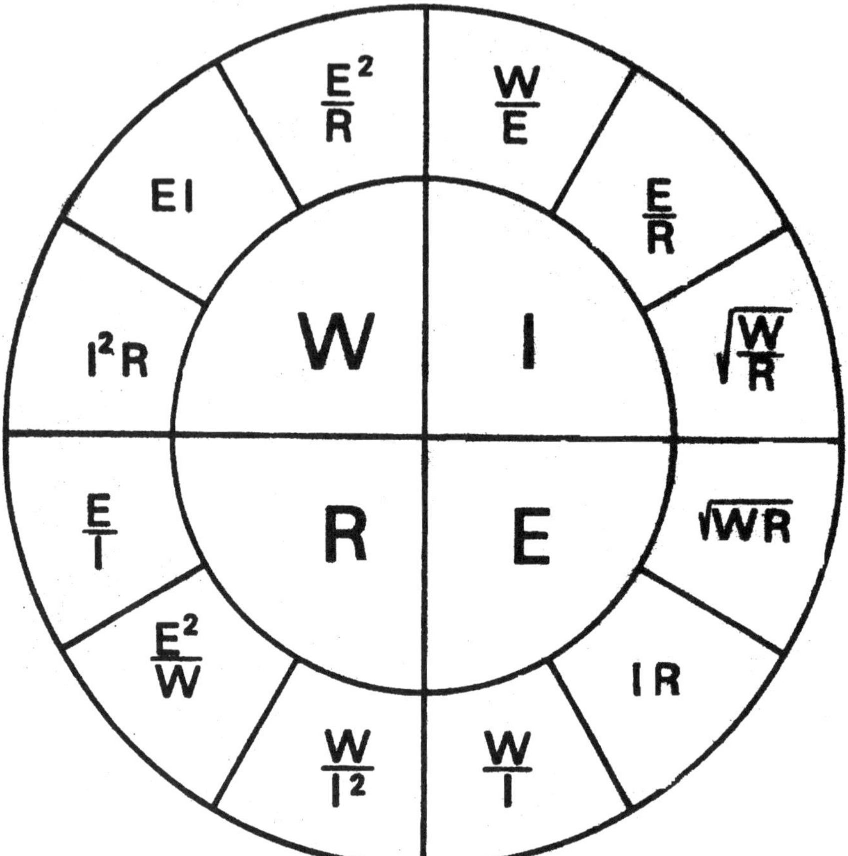

W
I
R
E
E²/R
W/E
EI
E/R
I²R
√(W/R)
E/I
√WR
E²/W
IR
W/I²
W/I

10K to drop supply voltages in the preamp. How do you know what wattage-rating resistor to use? You need to know how much wattage is dropping across the resistor. You quickly look at the Ohm's Law Math Chart and look for "W" (wattage). There are three formulas. The easiest one to use is the E squared divided by R. You measure the voltage across the resistor in question and read 50 volts. 50 volts squared equals 2,500. Divide the 2500 by 10K and you get .25 watts. You decide to double it for safety and use a half-watt resistor.

Or let's say you are converting a Twin Reverb to cathode bias. It's too loud to use at your small club gig and you want to experience the compression of a cathode-biased amp. You use a 600 ohm cathode resistor and develop 50 volts across the cathode resistor. You use the same formula as in the previous example that is voltage squared divided by resistance. In this case 2,500 (voltage squared) divided by 600 (resistance) equal 4.16 watts. You decide to use a 15 watt resistor to allow a margin of safety and to allow for any additional A.C. (when the amp is jamming).

Or, let's say you want to know if that "re-issue something or other" can take a 12AY7 without blowing up the ¼ watt plate load resistors. You measure the voltage across the plate resistor and get 161 volts. Using the same formula as above, you square the 161 to get 25,921. Divide this by the 100,000 ohm plate resistor and get .25921 watts! Better change that ¼ watt reissue resistor to a ½ watt if you are going to run a 12AY7 in there.

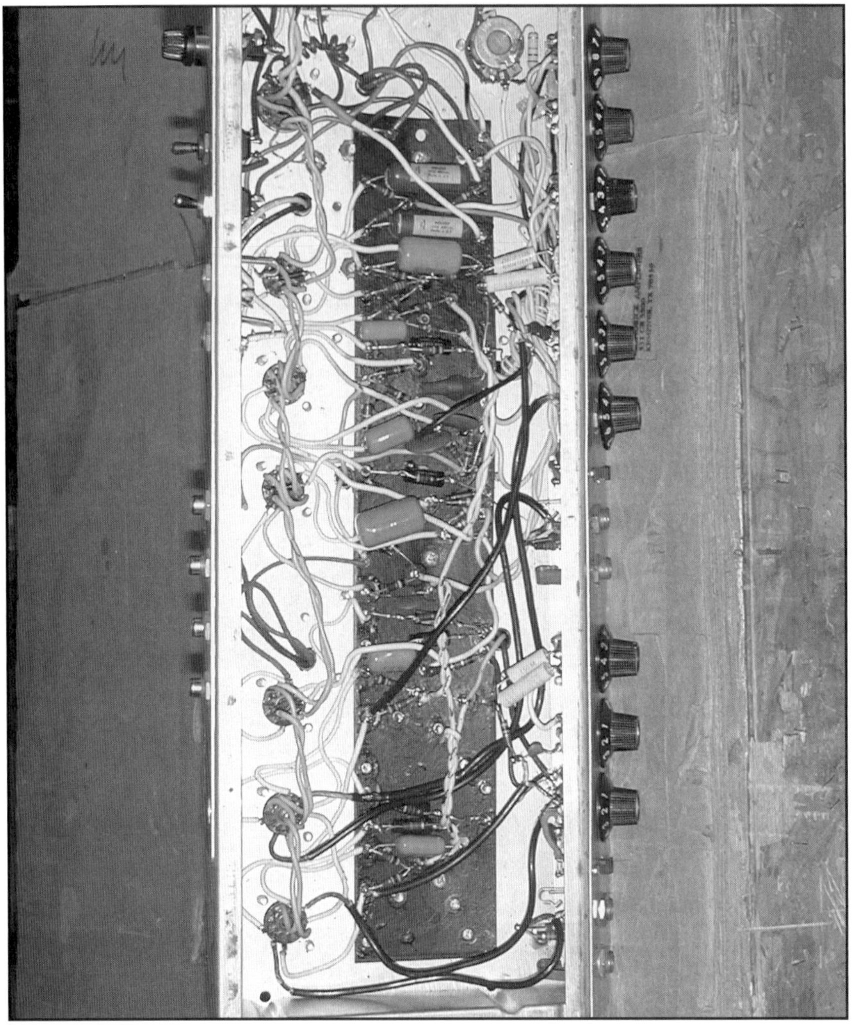

GUERRILLA TROUBLESHOOTING

As a young toddler in the 50s, I remember standing on my grandmother's kitchen counter, watching her bake bread. She would put a little of this, a little of that, and a lot of this, and she never measured with the conventional cup, tablespoon, etc. Her bread was always consistently wonderful. When I'd ask her, "Grandma, how much of this do you use?" She would reply, "Just enough, but not too much."

As an amp troubleshooter, that may troubleshoot many amps in a given day, it has never been advantageous for me to use conventional techniques. For one thing, these techniques take too long. By using quicker troubleshooter techniques, I can diagnose ten amps in the time it takes someone else to troubleshoot one or two amps. Don't get me wrong: I'm not anti-signal generator and anti-scope; however, I would only use a scope as a last resort, which translates to almost never. There are much better and quicker ways to troubleshoot amplifier problems. I like to think of troubleshooting amps in the same spirit as my grandmother baking bread.

My main troubleshooting tools are: a chopstick, a jumper wire, a good multimeter (I use a Fluke 8060A that can also measure relative dB gain and frequency), a few "known good" tubes for substitution troubleshooting, a homemade current limiter that simply puts a 100 watt light bulb in series with the amp I'm troubleshooting, and a high impedance signal tracer which consists of some high-impedance headphones in series with a 600 volt non-polarized cap. (Instructions for building the limiter and tracer appear on page 325 of my second book, *Tube Amp Talk for the Guitarist and Tech*.)

USE YOUR BRAIN

Before you can troubleshoot successfully, you must understand what kind of problem you are having. Are you having a problem with the amp drawing too much current? No sound? Bad sound? Is it a hum problem? Is it an oscillation problem? Is it a tonal problem? Let's define what kind of problem it is. Now that you know what kind of problem it is, use your brain.

USE YOUR EYES, EARS, NOSE, AND HANDS

Oddly enough, a simple inspection is sometimes the quickest way to troubleshoot an amplifier. I once had a technician working for me who had studied electronics in college and was well studied in electronic theory. He worked on an amp for several hours with a signal generator and a scope and could not find the problem. An apprentice who had been hanging out with us for about week and had never had any formal training whatsoever, walked past the amplifier and noticed a cooked resistor. He asked, "Is that resistor supposed to be "burnt-looking" like that?" The resistor was replaced and the amp was immediately repaired. How much more simple would it have been for the schooled technician to spend five minutes looking over the amp for anything amiss?

Similarly, there are other problems that can be found with the eyes. Sometimes input jack switches stick in the closed position killing the gain in the amp. Output jacks will do the same on occasion. All of these can be visually inspected. A wire may be broken. Solder joints can be dull and bad looking. These can be found with the eyes in a relatively short period of time.

Another thing to look for is capacitors that have bubbled on the positive side (I'm referring to electrolytic caps. These are used in the bias circuit, bypass circuits, and the power supply). Look at the positive ends. Are they bubbled? Are they leaking? If so, they need to be replaced.

Use your ears. Let's see what a bad output transformer sounds like. Take a two-output tube amplifier. Remove one of the output tubes, turn the amp up, and play it. Doesn't it sound awful? That's what a bad output transformer sounds like. The next time you hear that sound you will immediately know it's a bad output transformer.

Here's a test to narrow down a bad output transformer sound. On the amp in question, remove one of the output tubes. Listen. Replace that output tube and remove the other tube. Listen. From this simple test you can narrow the problem. The side that does not have any difference in sound when the tube from the corresponding side is removed either has a bad output transformer, a blown screen resistor, a disconnected cathode or an open coupling cap (feeding the grid from the phase inverter). Using a voltmeter, check the screen voltage, the grid voltage and the plate voltage. If there is no screen voltage, the screen resistor is probably burnt open. (In this case, the tube was probably shorted plate to screen and the tube must be replaced.) If there is no plate voltage, the transformer is open on that side. If the cathode voltage is equal to the plate voltage, the cathode is not properly grounded. If none of these are problematic, it is probably a coupling cap that is feeding the grid (from the phase inverter).

Another trick is using the God-given gift of the olfactory glands—your sniffer! If you think a part has burned up or a transformer is fried, smell it. It will smell burnt, if it is.

You can also use your hands. I use my finger as a signal-generator. Take your index finger and hold open the input jack. You should hear a nice 60 Hz hum coming from the speaker. This is due to the capacitance of your body picking up the A.C. hum that's present in the air. I've also used my hands to troubleshoot parasitic oscillations. Often times, the capacitance of your body, when you get it close to a component, will effect the parasitic. In this case, you can isolate more clearly where the parasitic is actually coming from.

USE OF A JUMPER WIRE

You can use a simple jumper wire to further isolate problems occurring within a stage. For instance, I can use a jumper wire to short across the plate load resistor, which would kill the output of the tube. If the problem still persists, it is after the plate resistor, in the circuit. Let's follow it down line using the jumper wire again. Short the cold side of the coupling cap to ground. If the problem still persists, it is after the coupling cap in the circuit. If the problem does not persist, it is before the coupling cap.

We can also use a jumper wire to short the grid of a preamp tube.

You short it to ground. This will cut the signal going into the tube. Therefore, if the aberrant problem still occurs, it is after this grid circuit. By using a jumper wire, we can isolate exactly where the noise or problem is coming from in the amp.

I sometimes use a jumper wire with one end at the chassis ground and the other end is touched to the grounded side of any component whose grounding is suspect. If this cures a problem, the ground in question is bad. I can check ten grounds in a few seconds with this technique.

USE OF A HIGH IMPEDANCE SIGNAL TRACER

I use a pair of high impedance headphones with a capacitor on one lead to listen to anything occurring inside an amp. One end of the headphones goes to the chassis ground and the other end goes to a 600V non-polarized capacitor. The value is not important. I use a .1 uf, but any capacitor would work. You simply take the capacitor and touch any point in the circuit. You can hear what's going on in that particular part of the circuit. This is especially useful when troubleshooting an amp that has no sound coming out of the speaker. We can play guitar through the input and trace the signal from one tube to the next until we find the part that the signal stops. Where the signal stops, you start backing up towards the input and check it out until you can isolate the exact spot where the signal is stopping. This is much faster than a scope. It's a lot easier than a scope. Although it won't do the same things that a scope will do, it has the homely virtue of getting the job done correctly and in a short amount of time.

ISOLATE THE PROBLEM

For instance, if it's a "hum" problem, is it 60 Hz or 120 Hz.? If it's 60 Hz, it's in the filament heater or in the A.C. line. If it's 120 Hz, it's in the D.C. power supply of the amplifier. If it's a "current" problem, where is it drawing too much current, pull the output tubes. If the problem persists, then we know it's not the output tubes and we've ruled that out. If the problem stops, then we know the output tubes were drawing too much current. In this case, the output tubes were not biased properly or one or both tubes are bad or shorted.

In the case of hum, we simply pull the phase inverter tube. If the hum persists, then it's in the output stage. If it does not persist, then it's in the preamp stage, in which case you would replace the phase inverter tube and start pulling preamp tubes until you can isolate which stage the problem is coming from.

Let's say you think you have a bad power transformer. The scenario is this: the amp is drawing way too much current and blowing fuses. You plug the amp into a current limiter and the light bulb on the current limiter shines bright, indicating that the amp is drawing too much current. At this point, you simply check the primary to make sure that the A.C. cord is not shorted. Do this by checking voltage across the transformer primary. If it is zero volts and the amp is drawing current, the A.C. line is shorted. If the A.C. cord is not shorted, the next step would be to begin clipping transformer secondary wires, one at a time. In noticing the light bulb of the current limiter, when a wire is cut, check to see if the bulb is still burning bright. When the wire that gets cut causes the light bulb to go out, you know which circuit the problem is in. For instance, you clip one of the red B+ wires and the amp quits drawing current, which indicates either a shorted diode or a shorted filter cap in the power supply circuit. What happens when you clip every secondary wire and the amp still is drawing too much current? It's simple: you have a bad power transformer that needs to be replaced. At this point, the secondary would be completely disconnected, making it easier to install a new one. (Hint: When clipping transformer wires, leave ¼" of insulation on the lead that the wire is being clipped from. The color-coded insulation will facilitate re-installing it correctly later without having to think about it.)

LEARN TO RECOGNIZE PARASITIC OSCILLATIONS

Unstable amplifiers will sometimes oscillate. These oscillations can occur at low frequencies, high frequencies, and even at frequencies not audible to humans (in which case the amp will appear to have shut down even though it is drawing major current). Learning to recognize these oscillation problems and learning their causes and remedies can save weeks of troubleshooting time. For instance, most oscillations are caused by one of three things. One is an incorrect negative feedback loop that is wired positive. (Hint: This can be caused by either the output transformer primary or secondary wired out of phase. This makes the negative feedback loop change to positive, which causes oscillation.) Second is improper grounding, such that there is a load resistance between what should be a ground and true ground, in which case, a signal from a previous or later stage is fed back over this load resistance, causing a positive feedback. Third is improper lead dress. Production amps sometimes suffer from improper lead dress. For example, on a Tweed Deluxe amp, the second channel input jack is too close to a certain coupling cap. The amp will make a sound that sounds like a bad speaker, but if the speaker is changed there will be no improvement. Moving the proximity of the cap will stop the oscillation.

When encountering parasitic oscillations, shortening the grid wires, particularly the ones on the output tubes, would be well advised. This will solve the problem, most of the time, and takes very little time and no parts.

THE TEXAS SHOTGUN APPROACH

Often times it is easier to replace a few suspect components rather than spending hours trying to find which one is bad. A good example of this is when troubleshooting an oscillator circuit for a Vibrato. Let's say you have an oscillator that is not oscillating. Nine times out of ten, if you change the bypass cap and all four coupling caps (three that couple the plate back to the grid and one that couples the oscillator to the next stage), then the problem will go away. It takes ten minutes to replace those three caps and the bypass cap. Why not just replace them all and be done with it? If one of the caps is bad, who cares which one? Replace them all and you'll get the right one and you won't be bothered with another hour of trying to figure out which one it is. Here's another example of the Texas Shotgun Approach: let's say you have some crackling sounds coming from the amp and you swap tubes around and you're convinced it is not the tubes. There is a 95% chance it's the plate load resistors. In most amps there are at least six of these resistors. Why not replace them all? Put brand new plate load resistors and you'll get rid of the noisy ones. You won't have to spend hours trying to find which ones were noisy and which ones weren't. Who cares? Replacing them all and you will get the offending parts in a fraction of the time.

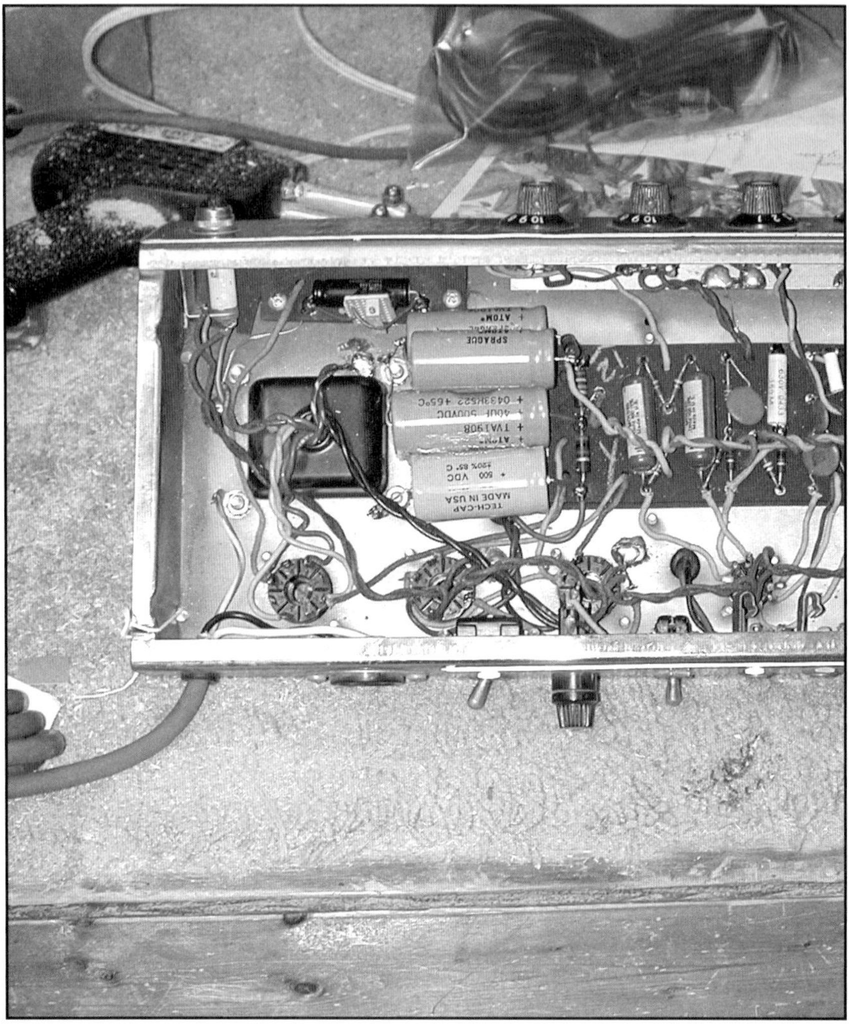

TAMING THE PARASITIC BEAST

Have you ever plugged into a Blackface Super Reverb and noticed a harsh non-musical, brittle, high-end raspiness (especially when pushed hard) that didn't sound like it could be made by a guitar? You've got a parasitic problem. Have you ever thought you had a blown speaker, changed it and then found out the new one sounds blown — just like the first one? You've got a parasitic oscillation. Or let's say you hear a sound that sounds like a mosquito riding on the crest of the note. You've got a parasitic.

Or you think there's a noisy tube socket. Every time you touch the tube in the socket, you hear a noise. You suspect it's the tube, but every new tube you try does the same thing. It must be in the socket, you think. In desperation, you change the socket, only to have the problem remain. Is it the socket? Nope — it's a parasitic.

What's a parasitic? It is an invisible circuit that doesn't appear on the schematic. It occurs when one or more components in one part of the circuit couples to another part of the circuit either by capacitive, inductive, magnetic or other means. The parasitic circuit may oscillate at frequencies beyond human hearing. In this case, the amp may seem to shut down and yet draws major current because it is oscillating above 20 Kilohertz.

Many amps have parasitic problems directly from the factory. For instance, Plexiglass-front Marshalls will go into parasitic oscillation if you use the bright channel and turn the presence and treble and volume full up. Turn the presence control down, and the oscillation clears up. Notice the 5600 ohm grid resistors on the vintage Marshalls. Those resistors are to suppress parasitic oscillations.

Most Blackface Fender's (with reverb) are prone to parasitic oscillations. In fact, the 2000 pf ceramic caps that were added to the grids of the output tubes (on the Silverface Fenders) are clearly a parasitic suppression modification.

Early Boogies had a parasitic suppression circuit that was most unusual. A wire was soldered to the plate of one output tube (the one whose signal is 180 degrees out of phase with the input signal). The other end of the wire was not connected to anything, but was routed back to the input wire that connects the input jack with the grid of the first preamp tube. There was no direct connection; the wire was simply wrapped around the input wire two or three times (enough to measure about 5 to 10 picofarads of capacitance). This circuit is extra cool because it uses a man-made parasitic to suppress an unwanted parasitic. I guess the guys at Boogie have an ironic sense of humor. (This type circuit sounds nasally.) Even though this type circuit can stabilize an otherwise unstable amplifier, because of the nasal quality it surely imparts, I would suggest this type of parasitic suppression circuit only as a last alternative.

Take the example of the tweed Deluxe. One in ten have a parasitic that manifests itself occasionally when you play an open low "E." As a player, you are likely to think it is a rattle in the speaker or the string is rattling on the fretboard, or in severe cases you may think the output transformer is going out. I spent weeks researching this problem. It is caused by a coupling capacitor in the amp that makes a parasitic capacitive coupling with the metal on the bright channel input jack. Is this bizarre? I would have never imagined this to be the case, yet moving the cap or the jack or even repositioning the cap so that the surface area of the cap is perpendicular to the metal on the input jack can easily prove it.

There are many ways that a parasitic problem can manifest itself. You can begin to think there is a poltergeist living in your amp. Oddly enough, not much is mentioned about parasitic oscillations. You hardly ever see anything written about them. Perhaps those who have been beaten for days and weeks are probably not jumping up and down to share such hard earned information. My first encounter with a parasitic was with a Brown Fender Super that would seem to "cut out" intermittently when the volume was cranked. It would just seem to shut down, even though multimeter testing revealed it was drawing major current. This amp was one of those that would oscillate at frequencies humans can't hear. You know how a PA system can feedback and get that high pitched feedback squeal? Imagine the squeal at just beyond the frequency of human hearing, but with an intensity that will allow no other signal to pass. That's what this amp was doing. I spent a week of my life with that amp.

HOW TO FIGHT THE PARASITIC

There are only four ways to fight a parasitic oscillation problem. You can either: modify layout/lead dress, suppress some high-end response, reduce the gain, or install a parasitic suppression circuit. The best solution is always to modify layout/lead dress. When you do this, you are addressing the source of the problem and not just the symptom. The problem with modifying the layout or lead dress is that you must know what is causing the parasitic. That is the hard part. The other solutions mentioned may solve the symptom, but they will all alter tone at least to some degree. Altering lead dress will most probably not affect tone and that is why it should be looked at as the first solution.

There are general rules of good layout/lead dress that are a good place to start looking for the problem parasitic. In general, the input signal starts on one side of the chassis and the layout progresses towards the other side gradually, as the signal is amplified. That is to say that you would never want the layout to criss-cross towards one side and then come backwards toward the input side. If you did this, you would be asking for parasitic problems. I remember a Dual Showman that I modified years ago. I used the vibrato tube for a normal channel extra gain stage and that was a mistake. By criss-crossing the signal from channel one, all the way across channel two to the vibrato tube and back to channel one, I had a parasitic problem that wouldn't quit.

In the case of the tweed Deluxe mentioned earlier, rotating the coupling cap by 90 degrees fixes the problem without any change in tone!

OTHER GENERAL RULES OF GOOD LAYOUT

In general, all grid circuits should be short and plate circuits should be long. Here is why: A grid circuit is ultra high impedance, so a long grid wire acts exactly like an antenna to pick up stray signals. Keeping this grid length to a minimum avoids this. For instance, when I first started building the Climax amplifiers, I had a parasitic problem to address. The clean channel of the Climax uses a tone circuit similar to a 60s Fender. Once the plate current signal goes through the tone caps, it becomes part of the next stage's grid circuit. I had to move the tone caps (which are also used as the coupling caps, in this case) off the board and mount them directly on the tone pots. This change of layout actually lengthened the plate circuit and shortened the grid circuit of the next stage — simultaneously. This solved the problem without any change in tone. What a difference a few inches of grid wire mean.

When I think of shortening grid length, I can't help but think back to when Kendrick Amplifiers began manufacturing the 4212 amp. This amp was basically a copy of the tweed Twin — a four output tube 2x12 combo. In this particular design, like the original tweed Twin, the length of wire from the phase inverter output to the actual grids of the output tubes is critical. If you have an inch too much wire length, you will get a parasitic that sounds like a blown output transformer or blown speaker. Changing either offers no help. Shorten the grid wire and the problem clears. Here is a perfect example of why there is more to building an amp than copying the schematic.

Another rule of good lead dress: Ground the main filter caps (that supply the output transformer), the screen supply filter caps, the cathodes of the output tubes and the center tap from the power transformer all at the same point. This keeps from superimposing the output signal across any stray load resistance between adjacent grounding points of the chassis. I bring this up, because many amps (including most Fenders) need modification to correct the ground of the screen supply. If you look underneath the cap pan board of a Blackface Fender, for example, you will find the screen supply filter cap grounded to the phase inverter filter cap ground. The screen filter's ground should be disconnected and tied to the main filter ground instead. This simple procedure has made a difference in terms of parasitic problems in certain amps.

Another rule of good lead dress: Grounds should not offer any resistance. Why? Because if they do, any signal that goes through that ground will use that resistance as a load resistance to develop a signal. This developed signal can now superimpose itself on something else. This is particularly bad if it can superimpose to a part of the circuit that is "in phase" with the developed signal. In this case it can cause positive feedback.

This is where checking the resistance of the ground with a very accurate meter can be useful. I like to use my trusty Fluke 8060A multimeter. It has a relative function, which means I can zero out the resistance of the test leads. I touch the two test leads together and get a reading. This is the resistance of the actual test leads themselves. When I press the "relative" function, the meter reads zero. It now is compensated for the test lead resistance. In this way, I can read very small resistances.

MORE ON LEAD DRESS/LAYOUT

When troubleshooting a parasitic, look for two parts of the circuit that are "in phase" with each other AND come within 3 inches of each other. Since a preamp tube will flip phase by 180 degrees, this means you should look at the grid circuit of the first gain stage and see where it is physically located to the plate circuit of the next stage — or even the grid circuit of the stage after that! If any of these are too close physically, you will get the possibility of positive feedback. If the gain of the circuit overcomes the loses, you will have oscillation. The cure is simply to rearrange lead dress to stop this unwanted coupling.

Now look at the next grid circuit and see where it is physically located in relationship to the plate circuit after that stage, etc. Sometimes this will give clues to where the parasitic coupling is occurring.

When we talk about keeping grid circuits short, sometimes that is not easy to do, especially on 60s and later Fenders that have long grid circuits on the input jack and the volume control. When you cannot keep the grid circuit short, try using shielded cable and ground the shielding only on one end.

A TRICK OF THE NINJA

What I'm about to tell you was obtained on the firing line of experience. There is a correct and incorrect polarity of a non-polarized cap, and once you figure this out, you can sometimes correct parasitic problems by going through an amp and correcting the polarity of all non-polarized caps.

When a capacitor is made, it is basically two conductors separated by a non-conductor. To get enough capacitance in a small component, two strips of metal foil are cut in very long strips and rolled up—each foil has its own lead. The whole thing is then encased in epoxy. Only one of the strips will be nearest the outermost edge of the cap. The lead that goes to this foil goes to the most grounded (least positive) side of the circuit. Why is that necessary? When you connect the outermost lead to the most grounded part of the circuit, it is as if the component itself is shielded by this more grounded connection.

How do you know which lead is the outermost? A simple test with a capacitance meter will tell the story. Take a piece of tin foil and wrap it around the capacitor. Connect one lead from the capacitance meter to the foil and the other meter lead to one of the cap leads. Take a reading. Now test from the foil to the other cap lead. The lead with the highest capacitance to the foil is the outermost lead. Most currently manufactured caps have the outermost lead on the "right" side when reading the writing on the cap from "left to right." Older manufactured caps sometimes had a black line around the end of the cap that had the outermost foil.

This would apply to tone caps as well as coupling caps. For instance the outermost lead on a tone cap always goes towards the tone controls, for instance, and the innermost lead goes to the plate circuit. Likewise, on the coupling cap, the outermost lead goes to the grid circuit of the next stage while the innermost lead goes to the plate circuit (high voltage).

OTHER CURES

So let's say you've gone through the amp, corrected all grounds, shortened all grid circuits or shielded those that were too long, and even corrected the polarity of all non-polarized capacitors; but the parasitic is still there. What next?

If you have an idea which part of the circuit the parasitic coupling is occurring, you could put a small value resistor directly on the grid of that tube (in series with the grid circuit, but mounted directly on the tube socket). High frequencies do not like resistances. In fact, when a signal is run through a resistance, the first thing to go is the high-end. (You know this from rolling down the volume on your guitar and noticing how the high-end goes away.) A small resistor installed in the exact proximity of the grid can sometimes be just enough to stop an oscillation. A typical resistor value would be ½ watt—anywhere from 820 ohms to 10K. You would want to experiment and use the smallest value that would stop the parasitic. You cannot use a decade box to experiment because the proximity of this resistor is essential to it stopping the parasitic. The resistor must be mounted with zero lead length directly on the socket grid pin. I would start with an 820 ohm and see if it stops it, if it doesn't, try a 5K. Then try either a 7.5K or a 2.5K, depending on what works and continue in a like manner until you find the value that just stops the oscillation. You have seen this circuit many times on power tubes, but it also works on preamp tubes! The Fenders typically used 1.5K and the Marshalls generally a 5.6K.

Here's another little trick that works, if you know which stage the parasitic is occurring. Short the plate load resistor with a small value cap. Depending on the type of oscillation, sometimes a small value cap 10 pf to 500 pf across the plate resistor of the offending stage will stop the oscillation. This is especially effective if you are trying to stop that really high frequency stuff. Why? Because a high frequency signal sees a small value cap as a short circuit and the high frequency gets bypassed to ground without ever making it to the next stage. Also if the cap is small enough, there will be no audible difference in tone. Pretty slick, eh?

Here's another trick, but once again you have to know which stage the oscillation is occurring. Let's say you tried shorting the plate resistor with a small cap. The other version of this is to short the grid circuit with a small cap. You've seen this on many Peaveys and Silverface Fenders. Remember the 2200 pf caps on the power tube grids to ground? You don't have to use that value, in fact, the smaller the value the better, in terms of it not messin' with your tone.

Here's another variation: You can use a small cap to inject high frequency interstage negative feedback to stop the oscillation. I'm talking about a small cap (5 pf to 500 pf) going from the plate to the cathode (or grid) of the same stage. This would cause only high frequencies to be fed back and phase cancelled — thus stopping oscillations.

MO' TRICKS OF DA NINJA OR USING PARASITICS TO FIGHT PARASITICS

Here's a trick I have used many times on 60s Fenders. Every now and then, you get a Super Reverb (or Pro, Bandmaster, etc.) that sounds like it wants to pick up a radio broadcast when you touch the input jack open with your finger. There's a certain audible oscillation sound that is the tip-off that this amp is unstable. I have a non-conventional way to stop this with a shielded wire. It works because every shielded wire is also a capacitor — of sorts. A capacitor is by definition two conductors separated by a non-conductor; so a shielded cable is a capacitor. It will have a certain amount of capacitance per foot. What you do is this:

There is a non-shielded wire going from the apex of the two 68K resistors on the input jack that go to the grid of the preamp tube (pin #2). Replace this wire with a shielded wire. Do not ground the shielding. Instead, simply hook the shielding to the plate of the same tube. In other words, your grid wire goes to pin #2 (grid) and the shielding goes to pin #1 (plate). The shielding isn't terminated on the input jack side. In fact, I like to cut the shielding short on that end and then pull the remaining insulation back to cover the shielding completely. This looks good and since there is high voltage on the shielding, prevents an accidental short to ground.

This works because would-be high frequency oscillations are injected back into the grid circuit at 180 degrees out of phase. This phase cancels the oscillation, but also phase cancels some high end. The exact amount of high-end phase cancellation is determined by how long the shielded wire is and how much capacitance per foot we are dealing with. If you find that the loss of high end is noticeable, you can remove some of the shielding on the input side. If the amp has a harsh or brittle high end, this mod may actually smooth things out a bit. You really need to listen and see what the amp is doing.

This same modification is also useful in another place on 60s Fenders. There is a long wire going from the volume pot center terminal to the grid of a preamp tube. This wire also may be replaced with a shielded wire. Again we do not ground the shielding and there is no shielding connection on the volume pot side. Instead, the shielding is connected to the plate of the same tube. It works exactly the same way — by injecting 180 degree out of phase high frequencies back into the grid circuit thus phase canceling unwanted oscillations.

Don't go crazy with these mods. Use them sparingly. On certain amps, the improvement is so dramatic that you will be tempted to modify every amp you own. Don't do it. You would not use both mods on the same amp except in extreme cases.

TRIAL AND ERROR INTERSTAGE FEEDBACK

This is a take-off of the Boogie trick that was mentioned earlier. I used it myself once in an emergency. I told you how the first Boogies had a wire attached to one output tube plate (pin #3) and the other end simply wrapped around the wire that goes from input jack to first gain stage grid. This circuit will stabilize an otherwise unstable amp, but will affect the tone and impart that nasally sound.

Here's the variation: don't have the feedback going from output tube plate to input jack, instead hook a 5 or 6 inch wire to the plate of the phase inverter tube. The other end of the wire doesn't connect electrically with anything. Instead, the insulation is left on and the tip of the wire is wrapped three times around other wires. You would experiment by wrapping it around other wires that occur previously in the circuit. You will notice that when wrapped around certain wires, the stability problems worsen, and with other wires the situation improves. When you find a spot that makes it better, leave it. You might even try another interstage feedback wire, or several.

I have found this type interstage feedback to have little effect on tone. What's cool is that you can hook a wire to the plate of any tube and then experiment with the free end. Put it anywhere you want and see what happens. You can't blow anything up, because the wire doesn't connect at both ends, it is never really hard connected to anything; we are simply enjoying a good parasitic coupling.

MODIFICATIONS

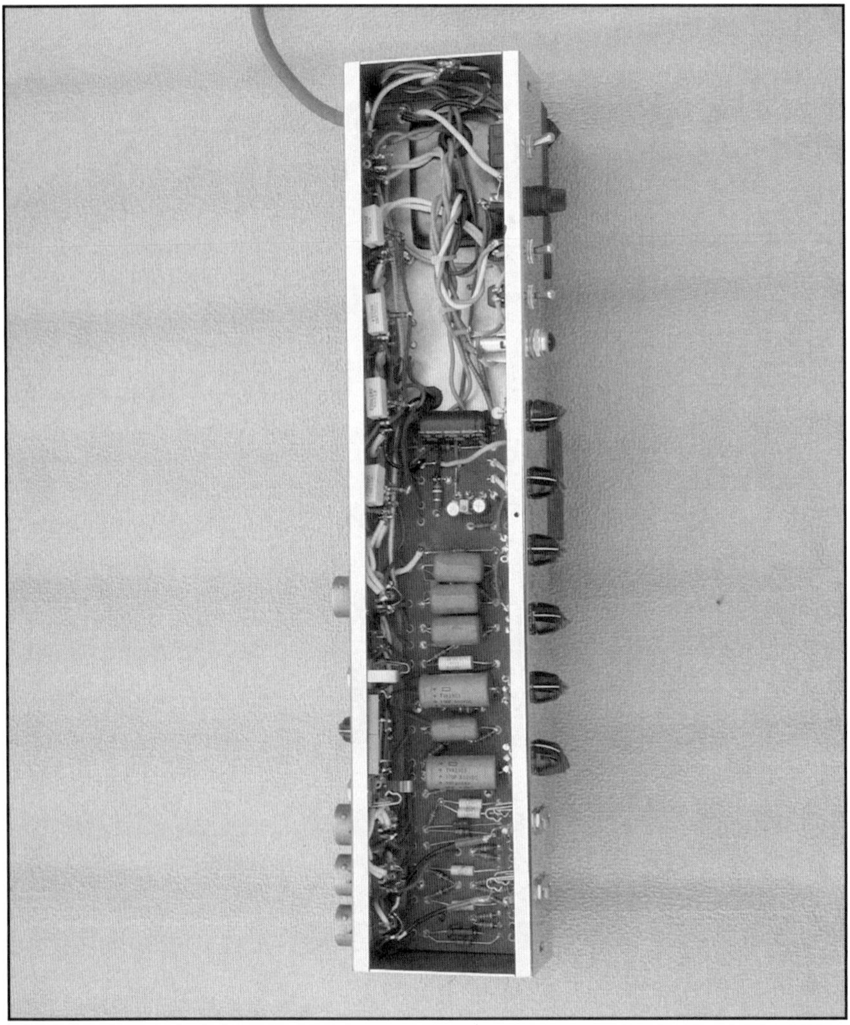

CORRECTING THE VINTAGE AMP DEFICIENCIES

What a difference 40 years of hindsight makes. For most of us baby boomers, we started out playing tube amps in the 50s and 60s; went with that overcompressed, buzzy and homogenized California tube distortion in the early 70s; changed over to emotionless transistors at some point; went to a rack system in the 80s; and finally went full circle and changed back to tube amps in the 90s. Whew, that was a journey! Can you remember when no one wanted a tweed amp because it had "too much distortion"? You could get them for under $100. Rectifier tubes went out of style in the 70s!

Even though we've gone full circle, the vintage amps perform differently now than they once did. For one thing, the wall voltage now is 120 volts and those vintage amps were originally designed when the wall voltage was 110 volts! (The voltages printed in the original 50s schematics are only accurate when using a 110 volt wall outlet!) A real vintage amp plugged into 120 volts will have all internal voltages about 9% higher than what is written on the schematic. So the vintage amps of today really do sound better than they did in the 50s.

Nowadays, we like to overdrive those tubes and really make them work to get "that tone." Since few of our forefathers of tube amp wizardry could have imagined how players would abuse their amps in the future, there were power supply deficiencies in the vintage designs.

THE OUT-OF-TUNENESS PROBLEM

Because players in the 50s and 60s did not turn up very loud, almost all vintage amps were designed with underfiltered power supplies. This means the filter caps (in the power supply) have a microfarad value too small to accommodate the current the amplifier draws when overdriven. Not only that, on certain amps, if you increase the microfarad value of the filtering, the rectifier tube arcs or the fuse blows when the amp is switched from standby to play!

On most 50s and 60s era amps, there are two 20 uf capacitors in parallel as the main filter. This is a net total capacitance of only 40 uf. On some of the 60s amps, there were two 70 uf capacitors in series. Two 70 uf in series is a net total of only 35 uf. This is barely enough filtering if the amplifier volume is set less than halfway up. At overdrive settings, the current is so high that the filtering cannot get rid of the annoying 120 cycle ripple current that occurs when an A.C. wall voltage is rectified to make the D.C. voltage required to operate tubes. You end up with a guitar tone that is modulated by the 120 cycle ripple current and that always sounds out of tune. Listen to any Beatles recording where the amps were cranked during the recording. The guitars always sound out of tune. This is very annoying when you are playing and everything you hear is out of tune. Also, when there is not enough filtering, at loud volumes, the power supply may not be able to keep up with the amp's power needs. This results in "wash out" and the volume and tone just "go away"!

THE SOLUTION

You need to increase the filtering but without stressing the rectifier tube. I like to use two 220 uf capacitors in series. I like using 350 volt caps. When you put two of them in series, you get a solid 700 volt rating (providing you put a 220K ohm 1 watt resistor across each capacitor). It is important to keep that voltage rating up, because there will be voltage spikes 100 volts or higher than the B+ voltage (voltage coming directly off the rectifier tube). When you put the two 220 uf caps in series, you will have a net of 110 uf of capacitance at 700 volts for your main power supply. This is about triple the filtering of the stock design. This will enable you to turn the amp up and still have pure tone that sounds in tune with itself!

THE RECTIFIER TUBE PROBLEM

If you are playing an amp that has the main filter supply connected to the cold side of the standby switch (almost any tweed amp), you will need a small modification to eliminate stress on the rectifier tube. With the stock wiring, none of the filter caps are charged during warm up. When the standby switch is thrown, the rectifier is operating into an almost direct short for the few seconds it takes to fully charge all the filters in the amp. This could result in an arced rectifier tube or blown fuses or both. With Mullard GZ34 rectifier tubes selling for $100 or more, we don't need to ruin one by encouraging it to arc. Also, if you beefed up the main filters as described above, it will be even harder on the rectifier tube because bigger caps take more energy to charge.

SAVING THE RECTIFIER TUBE

Move the main filter connection and only the main filter connection (not the center-tap of the output transformer) from the cold side of the standby switch to the hot side of the standby switch. If the filters are connected to the hot side of the standby switch, when the amp is turned on and as the rectifier tube is heating up, the filters will begin to trickle charge. By the time the rectifier is completely heated up, the filters will already be completely charged! When the standby switch is thrown and the other filters are trying to charge up, the power stored in the main filters will charge the uncharged preamp tube filters and there will be much less stress on the rectifier. You will hear a loud "pop" coming from the speakers, but this is normal and not to be of concern. If you compare the tweed amps to the Blackface amps, you will notice that Fender decided to move the main filter supply to the hot side of the standby switch as we are suggesting. You will also notice that all Blackface Fenders have the loud pop when they are turned from standby to play. That "pop" is the sound of all the energy leaving the main filters all at once to charge the other caps. It is better the energy come from a capacitor rather than having the rectifier operate into a dead short for a few seconds!

BIAS ADJUSTMENT

Many of the amps from the 50s incorporated non-adjustable fixed bias. When you put an amp designed for 110 volts into a 120 volt wall outlet, all of the voltages will be about 9% higher. With the voltages up 9%, the idle current will also go up. This is a very good reason for putting a bias adjustment pot on vintage amplifiers that lack it.

With any fixed bias amp, there is a negative voltage supply. There will be two resistors that divide off a certain amount of voltage. The two resistors will consist of a dropping resistor (connects to the diode) and a load resistor (goes to ground). The load resistor can be replaced with a cermet trim pot in series with a fixed resistor. For example, if the stock load resistor is 56K, you could use a 50K cermet pot in series with a 30K resistor. With this circuit, you could adjust the range all the way down and have 30K resistance, or you could adjust it all the way up and get 80K. This would allow you to adjust the bias voltage — either up or down as needed.

For an additional example, if you had a 40K load resistor in your negative bias voltage supply, you could replace it with a 15K resistor wired to a 50K cermet pot. This would give you a range from 15K to 65K.

When installing adjustable bias, always use a cermet element pot. The bias voltage supply is D.C. and the cermet pot can take the D.C. without malfunctioning. Cermet pots never malfunction. I have used them extensively for years now and never seen one go south.

THE SPEAKER PROBLEM

Vintage amps have old speakers. Most of these old speakers have a paper bobbin voice coil former. A voice coil former is a bobbin that a coil of wire is wound around. The coil of wire gets hot when the speaker is being used. Have you ever seen a piece of 40 year old paper? Imagine what that paper bobbin would look like with the coil heating and cooling, heating and cooling over a period of 40 years. If you use a vintage amp, and you have a vintage speaker, you will blow that speaker. Trust me, I know. You will be playing that amp and loving the tone and then...Uh Oh, the speaker is history. Either the voice coil will disintegrate, the glue holding it to the paper will disintegrate, or the coil will burn up. If you recone it, that costs almost as much as a new speaker and with the devaluation of your amp, it ends up costing even more than a new speaker.

REPLACE THE SPEAKER

Replace the speaker BEFORE you blow it. That way, you will still own a working original speaker. If you ever want to sell the amp, you can sell the amp with the original speaker and it will bring much more dineros than if you had a blown or reconed speaker. Also, by having a new speaker in there, you don't have to worry about blowing it. You can crank the amp with confidence.

GET YOUR AMP OVERHAULED

Vintage amplifiers need to be overhauled in order to perform their best. Parts wear out. Component values drift. Tubes begin to lose their output. Capacitors dry up. Get your amp overhauled and use quality American parts. The Sprague Atom electrolytic capacitors are the best. They will sound "head and shoulders" better than the cheap Taiwanese caps being sold everywhere. Replace drifted resistors with Allen Bradley carbon composition resistors, not Radio Shack carbon film resistors. Make sure and check coupling caps for D.C. voltage leakage. Even a half a volt of D.C. leakage can ruin the sound of your amp. If a half a volt leaks from the coupling cap to the grid of the next stage, then the biasing scheme of the next stage is thrown off and the amp sounds horrible.

With a simple overhaul, new speakers, a beefed up power supply and adjustable bias, you could have your vintage amp sounding better than it sounded when it left the factory.

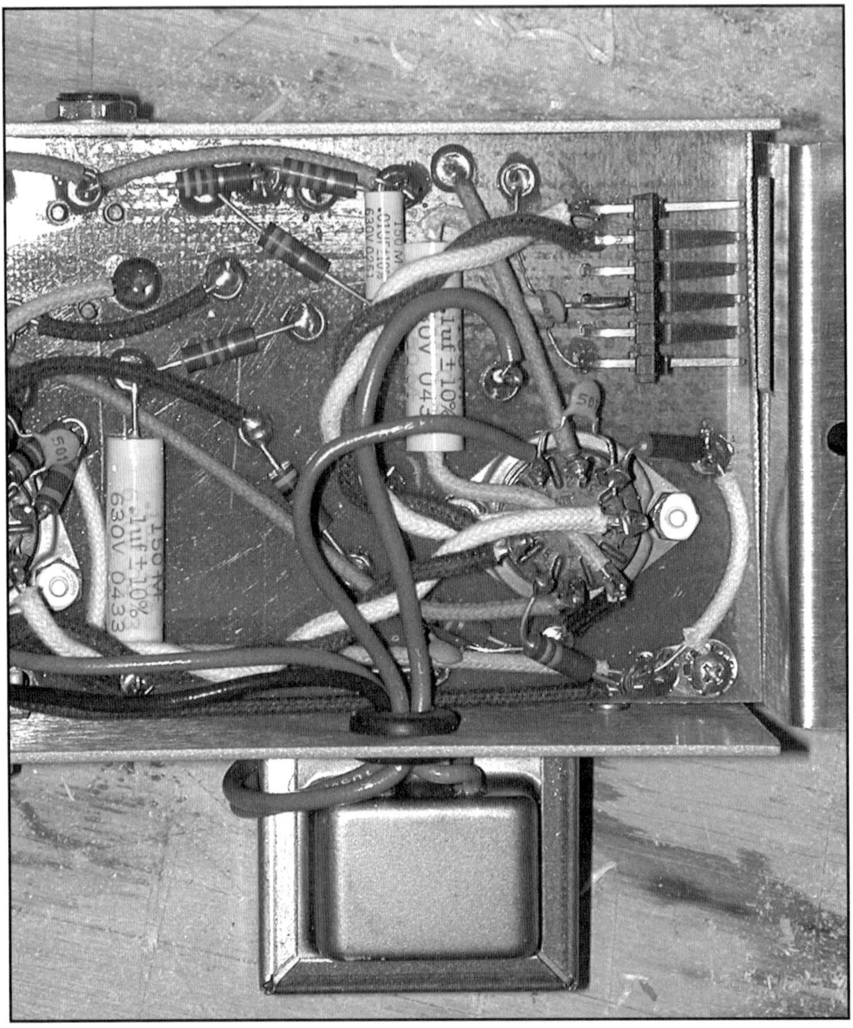
.1uf ±10%
630V 0433

AMPLIFIER BLOOPERS AND THEIR CORRECTION

Forty years hindsight may be even better than 20/20. When we look back at familiar amps over and over again, we begin to see problems (and accompanying solutions) that an occasional glance wouldn't have revealed. Amp builders in the 50s and 60s didn't have the advantage of hindsight (nor did they dream that the players of the future would be running tube amps with the volume controls up!) Surely the lower testing volumes of yesteryear would have obscured noises, hum, and instabilities enough to make most inherent flaws seem non-existent.

For example, who would have ever thought that someone would turn a Marshall full stack up enough to force the high pitched parasitic oscillation that occurs when the treble and presence controls are at more extreme settings? Or what about the buzz that sounds like a blown speaker that occurs on some tweed Deluxes? Or what about the loud grounds hum that occurs on Hiwatt, Gibson, and Ampeg? Perhaps the more conservative test volumes of yesteryear were not enough to reveal these as deficiencies. Let's look at some examples:

Problem: Noise that sounds like intermittent radio noise
Offending Amplifier: Most Blackface Fenders
Solution: First, I would recommend installing shielded wire to replace the wire that goes from the two 68K input resistors to the grid of the first preamp tube. The shielding should only be grounded on one end. I like to ground the shielding on the end nearest the input jack.

In a similar manner, the wire that goes from the volume control wiper (center lead) to the grid of the second stage should also be replaced with shielded wire. Ground the shielding at only one end.

To avoid losing high-end, select low-capacitance shielded wire. Keep the length of the wire as short as possible.

PROBLEM: Excessive 120 cycle Hum
OFFENDING AMPLIFIERS: Gibson, Ampeg, Hiwatt, and Vox
SOLUTION: There are many causes for hum and therefore many solutions, but in some tag board construction amps such as Vox, Gibson, Ampeg, Hiwatt and certain other amps; the grounds for the cathode resistors and grid return resistors are daisy-chained and then grounded at one end. This actually encourages hum. One solution is to give every cathode circuit a separate ground wire and give each grid resistor its own separate wire to ground. If the cathode circuit has a by-pass capacitor, it is OK to use one wire for both the by-pass capacitor and the cathode resistor circuit. Each cathode, each grid and each filter cap should have its own wire that goes to a 'star ground'; that is, all ground wires terminating at on point.

In fact, I like to take it a step further and use two star grounds. I like to put the first star ground near the power transformer. In fact, the output tube sockets sometimes have a metal grounding ring that works great as a star ground. This star ground is used for:
1. The cathode circuit of the output tubes
2. The main filter cap ground
3. The screen supply filter cap ground
4. The bias supply ground (or output tube grid return resistor circuit in self biased output stage)
5. The transformer B+ center-tap

I like using the ground lead on the input jack as the second star ground. The second star ground is used for:
1. All preamp cathode circuit grounds
2. All preamp grid return circuit grounds
3. All preamp filter caps
4. Input jacks

When you are soldering a ground to a metal chassis, make sure and use a big solder gun (I use a 175 watt iron that we affectionately refer to as "Big Bertha"!) Also, you want to scrape off any chrome or nickel-plating from the chassis. I use a Dremel tool for this. I leave the soldering iron on until it is very hot and then I heat up the chassis for a while before applying any solder. The biggest problem that most people have with chassis grounds is not getting the chassis hot enough before applying solder. When you consider that the chassis acts as a heat sink, then you can understand why you must use a big iron and preheat the iron and the chassis. If you apply the solder too soon, the rosin will melt and deposit a film-like coating between the chassis and the wires to be grounded.

PROBLEM: Insufficient voltage rating on bias filter capacitor
OFFENDING AMPLIFIER: Certain Blackface Fenders
SOLUTION: Many Blackface Fenders use a 50 volt electrolytic filter capacitor in the negative voltage bias supply. On certain Deluxe Reverbs, I have measured the voltage at as much as 60 volts.

I like to change these to the same mfd. value, but with a 100 volt rating. Simply observe correct polarity and change the capacitor and you are done.

PROBLEM: Excessive 60 cycle hum
OFFENDING AMPLIFIER: Almost any tube amp
SOLUTION: Most amp builders of yesteryear paid zero attention to filament heater polarity. With a push-pull output stage, the filament hum is self-canceling — IF THE FILAMENTS ARE WIRED IN CORRECT POLARITY. If the filaments are wired in reverse polarity, the output stage becomes hum inducing.

The bad news is this: The odds are 50/50 that the output tubes are wired correctly, so this is something everyone should check and correct, if needed.

The pair of filament wires that terminate on pins #2 and #7 of most octal output tubes should be wired such that pin #2 of one output tube terminates on pin #2 of the adjacent output tube. Likewise, the wire that terminates on pin #7 of one tube should go to pin #7 of the adjacent tube. Of course, if there are four output tubes, all of them would be wired with the same polarity.

The early amp builders usually used the same color wire for wiring up filaments and since they are twisted pairs, it is very difficult to see if the filaments are wired in correct polarity. If you clip one lead of an A.C. voltmeter on pin #2 of one tube and the other lead to pin #2 of the other tube, then the voltage should read, "zero." This would verify that the tube sockets are wired correctly. If the reading is 6.3 volts, then you must reverse the polarity on one of the tube sockets.

Amplifier Bloopers and Their Correction

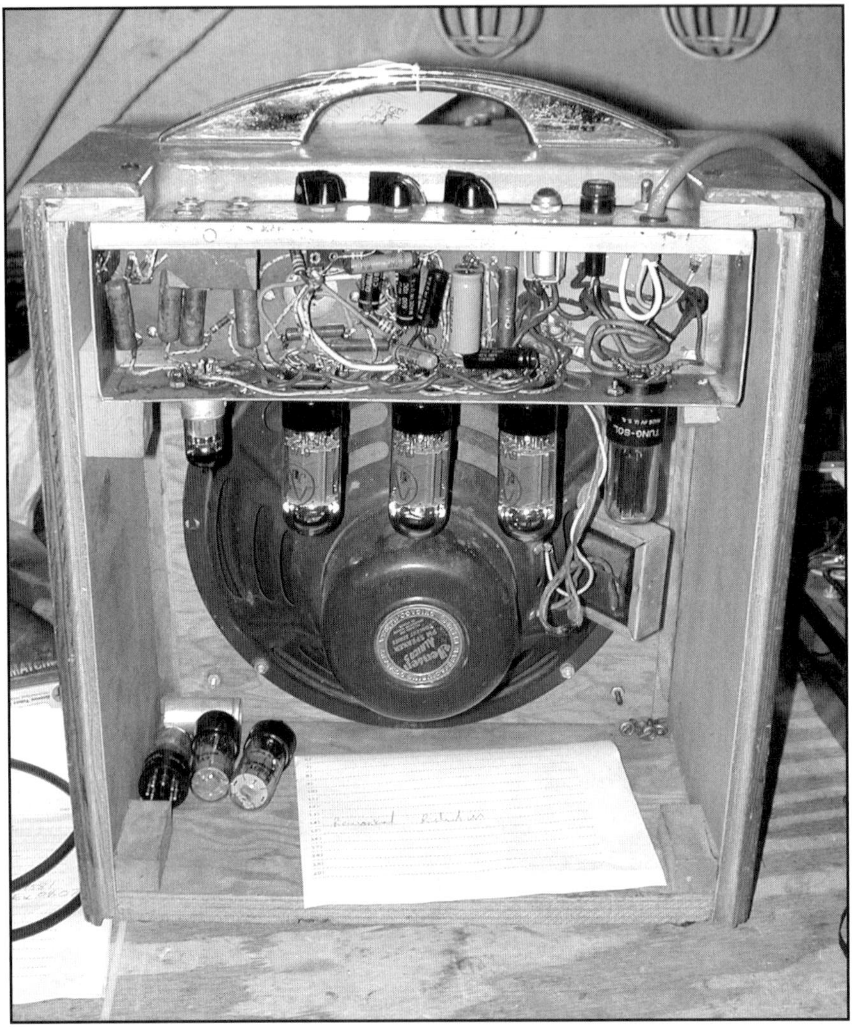

GETTING THE TONE YOU DON'T HAVE

Most guitarists need only two really great tones — namely: a great lead tone and a great clean tone. Most vintage tube amps give only one good tone, either a lead or clean tone.

LET'S LOOK AT BLACKFACE AND SILVERFACE AMPS
Consider a Blackface or Silverface Fender for example. The voicing of such an amp is such that the mids are somewhat scooped out, the highs are jangly and the lows are fairly focused and clear. Because the mids are somewhat scooped, there is plenty of "air" or "space" in the notes, so the notes don't crowd each other. This voicing lends itself for a great clean tone.

When you turn such an amp up to get overdrive, there is not really enough midrange or gain to get a thick lead tone. That is why many players (Steve Vaughan included) used an overdrive pedal to get a thicker overdriven lead tone from the mid 60s/70s Fenders.

LET'S LOOK AT TWEEDS AND MARSHALLS
Now consider a tweed Fender or a (four input) Marshall. Both of these amps have that fat midrange that makes a plain string so thick, it sounds wound. These amps are wonderful for lead tones, but they are difficult to get a good clean sound. The middle of the note is so thick, that adjacent chord notes compete for "space" and then both notes distort.

LET'S LOOK AT BOTH OF THEM
Short of carrying multiple vintage amps, how does one get the clean tone from a tweed amp and how does one get the lead tone from a Black or Silverface amp? Tweed amps, four input Marshalls, Blackface, and Silverface amps have two channels. What if we could select the

best sounding channel of an existing amp and modify the other channel to get the tone we don't have? You could take a Blackface Fender, for example, and select the reverb channel for your clean tone, then modify the other channel for your lead tones. Or you could take a tweed Super, decide you like the instrument channel for lead tones, and modify the other channel to get a better clean tone. We are not going to drill any holes; we won't do anything that can't be easily reversed (you can put it back to stock if you ever want to sell the amp).

CREATING A LEAD CHANNEL ON A BLACK OR SILVERFACE FENDER

We will start with the Blackface or Silverface Fender. We will keep the reverb channel as our clean sound and modify the normal channel (which normally isn't used by most players anyway). The normal channel needs more gain and a thicker midrange to get that killer lead sound. You don't really need reverb for lead tones because lead tones will cut through a mix better without reverb.

The tone stack of any amp causes a reduction in gain (sometimes up to 35 dB reduction!) Also, the tone stack of a Blackface or Silverface Fender is a type of midrange scoop filter that gives it its characteristic "scooped midrange" tone. To get this great lead tone on the normal channel, we will add a bypass circuit, where some of the guitar signal bypasses the tone stack. This will improve gain considerably and by bypassing the tone stack, the tone won't be so "midrange scoop" filtered. All you need for this mod is a 1 Meg ½ watt resistor and a .01 mfd 400 volt capacitor (I like the Mallory brand, 150 series capacitor for this purpose).

Remove the chassis from the amp and look at the first preamp tube socket. This is the 12AX7 that is closest to the end of the chassis and it is also the one that is used for the normal channel. If you look at the underside of the socket, you will notice space for 10 pins, but only 9 pins are used. Look at the space where the tenth pin could have gone but is not, that space is called the "key." Going clockwise from the "key," and looking from the bottom of the socket, the first pin is pin #1. Solder one end of the 1 Meg resistor to pin #1 of the first preamp tube. Leave the other lead of that resistor pointing up in the air.

Now we are going to look at the back of the volume control on the normal channel. Notice there are three leads on the top of the volume control. Look at the lead on the right (looking from the back of the pot). Take one end of the .01 mfd 400 volt capacitor and solder it to the right lead of the pot. If you hold the .01 mfd cap and read the markings from left to right, it is the right lead that should be soldered to the pot. The left lead should be left alone for now.

Now we are going to take a short piece of hookup wire (use the shortest length possible) and connect the open lead of the resistor to the open lead of the .01 uf capacitor. Each connection should also be soldered. Now the modification is complete. Your normal channel will have considerably more gain and a thicker overall response.

CREATING A CLEAN CHANNEL ON A TWEED OR MARSHALL

On almost all tweed amps and all 4 input Marshalls, the first preamp tube is configured the same. Pin #1 of the first preamp tube is the plate circuit of the first channel (or normal channel, or microphone channel — depending on how it happens to be labeled). Pin #6 is the plate circuit of the second channel (or bright channel or instrument channel — depending on how it is labeled).

First, you want to play the amp and find out which channel works best for your lead tone. Once you determine this, you will be modifying the other channel to get a great clean tone.

We are going to make a filter that "scoops" the mids and drops the gain slightly and then install this filter in place of a coupling capacitor. This filter will simulate the tone stack sound of the Blackface or Silverface amps. This will give you more bottom-end focus, more space around all the notes, and a clearer top end.

FIND THE CAPACITOR TO BE REPLACED

First lets locate the coupling capacitor that will be replaced with the filter. If you are modifying the first channel, look at pin #1 of the first preamp tube. Follow the wire on pin #1 back to the board and you will notice a coupling capacitor (almost always a .02 uf at 400 volt). This is the capacitor that will be replaced to get the first channel as the clean channel.

If you are modifying the second channel, look at pin #6 of the first preamp tube. Follow the wire on pin #6 back to the board and you will notice a coupling capacitor (almost always a .02 uf at 400 volt). This capacitor will be replaced to get the second channel as the clean channel.

LET'S MAKE A BLACKFACE FILTER

The filter consists of a subassembly that replaces the coupling cap that is associated with either pin #1 of the first preamp tube (if channel #1 is being modified) OR it will replace the coupling cap associated with pin #6 of the first preamp tube (if channel two is being modified). This filter consists of only three components: a 220K ½ watt resistor, a .1 uf at 400 volt capacitor and a 100 pf capacitor at 100 volts or higher.

The 100 pf capacitor and the 220K resistor get wired in parallel to each other. We then take one end of the 100 pf/220K subassembly and wire it to one end of the .1 uf capacitor. This puts the .1 uf in series with the 100 pf/220K section. Now that wasn't so hard, was it?

You are going to use this subassembly as a substitute for the first gain stage coupling capacitor for the appropriate channel you are modifying. Remove the stock coupling capacitor. The free lead of the .1 uf capacitor goes on the board in the eyelet that is facing the plate of the preamp tube (either pin #1 or pin #6 depending on which channel you are modifying). The other free end of the subassembly (this will be the free end of the 100 pf and the 220K) goes into the eyelet that is closest to the front of the amp.

LOOK AT WHAT WE'VE DONE

We've simply replaced the stock .02 coupling cap with a filter. The filter consists of a .1 uf that faces the preamp tube plate. This .1 uf is connected to a free lead from a 100 pf cap and the free lead of a 220K resistor. The other ends of the 100 pf and 220K are twisted together and are soldered to the eyelet closest to the face of the amp.

EPILOGUE

No matter what type of tube amp you are playing, whether you play an amp with a naturally great lead tone and a modified channel that has usable clean voicings; or a naturally clean amp with a second channel modified for lead; remember that a tube amp should inspire the player to play his best. If your amp inspires you, it is passing the only true test for tone.

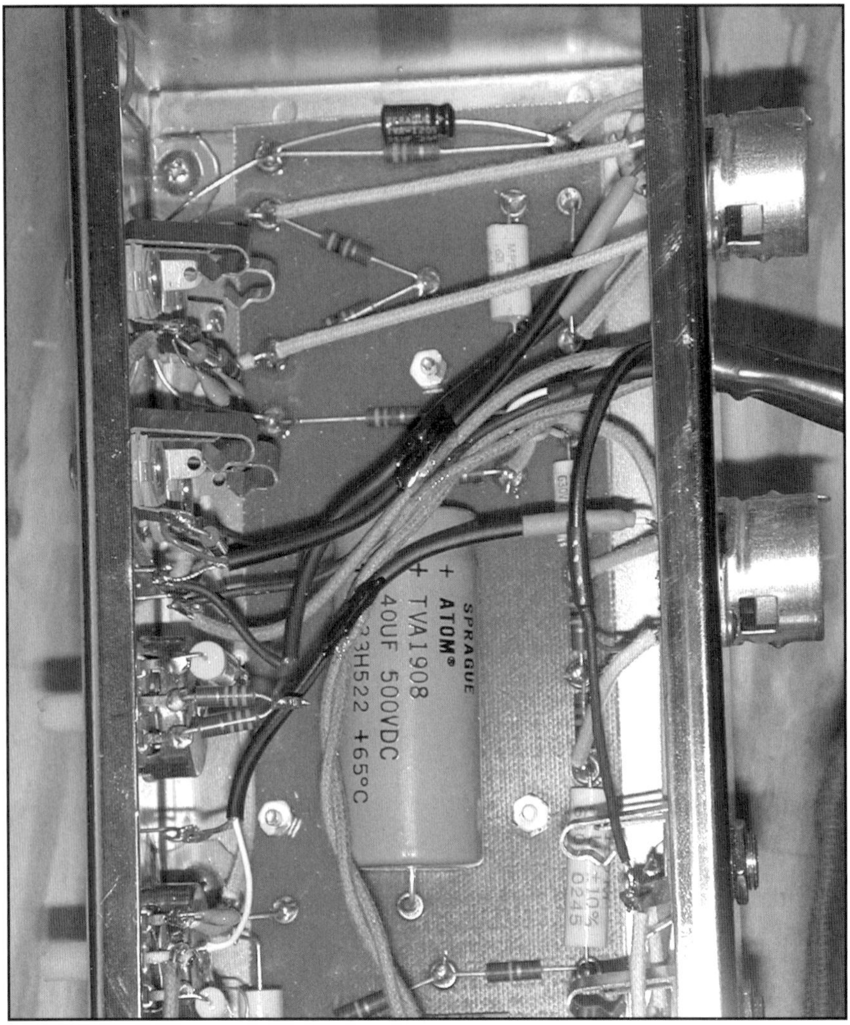
SPRAGUE
+ ATOM®
+ TVA1908
40UF 500VDC

HOT RODDING YOUR VINTAGE TUBE GUITAR AMP FOR MORE GAIN

Have you ever had an amp that was working perfectly as designed, yet it just didn't seem to have enough gain? I am not talking about a tired old tube amp that needs an overhaul. I am talking about a tube amp with a recent cap job and overhaul, good tubes and good speakers — yet it just lacks the "umpha" that it needs in order to be usable. I had a Magnatone come into my shop one day that had been recently overhauled. The customer complained about the amp's lack of responsiveness. All of the voltages checked closely with the schematic. It had excellent tubes and everything was working correctly — yet the amp was lifeless. It had no punch and its "get up and go" seemed to have gotten up and gone! This amp could inspire no one.

A quick check of the preamp voltages confirmed that the design used around 110 volts D.C. on the plates of the preamp tube. This might be fine in other situations, but the amp sounded constipated. I realized I needed more voltage on the first gain stage. Remember that if you increase the voltage on a preamp tube, the gain will go up and so will the headroom. The way to get more D.C. voltage on the preamp stage is have less voltage drop in the power supply dropping resistors. This type of modification could be done on any tube amp because all tube amps have power supply dropping resistors. These are the resistors that go between each filter cap. They actually connect one filter cap to another, but each resistor drops the D.C. voltage as the voltage is distributed to the next filter cap down line.

INCREASING PREAMP VOLTAGE

In all tube amps there is a rectifier circuit that takes the wall A.C. and makes it into the D.C. voltage that is required for the tubes to work. To isolate the various stages, a dropping resistor is used after the main filter caps to feed voltage to a screen supply filter cap (called the screen supply because it supplies the screens of the power tubes with voltage. Note: Sometimes a choke is used instead of the resistor.) Then another power supply dropping resistor is used to drop the voltage from the screen supply filter cap to the phase inverter supply filter cap. Then a power supply dropping resistor is used between the phase inverter filter cap and the next stage filter cap, etc.

You need those resistors in the power supply to help isolate each stage from the next (decoupling), but the resistor values don't need to be quite so high. The higher they are, the less voltage goes to the next stage. If you make the resistor between the main supply and the screen supply smaller, then all of the preamp voltages will go up. If you make the power resistor that is in between the screen supply and the phase inverter supply smaller, then all the voltages from the phase inverter back towards the earlier stages all go up. On this particular Magnatone, I made each power resistor a little smaller. I basically cut each one in half. This made all the voltages in the preamp section come up, which improved the gain some but still not enough.

The plates of section one and section two of a 12AX7 style tube are at pin #1 and pin #6 respectively. I was able to get the voltage on the plates of the preamp tube up to about 220 volts. This is pretty much optimum. You don't want to go too high because the tube will start getting hard sounding if there is too much voltage on it. The absolute design maximum plate voltage for a 12AX7 is 330 volts, but I would not recommend going that high.

CHANGING THE PREAMP CATHODE RESISTOR

Next, we want to look at the cathode biasing design of the preamp tubes — especially the first preamp tube. The cathode for the first section of a 12AX7 is pin #3. The second section cathode is pin #8. You can look at these pins and follow them to the resistor they are using to see if this modification is applicable. The Magnatone amp used an unbypassed 4.7K ohm cathode resistor on the first stage of the preamp tube (12AX7). If we make the cathode resistor smaller, the gain will go up. If that's the case, why not make it really small?

Although the smaller value will get you more gain, if you go too small, the amp will want to "hiccup" at higher volume settings. When it "hiccups" and you stop playing, the amp won't! A standard, "middle of the road" value to use is 1.5K, which is what I used for the Magnatone. To squeeze every last bit of gain from a tube, you could go to an 820 ohm and check to see if this makes the amp "hiccup." If it does, you can increase the value slightly until you find the point where the "hiccup" goes away. If it sounds fine at 820 ohms, leave it, but if you have a problem, try a 1K or a 1.2K.

ADDING A BYPASS CAPACITOR

If we use a bypass capacitor across the cathode resistor of a preamp tube, the gain goes up. In fact, there are modern amps that put a switch on the bypass cap and the switch might be labeled "fat" or "extra gain." With the bypass cap switched "on," the gain goes up. On the Magnatone, which originally used an unbypassed 4.7K cathode resistor, I used a 25 uf at 25 volt bypass capacitor. The 25 uf at 25 volt is a very common value. When choosing a bypass capacitor there are a couple of things to remember. First, the 25 uf at 25 volt will boost all frequencies for the guitar when used with a 1.5K cathode resistor. If you have a boomy sounding amp, you may want to use a smaller value to help rid some of the bottom-end boominess. The smaller value cap will boost the highs and mids but not as much of the bottom-end. For example, you may want to go to a 10 uf or a 5 uf to lose some of the bottom-end boominess. If you want a more trebly sound with more bite, you could go even smaller than that, to perhaps a 1 or 2 uf. Marshall used a .68 uf cap on some of their designs. This gives that biting treble which slices right through you. When choosing a bypass cap, you want to listen to the amp and see what value it needs. This way you can increase gain AND voice the amp in the same process.

Also, the bypass cap is chosen is relationship to the cathode resistor. While a 25 uf bypass cap may boost all guitar frequencies when used with a 1.5K cathode resistor, you will need a larger cap to get the same result with a smaller value cathode resistor. Vice versa, you would use a smaller value cap to get the same result with a larger cathode resistor. I like to forget the math and just go with what sounds good. If the amp is too boomy and needs more top-end to make it sound good, make the cathode bypass cap smaller. If you don't have enough bottom-end, make it larger. You can go to a 50 or 100 uf cap if you like. The original 5F6A Bassman used a 250 uf cap for the first stage!

CHOOSING THE GRID RESISTOR

Pin #2 is the grid of the first section of a 12AX7 style tube. The second section is pin #7. Look at these pins and you will notice they go to some type of resistor (or pot) that goes to ground. The value of this resistor affects gain. On the Magnatone, the resistor was too small (low gain) and it was part of a voltage divider from the input jack. A voltage divider is where two resistors are used. One resistor connects to the source (in my case this was the input jack), the other resistor connects to ground; and the junction of the two resistors goes to the grid of the tube. Usually both resistors are the same value (which would cut the signal exactly in half) — but they don't have to be. In my case, they were the same value. This meant that the signal going to the grid of the preamp tube was cut in half, resulting in a loss of 3 dB! Also, the grid resistor (that's the one that goes from the grid to ground) was smaller than 1 Meg. I removed the voltage divider and had the input jack go directly to the grid. I used a 1 Meg resistor going from the grid to ground. This improved gain quite a bit also.

Using the 1 Meg value grid resistor is most common. You could go to a 2 Meg or higher, but there is not much difference in gain once you go past 1 Meg and the 1 Meg is more stable than the 2 Meg.

SELECTING THE PREAMP TUBES

With the Magnatone amp I was modifying, the preamp section used 12AX7 tubes, so I already had the highest gain 12 volt preamp tube already installed. But let's suppose you are going for more gain and you notice a lower gain preamp tube in your particular circuit. You could always try substituting a higher gain preamp tube for a lower gain stock tube. For example, the amplification factor of a 12AU7A is 20. You could change this tube to a 12AY7 (amplification factor 44) and squeeze another 3 dB of gain! Or you could possibly use a 12AT7 that has an amplification factor of 60. The next one to try would be a 5751 (amplification factor of 80) and then finally the 12AX7 (amplification factor of 100).

EPILOGUE

There are many cool vintage hand-wired tube amps that are completely unusable in a gig situation, yet they could be useable with only a few very slight modifications. When I finished with the Magnatone, it had beautiful overdrive, rich harmonics, and plenty of sustain. I would have been proud to gig with it. In its stock condition, I would have never used it in a real live situation. When you add it all up, a few dB's here and a couple there and a few over here can add up to make a difference between a lame sounding amp and one that inspires you to play your best. And if you are worried about keeping it original, save what few resistors you remove and put them in a zip lock baggie with a written documentation of what you did. Staple the baggie into the bottom of the amp. If you ever want to sell the amp and put it back to stock, you have the original parts and you have documentation so you can remember what you did. But if it sounds so much better than stock you may never change it back.

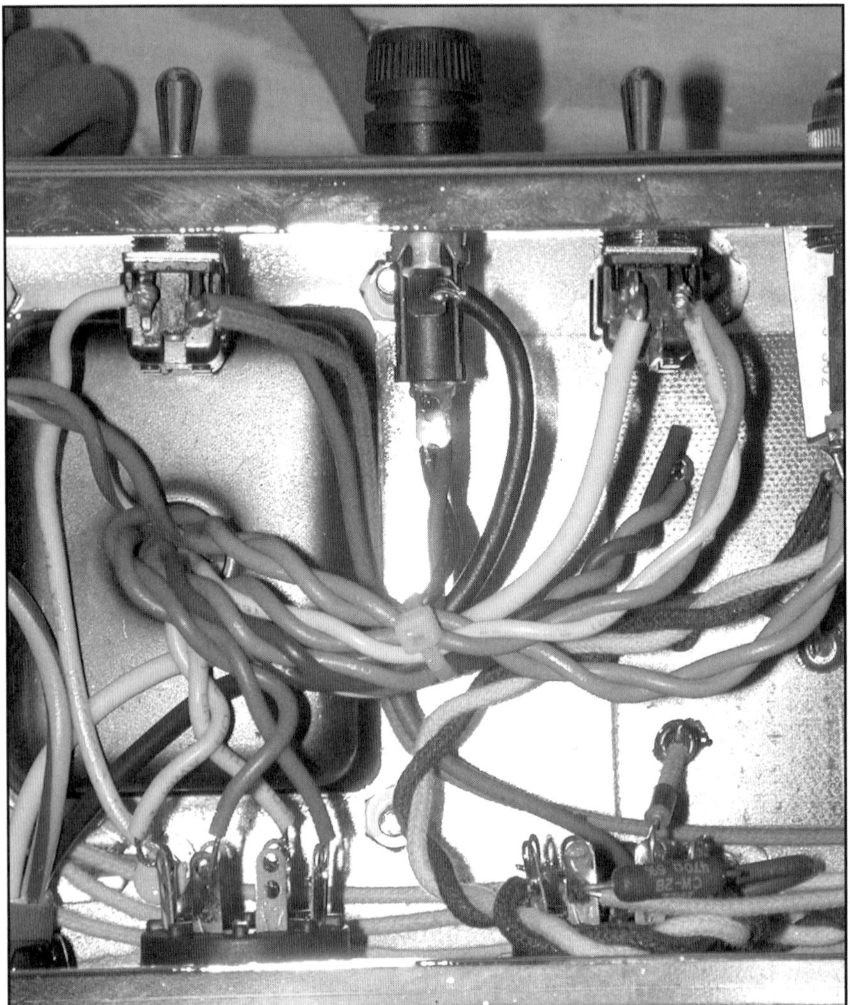

WHAT TO DO "AFTER" THE BLACKFACE MOD

Most players prefer the dynamic aliveness and organic tonal qualities of the Blackface Fender Twin Reverb to the Silverface Fender Twin Reverb, so the Silverfaces sell for considerably less. Several years ago, I published the four simple steps for converting a Silverface Fender amplifier circuit into a Blackface Fender amplifier circuit. This modification simply duplicated the circuitry of the Blackface and actually worked beautifully on most amps.

Because the Silverface amps (in general) suffered from bad layout and sloppy wiring, changing to Blackface specs and opening up the tone would sometimes unleash parasitic "ghosts" circuits. The result could manifest itself as a louder than normal noise floor or an unmusical high frequency oscillation, or even a mosquito-like sound on top of the note! The easy way out would be to abandon the Blackface modification, settle for bad tone when you could have great tone, and just put those 2000 pf caps back on the grids of the output tubes. CBS engineers added these capacitors to ground out high frequency parasitic oscillations. You removed these caps as part of the Silver to Black conversion!

If your converted amp exhibits such instability problems, I can tell you some things to do, without altering the Blackface circuit, that will more than likely "cure" the problem. Good lead dress; good layout and proper grounding should eliminate all of these instability problems.

GOOD LAYOUT

One problem with both the Silverface and the Blackface layout is the physical placement of the tone caps. These tone caps (typical value .1 mfd, .047 mfd, and 250 pf) are on both channels, and they are actually used in place of coupling caps. In other words, the tone caps ARE the coupling caps in this case. On a coupling cap, the side facing the plate of the tube is the plate circuit and the side facing away from the plate becomes the beginning of the grid circuit (of the next stage). For best layout, we should always keep grid circuits as short as possible. A long wire on a grid circuit acts as an antenna and the tube amplifies any signal that develops.

What does all this mean? The tone caps in both Silver and Black amps should have been mounted on the actual pots to which they are connected rather than the way they are on the board. To have done so would have eliminated several inches of antenna, err, hook-up wire in the grid circuit.

Look at Figure 1 and notice that this is how the Silverface normal channel comes wired stock. What we are going to do is relocate the tone caps (these are the three caps on the end of the board whose values are 250 pf, .1 mfd, and .047 mfd.) and the 100K resistor that connects the two larger tone caps with the smaller. We start by removing all three caps and the 100K resistor. We also need to remove all three wires that connect the tone caps to the treble and

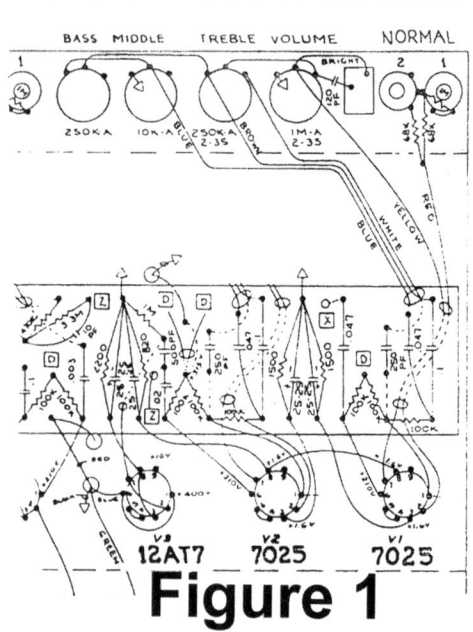

Figure 1

middle controls. These wires, shown in Figure 1, are labeled: blue, white, and brown. Your particular amp may or may not use the same color code.

As a side benefit, by moving these caps to the pots, we only need to run one wire (see Figure 2) from the tone stack to the plate resistor instead of using the three stock wires. This alone will eliminate a foot or more of excess wire per channel!

Figure 2 shows what the normal channel should look like after the three caps and the resistor are moved and a wire is installed connecting the 250 pf cap (and 100K slope resistor) to the plate resistor.

Next, in a like manner, let's do the exact same thing to the vibrato channel. Begin by removing the tone caps, slope resistor and the wires going to the treble and middle pot. Re-install the tone caps on the pots, using the 100K slope resistor to connect the 250 pf to the other two caps. Remember to install a wire from the 250 pf and 100K slope resistor junction to the associated plate resistor that terminates on pin #1 of V2. When you are done, the wiring for the vibrato channel tone circuit should be wired exactly like the tone circuit of the normal channel. The circuit will be the same electronically as before. We are not modifying the circuit, but just getting rid of a lot of wire and shortening the grid circuits for both channels.

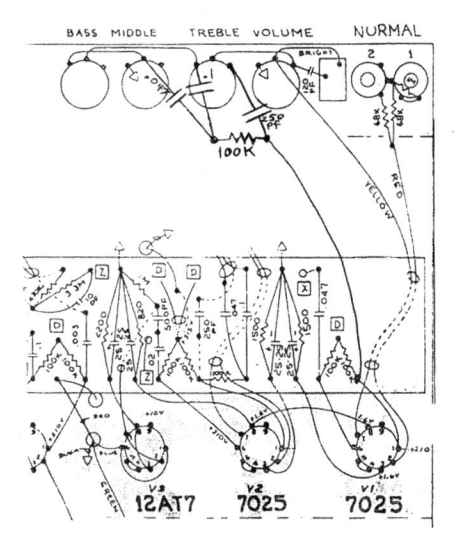

Figure 2

GOOD LEAD DRESS

The next thing we want to do is remove extra wire feeding the reverb, speed and intensity controls. In all, there are five wires that go from the board to those three controls. Unsolder the wires, one at a time, on the end connecting to the pot. Shorten the wire as much as possible and re-solder. Again, we are not modifying anything electronically, just removing a lot of extra wire.

There are four wires that need to be replaced with shielded wire. These are all long grid wires that cannot be shortened. When you cannot shorten a grid wire, the next best thing is to shield it. This helps keep it from becoming so much of an antenna. The problem with shielding is that shielded cable has capacitance and therefore can cause a loss of high-end. Therefore, when choosing cable for this modification, opt for low-capacitance shielded wire. To minimize the capacitance, this wire should be kept as short as possible.

Look again at Figure 2. Notice the wires on the input jack and volume control marked red and yellow respectively. (Your particular amp may or may not use the same color-coding.) These terminate on pin #2 and pin #7 (respectively) of V1. Replace each wire with shielded wire. Terminate the shielding to ground only on one end. I like to ground on the faceplate side. I ground the shielded input wire on the input jack and I like to ground the shielded volume pot wire on the volume pot. Another little tip: Install the tube-side connection first. Start by stripping the insulation and shielding back on the tube-side end of the wire. Try stretching the outer insulation back over where the shielding was trimmed away. This prevents accidental shorting (of anything) to the shielding.

Let's finish up the lead dress by shortening all other grid wires in the amp. On the preamp tubes, the wire that feeds pin #2 and pin #7 is the grid wire. On the output tubes, the wire that feeds the 1500 ohm resistor that is located on pin #1 of the output tube is the grid wire. Remember, when it comes to grid wires, shorter is better!

PROPER GROUNDING

Under the cap pan, there are several filter caps. The main (totem pole) filters connect to the rectifier, the screen supply filter, phase inverter supply filter, and the preamp supply filter. If you lift the circuit board that the capacitors are mounted to and look at the ground-side of the capacitors, you will find the negative connection on the screen supply filter connected to all the other preamp and phase inverter filter's (negative) grounded side! There is a ground wire attached to this circuit and the wire goes through the chassis and grounds directly on the grounding buss. There is also a different ground wire that goes from the groundside of the totem pole main filter, through the chassis, and grounded near the power transformer. The problem is that the screen supply filter should not be grounded with the preamp filter grounds. It should be grounded with the main totem pole filter.

Here's how to fix it. With the filter capacitor circuit board lifted, disconnect the screen supply filter ground from the preamp and phase inverter grounds. Now you run a single wire from the screen supply filter groundside (on the board) to the same ground as your main totem pole filter (also on the board). I like to run this wire underneath the board so it is hidden.

CONCLUSION

At this point, your amp probably sounds wonderful. If it does not sound wonderful, it might be time for a simple overhaul which would include: replacing all filter capacitors, replacing all tubes and re-biasing output tubes, changing any resistors that are out of tolerance, and perhaps changing out the coupling caps to Sprague Orange Drops or Mallory 150 series.

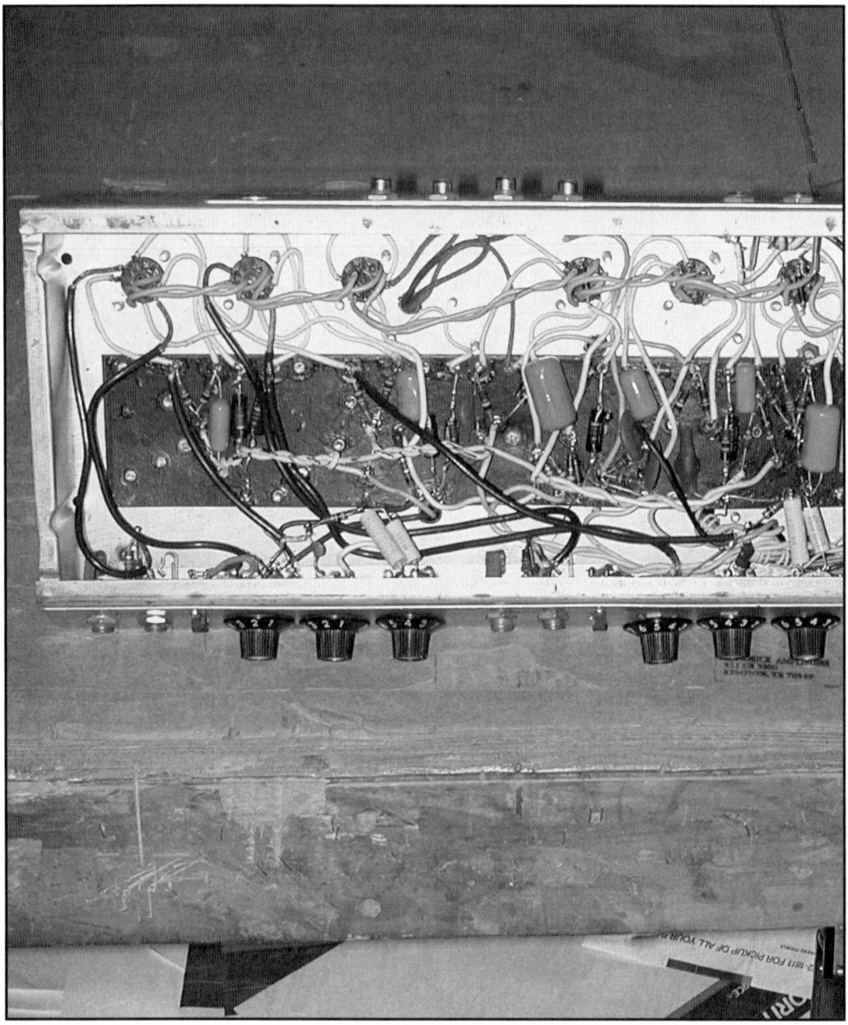

TWEED DELUXE TONE FROM A BLACK OR SILVERFACE AMP

Sometimes particular modifications come from customer's ideas and tonal requests. One of my good customers uses a Silverface Deluxe Reverb that was recently converted to Blackface specs. For versatility, he wanted a tweed Deluxe tone added to his Blackface tone. Since he was not using the normal channel for anything anyway; he asked me to make the normal channel into a tweed Deluxe preamp circuit. He wanted to use an AB switching device to go from Blackface tone (vibrato channel) to tweed tone (what used to be the normal channel). This gave him both tones, but without having to schlep another amp to the gig.

This seems like a simple task except the Blackface/Silverface circuitry is much different than the tweed circuitry.

What are the differences?

There are obvious differences such as fixed bias (Black and Silverface) verses cathode bias (tweed). And there are other differences such as the Black and Silverface having more loss in the tone section than the tweed.

Electronic differences include the distributive load phase inverter (50s) verses the grounded grid phase inverter (60s). The distributive load phase inverter actually loses gain, while the grounded grid type picks up gain.

Also, the gain in general of the tweed circuit is much less than its Black or Silver cousin. Even though the gain is less on the tweed, the tweed seems to have more distortion. Why is this? Well for one thing, the tweed is voiced for more mids, which have a tendency to break up easier. Also not to be overlooked, the tweed Deluxe does not use a voltage divider for the volume control.

The tweed Deluxe does not use the conventional voltage divider volume control!

How does the volume control work if it isn't a voltage divider? It loads down the source impedance to reduce gain! This results in a distinctive distorted tone, unlike the Black or Silver counterparts. This is a circuit that I have used myself on many Kendrick amps. Boogie used this type of volume on the first Boogies. It really does have a unique sound.

Here's the challenge: make a circuit that sounds like a tweed Deluxe, but by compensating for the fact that we are using a Deluxe Reverb output stage and phase inverter.

LET'S GET STARTED!

Remove the chassis from the cabinet and inspect the normal channel wiring. It should look like Figure 1. Remember when modifying a vintage amp, never drill holes or lose parts. If you are going to take any small parts out, put them in a plastic bag and staple them to the inside wall of the amplifier cabinet. They won't get lost. If you ever sell the amp, or if you want to put it back to stock, there will be no question as to the whereabouts of original parts.

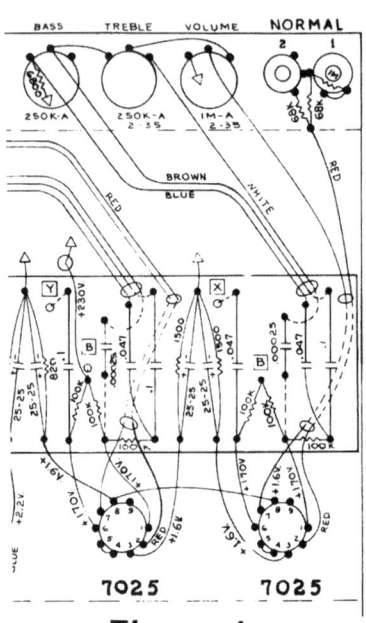

Figure 1

PARTS LIST

Here are the parts you will need to do this modification:
One 1 meg audio taper pot
One .005 mfd capacitor 100 volt or better
One 500-pf cap 100 volt or better
One .02 mfd capacitor 400 volt
One 10 K ½ watt resistor
One 100 K ½ watt resistor
One 470 K ½ watt resistor

280   Tube Guitar Amplifier Essentials

Let's rewire the channel.

We are going to rewire the 1st preamp tube and the volume and tone control. We will also install a 470K mixer resistor (not shown, but more on this later).

Using Figure 2 as a guide, rewire the channel. You will use many existing parts. You will not be using the bass control, but I would recommend leaving the pot installed for looks and safekeeping. You will need to change the treble pot to a 1 meg to make the tone control. Pay particular attention to the 100K resistor that goes from pin #6 to the board junction of the .02 mfd and the 10K.

I used the existing .1 mfd tone cap as a coupling cap. You want to leave it where it is, but replace the 100K slope resistor with a straight wire.

You will notice that figure 2 does not show the 470K ohm resistor that is listed in the parts list. If you look at point X on Figure 2, you will notice it goes to a 220K resistor that feeds the phase inverter. In fact, the output of the vibrato channel also feeds a 220K resistor. These two resistors apex together to feed the input capacitor of the phase inverter. This point is where the channels mix together into the phase inverter. If you are not sure where to find this, look at the phase inverter tube next to the power tubes and follow pin #2 back to the board. It will go to a capacitor and the other end of the capacitor will have the two 220K resistors — one for each channel. The 220K resistor coming from the normal channel gets changed to a 470K and you are done.

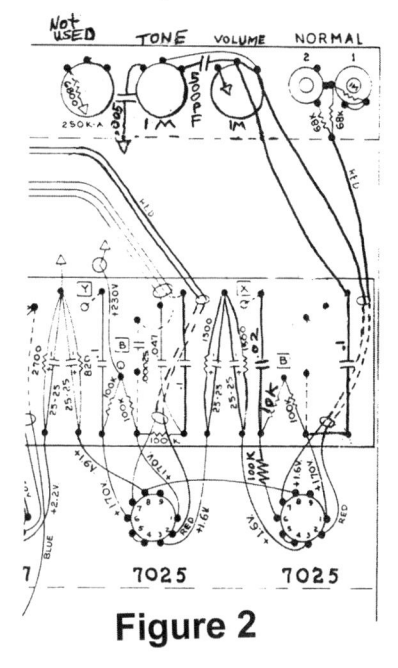

Figure 2

HOW DID I DESIGN IT?

I took a decibel meter and checked the gain of a tweed Deluxe style amp (Kendrick 2112) that was tubed with a 12AX7 on the first stage. I put signal (about 125 millivolts) on the input jack and zeroed out my decibel meter. I then checked the gain by putting the decibel meter on the grid (pin #5) of each power tube. With the volume control maxed, I measured about 30 dB preamp gain on one tube and 32 dB on the other. Now I knew I needed about 32 dB gain overall in designing this tweed channel modification.

I rewired the normal channel Deluxe to tweed specs. I checked decibels gain again and ended up with about 45 dB gain. I needed to lose some gain. I did this by using a voltage divider on the second stage plate circuit. Instead of using a 100K plate resistor, I used two resistors in series, a 10K and a 100K. The resistors are situated so that the signal is taken off the 10K. This means the 100K drops gain while the 10K is the load resistor. This lowered my gain to about 35 dB. I then changed the 220K mixer resistor with a 470K and I was there. There were other ways to lose gain, but I felt these methods would give the best overall performance.

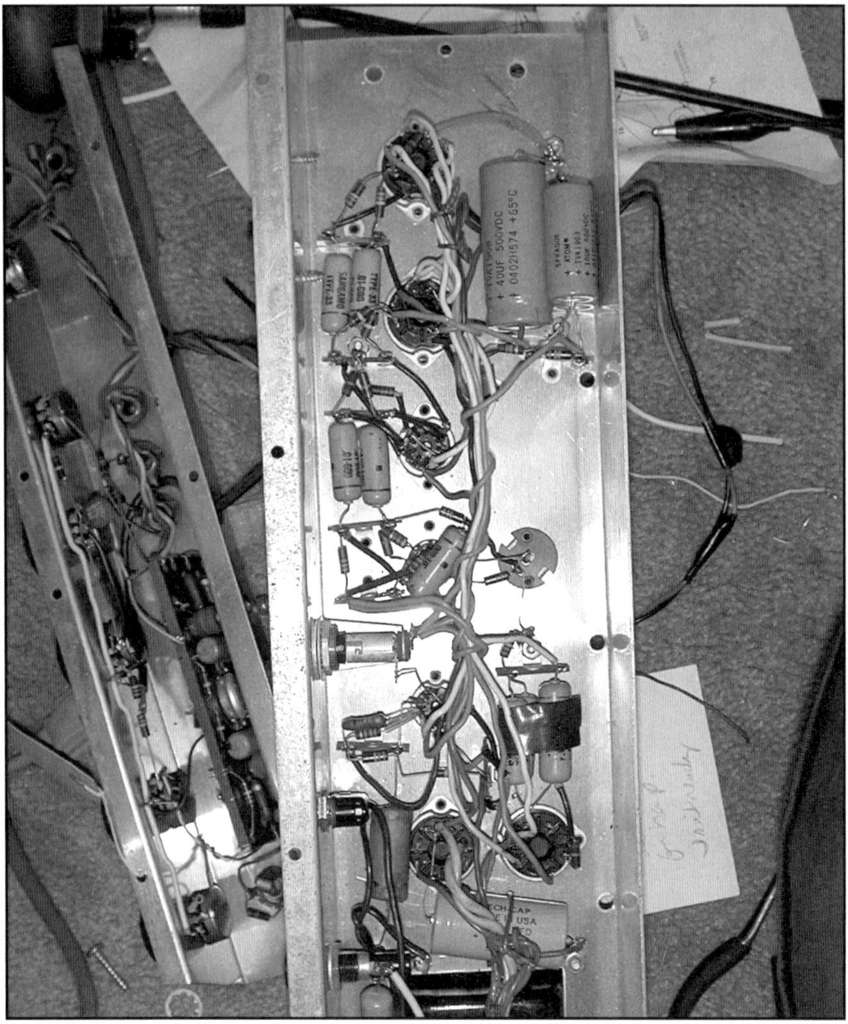

HARP AMP SECRETS AND TIPS

Before 1993, when I designed the first tube amp specifically for blues harmonica, little research had been done on how to make a tube amplifier sound best for harp. We all know that tube circuits can be voiced to perform a certain way, but the question is, "How should they be voiced for harp?" In addition, harp players use "industrial grade" high-impedance vintage PA microphones such as the Astatic and the Green Bullet. These type microphones are prone to feedback.

I am going to share some of my research with you and show you how to modify an existing tube amplifier for use with a blues harmonica; or you can build your own harp amp.

Although I had previously spent time with Kim Wilson (The Fabulous Thunderbirds) listening to various speakers and speaker configurations to determine what was best for harp; it was the internationally famous blues harp player, Paul Orta (The Kingpins), that convinced me to design the first tube amp specifically for harp. Paul brought in an old wooden cabinet National tube guitar amplifier. This particular amp originally belonged to Jimmie Vaughan and was his first guitar amp. It sounded horrible for guitar. It was over-compressed without any clean tone whatsoever. Although I did not date it, I would guess it to be late 40s. It had a field coil speaker driven by two 6L6Gs running Class A push-pull. Paul had bought this amp because he liked the tone for harmonica, but he found he could not use the amp in a live gig situation. It was not loud enough and there was too much hum. Even if the amp was miked through the PA, the hum level was beyond usable. Paul loved the tone of this particular amp and felt it to be the definitive tone for harp. We just needed to get rid of the hum and increase the volume about five fold.

Paul asked me to analyze this amp to find the essence of its tone.

I would then use what I learned to design and build the perfect harp amp for him.

After studying the old National Amplifier, I broke its essence down into basics. I believe these basics to be perfect for harp amp tones. In the process of analyzing this amp, I stumbled onto a way to fatten the tone and eliminate feedback (more on this later.) Here are the basics along with an explanation:

1. Low plate voltage on the preamp tubes. The National had very low voltage on the plates of the preamp tubes. This would be a terrible idea for guitar but worked great for harp. The plate voltage determines both the frequency response and the headroom. With low voltage, the tube breaks up at almost any volume and the frequency band shifts to a lower register. Since harp frequencies are relatively low compared to guitar, this lower voltage fattens the notes while helping reduce high frequency feedback. Although the National had voltages running around 95 to 100 volts, I experimented with different voltages and found 80 to 90 volts to be ideal for harp.

If you have a guitar amp you are modifying for harp, you could simply increase the value of the power supply dropping resistor that feeds the plate resistor of the preamp tubes. Since preamp tubes draw very little current, the dropping resistor may have to be replaced with a much larger value. I would use a decade box in place of the dropping resistor and by trial and error find the appropriate value resistor. Do not change the plate resistor, only the power supply dropping resistor!

2. Larger than normal coupling caps. The exact value of a coupling cap determines how much lower frequencies get through the circuit. Larger values simply let more signal pass. Through experimentation, I found the .1 uf coupling cap to be best for harmonica. Of course, if you were modifying an existing guitar amp, you would simply change the coupling caps (typically .01 uf or .02 uf and sometimes .047 uf) to a .1 uf. You would use a 400 or 600 volt rating.

3. Simple two-stage design. Less is more. If you get more stages of gain, you are amplifying the feedback problem and you will just have to turn down the volume. This explains why the normal channel on a Blackface Fender works better for harp than the Vibrato channel.

The National actually had only one stage of gain and a paraphase style inverter that acted as another stage of gain. A tweed Champ, tweed Princeton and tweed Deluxe are examples of amps with simple two-stage design. It is interesting to note that all of these amps work great for harp.

4. Paraphase style Phase Inverter. This obsolete design has not been used since the mid fifties. The paraphase inverter takes advantage of the fact that a tube inverts the signal by 180 degrees. A very small signal is divided off the signal path that is driving the first output tube. The small signal is run through another preamp tube, which drives the other output tube. Since running it through the additional preamp tube inverts the phase by 180 degrees (with respect to the signal driving the first output tube), phase inversion is achieved.

You can not get a clean tone with a paraphase style inverter because one of the output tubes is being fed by a signal that was run through an extra tube. Any distortion introduced by this extra stage is amplified by one output tube, but not on the other. The result is a "not so clean" tone.

There are two types of paraphase inverters: the fixed and the self-balancing. A good example of the fixed paraphase inverter would be the 5C3 Fender Deluxe. A good example of the self-balancing type would be the 5D3 Fender Deluxe.

The National amp had a fixed paraphase inverter, but I opted for the self-balancing type instead. In the self-balancing type, a resistor that is common to both circuits goes to ground. If one side is driving too hard, it phase cancels some of the signal developed across this common resistor, thus balancing everything out. This is where I had a happy accident.

5. A cathode-biased, Class "A" push-pull output stage. Cathode biased amps are generally more compressed with a more singing quality. In general, a spongier response is achieved. The Class "A" push-pull output stage simply means the tubes are driven by a phase inverter and they never go into cutoff.

I used a 250 ohm 10 watt cathode resistor with a 33 uf 100 volt bypass cap. I like going with a higher voltage rating on the cathode capacitor because the higher voltage cap can take plenty of heat and still be within its operating parameters.

6. High idle plate current in the output stage. The high idle current is typical of Class "A" style amplifiers. The output tubes on the National were running about 60 mA per 6L6 tube. Since the National used 6L6G tubes (rated for only 19 watts plate dissipation), I opted to run 6L6GC (30 watts plate dissipation) at an even higher 70 mA per tube.

If you are converting a guitar amp from fixed bias to cathode bias, the cathode resistor, by developing a voltage on it, makes the tube "think" it is operating at a lower plate voltage. Why? Because the tube only "sees" the difference between the cathode voltage and the plate voltage.

Let's say you have a Super Reverb that normally operates at 445 volts, and you change from stock "fixed bias" to "cathode bias." You add the typical cathode resistor/cathode capacitor to the output tubes and measure 45 volts across the cathode resistor. This means the tube only "sees" the difference between the 445 volts plate voltage and the 45 volts cathode voltage. It performs "as if" it were operating at 400 volts. Given this scenario, one could see how we could "idle up" quite high compared to stock. Perhaps 60 mA per side would work fine without the tubes glowing cherry red.

7. Tube rectifier. Of course, the National amp had a tube rectifier. I would always recommend a tube rectifier with a harp amp setup. You need the compression that a tube rectifier gives. I used the GZ34, which is my favorite rectifier tube.

If you have an amp that does not have a rectifier tube, one can be added by using a 5 volt 5 amp auxiliary filament transformer and an octal tube socket.

HOW TO STOP FEEDBACK AND FATTEN THE TONE

I told you about the self-balancing paraphase inverter and I told you I had a happy accident. When I was designing the harp amp for Paul Orta, I thought I would use a potentiometer instead of a fixed resistor so I could dial in the exact value by ear. To my surprise, I found that if I deliberately made the waveform non-symmetrical, the harmonica tone actually fattened up!

Here's the other part of the accident. I found if I connected the speaker reverse polarity with respect to which half of the waveform is bigger, then the threshold of feedback goes up. This means the amp can be turned up to ridiculous volume levels before acoustic feedback occurs! I decided to leave the potentiometer as a "waveform symmetry" control so Paul could fatten his tone while reducing feedback!

I will never forget the time Paul called me after doing an outdoor gig with his new harp amp and said for the first time in his career a sound man actually asked him to "turn it down." It seemed he was burying the drummer and the guitar player in the mix!

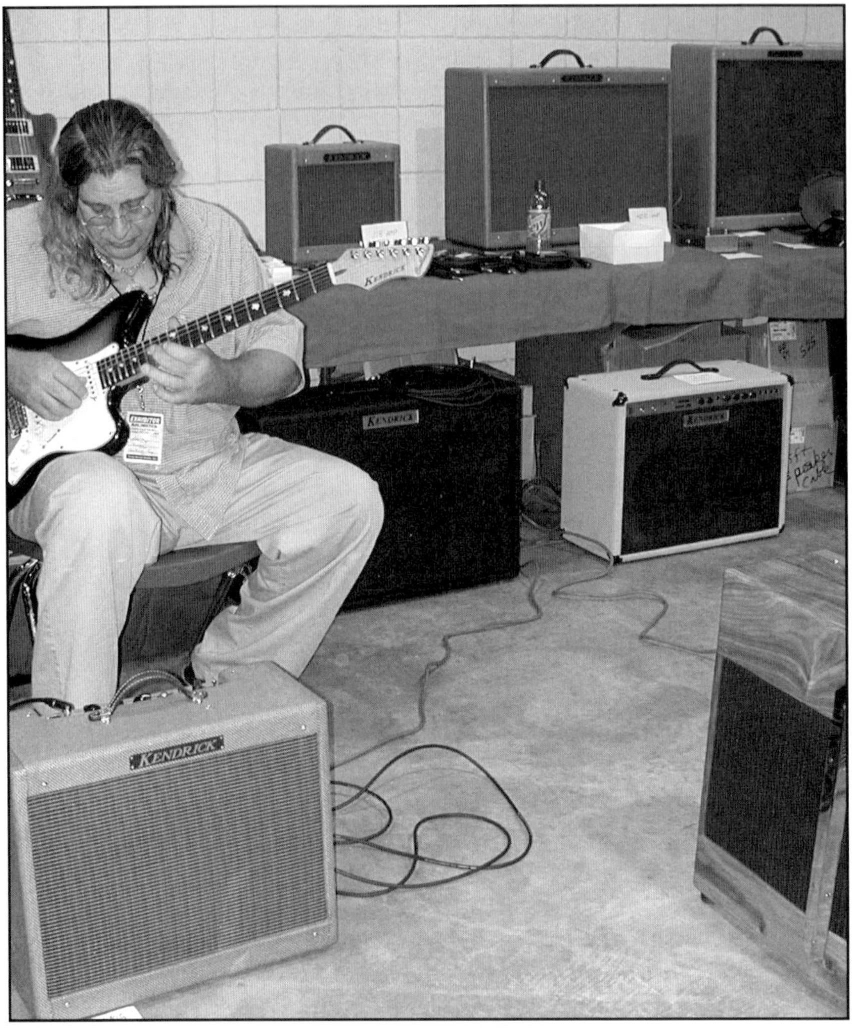
KENDRICK

"BEEFING UP" YOUR TUBE GUITAR AMP FOR MORE HEADROOM

Most stock tube guitar amps work great for rock and blues, but what if you are playing jazz or country and you need a louder, cleaner sound? Or maybe you just like to play loud and clean. Alternatively, you may have a tube guitar amp that you are setting up for bass guitar or steel guitar, or maybe even keyboards. How can you "beef up" your tube amp for more headroom? Here are some ideas to modify that tube amp and make it give you the biggest clean sound. You may want to try one or more of these modifications to enhance headroom.

1. "BEEF UP" THE OUTPUT TRANSFORMER — You can get greater clean from a "two output tube" amp by using a "four output tube" output transformer — Output transformers are wound to a turns ratio and not to a specific impedance. That is to say that a Twin output transformer which is wound for four output tubes going into a 4 ohm speaker load will have the same turns ratio as an output transformer with two output tubes going into an 8 ohm speaker load. It would then follow that you could use an 80 or 100 watt output transformer on a two output tube amp, simply by hooking it to a speaker load that is twice what one would normally use for 4 output tubes. This improves clean headroom dramatically.

My friend, Joe Barden, used to take those cheesy 2x10 Brown Vibroverb reissue amps and replace the stock output transformer with a Twin output transformer. He then changed to an 8 ohm 15" JBL speaker (complete with new baffleboard) and voila — instant Stevie Ray Vaughan.

2. USE "BEEFIER" OUTPUT TUBES — In most amps, using a more powerful output tube will result in a cleaner sound. The 6V6, 6L6, 5881,

EL37, 7581A, 6550, KT66, KT77, KT88, KT90 all have the same pin out. What is different is their filament current, biasing and, of course, power output. When changing to a different type of output tube, how do you know if the power transformer can handle the filament current of the new tube? Simple; just check the filament voltage (pin #2, pin #7). If your filament voltage is stable at 6.2 to 6.5 volts, the power transformer can tolerate the change. If the new tube is drawing too much filament current, you will know because the filament voltage will drop to below 6.1 volts. If your power transformer does not like the new output tube, you can still use it; you will just have to install an auxiliary filament transformer. On Fender amps, I like to disconnect the preamp tube filaments from the main power transformer and just connect the preamp tubes to the auxiliary filament transformer. This gives me an extra two amperes of filament current for the output tubes, which is plenty in almost all cases. (Note: When adding an auxiliary filament transformer, make sure there is a ground reference to the new filament supply. If the filament winding is center-tapped, use it; or else ground one leg of the new filament supply. Or you could make an artificial center-tap with two 100-ohm resistors — each tied to a leg of the filament winding and to ground).

You would want to replace the 6V6, 6L6, EL37 or the 5881 with the 6550, 7581A, KT66, KT77, KT88, or KT90. For example, we could take a Deluxe Reverb that normally uses 6V6's, and replace the tubes with KT66's. (The KT in KT66 stands for Kinkless Tetrode. This tube can be used for push-pull and still have that single-ended, class A, and flute-like roundness. The waveform does not have the normal "kink" as with other tubes used in push-pull). The KT66 is a more powerful version of the 6L6. With the KT style tubes, the power increases as suffix numbers increase. In other words, the KT77 is a more powerful version of the KT66 and the KT88 is more than the KT77, etc.

There is a KT66, being made in Slovakia today, that sounds almost exactly like the original Genelex KT66. This tube is extremely round with good headroom. I set up a Bandmaster last week for a bass player and we used the KT66 Slovakian tube. This tube was too long to fit into the Bandmaster, but only by a $1/16$ of an inch. I reinstalled the output tube sockets and mounted them from the inside of the chassis (as opposed to outside stock mounting) to make it work. This gave me an extra ⅛"! They sounded great. Of course, I replaced the output transformer with a Kendrick 4212A (Kendrick's Tweed Twin copy) which gave me a bass guitar tone like a huge bass flute! This setup actually sounded great for guitar as well. It reminded me of the Vox AC30 tone — cutting through with the roundness of the fundamental, plenty of British bark; but with the clean holding together well.

Changing from 6L6, 5881, or 6V6 to a 7581A or a 6550 can also help headroom. The 7581A can handle 5 watts more (per tube) than a 6L6GC. The 6550 is yet even more powerful than the 7581A!

3. "Beef Up" the main B+ filter caps — It takes power for tubes to have headroom. The output tubes get their power from the main filters. These filters connect to the center-tap of the output transformer. Increase the value of these two or three times to get improved headroom. For example, a stock Fender Blackface amp might use two 70 mfd in series. When you put two caps in series, the total capacitance is only half of the value of one of those capacitors. That is to say that a Blackface Twin only has 35 mfd. of filtering on the mains! This simply is not enough. I like to change those 70 mfd caps to 220 mfd. Put two of those in series and we end up with 110 mfd of filtering. Now that will provide some punch and clarity when you slam a low "E"!

4. "Beef Up" the screen supply filter caps — Stabilizing the voltage on the screen supply tightens the envelope of the clean sound. Look at the filter capacitor that feeds the screen resistors. Whatever the value, double it — for best clean. Most amps use a 20 mfd capacitor for the screen supply. I like to use 40 mfd for this position.

Caution: You do not want to increase any filter capacitor values that feed the preamp. The preamp section of an amp is RC (resistor capacitor) coupled and to increase the microfarad value of filter caps feeding the preamp will hurt your tone! Such is not the case with the main filters or the screen supply filter.

5. "Beef Up" the rectifier — When we "beef up" the main filters and the screen supply filters; we may need to improve the rectifier circuit. The solid-state rectifier will produce higher supply voltage and therefore more headroom. If the rectifier circuit is solid state, change the stock diodes to a higher amperage rating. For example, if the amp uses 1N4007 diodes, which are rated at one ampere; change to either the 1N5399, rated at 1½ amps or the 1N5408 that is rated at

3 amps. If the amplifier has a tube rectifier, replace it with a solid-state replacement. I like to make my own rectifier replacer by using a male octal socket (could be made from discarded output tube base), and six diodes. Details for making this can be found on page 97 of my second book, *Tube Amp Talk for the Guitarist and Tech*.

6. "BEEF UP" THE VOLTAGE GOING TO THE PREAMP TUBES — With preamp tubes, higher plate voltage means greater headroom. This voltage can be adjusted, but you do not adjust the plate resistors. Leave those 100K plate resistors alone! The power supply of a tube amp will have a power resistor coming from the output stage, that feeds voltage to the plate resistors of the preamp stages. You usually only have to decrease the first one of the series and all preamp voltages will go up. This alone will give better headroom for each stage of gain. You increase plate voltage by decreasing the value of the power resistor that feeds the plate resistors. There will be a filter capacitor tied to each power resistor.

7. "LESS GAIN" IS "MORE CLEAN" ON THE PREAMP TUBES — When we replace a 12AX7 style tube (amplification factor of 100) with another tube of the same "12A—" style, but with lesser gain, for example a 12AY7 (amplification factor of 44); we will clean up the sound. Less gain per stage results in less distortion. Less distortion equals more clean. You could also experiment with the 12AT7 (amplification factor of 60), or a 12AU7 (amplification factor of 17).

I remember a few years ago manufacturing a bass amp that was based on a 4x10 Bassman 5F6A circuit. By actual A/B experimentation we found using the 12AY7 for the first preamp tube, a 12AT7 for the second, and a 12AU7 for the third (phase inverter) gave us the best clean tone. Likewise, you could experiment yourself by A/B experimentation with simple tube substitution, to determine what works best with your amp.

8. "BEEF UP" THE SPEAKER CABLE THAT FEEDS YOUR SPEAKERS — Unless your output transformer goes directly to your speakers, now would be a good time to look at your speaker cable. If you want good headroom, the speaker wire has to be big enough to get the current to the speaker. Choose big wire, such as 12 gauge or 14 gauge.

9. "BEEF UP" CLEAN WITH CLEANER SPEAKERS — The speakers are what "makes" the sound wave. Why not critically listen to your

speakers to see if they are giving you the tone you need. Are they wired correctly? They must be wired in correct polarity so that the cones are moving in the same direction at the same time. Does the impedance match the amp? You will get the cleanest sound when the speaker impedance matches the amplifier impedance. Do you like the clarity of the speakers you are using?

Whether you choose one of these modifications or possibly a combination of several, one thing is for sure: It is good tone only if you like the way it sounds. If you try one of these mods and do not like the way it sounds on your amp, put it back to stock. These modifications are merely suggestions for you to try. The acid test remains: Does it give you the tone you want?

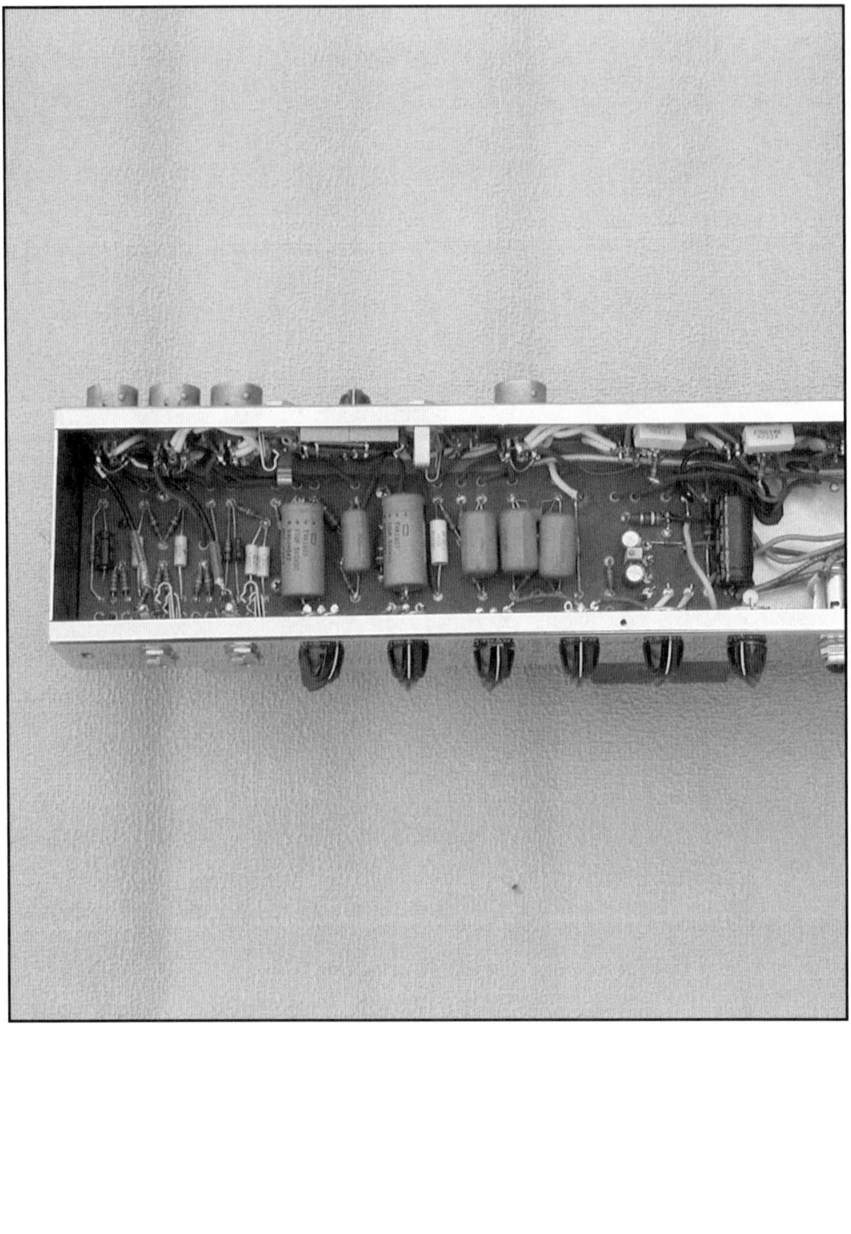

CONVERTING YOUR NORMAL CHANNEL TO BRITISH

There are many Blackface and Silverface Fender amps of which the normal channel is never used. If you don't mind giving up your vibrato, I can show you how to get that big British bark out of the Normal Channel of your Blackface or Silverface Pro Reverb, Super Reverb, Deluxe Reverb, Twin Reverb, Vibrolux Reverb, Bandmaster Reverb or Showman. It is a simple modification that can be performed with only two capacitors and five or six resistors.

With the normal channel sounding like a Vox AC30 at lower volumes and an overdriven Marshall at higher volumes, one could switch between the stock reverb channel and the modified normal channel and have quite a tonal palette. All of this is possible, without defacing the amp or drilling any holes. This mod is completely reversible; just remember to save the old parts.

PARTS NEEDED
The additional parts you will need are:
One 100 K ohm ½ watt resistor
One 2700 ohm ½ watt resistor
One 10 K ohm ½ watt resistor
Two 330 K ohm ½ watt resistors
One .68 microfarad (25 volt or better) capacitor
One .02 microfarad 400 volt capacitor
One resistor (optional), for adjusting midrange amount

Even though this is a simple mod, don't try it unless you feel confident in your ability. Perhaps you could enlist a trustworthy helper or you could take it to a competent shop.

PREPARATION FOR THE MODIFICATION

To start with, you will remove the chassis. If you look at the chassis it will resemble this picture.

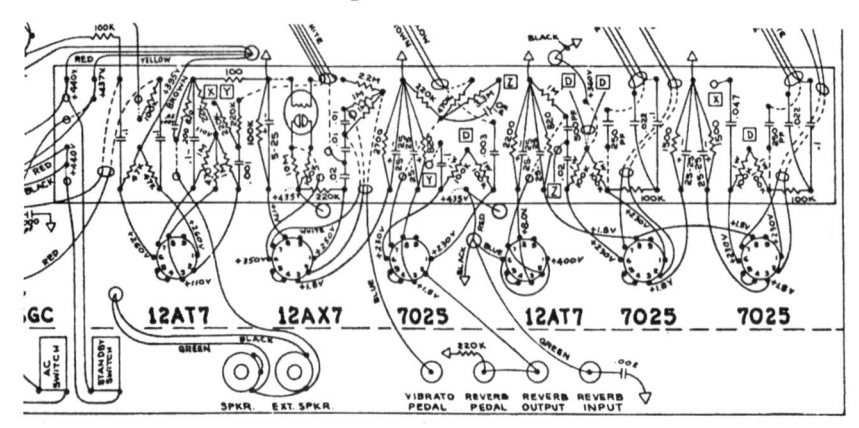

We will basically remove everything from the vibrato tube (12AX7) except the heater wires (pin #9 and pins #4 + #5), and the cathode wire (pin #3). All of the associated vibrato tube components on the board are also removed.

Here's a hint: you will notice there is a wire coming out of the chassis and terminating on the board near the vibrato tube. Leave this wire connected because it is live (400+ volts) and by leaving it on the board, you don't have to worry about it shorting against something else in the amp.

Also, you will be removing the cathode resistor and the cathode capacitor from the first preamp tube. Look at pin #3 of the first preamp tube and trace it back to the board. You will notice it goes to a 1500 ohm resistor with a 25 microfarad cap across it. Remove both of these components.

When you have removed all of the parts, your circuit board should resemble this picture (top of next page).

LET'S START BUILDING

First, we will replace the cathode components of the first preamp tube (going to pin #3) with a 2700 ohm resistor and a .68 microfarad capacitor. These two components will replace the 1500 ohm and the 25 microfarad you removed earlier.

Second, you will need to locate the two 220K resistors that are feeding the input of the phase inverter. If you don't know which ones these are, look at the 12AT7 preamp tube next to the vibrato tube. Look at the drawing and you will see these resistors. In the amp, each resistor has a wire going to it. But in the drawing, these points are labeled with "X" and "Y." Unsolder both wires. Put the wire that went to "Y" on the other 220K resistor (that was marked with an "X"). The wire that went to "X" will be soldered to a 330K resistor later. More on this later.

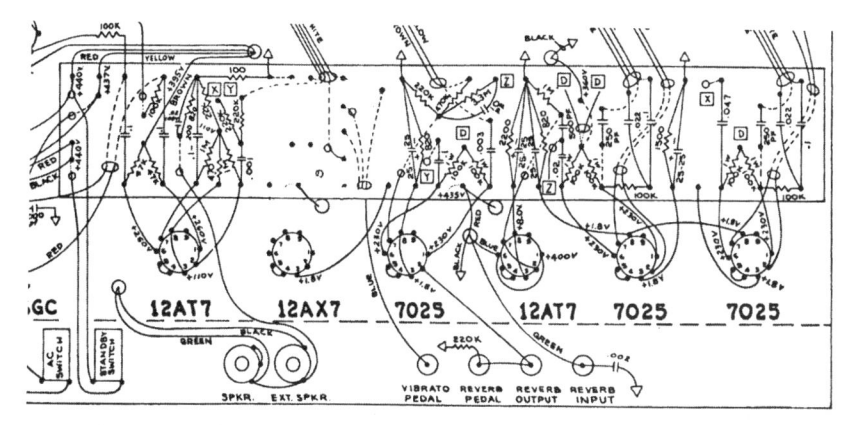

Third, look at the back of the intensity pot. Disconnect the wire going to the right side of the intensity pot.

Fourth, solder in the .02 capacitor, the 10K cathode resistor, the two 330K voltage divider resistors and the 100K plate resistor. Refer to this drawing.

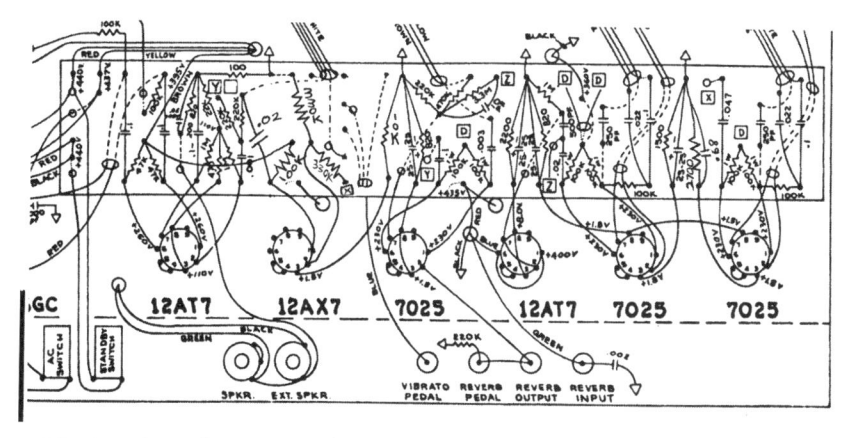

Notice that the 100K plate resistor gets its power supply voltage from the phase inverter supply. You will simply solder a jumper wire from the two phase inverter resistors to the 100K.

Notice that the .02 microfarad capacitor connects between what

Converting Your Normal Channel to British 299

used to be point "Y" and the 100K plate resistor.

Notice how the two 330K resistors are situated. One is grounded. Solder a wire from the junction of the two resistors to pin 2 of the tube.

Remember the wire that originally went to point "X"? That one goes to one of the 330K resistors. Refer to the drawing and you will see we have relabeled point "X" to be the proper end of the 330K resistor.

Hint: since some of the eyelets have wires going to them from the underside of the board, I highly recommend you assemble the components of this mod in the exact location indicated by the drawing.

Double-check your work against the drawing to see if it matches. When you are certain you have completed the mod correctly, plug the amp in and play some hip licks.

Notice how the gain from the normal channel picked up a few dB. Also, notice that barky British thang coming out of the normal channel. Notice how it overdrives when driven hard.

If you have a midrange control, you may want to dime it. If you don't have a midrange control, you will have a resistor (probably a 6.8K) soldered to the back of the normal channel bass control. If you feel you need more midrange, take a 25K pot and temporarily substitute it for the resistor. Dial in the best tone. Being careful not to disturb the pots setting, remove it from the circuit and measure the resistance with a good meter.

Find a resistor of this same value and replace the resistor on the back of the bass control. You are done with the mod. Now put it all back in the cabinet and jam out. Get yourself an AB switch and go from bark to chime.

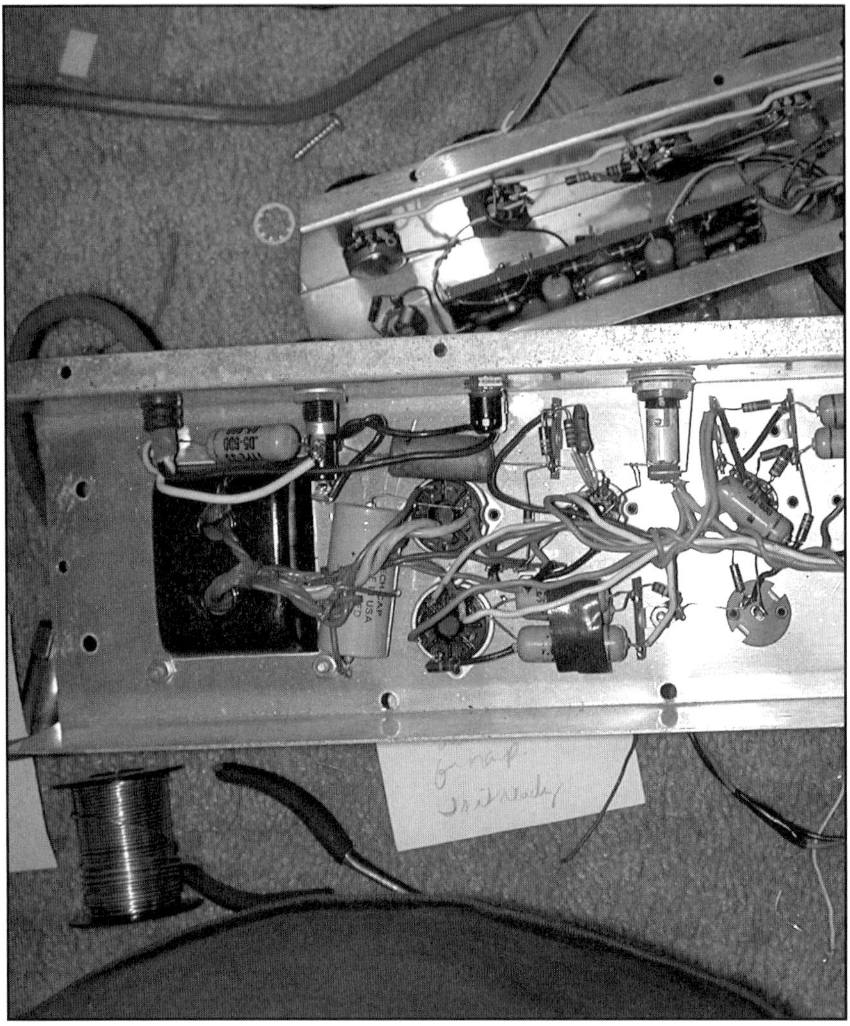

SAVE THAT BLACKFACE DELUXE!

Most amp enthusiasts know the Blackface Fender Deluxe amp lacks the gain of its more popular brother, the Deluxe Reverb. When the reverb circuitry was added to the Deluxe circuit, an extra gain stage (extra 12AX7 tube) was used to mix the reverb with the dry signal. In simple terms, the Deluxe Reverb has an extra stage of gain the non-reverb Deluxe is missing.

An obvious cure would be to sacrifice the vibrato circuit. This would free the 12AX7 (used for the vibrato) for another stage of gain. One could simply duplicate the circuitry of the Deluxe Reverb, but that would be a major undertaking and not easily reversible. Let's look at some easier cures that require a minimal amount of modification. In fact, all of the tricks I will suggest require only a wire moved or a one-resistor-value-change mod. These can easily be put back to stock and most importantly; no holes are drilled in the amp chassis.

USE A FOOT PEDAL

Perhaps the easiest cure of all would be to try a clean-boost foot pedal—like the Klon, Kendrick Buffalo Pfuz, Electro-Harmonix LPB1. The idea is to feed the amp more signal at the input to afford greater gain when the signal gets to the output tubes. Using a guitar with a hotter pickup may also make a favorable difference.

INCREASE THE PHASE INVERTER OUTPUT

PARTS NEEDED: a ½ watt 10K resistor (brown/black/orange).

Remove the chassis from the cabinet and look at the phase inverter tube (the little preamp tube next to the output tubes). You'll notice pins #7 and #2 have wires that connect to the board. Each wire goes to the board and connects to a 1 meg resistor (brown/black/green). Both

1 meg resistors apex and connect to a 22K resistor (red/red/orange). Replace the 22K resistor with a 10K resistor, and you're done.

HOW IT WORKS: voltage develops across the 22K resistor as current flows through the resistor to the cathode of the tube. The tube only "sees" the difference between the cathode voltage and the plate voltage. In fact, that is the only voltage that is real for the tube. For example, if you had 180 volts on the plate and 80 volts on the cathode, the tube is really only "seeing" 100 volts. If we decrease the long-tail cathode resistor value (stock was the 22K), then less D.C. voltage will develop across the cathode circuit. With less cathode voltage, the tube sees more voltage across itself. More voltage will give more gain.

DECREASE THE AMOUNT OF NEGATIVE FEEDBACK

PARTS NEEDED: a ½ watt 4.7K resistor (yellow/purple/red).

With the chassis removed, look at the extra speaker output jack. Notice a wire from the hot side of this jack to the board. It goes under the board to an 820 ohm resistor (gray/red/brown) situated above it on the board. This is the negative feedback resistor. Change it to a 4.7K and you're done. Hint: you might do this mod when you do the phase inverter mod because both go to a common eyelet.

HOW IT WORKS: negative feedback is a portion of the signal taken off the speaker and re-injected into a particular place in the circuit where it is 180 degrees out of phase with the signal. This lowers gain quite a bit, but is used to smooth out frequency response. If a particular frequency is louder than others, it will be fed back louder, thus reducing that particular frequency's gain without affecting any others. When you use a 4.7K feedback resistor, you are reducing the amount of signal fed back, thereby increasing overall gain. This also makes the amp sound a little more raw, with easier distortion.

ELIMINATE DROPPING RESISTANCE ON MAIN CHANNEL

PARTS NEEDED: a piece of wire

If you look at where you changed the 22K to a 10K, you'll notice there are two 220K resistors next to it. These resistors apex and connect to the phase inverter input cap, which is usually (but not always) a .001 ceramic cap. The 220K closest to the 22K (which you just changed to a 10K) is the coupling resistor for the normal channel. The other resistor is the coupler for the vibrato channel. Decide which channel you want the most gain from and replace the resistor with a straight wire. Don't short both resistors, only one. Hint: you don't need to remove the resistor. Simply solder a wire across the resistor, thus shorting it. If you ever want to put it back to stock, the original resistor is already installed; you need only remove the shorting wire.

How it works: the two 220K resistors allow signal from each channel to merge and be fed into the phase inverter. The resistors act to isolate one channel from the other. The phase inverter's input impedance is approximately 1 meg. When a 220K resistor is placed in front of the phase inverter, the circuit "sees" this as a voltage divider with the 220K being the dropping resistor and the 1 meg being the load resistor. When we short the dropping resistor, we have reduced the dropping voltage to zero, thus eliminating any loss.

DISCONNECT INTENSITY POT

Parts needed: none

With the chassis removed, look at the back of the intensity pot. You'll notice three leads. The left one is grounded to the housing of the pot, the middle one goes to a brown wire and the right lead goes to a yellow wire. Disconnect the yellow wire from the pot and you're done. This will disable your vibrato but improve the gain and tone.

If you must have functional vibrato, install a push/pull pot to replace any pot on the control panel and then wire the switch on the push/pull pot so it reconnects the yellow wire to the intensity pot. Ordinarily, you would want to put it on the intensity pot itself, except you might have a hard time finding a 50K reverse-audio-taper pot with a push/pull switch. You may have to settle for a 250K or a 1 meg pot. When you need vibrato, you simply pull the pot and the vibrato is working as a stock circuit. On the other hand, when you're not using the vibrato, you can disable the intensity pot to get better tone and better gain!

How it works: when a vibrato circuit was added to the Blackface design, a 50K intensity pot was used as the load resistance in parallel with the 1 meg input resistance of the phase inverter. When signal leaves the preamp it has two basic paths to ground — through the 50K intensity pot or through the phase inverter grid resistor/long-tail cathode resistor circuit. Most of the signal will go the 50K intensity pot, thus

Save That Blackface Deluxe!

starving the phase inverter. Disabling the intensity pot forces more signal to the phase inverter.

RE-VOICE MIDDLE RESISTOR

After all modifications are performed, you might like to adjust the final voicing of the amplifier. Depending on what your speaker sounds like and what kind of tone you are going for, you will want to adjust the midrange frequencies by adjusting a resistor value on each channel.

On the back of the bass potentiometer on each channel you'll notice a 6.8K resistor (blue/gray/red). As this resistor value is made larger, there will be more midrange and more gain. Disconnect the stock 6.8K resistor and temporarily install a 25K pot. This will allow you to adjust the value by ear, thus finding the best resistor value. After the pot is adjusted by ear, you will disconnect the pot without disturbing the setting, and measure the resistance it provided the circuit. Next, simply take a standard value resistor and substitute for the pot, taking care to solder it properly. You may have to get the closest value.

HINT: to wire the pot correctly, the left and middle leads are joined and connected to the amp's ground. The right lead of the 25K pot goes to the left lead of the bass pot on the channel being voiced.

After you have voiced one channel, be sure to do the other in like manner. Remember — increasing midrange frequencies will help the amp break up sooner, and decreasing the midrange will provide more space between the notes and a cleaner overall sound.

HOW IT WORKS: many Blackface amps have a middle control to adjust midrange frequencies. Since the Deluxe was not Fender's top model, the company eliminated the middle control and substituted a 6.8K fixed resistor. When you install the 25K pot, it becomes the middle control. Once adjusted, a fixed resistor provides your preferred fixed value.

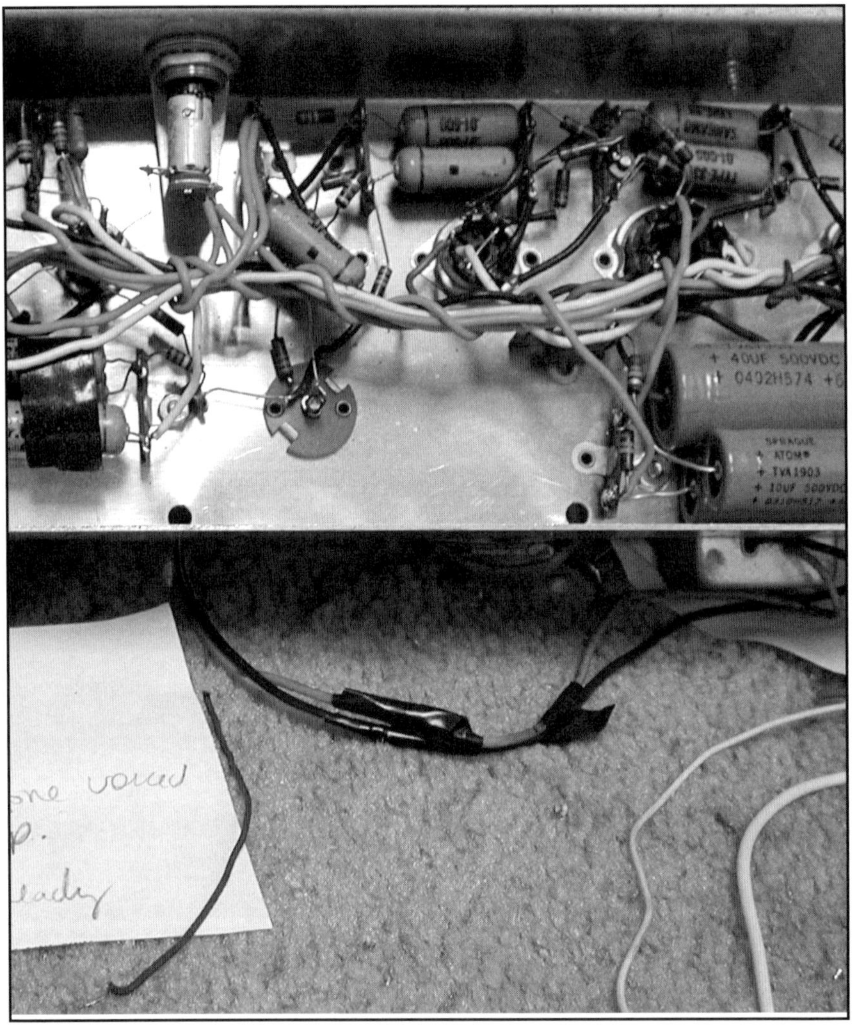
SPRAGUE
ATOM
TVA1903

ADJUSTABLE FIXED BIAS FOR SMALL PRACTICE AMPS

With more and more musicians playing and practicing at home, there seems to be a surging popularity with smaller tube amps. The advantages of a small tube amp are enormous. First, you can turn it up to the point of tube overdrive without the deafening loudness of a big amp, so you save your own ears. Your dog won't go for your jugular, the neighbors won't call the police, and your wife won't leave for an evening at the shopping mall. If you need to change the output tube, you only need one tube (no need for the expense of matched pairs!) These amps cost less to buy and less to maintain.

A tweed Champ or a Kendrick 118 is what I call the "lowest common denominator amp." If we were studying "Tube Guitar Amplifiers 131" at the University, and our assignment was to build a tube guitar amp; at the very least we would need a rectifier circuit (to change the wall A.C. into D.C., which is required to operate a tube circuit), a preamp tube (to add gain to the weak guitar pickup signal), and an output tube (to add enough power to drive a speaker). That's all you get in the tweed Champ or Kendrick 118. There is no pre-gain stage, tone driver circuit, tone recovery circuit, reverb drive circuit, reverb recovery circuit, FX loop send, FX loop return, master volume circuit, graphic EQ circuit, phase inverter, differential amplifier, etc. The smaller amp's simplicity allows you to hear less of the circuitry and more of the tubes. That is why tube aficionados prefer a bare bones amp to listen to different types of tubes. They can hear more of a difference because they hear JUST the tubes and not a bunch of extra circuitry.

But the problem with these minimalist amplifiers is that they are cathode biased. Although cathode biasing allows more compression and longer sustain, it can also account for a mushy bottom-end and lack of punch. Forget about getting a great clean tone with a cathode biased practice amp. And forget about a Stevie Ray tone with a cathode biased amp! The smaller amps already have enough compression with the rectifier tube, the output tube and preamp tube, but by modifying the bias circuit from cathode bias to adjustable fixed bias, one can get the punchy and clear bottom-end that is normally only associated with bigger amps.

LET'S DO THE MODIFICATION

Modifying a Champ or Kendrick 118 from cathode bias to adjustable fixed bias involves only five steps. If you are technically challenged, get a friend that knows what he is doing to help you. We are working with the bias circuit. If you screw something up and the output tube doesn't get proper bias, it could cause the output tube to draw too much current. This could end with a burnt transformer or a burnt power tube. We are going to take the five steps one at a time. They are:

1. Create adjustable negative voltage bias supply
2. Ground the cathode of the output tube
3. Unground the grid return resistor of the output tube
4. Connect the ungrounded grid return resistor to the adjustable bias supply.
5. Set the output tube bias to the proper operating level and test the amp.

CREATE ADJUSTABLE NEGATIVE VOLTAGE BIAS SUPPLY

To create a negative voltage supply, we are going to take A.C. voltage off the B+ winding (the red wire that terminates on pin #4 of the rectifier tube), drop it down, rectify it, filter it and run it through a voltage divider to adjust for the exact negative voltage needed. To do all of this, we will make a small subassembly that is self contained and can be glued into the amp with silicone glue. I am not in favor of drilling holes in an amp chassis. The silicon glue will hold just fine, and if you ever want to put it back to stock, there won't be any signs that it had ever been modified in the first place. You will need some parts to make this subassembly:

1. A 220K 1 watt dropping resistor
2. A 1N4007 diode. This is a 1000 volt 1 amp diode

3. Two 10 mfd at 160 volt electrolytic capacitors
4. A 50K cermet element pot. I use the 20 turn type with the brass adjusting screw
5. A 10K load resistor
6. Perfboard or some other suitable component board material. The fiberglass perfboard can be purchased with holes pre-drilled every $1/10$ of an inch. This works great for making a small subassembly, because you can mount the components in a small space and glue the component board to the inside of the chassis.

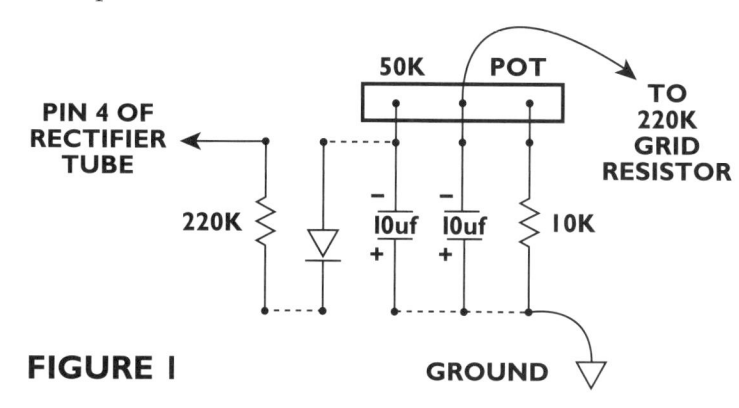

FIGURE 1

Look at Figure 1. (Note: the dotted lines are connections to be made underneath the perfboard or other suitable component board.) You are taking A.C. voltage from pin 4 of the rectifier tube. This A.C. voltage is going to the 220K 1 watt dropping resistor. The other end of the 220K goes to the 1N4007 diode. The diode is mounted such that the cathode faces the 220K. The other end (anode) of the diode goes to both the negative lead of one of the 10 mfd at 160 volt capacitors and one of the end leads of the cermet element pot. The wiper of the pot goes to both another 10 mfd at 160 volt cap's negative lead and to the grid return resistor from the output tube. (More on this later). The other end lead of the pot goes to a 10K load resistor and the other end of the load resistor gets grounded. Also the positive leads from both 10 mfd capacitors get grounded too.

GROUND THE CATHODE OF THE OUTPUT TUBE

In a cathode biased amp such as a Champ or a Kendrick 118, pin #8 from the output tube socket is the cathode. There is a wire going from pin #8 to the cathode resistor and cathode bypass capacitor.

The other end of this cathode resistor and bypass cap normally go to ground. In the adjustable fixed bias design, pin #8 needs to go directly to ground. To simplify the mod and to keep it 100% easily reversible, simply put a jumper wire across the cathode resistor/bypass cap that is attached to pin #8 of the output tube socket. When you short across the cathode resistor/bypass cap, it is the same thing (electrically) as running a wire from pin #8 directly to ground. If you ever want to put the amp back to stock, it is much easier to simply remove the jumper wire that you used to short the cathode resistor/bypass cap to ground.

UNGROUND THE GRID RETURN RESISTOR OF THE OUTPUT TUBE

If you look at pin #5 of the output tube, and follow the wire back to the board, it will go under the board and terminate on a 220K ½ watt resistor. It is the only stock 220K resistor (red, red, yellow) in the amp! The wire coming from pin #5 (the grid of the output tube) actually terminates where the 220K resistor meets with the coupling cap from the previous stage. The other end of the 220K resistor is grounded. You are going to unsolder the grounded end and lift it slightly off the board. You must lift the grounded end of the 220K slightly off the board, because the eyelet it was mounted in was grounded and you don't want this component grounded. We are going to attach the output of the negative bias voltage supply here in the next step.

CONNECT THE UNGROUNDED GRID RETURN RESISTOR TO THE ADJUSTABLE BIAS SUPPLY.

Next, you want to attach the output wire coming from the wiper of the cermet element pot to the lead of the 220K resistor which has been lifted off the board. This will provide negative voltage to the grid return resistor and ultimately to pin #5 of the output tube.

SET THE OUTPUT TUBE BIAS TO THE PROPER OPERATING LEVEL AND TEST THE AMP.

It is best the check to make sure everything is right before we actually bias the amp. Remove the output tube, turn the amp on and check pin #5 of the output tube for negative voltage. If there is no negative voltage on pin #5, you must troubleshoot the amp and find out why. Do not, under any circumstances, install the output tube if negative voltage is not present on pin #5.

With the meter still connected to pin #5, adjust the cermet pot a few turns each way to learn which way makes the voltage go up and which way makes it go down. We are now going to set an arbitrary amount of negative voltage.

We want to get enough bias voltage on pin #5 so that we can install an output tube without fear of it burning up. If you are using a 6V6, set the voltage going to pin #5 to about -30 volts. If you are using a 6L6 or some other more powerful tube, start out by setting the voltage on pin #5 to about -50 volts. This will idle the tube very low when the output tube is re-installed. We want the idle to be low while we are setting the bias, so we are adjusting to an arbitrary amount of bias voltage that we know will tame down the output tube when you install it.

Now we are going to set the idle plate current of the output tube by adjusting the negative bias voltage. To do this, we want to change our multimeter to the D.C. milliamp setting. The positive lead of the meter goes to pin #8 of the rectifier tube and the negative lead goes to pin #3 of the output tube. Next, with the amp still off, install the output tube. Turn on the amp and let it warm up.

As the amp is warming up, you should see some current reading on the meter. Remember which way made the negative voltage go lower? That's which way we want to turn the bias pot to make the plate current go higher! We want to adjust the negative bias voltage until the plate current we are monitoring gets to around 45 mA. Remember that these type amps are Class A single-ended design and draw more current at less voltage than similar push-pull Class AB amps. You can experiment with more or less current but don't set it for so much that the plates glow cherry red. If the plates are glowing, the tube is exceeding its plate watt dissipation and should be tamed down. 40 to 60 mA of idle current is about average.

GET YOUR GUITAR AND LISTEN TO YOUR NEW AMP!

Now comes the fun part, playing the guitar through the "new" amp. It will sound completely different. You will notice some bottom-end focus that you are not used to hearing coming from an amp that small. The low "E" will hold together better than ever before. Bon Appetit!

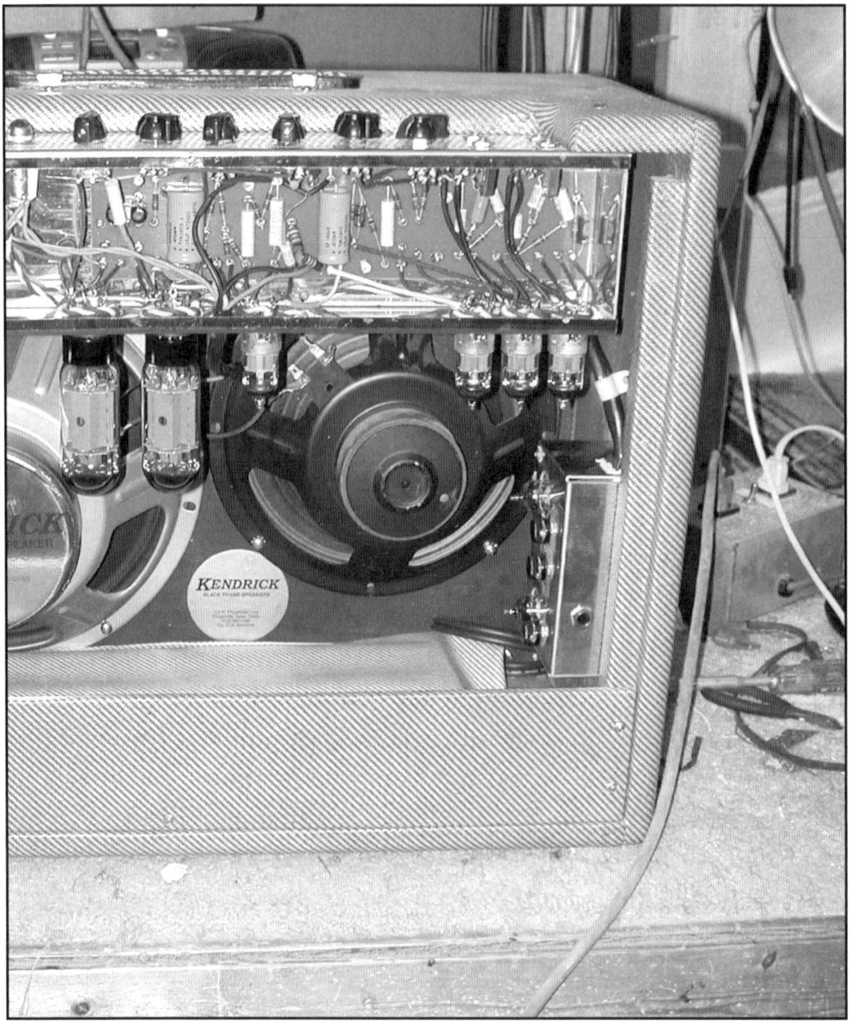
KENDRICK

ADJUSTABLE FIXED BIAS FOR YOUR NON-ADJUSTABLE FIXED BIAS AMP

Many of the amps built in the 1950s and 60s were designed with fixed bias output tubes but did not have an adjustment pot to set the bias! For that matter, almost all Mesa Boogie amps are fixed bias; yet all lack an adjustment pot! If you bring such an amp to a tech, he may use a resistor substitution box (also called a decade box) to "dial in" the correct bias voltage and then replace the substitution box with the appropriate value resistor. This is a real hassle. Who wants to "dial in and change" a resistor value every time you set bias for the output stage?

Anytime such an amp comes into my shop, I highly recommend a minor modification to make the bias supply circuit adjustable. Adding a bias adjustment pot is a simple modification that is strictly internal and can be done without defacing the amp. With a small cermet element pot and a resistor, one can modify the bias supply circuit so that bias can easily be set without having to solder anything in the future. I am certain that any tech that adjusts bias voltage in the future will appreciate the ease that an adjustment pot affords.

UNDERSTANDING THE BIAS SUPPLY CIRCUIT

A fixed bias supply consists of an A.C. voltage supply, a solid-state rectifier, a dropping resistor, a load resistor and one or two filter capacitors. The A.C. voltage supply is usually a tap off the B+ winding, but it can also come from a resistor or a capacitor connecting to the end of the B+ winding. The rectifier is usually a silicon rectifier (aka diode) such as a 1N4003, a 1N4005 or a 1N4007. In the case of 50s Fender amps, a selenium rectifier was used. The rectifier changes the A.C. voltage (electricity that goes both directions) to pulsating D.C. (electricity that only goes one direction). A filter capacitor is attached to the anode side of the rectifier. This filter cap changes the pulsating D.C. to smooth D.C. It is almost always an electrolytic capacitor. The polarity of the capacitor is such that the "minus" end goes to the diode while the "plus" end goes to ground. If you follow the circuit, there will be a dropping resistor between the rectifier and the bias voltage output. There is also a load resistor between the bias voltage output and ground. Many times there will be another electrolytic filter capacitor in parallel with the load resistor. The polarity of this capacitor is also such that the "plus" end goes to ground and the "minus" end goes to the bias voltage output. This assures smooth D.C.. (Pulsating D.C. will sound like 120 Hz hum if it is not smoothed out.)

The dropping resistor and the load resistor are the components of a voltage divider. If you add their resistance together and divide by the load resistance, you will have the same ratio as the total voltage (from the rectifier) divided by the bias voltage output.

Let's look at a 5F6A Bassman as an example. There is a 15K dropping resistor and a 56K load resistor. If you increase the dropping resistor value, the bias voltage goes down. If you increase the load resistor, the bias voltage goes up. The converse is also true: decrease the dropping resistor and the bias voltage goes up; decrease the load resistor and the bias voltage goes down.

LET'S DESIGN A BIAS ADJUSTMENT CIRCUIT

We will start with the bias circuit of a 5F6A Bassman amp. There is more than one way to design a bias adjustment circuit. I would go the simple approach and replace the 56K load resistor with a variable resistance. To create a variable resistance, I would use a 39K resistor in series with a 50K cermet element pot. (It is important to use a cermet element pot because we are dealing with D.C. voltage and D.C. voltage will burn up a carbon element pot!) This would give me a variable resistance from 39K (pot adjusted to zero ohms) to 89K (pot adjust to maximum setting).

Here is how to place the resistor in series with the pot. There are three leads on the cermet pot. Solder the middle lead and one of the end leads to one of the resistor leads. When you put it into the circuit, the other resistor lead counts as one lead and the unsoldered lead on the cermet pot counts as the other lead, with respect to the 56K resistor it will replace. In this configuration, you could think of this as one component — a variable resistor whose parameters can be varied 39K to 89K. You are simply replacing the stock 56K resistor with this variable resistance (which consists of the 39K resistor in series with the 50K pot).

The 39K resistor coupled with a 50K cermet pot allow for a continuous voltage adjustment from -43.94 to -52.07. Here is how I got that.

STOCK SETUP

First, let's look at the stock setup which does not have an adjustable bias. Add the 15K dropping resistor to the 56K load resistor and get 71K total resistance of the circuit. So the ratio of 71K (total resistance) divided by 56K (the load resistance) equals the same ratio as the D.C. voltage on the anode of the rectifier -60.85 (total voltage) divided by the actual bias voltage (-48). The schematic of the Bassman shows the bias voltage to be -48 volts. 71K (total resistance) / 56K (load resistance) = - 60.85 (total voltage) / -48 (load voltage or bias voltage output).

MODIFIED SETUP

Let's look at the math for both the minimum and maximum bias voltage output when we replace the 56K with a variable resistance (that can be varied from 39K to 89K.)

We will start with the 39K load resistance, which is the minimum adjustment. This would occur if the 50K pot was adjusted to zero ohms and the only resistance in the load circuit would be the 39K resistor. You would have 15K (dropping resistor) + 39K (load resistor) = 54K (total resistance.) To calculate the lowest bias voltage: 54K (total resistance) / 39K (load resistance) = -60.85 (total voltage) / -43.94 (bias output voltage.)

For the maximum adjustment, the pot would be set for maximum ohms (50K). Remember that 50K pot is in series with a 39K resistor, so the total load resistance is 89K. You would have 15K (dropping resistor) + 89K (the 39K plus the 50K pot) = 104K (total resistance.) 104K (total resistance) / 89K (load resistance) = -60.85 (total voltage) / -52.07 (bias output voltage.)

Adjustable Fixed Bias for your Non-adjustable Fixed Bias Amp

VARIATIONS ON A THEME

Sometimes the bias circuit of certain amps will differ from the standard bias circuit described. For example, sometimes the dropping resistor is between the transformer and the rectifier instead of after the rectifier. In this case, the load resistor can still be replaced with a resistor in series with a pot. You might wonder why do we need the resistor? Couldn't we simply use a 100K pot and adjust it down? Yes we could, but we want to design enough resistance into the circuit so there is no chance of completely grounding out the bias supply. To do so would cause your output tubes to draw extremely high current and possibly burn up. Also, if we draw too much current in the bias circuit, we risk burning something up there also. Having a fixed resistance builds safety into the design.

Certain amps have tremolo of the type that modulates the bias supply. For example, the 6G16 Vibroverb and the 6G2 Princeton both use this type of tremolo. In both of these designs, the dropping resistor is between the rectifier and the transformer and the load resistor goes from the anode of the diode to ground. One could simply replace the load resistor with a resistor tied to a pot. On the 6G2 Princeton there is a 30K load resistor. Change this to a 22K in series with a 50K cermet pot. This would give you parameters of 22K to 72K. The Vibroverb uses a 33K load resistor, but it could also use the 22K resistor in series with a 50K pot; thus giving a range from 22K to 72K.

UNCONVENTIONAL BIAS CIRCUITS

Although most bias supply circuits are designed as previously described, there are certain designs that would require a different modification to make them adjustable. For example, on certain Ampeg amps, the bias circuit is designed without a dropping resistor, but with two load resistors. One load resistor is before the diode (this one loads A.C. current) and the other load resistor is after the diode (this one loads D.C. current. Note: On these circuits, a small value capacitor is used to bring A.C. current from the B+ winding to the diode (and the A.C. load resistor, too.) The load resistor on the A.C. side would be the place to substitute the variable resistance components. A typical A.C. load resistor value is 56K, so the 39K resistor in series with the 50K cermet pot would work fine.

On certain other rare designs, the Vox AC100 comes to mind; one or more zener diodes are used to regulate the bias voltage. These bias circuits are very tricky to adjust, because the zener diode is used as a voltage regulator. Any change in voltage will cause the zener diodes to regulate it back to what it was! The bias voltage supply could be made adjustable with a circuit re-design.

AMP BUILDING

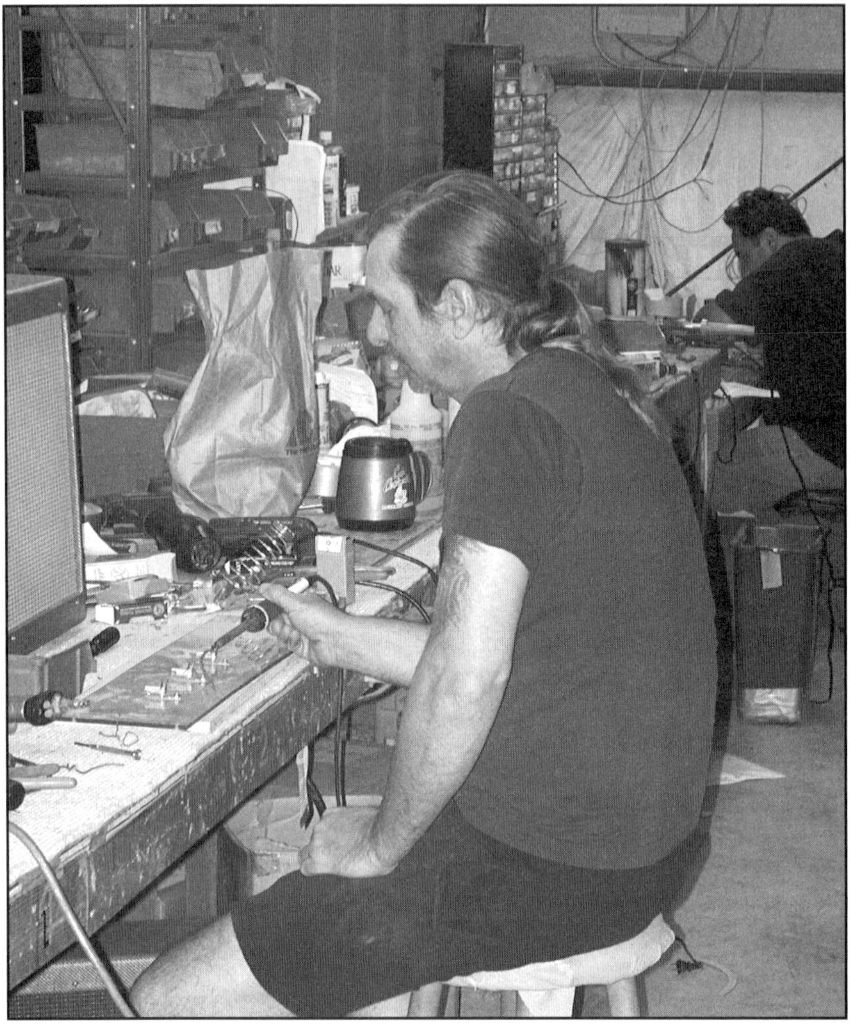

TEN AMP BUILDING TRICKS

I know there are many guitar players that either have the itch to build a tube guitar amplifier or will get the itch soon. With a good dose of beginner's luck, quality components and little blind faith, one could probably turn out a great sounding amp. When I built my first amp, I did not fully understand what was going on inside an amp, but I was very lucky. The amp sounded great which fed my confidence to build a second amp. The next thing you know, I was building amps for friends and family. I look back now and see I have built tube amps professionally for 15 years!

It is possible to build an amp exactly like the schematic diagram and have the amp not work at all! It is possible to have everything wired correctly with correct voltages and yet the tone sounds horrible.

I produce Tube Guitar Amp Seminars in major cities all over the country. A few days ago, I led one of my Tube Guitar Amp Seminars at my amplifier factory. Many of the participants brought their problem amps. One such amp was a homemade tube guitar amp, built from a kit purchased from a well-known manufacturer/designer. There were layout mistakes and design errors that made the amp sound horrific. The guys called it the "Kazoo Tone." Just by replacing the Illinois Capacitor Brand Filter caps (these are actually made in Taiwan and not American as the name "Illinois" implies) and moving a few components, the tone became beefy and rich.

Here are some tips for amp building. Some of these were expensive, hard won lessons. They are yours to keep for free.

BUILDING AXIOM #1 — **Spend more time planning and less time building.** Even after you have planned, you will be better off to check and re-check constantly.

If you check and re-check, you will have an amp that works the first time you turn it on. What a thrill it is to "fire up" the amp (that you made) and have it work perfectly. This may be a guitar player's way of giving birth.

BUILDING AXIOM #2 — **Do not skimp on components.** For example, there is a reason why cheap transformers are cheap. The transformers are the most important part of the amp. They make the most difference. If you get everything else right and the transformers are not happening, your amp will not be happening either.

Almost as important as the transformers are the tubes and speakers. The tube is the character of the amp and the speaker is what is vibrating the air to make a sound.

Always remember that it only costs three times as much to go first class. If you are planning to keep your baby, you will soon forget what it cost. You will never forget what it sounds like.

AMP BUILDING AXIOM #3 — **Always use shielded cable on the grids of the first two gain stages.** The amplification going on in a preamp is geometric, not algebraic. We are talking 100X100X100 and not 100+100+100. Any instabilities or noise will become a problem once they are amplified a million times. Be sure to ground the shielding ONLY ON ONE END, lest you want to create a ground loop hum.

On a 12AX7, pin #2 is the grid for one triode section and pin #7 is the grid of the other. It is not necessary to use shielded wire on the plate or cathode, only on the grid.

BUILDING AXIOM #4 — **Overdesign by 100%** and you will not blow things up. Let us say your amp uses two 6L6 and three 12AX7 tubes. You add up the filament current and calculate it to be 2.7 amperes. (.9 amperes for each 6L6 and .3 amperes for each 12AX7.) You need at least a 5.4 amp filament winding on your power transformer. (2.7 amperes needed times two) Hint: Since 5.4 amps is a non-standard rating, use a 6 amp. Do not use a 3 amp filament winding, lest you desire a mushroom cloud that has a funny burning smell.

Here is another example. You calculate the wattage of a particular power resistor to be .9 watts. (This can be done easily by squaring the voltage drop across the resistor and then dividing by the resistance of the same resistor.) By overdesigning by 100%, you need at least a 1.8 wattage resistor. Standard value is 2 watts, so that is what to use. Do not use a 1 watt resistor, lest you yearn for service problems later.

AMP BUILDING AXIOM #5 — **Layouts should be such that the signal NEVER crosses back over itself.** Typically the input will be on one side of the amp and the A.C. power is on the opposite side. The signal should move from input to output transformer without crossing back over itself, lest you want to build an oscillator. Can you say parasitic oscillation?

In general, you want the input jack as far away as possible from the power and output transformer.

AMP BUILDING AXIOM #6 — **Keep your grid wires short.** Grid wires act as an antenna for instability, noise, parasitic oscillations, etc. The shorter the antenna, the less likely you will encounter a problem. It is better to lengthen the plate wire of the preceding stage to keep the grid wire of the next stage as short as possible. When the signal leaves the plate in a preamp, it is considered a plate circuit until it reaches the coupling cap. Once it passes the coupling cap, it becomes the grid circuit of the next stage. Keep it short lest you want to build an unpredictable oscillator.

In certain amps, if the grid wires on the output tubes are too long; the amp will develop a parasitic oscillation and simply not work. For example, in a Tweed Twin circuit, if the grid wires are an inch too long, the amp will not work! (The grid wire is pin #5 in most popular output tubes (6L6, 6V6, EL34, etc.)

Also, if you are using a grid resistor on the output tubes, it should be mounted with the body of the resistor as close as possible to the socket lead. In other words, it should have zero lead length. Grid resistors are used on the output tubes to help stabilize the amp and stop parasitic oscillations. If the lead length is too long, the grid resistor will not help stabilize the amp. Also, if you are having stability problems with an amp, using a larger value grid resistor on the output tubes may help improve the stability of the amp.

AMP BUILDING AXIOM #7 — **When mounting transformers, make sure the laminates of one transformer are at right angles to the laminates of the adjacent transformer.** You do not want the laminates to be co planar, lest you are building a boat anchor or a doorstop.

BUILDING AXIOM #8 — **The main filter capacitor ground, screen supply ground, B+ center-tap ground, and cathode ground from the output tubes should all be grounded at the same point.** The grounds for each of the other filter caps should be at or near the cathode ground of the preamp tube it is supplying voltage to.

If you do not follow this rule, brush up on your parasitic oscillation troubleshooting skills.

BUILDING AXIOM #9 — **Whenever possible, mount your tone capacitors on their related potentiometers.** If you look at a Blackface or Silverface Fender, you will notice they mounted their tone caps on the board. This is one of the reasons those amps sometimes sound bad. By mounting them to their related pots, you are able to use about 2 feet less wire. This is a dramatic difference, tonally. You are taking 2 feet of wire from the grid circuit!

BUILDING AXIOM #10 — **Take your time to do it right the first time.** How many times are you going to build your amp? If you do it right, you will be playing that amp for decades and possibly handing it down to a son or in some cases, a grandson. How good do you want it to sound? If the tone does not matter, why are you building a tube amp in the first place?

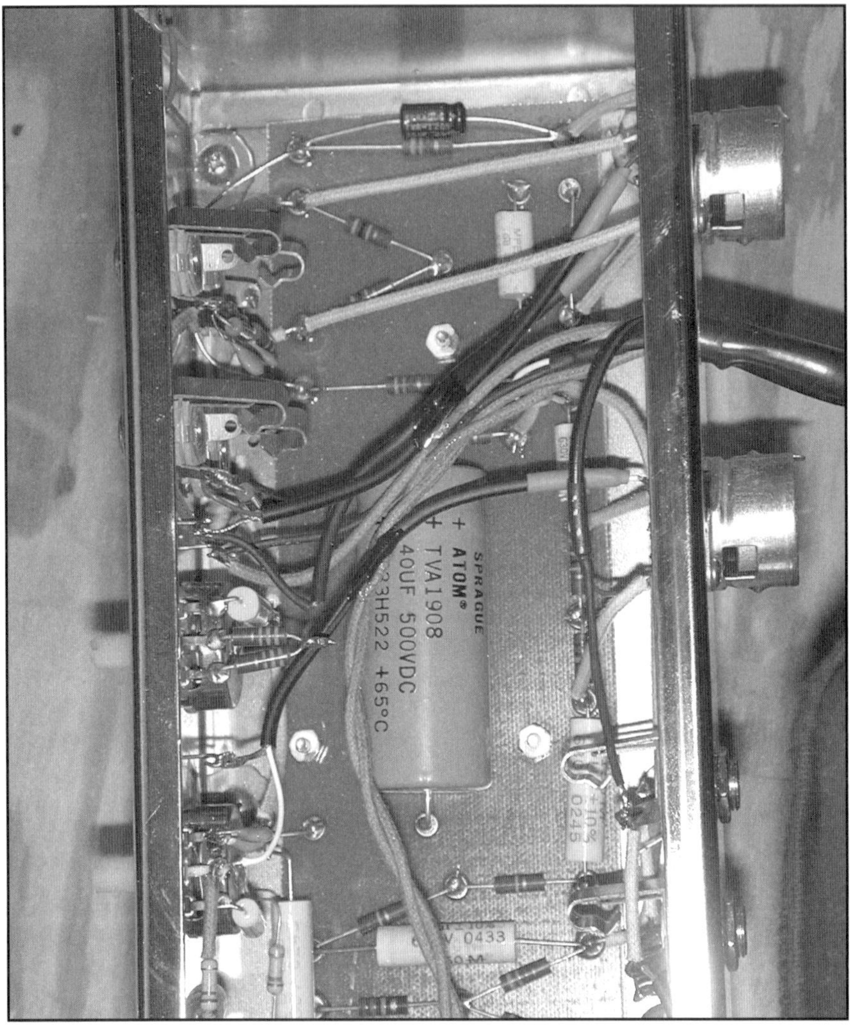
SPRAGUE
ATOM®
+ TVA1908
40UF 500VDC

AMPLIFIER CIRCUIT LAYOUTS

When I look at a vintage tube amplifier, I love to check out the actual circuit layout, how components are grounded, the lead dress, and some of the clever little tricks that builders have used to "help" their designs. You may ask, "Why does it matter how a circuit is laid out in an amp chassis?" A capacitor is simply "two conductors separated by a non-conductor." Since every wire in the amp is a conductor, and each wire has non-conductors between it and all the other wires: doesn't that qualify as the definition of a capacitor? Stray capacitance could occur between any two wires in the amp! Of course, the closer the two wires are together, the more capacitance they will have and the easier it is for the signal from one wire to appear on the other one! One can actually measure the capacitance on two adjacent wires with a capacitance meter.

Besides capacitive coupling, there is also inductive coupling. I remember working on an Vox Super Reverb Twin piggyback amp on day. There is not a worse sounding reverb on this planet. The reverb in that design is really a joke. The reverb pan contains what looks like the spring off a screen door with a phonograph ceramic cartridge attached to each end! I am not kidding. The phono cartridges were used for both sending signal to the spring and returning signal off the spring!

I spent a week redesigning the reverb circuit to a transformer driven Hammond pan circuit. While I was working on this, the chassis was on the bench and out of the cabinet. When I finally finished and the reverb sounded absolutely great, I put everything back together only to hear a loud hum in the reverb circuit — rendering the reverb unusable. When it was being tested, the unit was "church mouse quiet" and the reverb had zero hum. When the chassis and reverb pan were put back in the cabinet, A.C. hum from the power transformer was induced into the wirewound transducers on the Hammond style reverb pan. The pan was physically near the power transformer and no matter where the pan was put in the cabinet; there was nothing that could be done. Stray inductive coupling had done me in.

In short, the way a circuit is laid out in an amplifier design can sometimes make as much difference as the circuit itself. Basic rules of good circuit layout must be followed to assure that the circuit is stable and the amp does not become an expensive oscillator! Depending on the frequency an amp oscillates, the symptoms could vary from motor boating (putt, putt, putt), to squealing, to buzzy distortion on the edge of the note, to completely cutting out, and possibly others. For the amp builder looking for some easy rules to follow, I offer these.

RULE #1 The layout should be done such that the input signal starts on one end of the amp chassis and "flows" (as the signal becomes stronger) towards the other end. For example, you would avoid having the signal path cross back over itself. To violate this rule is to allow one or more parasitic feedback circuits to occur which are not drawn on the schematic! These unwanted phantom circuits could cause motor boating; mosquitoes on the note, oscillation and in severe cases — prevent the amp from working at all. The most stable circuits are those whose output is far away from the input and the signal gain gradually moves from input to output without crossing over itself.

RULE #2 Grid wires should be as short as possible. Any signal appearing on a grid will be amplified many times over. You could think of the grid wire as an antenna. The longer the antenna, the easier it is to pick up stray signal. You want the grid wires as short as possible so it does not pick up some other signal that is near it physically. Remember, if one stage of an amplifier has it's output sent to an earlier stage's grid, then it could begin oscillating. Various different symptoms would occur, depending on the frequency of the oscillations.

RULE #3 Plate wires should be long. Longer wires have more inductance and inductance on a plate wire is good. They don't have to be really long, but having them longer than the grid wires helps.

RULE #4 The A.C. cord and all the internal 120 volt A.C. wiring (230 volt in Europe) should be as far away from the input as possible. You don't want that 60 Hertz (50 Hertz in Europe) to be picked up by any of the early stages as it will be amplified and become very loud hum.

Rule #5 The main B+ centertap ground (or the bridge rectifier ground on a full wave bridge rectifier configured circuit) should be located as far away from the input circuit as possible. The power supply main (1st section) filter capacitor ground, the power tube cathode ground (or power tube cathode resistor ground, if cathode biased) and the filter capacitor ground for the screen supply should all be grounded at or near the Main B+ centertap ground. Remember, the power tubes are drawing enough plate current and screen current to superimpose a signal on even the slightest resistance. So don't take chances. If the main filter ground, B+ centertap ground, screen filter ground, and power tube cathode circuit ground are at the same point, then there is no resistance for the current to superimpose a signal upon.

Rule #6 The early preamp stage filter capacitor ground should be near the cathode resistor ground of the associated gain stage. Ideally, the grid return resistor ground of the next stage (sometimes this is a volume control resistance) should be grounded near the cathode resistor and filter cap ground of the previous stage. This is because the next stage grid return resistor is in parallel with both the cathode resistor/tube circuit and the filter capacitor of the previous stage.

Rule #7 Always use a twisted pair of wires for the filament heater circuit. Twisted pair filament wires must have a ground reference. This can be done easily if there is a centertap on the filament winding, in which case the centertap should be grounded at or near the main B+ ground. If the filament winding on the transformer lacks a centertap, use two 100 ohm ½ watt resistors configured with one on each side of the 6.3 volt winding. The other free end of each one goes to ground. This is known as an artificial centertap. It will balance out A.C. filament hum.

Rule #8 When using a twisted pair for the filament circuit of a push-pull amp, always make sure the polarity is constant throughout the output tube sockets. That is to say, for example, that the filament wire that terminates on pin #2 of one 6L6 tube should terminate on pin #2 of each output tube and the filament wire that terminates on pin #7 should terminate on pin #7 of the other output tubes. By following this rule, you are allowing the hum that is induced in the filament circuit to phase cancel each other — thus avoiding annoying hum.

Rule #9 If long grid wires are unavoidable, use shielded wire. Only one end of the shielding is grounded. The shielded wire will protect the grid wire from picking up unwanted signals. This is especially important on the grid wires of the input jack and the volume pot of Blackface and Silverface Fenders. These grid wires are too long and need shielding.

Rule #10 Keep 6.3 volt a.c. filament wires away from grid wires. The hum can be induced into the grid circuit, amplified a few thousand times and result in loud hum.

LAYOUT TRICKS

Here's a trick to make sure the grid wires are in the quietest place.
1. Remove the chassis from the cabinet and put the amp in the play mode.
2. Turn the controls up and listen to the background noise.
3. Using a non-conductive probe (I use a wooden chopstick), simply move the grid wires while simultaneously listening to hum and background noise.

You will notice the grid wires make less hum and noise in a particular location. That location is the correct place for the grid wire to be dressed.

Here's another cool designer's trick, used to tame an unstable circuit. Use a shielded wire for the grid circuit but instead of grounding the shielding; one end of the shielding is attached to the plate of the same tube while the other end of the shielding is not attached to anything. This adds a slight amount of negative feedback to the circuit. You will lose a tiny bit of high end, but you may also lose an annoying parasitic oscillation! Doing this to the input grid of an amp will usually cure the dreaded "d.c. on the guitar volume pot" syndrome. This is when a very small amount of d.c. (usually only a few millivolts) is imposed on the grid wire making the guitar volume and pickup switch sound scratchy/noisy.

Here's one more trick to correct the improper layout found in most Fender amps. This is done when the tone caps are physically located on the component board and long wires span from each tone cap to the tone control pots. You can dramatically reduce the length of the grid circuit of the second stage by mounting the coupling capacitors, directly on the potentiometers. You will want to mount the slope resistor on the other end of the tone caps. All together you will end up removing about two feet of grid wire from the amp.

In the Silverface Fenders, when converting the circuit to a Blackface style the parasitic suppression caps (2000 pf) going from the grid of the output tubes to ground must be removed. When these are removed, sometimes the amp will develop a parasitic oscillation. Moving the tone caps on both channels to the pots and thus shorting the length of the second stage grid circuit wires will almost always cure that parasitic oscillation.

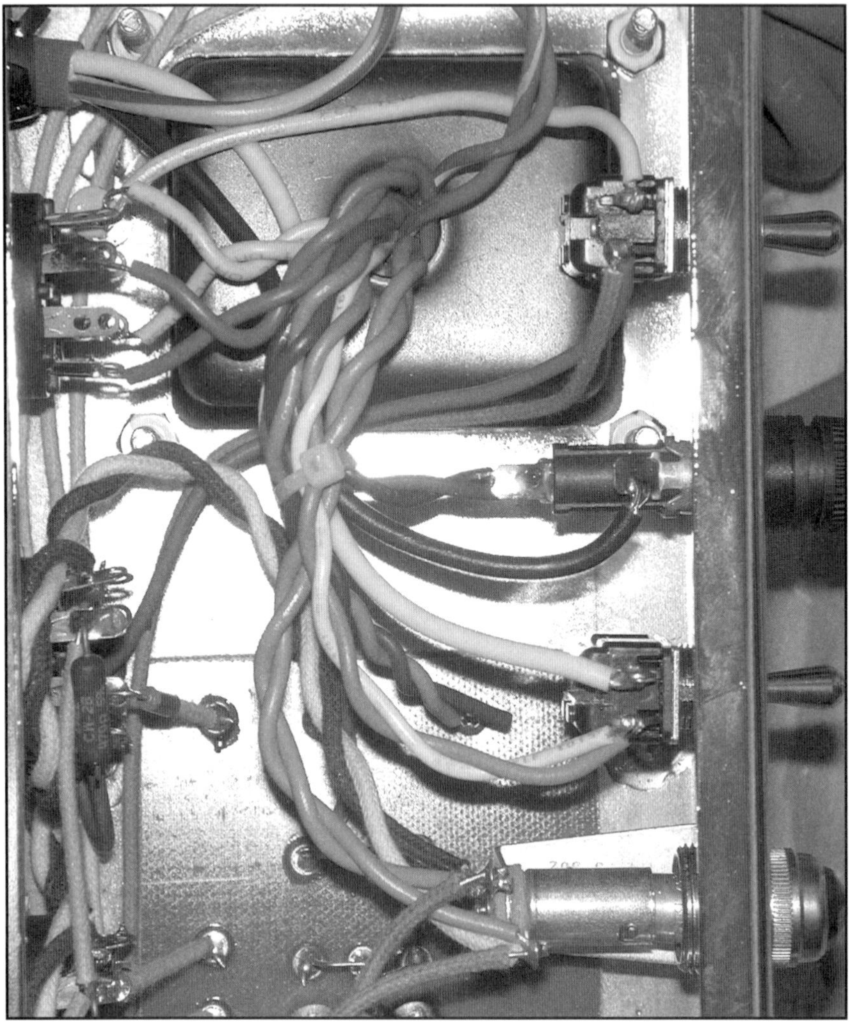

TUBE GUITAR AMP POWER SUPPLIES

All tube guitar amplifiers operate on Direct Current, or D.C. electricity. Direct current is electricity moving in one direction and not the other. Your wall outlet only gives out A.C., or alternating current. This is called alternating current because it goes both directions. In fact, you could say the directions of current flow alternate, hence the name: Alternating Current. In order to create D.C. electricity from an A.C. wall supply, a rectifier power supply is needed. The power supply consists of a transformer with a step-up secondary winding, a rectifier (this could be either a tube or solid-state device) that acts as a check valve so that the current can travel in one direction but not the other, filter capacitors to smooth out the D.C. electrical current, and sometimes a choke which resists any change of current.

THE HALF-WAVE RECTIFIER POWER SUPPLY

The simplest type of rectifier and perhaps the least efficient is the half-wave rectifier. With this design, the anode of a rectifier device is connected to one end of a transformer winding. The other end of the transformer winding is grounded. The circuit, or load, would then be connected between ground and the cathode of the rectifier device. The rectifier acts as a check valve, only letting the current move in one direction. During one half of the A.C. cycle, the rectifier will conduct and current will flow through the rectifier to the load. During the other half cycle, when the alternating current tries to go the other way, the rectifier will not conduct and no current will flow; hence the name: Half-Wave rectifier. This will produce D.C., except it will be pulsing D.C. — in tempo with the wall A.C. alternations. To smooth out the pulsations, a filter cap is placed between the cathode of the rectifier device and ground. This keeps the D.C. smooth, because between pulses, the capacitor discharges and during the pulse, the capacitor charges — thus keeping the voltage constant. Think of the capacitor as always trying to average out the pulsating D.C.

With proper filtering, this type of rectifier produces smooth D.C. voltage that is roughly 70% or less of the A.C. input voltage at the secondary. That is to say, if the A.C. input voltage to the rectifier is 100 volts A.C., the D.C. output voltage will be roughly 70 volts.

The Fender 6G15 stand-alone Reverb is a common example of a half-wave rectifier type power supply. In the 6G15, three diodes are placed in series as the rectifier device. Using three diodes together triples the Peak Inverse Voltage rating of the rectifier assembly. (Remember, semiconductor technology wasn't advanced in the 60s.) The PIV should be 2.8 times the RMS A.C. voltage; so many vintage designs use multiple diodes to get that rating up. If the diode has a 500 volt PIV rating, then three of them wired in series would have a 1,500 volt PIV rating. In the 6G15 design, a choke is placed in series with the cathode of the rectifier and on each end of the choke; the plus side of a 40 mfd capacitor is connected. The minus leads of both capacitors are connected to ground. The capacitors oppose any change in voltage, while the choke opposes any change in current. This minimizes pulsating D.C. and filters everything down to pure and smooth D.C. current.

The more current a circuit draws, the higher microfarad value the filter capacitors must be in order to filter out those pulsations. That is why half-wave rectifiers are generally used on circuits that do not draw much current (i.e., a reverb unit, a separate bias circuit, a preamp device). Circuits that don't draw much current are easily filtered down to pure D.C. If the circuit draws a lot of current, it is best to use a full-wave rectifier.

THE FULL-WAVE CENTER-TAP RECTIFIER POWER SUPPLY

With the half-wave rectifier described above, only half of the A.C. input cycle is used and the other half is wasted. If we took a center-tapped secondary transformer, the center-tap of the secondary could be grounded. With the other ends of the windings, two half-wave rectifiers could be made, so that both halves of the A.C. cycle could be used. Two half-wave rectifiers make a full wave, get it? Remember the center-tap gets grounded. One end of the transformer secondary winding goes to the anode of one rectifier device and the other end of the transformer goes the anode of another rectifier device. The cathodes of both rectifier devices connect together to the load. In a guitar amp, the two rectifier devices could be a simple 5AR4 or 5Y3 or 5U4 or 5V4 rectifier tube. Remember these rectifier tubes are very common with full-wave rectifier power supplies as they all have two anodes.

With the first half of the A.C. cycle, the rectifier on one end of the transformer winding conducts while the rectifier connected to the other end doesn't conduct. On the next half of the A.C. cycle, the process reverses and the first rectifier quits conducting and the other starts conducting. The cathodes of the rectifier devices are connected together and ultimately connect to the load.

Because both halves of the A.C. cycle are converted to D.C., if the A.C. input is 60 Hertz, then the pulsating D.C. will be 120 Hertz. 120 Hertz is much easier to filter than 60 Hertz because the faster a D.C. pulsation, the easier it is for a filter cap to smooth out the pulsations. The cap simply doesn't have to stabilize the voltage very long before it gets charged again. Assuming proper filtering, the D.C. voltage of the full-wave center-tap transformer will be a maximum of 1.4 times the RMS voltage of half the transformer secondary (half being from the center-tap to one end).

All vintage Fender guitar amplifiers use the Full-Wave Center-Tap Rectifier Power supply. Almost all amps with a rectifier tube use this design. For tube guitar amps, it is the most commonly used power supply design of all time.

THE FULL-WAVE BRIDGE RECTIFIER POWER SUPPLY

With the full-wave center-tap rectifier described above, only one half of the center-tapped secondary is used at any one time during each half cycle of the A.C. input. That is to say, on the first cycle, perhaps the top half is used and the bottom half is idle. On the next half cycle, the process reverses and the top is idle while the bottom half is used. So one of the halves is always being used and one half is always not being used — regardless of which half of the A.C. input cycle we look at.

With the Full-Wave Bridge Rectifier, there is no center-tap and we are going to use the entire winding on every half cycle. Like the full-wave center-tap rectifier, one end of the transformer secondary winding goes to the anode of one rectifier device and the other end of the transformer goes the anode of another rectifier device. The cathodes of both rectifier devices connect together to the load. But there are two important differences that allow us to use the entire secondary winding on both halves of the cycle.

1. We use a non-center-tapped transformer that is designed for half the secondary voltage of the full-wave center-tap configuration described earlier. This is done because we will be using the full secondary winding on both halves of the A.C. cycle.
2. Remember each end of the secondary is already connected to the anode of a rectifier device as in the full-wave center-tap configuration described earlier. We will add a diode (think check valve) on each end of the secondary winding. Each end of the secondary winding connects to the cathode of the diode. The anode of each diode goes to ground. This allows a pathway to ground when necessary. You need that ground reference, because this transformer has no center-tap. On one half of the A.C. cycle, one of those diodes provides a ground return and on the other half of the A.C. cycle the other diode provides the ground return.

Everything else remains the same. Now on every half cycle, the entire secondary winding is being used. The extra diode that was installed is like a check valve that only allows the current to return to ground. During one half of the cycle, one diode is returning to ground and during the other half the process reverses.

The advantage of the full wave bridge is that the transformer can be wound for half the voltage and without a center-tap. It is more efficient because the entire secondary winding is used on every half of the A.C. cycle and nothing is wasted.

With proper filtering, the output voltage on this type of power supply is a maximum of 1.4 times the secondary RMS voltage.

THE FULL-WAVE ECONOMY POWER SUPPLY

Sometimes a capacitor voltage rating of more than 500 volts is needed. Modern electrolytic capacitors only go up to a 500 volt rating. If a larger rating is needed, two capacitors can be stacked in series, which doubles the voltage rating. This is sometimes called a totem pole stack. With high voltage rectifiers, sometimes a totem pole stack is used as the main filter. For example, on an AB763 Twin Reverb, you will see a totem pole stack of two 70 mfd at 350 volt filter caps. The totem pole stack is used to get the voltage rating high enough for safety. For example, two 350 volt capacitors are configured in series to make a 700 volt rating. A 220K resistor is placed across each capacitor in order to assure that the voltage is divided evenly across both capacitors. We don't want 400 volts across one cap! Remember, these are 350 volt capacitors. With the 220K balancing resistors across each capacitor, the voltage will divide perfectly across the two caps/resistors and we will have the full 700 volt rating. However, with the two resistors, there is a pathway to ground that is a constant drain on the power transformer. We can eliminate that drain with the Full-Wave Economy Power Supply.

If one takes a full-wave bridge rectifier, and uses a center-tapped transformer, the center-tap could be hooked to the junction of the two filter caps and the two 220K balancing resistors could be eliminated, further reducing loss incurred by the two divider resistors. Remember, with the full-wave bridge rectifier, the entire winding is used on every half of the A.C. cycle, so the winding is always being used. Furthermore, the center of the winding will always have exactly half the total D.C. on it, so this perfectly balances the totem pole stack of capacitors.

The full-wave economy supply can be found in many Marshalls and all Orange amps. It is used generally where there is high voltage and the filter cap voltage rating needs to be higher than 500 volts. It was used on the Fender Vibro King. It is the most efficient way to rectify A.C. into high voltage D.C. Assuming proper filtering, the DC voltage of the full-wave center-tap transformer will be a maximum of 1.4 times the RMS voltage of the entire secondary.

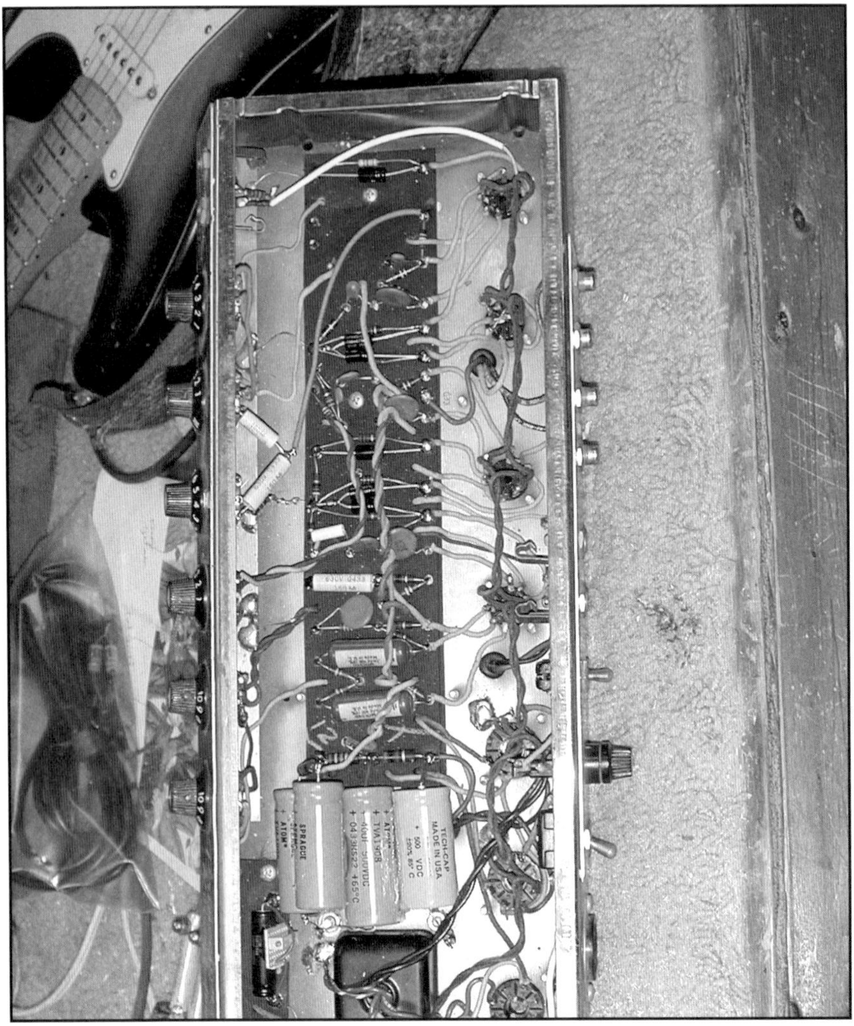

VINTAGE TUBE AMP DESIGN FLAWS

In the last decade, many people have become interested in building their own tube guitar amplifiers. When I first started building tube guitar amplifiers in the late 1980s, there were only a few custom tube amp builders, but now there are scores of novice builders that work part-time crafting tube guitar amplifiers.

For the most part, novice tube amp builders simply copy a vintage design that they know sounds good. This was the way Marshall amplifiers got started in the early 60s. Jim Marshall copied the 1959 Bassman circuit. You don't really need to know a lot about tube amp design to build an amp, if you copy an existing design that is proven. There are many flaws in vintage designs and if a builder doesn't really understand tube amp design, he is going to copy flaws without realizing it.

This can be a problem, especially if you go thru all the trouble of copying an amp design only to find out it has stability and oscillation problems. For example, it is possible to copy a 5F8A Fender Twin or 5F6A Bassman and have it wired exactly like the schematic and yet sound horrible — because the wires going to the grid of the output tubes are just one inch too long! Imagine the frustration of spending good money on good components only to build an expensive oscillator. Many times a novice builder lacks the expertise to know how to fix such an amp. I have had many such amps sent to my shop with the frustrated builder wanting to know why the amp, which is wired exactly like the schematic, doesn't work. Let's look at some of the design flaws.

VINTAGE DESIGN FLAW #1 — THE PHASE INVERTER OF MOST FENDERS AND MARSHALLS

On the 1959 Fender Bassman and many other Fender amps, the phase inverter layout is such that the plate resistors of the phase inverter are on the bottom of the circuit board. These connect, via coupling capacitors, to the 220K grid return resistors (going to the grids of the output tubes), which are mounted on the top of the circuit board. This results in long grid wires going from the 220K resistors to the output tubes. Get them an inch too long and the amp will have parasitic oscillations!

It is interesting to note that when Jim Marshall copied the Bassman, he copied the layout, but since the chassis were bigger, the wires were even longer. This is why on all Plexiglass Marshalls if you turn up the volume, treble and presence; you will hear a mosquito sound on top of the note. This is parasitic oscillation.

Here's the correction: Put the plate resistors from the phase inverter on the top of the board and put the 220K grid return resistors (for the output tubes) on the bottom of the board. The coupling caps remain unmoved. Of course you will have to move the grid and plate wires when the resistors are moved such that the circuit is unchanged. This will lengthen the plate wires of the phase inverter circuit (more inductance helps eliminate parasitic oscillation), but will shorten the grid wires by a few inches! The result is a stable amp that sounds great at any setting.

VINTAGE DESIGN FLAW #2 THE 5E3 TWEED DELUXE

There are two flaws on a 5E3 Deluxe layout that could make the amp sound horrible, with an ugly parasitic oscillation on top of the notes, even though the schematic and layout would still be done correctly. In fact, there was an amateur amp builder from the Midwest that would make copies of old Fenders. For every ten Deluxe copies built, two of them would not work. He didn't know why and would simply not sell the bad sounding ones. Amazing!

Both flaws are on the layout of the phase inverter tube. If you follow pin #1 back to the board, it goes to a .02 uf coupling cap that goes to a wire under the board and eventually terminates on pin #7 of the same tube. This results in an additional four inches or so of grid wire. Correction: The capacitor should be removed from the board and mounted directly on the tube socket. It is going from pin #1 to pin #7 of the socket anyway. Also, the board should be lifted and the wire that connected the coupling cap to the 1 Meg resistor pin #7 wire should be removed. This eliminates a four inch antenna going to the grid of pin #7.

The other flaw has to do with the proximity of the .1 uf capacitor that connects to pin #6 of the phase inverter tube. It is mounted on the board such that it sometimes parasitically couples to the bright input jack. This results in parasitic oscillation in about 20% of those amps. Correction: Unsolder the wire that goes to both pin #6 and a 1500 ohm resistor, on the inside output tube. Unsolder the top lead of the .1 uf capacitor and rotate the capacitor 90 degrees counter clockwise. Unsolder the 220K resistor (that went to the same eyelet as the .1 uf cap) and rotate it to the bottom of the board so that you can solder the loose end of the cap and resistor together. Also, solder a wire to the junction of this cap and resistor. The other end of the wire goes to pin #6 (and the 1500 ohm resistor) of the inside output tube. Now you are left with a loose wire that is hanging near pin #6 of the output tube and going under the board. You may lift the board and remove this wire completely or simply cut it off where it comes out of the board.

VINTAGE DESIGN FLAW #3 THE SCREEN SUPPLY GROUND OF MOST BLACKFACE AMPS

In all Blackface and Silverface Fender amps that have the filter caps mounted in a cap pan, the ground for the screen supply filter capacitor is grounded to the preamp filters. For best stability, it should be grounded to the main filter supply ground. Here's why: If there is substantial screen current, that current could superimpose signal on any stray resistance found in the preamp supply filter grounds. This could result in a parasitic feedback circuit — one that doesn't show up on the schematic! Correction: Lift the component board in the cap pan and locate the wire that connects the screen supply filter ground to the preamp filter grounds. Disconnect it from the preamp filter ground and move the ground to the main filter supply ground.

VINTAGE DESIGN FLAW #4 THE OUTPUT TUBE FILAMENT HEATER POLARITY IN MOST PUSH-PULL AMPS

Most amps with two or more output tubes are push-pull design. In a push-pull output stage, the hum that comes from the 6.3 volt filament heater can be hum cancelled if the filament heater going to both output tube sockets is wired with correct polarity. The filament supply is a twisted pair of wires that brings 6.3 volts A.C. to each output tube socket. For example, the two leads on a 6L6, 6V6 or EL34 output tube are pin #2 and pin #7. The filament supply should be wired so that the wire that goes to pin #2 of one tube is connected to pin #2 of the other tube. Similarly, the wire that goes to pin #7 of one tube should connect to pin #7 of the other tube. By wiring them this way, in a push-pull application, any hum induced in one tube is canceled by the hum induced in the other tube.

CORRECTION: Simply inspect the wiring and see if the wire going to pin #2 of one tube goes to pin #2 of the other. If it does not, simply reverse the wiring of one tube. If you are building an amp, pay attention to get this right and your amp will have less hum.

With a 12AX7 preamp tube, filament polarity makes no difference because the filament of a 12AX7 is a humbucking design.

VINTAGE DESIGN FLAW #5 SCREEN SUPPLY VOLTAGE AT HIGHER POTENTIAL THAN PLATE

On some vintage amps, the screen supply comes directly off the centertap of the output transformer. This is a mistake because it results in the screen having a higher voltage potential than the plate. Although the plate has more mass than the screen, having higher voltage on the screen is inviting too much screen current, and we certainly don't want to burn up those NOS tubes when we crank the amp! Some amps that come to mind are the Fender 5E6 Bassman and the 5E7 Bandmaster. Gibson did it on the GA88, GA30RV and the GA70.

Correction: If the amp has a pi filter (two filter capacitors separated by a choke) for the main supply, such as the 5E6 Bassman or the GA30RV, simply moving the centertap of the output transformer to the other side of the choke (the higher voltage side nearest the rectifier) will do the trick. Depending on the circuit, to drop the screen supply voltage, you may need to add a small dropping resistor (500 to 1000 ohms for example) and a filter cap (20 uf for example).

VINTAGE DESIGN FLAW #6 LACK OF SCREEN RESISTORS

On some vintage designs such as very early Marshall amps, the Fender 6G15 Reverb unit, and a few others, there are no screen resistors on the power tubes. If the design uses fairly high voltages, this can result in premature tube failure. I remember the first time someone in my hometown ordered a Marshall amp (back in the late sixties). He called his friends over to hear it. He cranked it up and it sounded great for about 5 minutes then — Kaput! The EL34's blew. At the time, we didn't know that a 6CA7 American tube, which could be bought at the local drug store, would have worked fine as a replacement tube. He waited 3 months for Marshall to ship him another pair of EL34's only to have them blow within minutes again. Later, Marshall issued some sort of service bulletin for shops to install screen resistors in their amps whenever possible.

This may not be a problem if the power supply voltages are not very high. For example a Gibson GA30 RV lacks screen resistors, but excessive screen current is not a problem because of the relative lower voltages used (320 plate volts for the 6V6 output tubes).

On the other hand, a Sunn 200S Sorado amp which uses an ultra-linear output stage and runs the plate voltage (and screen voltage) around 620 volts or so, needs to have some sort of screen resistor to avoid screen arcing inside the tubes. Even a 100 ohm 2 watt screen resistor (in series with the ultra-linear tap) will work wonders to stop the arcing.

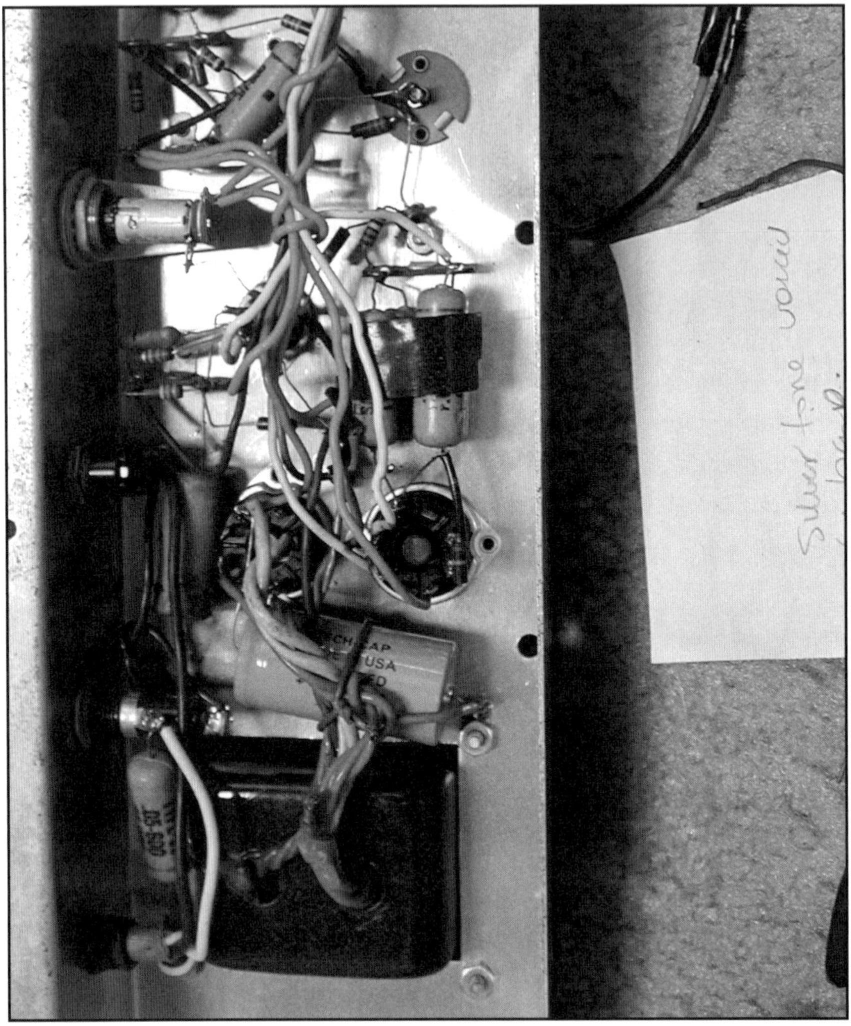

VOICING A TUBE GUITAR AMPLIFIER

How many times have you heard an amp that was "almost there tonally," but not quite? It's frustrating, isn't it? You get a good tube amp, listen to it and the tone is so happening, except for... maybe it has too much bottom; or the bottom it has is too boomy; or there's not enough top; or too bright, or too much headroom, or not enough headroom, too much compression, not enough sag, etc...

I would recommend starting with an amp that is "almost there" tonally, and work from there. If you have an amp that is fairly close to what you want, it will be fairly simple to tweak the tone to exactly what you want.

COUPLING CAPACITORS

Coupling cap values affect how much high-end and low-end gets through the circuit. For example, a smaller value cap lets less bottom through the circuit. Of course when you let less bottom-end through, it is another way of saying more highs. Conversely, a larger value cap lets more bottom through the circuit. This may or may not be good, because if you let too much bottom through, you will get boominess that flubs the bottom end. In other words, you can have more apparent bottom by restricting the bottom to the point that the bottom stays clear and punchy.

Coupling caps basically couple the plate of one tube (pin #1 or pin #6 on a 12AX7) to the grid of the next stage (pin #2 or pin #7 on a 12AX7). Typical values are anywhere from 500 pf (.0005 microfarads) to .1 microfarads. To hear an audible difference, the value must be changed by a factor of two. If you multiply by two, you get more bottom and if you divide by two, you get less bottom (more highs). In other words, changing a .02 to a .022 will not produce any audible difference. If you start out with a .02 cap and you want to make a change in tone, you will need to change to either a .01 or a .04 (.047 is standard value).

Almost as important as the microfarad value is the actual brand of coupling capacitor. In general, I like to think of the Sprague Orange drop capacitors as sounding something like a JBL speaker: clean with a transparent midrange, clear bottom and chimey top-end.

On the other hand, the Mallory 150 series (400 volt version) or the Mallory 152 series (600 volt version) capacitors tend to sound more like a tweed amp. That is a somewhat grainy and complex midrange with a slight flubbiness to the bottom-end and a smooth, rounded top-end.

I like to use these two different types for different parts of the amp. For instance, I like to use Mallory 150s or 152s in the front part of the amp and use the Orange Drops for the phase inverter. You may prefer them configured a different way, depending on what sound you are going for. For example, if you are going for a super clean sound, you might want to use Orange Drops throughout. Conversely, if you are going for a more complex tone, you might want to use Mallory 150s throughout. There is not a correct way, only the way that gives you the tone you are after.

Tony Nobles, my good friend that writes the Guitar Shop column for *Vintage Guitar* magazine, was complaining that his amp was lacking in bottom-end beefiness. He simply changed both of the .02 mfd coupling capacitors (that coupled the phase inverter to the output tubes) to .047 mfd Orange Drops and what a difference it made. He is now happy with his amp!

TONE CAPACITORS — In most amps, the tone capacitors are basically glorified coupling caps that are configured with resistors and potentiometers to allow frequency response adjustment. Let's take a Blackface Fender Twin for example. To couple the first stage to the rest of the amp, three different value coupling caps are used as tone caps. These are used in conjunction with a slope resistor and a matrix of potentiometers. As these pots are adjusted, one may adjust treble, bass and midrange.

Three coupling caps are used, namely a 250 pf (treble cap), a .1 mfd (bass cap), and a .047 mfd (midrange cap). The full signal comes into the tone circuit. The highs immediately go through the 250 pf, but the lows have a hard time going through the 250 pf so they go through the .1 mfd instead. A treble pot is connected, one end to the output side of the 250 pf and the other end to the output side of the .1 mfd. When the pot is rotated, the wiper can choose more treble by being rotated closer to the 250 pf. Rotate it closer to the .1 mfd and you get less treble.

The .047 mfd cap is connected to the same source as the .1 mfd, but the other ends of these are connected with a (bass control) pot configured as a rheostat (variable resistor). If the rheostat is turned all the way up (zero resistance), then the .047 mfd is in parallel with the .1 mfd! The circuit would see this as a .147 mfd capacitance, thus allowing more bass to get through the circuit. If the rheostat is turned all the way down (the full resistance of the pot between these two caps), then less bottom can get through the circuit.

The .047 mfd is also connected to ground with a potentiometer configured as a rheostat. As this resistance is lessened, more midrange is routed to ground, thus removing mids from the signal path.

These capacitor values can be manipulated to alter the way the tone controls work. For example, if you wanted a brighter sound, you could use a smaller cap for the 250 pf. In fact, that is exactly what Vox did on their AC30; they used a 50 pf cap for the treble cap. As the pot is adjusted for more treble, the treble will be brighter and glassier.

Let's say you wanted a beefier, rounder treble with more substance. You might want to change the treble cap to a larger value, let's say a 500 pf. That is exactly what Marshall did for their Plexis.

Perhaps you are finding yourself always turning down the bass because it is too boomy. You may consider using a smaller value bass cap. Maybe a .047 or a .02 mfd would be the way to go. There are many amps that use those values for the bass and midrange tone caps.

FILTER CAPACITORS — These are the large electrolytic capacitors that are part of the power supply. One could argue that a vacuum tube amp is nothing more than a modulated power supply. All tube guitar amps use D.C. power. The wall A.C. outlet supplies only A.C. power. Therefore, the wall electricity must be rectified to D.C. in order to have power for the tubes. In the process of rectification, the A.C.

Voicing a Tube Guitar Amplifier

gets converted to pulsating D.C. This pulsating D.C. must be filtered down to smooth D.C. and that's one reason why filter caps are used.

Consider that the filter capacitors are almost exactly like a rechargeable battery. Both filter caps and batteries store electricity by use of an electro-chemical process. I like to think of a filter cap as a battery that supplies power to the tube. The power supply/rectifier is there to keep the caps charged to full potential.

Actually, the main filters are used mainly to smooth out the pulsating D.C., while the earlier stage filters are used mainly to decouple or isolate one stage from another.

Let's say you play a loud low frequency note through the amp. If the filtering is inadequate, it cannot store enough electricity to keep the note full and rich. What happens is two-fold. First there is note "wash out." This is because the tube is not getting enough power to do its job. Second, there will be an ugly non-harmonic undertone that is the result of the note being modulated by the 120 hertz ripple current created when wall A.C. is rectified to D.C.

The filter caps are connected in stages. That is to say there will be a filter cap (or matrix of filters) connected to the output transformer, a filter cap connected to the screen supply, a filter cap connected to the phase inverter, a filter cap connected to the preamp stage, etc. Each stage is connected to the next stage by a resistor.

Increasing the value of the filter caps connected to the output transformer (mains) will allow more power to be available for the output tubes. This is really noticeable on louder and lower frequency notes. If increased enough, one could eliminate those ugly non-harmonic undertones (ghost notes) that are found on most vintage amps when those amps are cranked up in volume. Larger main filter caps will slightly reduce sag. It will make the amp less spongy in response. Bigger filter values can also prevent over-compression — where the front of the note is lost.

Increasing the value of the screen supply filter will reduce the sag (or envelope) of the note. Increasing either the main filters (output transformer) or screen filters will not affect the bass, midrange or treble content of the note.

On all the other stages of the amp, the tubes are almost always RC (resistor/capacitor) coupled. Therefore, changing the value of the filter cap feeding an RC coupled stage, will alter the amount of bass frequencies. Looking from the plate of a preamp tube, the plate resistor/filter cap is in parallel with the coupling cap. The larger the filter, the more signal goes through the filter instead of the coupling cap. For this reason, I would not recommend increasing the value of filter caps in an RC coupled tube circuit.

BYPASS CAPS — These caps get their name because they are used to "bypass" A.C. signal around the cathode resistor of a cathode-biased tube. Almost without exception, all preamp tubes are cathode biased. Sometimes the output stage is cathode biased and it too will have a bypass cap across the cathode resistor.

Let's say you removed the bypass cap from a cathode-biased tube. What would happen? Without a bypass cap, when signal amplifies, more current would go through the cathode resistor and alter the bias of the preamp tube (more towards cutoff). This would cause the gain of that particular tube to go down considerably. The sound would also compress quite a bit. The more the tube amplifies the more the bias would change.

Removing the bypass cap is a type of degenerative feedback. Sometimes it is useful to run a tube without a bypass cap. For example, if you have an instrument with a high output such as a bass guitar or a synthesizer you may want to have the cathode unbypassed so that the tube can take a big signal without clipping. Usually when this is done, a larger value cathode resistor is used, perhaps a 4.7K. I used this circuit on the Kendrick Six Shooter tube mic preamp. I wanted the first gain stage to take just about anything anyone could give it without clipping.

Here's another usage. Let's say you have a multi-gain stage amp and you don't want a particular stage to clip. Remove the bypass cap and use a larger value cathode resistor and you are there. For example, a popular Kendrick amp kit has a third stage that uses a 10K cathode resistor with no bypass cap. A tube configured this way can take a large signal without clipping. Instead of clipping, it compresses. This is heard as touch sensitivity. Play soft — it is clean as a whistle. Bear down and the front-end clips somewhat while the last preamp stage compresses.

I used this idea on the extra gain stage of the Kendrick 2410 amp.

I wanted the extra gain stage (which occurs in the circuit immediately before the phase inverter) to take a lot of signal before the onset of clipping. That is why I used an unbypassed 4.7K cathode resistor.

With a bypass cap across a cathode resistor, the quiescent D.C. current (idle current) flows through the resistor (D.C. cannot flow through a capacitor), but when the tube is amplifying signal and A.C. current is pulled into the cathode circuit, it bypasses the cathode resistor and goes through the bypass cap instead. The bypass cap's value is carefully chosen such that the capacitive reactance (think of this as the resistance the A.C. sees in the capacitor) is very small with respect to the cathode resistor value.

There is a formula for determining the capacitive reactance, but for our purposes, we will simplify and skip the math. We want the capacitive reactance at the lowest frequency to be considerably less than the cathode resistor value. This assures that the A.C. goes through the bypass cap and not the cathode resistor. To achieve a flat frequency response for guitar, the math works out to be a 25 mfd cap across a 1500 ohm cathode resistor. If you use a smaller value cathode resistor, you will have to increase the size of your bypass cap in order to have a flat response. Example: a 750 ohm resistor would use a 50 mfd. cap to get the same frequency response as the 1500 resistor using a 25 mfd cap. Similarly, if one used a 3000 ohm cathode resistor, a 12.5 mfd cap would give the same flat response. (12.5 mfd and 750 ohm are not a standard values, I am using those values to make a mathematical point.)

Maybe you don't want a flat response. Perhaps you need less bottom. Perhaps you would like more mids and upper end. You could change a 25 mfd bypass cap to a smaller value such as a 10 mfd, a 5 mfd or a 1 mfd and get less bottom and more mids. The smaller the value, the less bottom. Many Marshalls did exactly that. The first gain stage bypass cap was changed to a .68 mfd going across a 2700 ohm resistor. This gave a lot of bite and midrange punch.

On the other hand, you might need more bottom-end response. You could easily increase the value and get more bottom. Look at the original Bassman amps for example. They used a 250 mfd across an 820 ohm cathode resistor. This would bypass all A.C. frequencies around the cathode resistor, including very low frequencies.

RESISTORS — When a bypass cap is in a circuit, the larger the resistor value (for the cathode resistor), the more noticeable is the effect of the bypass cap. Let's just say that you had a circuit that used an 820 ohm cathode resistor with a 5 mfd bypass cap across it. If the resistor were changed to a 1500 ohm, you would hear the effect of the 5 mfd more. Why? Because the ratio A.C. capacitive reactance (of the capacitor) to D.C. resistance (of the resistor) is less as the cathode resistor's value is increased. The A.C. signal will want to take the path of least resistance and it will see the cap as the easiest path. Increase the resistor and the cap looks even easier to the A.C. signal.

Of course changing a cathode resistor in a preamp circuit will change the biasing of that particular tube. If you use too small of a cathode resistor, you might have a problem with the tone at loud volumes. On the other hand, if you use too large of a cathode resistor, you might have a problem with tone at lower volumes. How much is too much? It depends on a lot of factors. Why not use a decade box and dial it in? There is no substitute for listening with your own ears. You know what sounds good. If you don't have a decade box, use a 10K pot, dial it in, and then very carefully measure the pots value without disturbing the setting. Replace the pot with a resistor of this value and you are there.

Resistors are also used in many other parts of the amp. For example, the power supply uses dropping resistors to distribute power to different parts of the amp. In general, if the dropping resistor's value is increased, then there will be less voltage going to the circuit that it supplies. Less voltage on a preamp circuit means less headroom (easier breakup), slightly less gain and less high-end. Have you got a brittle sounding channel? Maybe you need to decrease the voltage feeding that stage. Brown it out.

I used this circuit extensively on the harp amp I designed. I designed the first gain stage preamp tube to operate with 80 volts on the plate. This makes the tube grind at any volume and takes off the ultra high-end, thus almost eliminating microphone feedback.

Besides being used in cathode circuits, tone circuits and power supply circuits; resistors are also used for grid return circuits, voltage divider circuits, plate resistors, bias supplies, hum balancing, channel mixing, and reverb mixing.

Here are some basics:

When I talk about a grid return circuit, I am talking about the resistor that goes from the grid of a tube to ground. This provides a load for the incoming signal to develop across and provides a ground reference for the grid of the tube. Use a larger value resistor and the highs have more chime. Use a smaller value resistor and the tone becomes warmer (slightly darker, with less crispness on the top). Typical values for a grid return resistor would range from 150K to several megohms. Most amps use a 1 meg as the grid return resistor of the first gain stage. You can tweak from there. Like most tweaking, double or halve the standard value and then listen to the result. For example, if you were tweaking a circuit that used a 1 meg grid return resistor, you might try either a 2 meg, or a 500K.

In a voltage divider circuit, two resistors are placed in series, with the second resistor usually terminated to ground. The signal is connected to the first resistor, which is the dropping resistor. The second resistor is the load resistor. The output signal is taken across the load resistor. The essence of voltage dividers is the ratio of one to the other. If both resistors are the same value, the signal will be cut exactly in half. If the dropping resistor is larger, the signal will be cut by more than half. If the load resistor is larger, the signal will be cut less than half.

PREAMP TUBES — Most amps use 12AX7 style tubes. There are many different versions of this tube that have varying amounts of gain. From highest to lowest in gain we have:

12AX7 – amplification factor 100
5751 – amplification factor 70
12AT7 – amplification factor 60
12AY7 – amplification factor 44
12 AU7A – amplification factor 20
12AU7 – amplification factor 17

Other factors to consider are the actual brands of tubes. There are some very good sounding new 12AX7s being made today. There are many NOS 12AT7, 12AY7, 12AU7 and 5751 tubes available.

One really nice sounding preamp tube is the Sovtek 12AX7LP. It works great in most circuits, but never put one in the second preamp tube position in a Bassman, Kendrick 2410, or an early Marshall. The reason is that the spiral wound filament in this particular tube is very sensitive with respect to heater-to-grid voltage. Amps that use a cathode-biased cathode follower circuit will exceed the Sovtek 12AX7LPs heater to grid voltage and the cathode will strip — thus ruining the tube.

OUTPUT TUBES — Although there are many different kinds of output tubes, there are a few common types that are generally used. The 6L6, 6V6, EL34, EL84 and 6550 are the most popular type of output tubes that are used for guitar amps. There are many tubes that can be substituted for a 6L6. In most cases, the KT66, 7581A, 5881, and EL37 can be substituted for the 6L6, and for one another. I will refer to this group as "6L6 style tubes."

Just as important as the types of tubes, the brands of tubes make a huge difference in tone. For example, if you took a NOS Tung Sol 5881 and compared it to a Philips 5881, and compared them to a Sovtek 5881, you would be amazed. The reason these sound so different is because the plates are made from different alloys, the cathodes are coated with different chemicals and there are many other variations in manufacture such as content of inert gases, grid material, base material, internal capacitance, etc. When I recorded 16 different brands and types of 6L6 style tubes, I was amazed at the difference in tone. The Genelex KT66 sounded very round and flute-like with lots of fundamental and very little harmonic breakup. The Slovakian KT66's sounded very close to the Genelex at a fraction of the price.

Sometimes you will see tubes labeled with 7581A/KT66. These are not KT66s. A KT66 is a "Kinkless Tetrode" whereas the 7581A is a beam power tube. Although these tubes are interchangeable, the beam power tube has a suppressor grid that is internally connected and the tetrode does not. The real KT66 is much rounder sounding.

Assuming the EL34 circuit runs at 500 volts or less, any of the "6L6 style tubes" can be used in an EL34 socket, but not necessarily the other way. The 6L6 style tubes do not have a connection for pin #1. Sometimes the amp designer used pin #1 (on the socket) as a mounting post because they knew that the 6L6 tubes didn't have a pin #1. The EL34 has a pin #1 which goes to a suppressor grid. The suppressor grid (pin #1) must be connected to pin #8 on the socket. This is why you can't use an EL34 in a 6L6 style socket unless you remove whatever is already on pin #1 of the socket, mount it elsewhere, and install a jumper wire from pin #1 to pin #8! The 6CA7 and the E34L are direct replacements for the EL34 so we will refer to these as "EL34 style tubes." All EL34 style tubes must be wired the same way as the EL34 when using them in a socket designed for 6L6. Usually the EL34, E34L and the 6CA7 tend to draw more screen current (than the 6L6-style tubes) so it would be advisable to use 1000 ohm 5 watt resistors with these tubes if you are converting a 6L6 style amp to take EL34's. One advantage to using the EL34 style tubes: they require less signal to drive them; thus when used in a 6L6 circuit, they are more easily overdriven!

Generally speaking, any of the 6L6 style tubes can be used in a 6V6 circuit, but a 6V6 cannot be used in a 6L6 circuit. Typical 6V6 voltages are generally much lower than typical 6L6 voltages. If you put a 6V6 in a 6L6 circuit, the increased voltage of the 6L6 circuit design will likely blow up the 6V6! If you have a 6V6 amp that needs more headroom, you can try a 6L6, 5881, 7581A, EL37, or KT66 to increase headroom. I would not try the 6550 in the 6V6 circuit because it draws considerably more filament current than the other 6L6 style tubes, even though it has the same pin-out.

When using a 6550 or EL34 one must be careful with regard to the heater current. The 6550 tube draws twice the heater current of a 6L6! The 6L6 draws twice the heater current of the 6V6. The EL34 draws almost as much as the 6550. When you consider that almost all amp designs will over-design the heater circuit current rating by 100%, it normally isn't a problem. An easy way to tell if the heater winding can take the extra current is to try the tube, but immediately check the heater voltage with an A.C. voltmeter (pins #2 and #7). If the voltage drops below 6.1 volts, it can't take it. If the voltage is stable at 6.1 to 6.6 volts, the heater winding will be fine.

The EL84 is a nine-pin miniature tube that is very popular. The 6BQ5, 7981, 7981A and EL84 are all interchangeable. The 7981A has the most headroom and can take a little more heat. It would be the most rugged of the EL84 style tubes.

SPEAKERS — When choosing speakers, you should choose the speaker that most compliments the amp. For example, if you have an amp with tons of bottom-end, you might want to use a speaker that lacks bottom-end. On the other hand, if you have an amp with lots of chime and plenty of highs, you may choose a darker sounding speaker so that the overall tone is even throughout the frequency range. Try to get the right speaker for the cabinet. If you have an open-back cabinet, you might want a speaker with more pronounced low end. Conversely, a closed back cabinet normally has more bottom, so you could get away with a speaker that did not have much bottom, for use in a closed back.

Almost all 12" speakers suffer from a phenomenon known as "edge yell" or "cone cry." This is where the cone distorts near the edge and sounds somewhat buzzy. When I first noticed this, I thought I had lost my mind. You may not have ever noticed this before, but notice it one time and you will hear it on almost every 12" speaker you listen to. This problem is more pronounced in brand new speakers than in speakers that have been broken in. The 10" speaker is not going to have this problem. The other advantage of the 10" speaker is that it has less cone inertia and is therefore more responsive (faster response).

BIASING — Tubes are sometimes called valves because just as a valve controls how many gallons can flow, a tube controls how much current can pass. When a valve (tube) is turned on full blast to where it is letting as much current pass as it possibly can, that condition is called saturation. When a valve (tube) is letting no current pass, that condition is called cut-off. Adjusting the bias of an amp is selecting an operating point somewhere between saturation and cut-off. If you select an operating point that is closer to saturation, the tube will break up more easily. It just doesn't have as far to go to achieve saturation. On the other hand, if an operating point is selected close to cut-off, the tube will stay fairly clean, as it will take a fairly large signal to drive the tube into saturation.

Preamp tubes are self-biased (also called cathode biased because of the resistor that is attached to the cathode of the tube that actually achieves bias) and never need adjusting. It is the output tubes that need to be biased. Some output tube designs such as the tweed Deluxe and the Champ are self-biased, and therefore do not need adjusting. If the output tubes are not self-biased, then they are fixed bias. Fixed bias does not mean they can't be adjusted, it means there is a "fixed" negative voltage on the grids. This can always be adjusted; it is just that some designs are not easily adjusted. The tough ones to adjust are the ones that use a resistor instead of a pot in the negative voltage bias supply. In this design, the resistor value has to be changed by using a decade box or replacing the resistor with a pot.

When adjusting the bias of an output stage, one must ask how he wants it to sound. If you want a clean sound that does not break up easily, you will want to adjust the bias such that not much plate current flows when the tubes are at idle (closer to cut-off). This gives you plenty of headroom before the tube saturates. On the other hand, if you want the tubes to break up quicker, you simply idle them at a higher current. This way it doesn't take much to "push them over the edge."

How much plate current? It really depends on the amp, because you don't want to exceed the plate watt dissipation of the tube. This is where experimentation with the bias of your particular amp is important to dial-in the exact character. A good rule of thumb for most guitar amplifiers is 35 milliamps of plate current. Try that, play it a while, then look and listen. Look at the output tubes. If the plates are glowing cherry red, they are idling too high. If they are not glowing cherry red, then you are not exceeding the plate watt dissipation and you are safe. If you want the amp to be cleaner, try 30 or 25 milliamps per output tube and see how that sounds. If you want quicker breakup, try 40 or 45 milliamps. Keep looking and listening. Any setting that sounds good to you AND does not make the tubes glow cherry red is the correct setting.

NEGATIVE FEEDBACK — If you played many different frequencies through an amp (that did not have a negative feedback circuit in its design) and recorded the exact volume of each frequency, you would notice that certain frequencies are louder than others. To help make all frequencies even with regard to volume, a negative feedback loop is sometimes used. This is a clever circuit in which a small portion of the output signal (that drives the speaker) is "fed back" into an earlier part of the circuit. This signal is 180 degrees out of phase with the output signal. This phase cancels part of the preamp signal and therefore reduces volume. However, it doesn't reduce the volume of all frequencies the same. If a frequency is louder coming out, then there is a larger signal being fed back and therefore more phase cancellation of that frequency. In other words, the louder signal gets reduced in volume more. If a particular frequency isn't as loud as other frequencies, then that note is not fed back as much, has less phase cancellation and becomes louder by comparison. In short, the negative feedback loop evens everything out, volume-wise, but CUTS OVERALL GAIN in order to achieve this. Not all amps employ a negative feedback circuit.

One can adjust how much actual feedback by changing the value of the feedback resistor. This is the resistor that is connected to your speaker output jack and leads back into the circuit. Make the resistor larger and you get less feedback. Make it smaller and you get more feedback. If your amp is too raw sounding and you need less gain and more headroom, you need more feedback and you would get this by using a smaller feedback resistor. On the other hand, your amp might be too clean and in need of more gain. In this case, you would want to use less feedback, which would require a larger resistor. When experimenting with the feedback resistor, you would go in multiples of two. For example, if the stock value were 20K, you would try a 10K if you need more feedback or a 40K if you need less. After you listen to that, you would go multiples again. (Example: You liked the 40K so you try an 80K next.)

Tube Guitar Amplifier Essentials

CONVERSATIONS FOR TONE

I first met Johnny Poe when he attended my Tube Guitar Amp Seminar. I could tell the tube amp bug had bitten him. Here was a man that had read all of my books, studied all of my instructional videos and was looking to expand from there. He called to request a "tone meeting." Thinking that the answers to his questions may be what you wanted answered for yourself, I recorded the conversation. Johnny Poe, an aspiring amp designer, is quizzing Gerald Weber on tone. The conversation unfolds.

Johnny: I took Radio and Electronics at TSTI back in Sweetwater, Texas in the early 70s, so I know enough about tubes to not kill myself with them. I never did get into tube amps until I started reading your books. I started messin' with them and learning more and more about them. I really enjoyed going to your seminar last fall, I learned a lot there, I took a lot of good notes; I still listen to the tapes I made from that. It has brought up some more questions I had in mind. I have been doing some work on amps for other people. The majority of the amps I get to work on are the stock Silverface Fenders. Everybody always ask me, 'Can you make it sound like a Marshall?' They always want it to sound like something different. I'll bet you get that question all the time?

Gerald: Unless they have a Marshall, in which case they want it to sound like a Fender.

Johnny: What I'm looking at is tweaking the amp. I can convert Silver to Blackface and put in the adjustable bias and get a fairly decent tone. I know that every one of these amps is going to sound different and everything in the signal chain affects the tone. Everything affects the tone. No two amps are going to sound exactly alike, but I'm looking at tendencies. If you change this, it tends to do this. If you change that, it tends to do that. I'm looking at what affects what, tonally.

Let's take the tonal characteristics of a British amp. First of all, how would you describe the sound of a good British amp?

Gerald: When I think of a British amp, I think of "bark." A British amp is gonna have that midrange barkiness that cuts through a mix. It's real round. It is not going to have that Fendery type of chime. It's going to compress on the high-end more. Generally, the British amps seem a little gainier. They don't really have that much more gain, its just that most of them use EL34's or EL84's which don't take as much signal to drive, so with the same amount of gain (as in a 6L6 amp) you end up driving them much harder.

The Fender amps are going to have more of a scooped midrange. They are not going to be barky. There will be a lot of space in there so that when playing chords, each note can be heard without crowding the other notes in the chord. On many of these amps, when they distort, the high end doesn't compress so much, instead it's more of a brittle type of chime, which I don't find very desirable.

Johnny: Let us say you had a stock Silverface Fender and you want it to sound British ...

Gerald: Well now there are a few things you could do. One thing you could do is change to an EL34 style tube; that would make it seem like it has more gain.

Another thing you could do — you need to bump up the mids. You could do this with some compensating caps, for example, across the volume pot. Instead of using a Fender value such as a 100 pf or a 47 pf, you would want to use something much larger that would let those mids cut through. For instance, a 5,000 pf (same as .005 mfd), or maybe even a .01 mfd or a 2500 pf could be installed across the volume pot as a compensating cap.

Alternatively, anywhere there is a voltage divider in the circuit; you could put a capacitor across the dropping resistor of the voltage divider. This would encourage the mids.

Of course, you would want to use a speaker that had a British type midrange. Perhaps a Vox Bulldog speaker, maybe a Fane, perhaps even a Kendrick Brownframe would give you that thick midrange voicing.

Johnny: Ok, now let's say you want a California type sound, you know, high-gain type sound. More of a Boogie type sound.

Gerald: The Boogie sound, though not one of my favorite sounds, had a novelty to it when it first came out. At that time, no one had heard that overdriven preamp sound before, so it was unique in that regard. Nevertheless, the Boogie sound is a high-gain preamp sound with a stiff power supply and therefore a stiff output stage. This type of gain could be gotten in a Silverface Fender by adding another stage of gain, perhaps a stage in front of the existing preamp.

In addition, the original Boogies did not use a voltage divider volume control for this extra stage. Instead of a regular voltage divider volume control, they used the Tweed Deluxe style volume control, which isn't a voltage divider, but is hooked up to load down the signal. I think this is part of the sound as well, because that circuit has a distinctive sound to it.

Also, the California sound, in general, has a lot more voltage and more filtering. Higher voltage on the preamp, higher voltage on the output tube, everything is higher with stout filtering.

Johnny: Another valid sound that people would be looking for, of course, is tweed type sound. Talk about the tweed sound.

Gerald: Most tweed amps had a .02 mfd coupling cap right after the first stage and then the signal went to a volume control, and then went on beyond that. With a Silverface Fender, this could be simulated with the Texas Tea control. This circuit is simply a .01 mfd cap that is in series with a 2.2 Meg pot wired as a rheostat. This circuit bypasses the stock Fender Silverface tone circuit. The cap goes to the plate resistor of the first gain stage and the rheostat goes to the top of the volume control. This circuit bypasses that raw, grainy midrange tweed tone around the tone circuit.

Another way this could be emulated, believe it or not, is by lifting the tone circuit ground! Now the tone controls won't work much at all, but you can tweak the tone controls a little for best tone.

The tweed sound is not going to have as heavy of filtering, and it's going to be lower voltage, so your tubes are going to break up a little quicker, they're going to have a frequency response band that is lower than if you used higher voltage.

Johnny: Ok, lets get a little tricky with it then. Let's say I had a two-channel Silverface Fender, a Pro Reverb for example — a standard two channel Fender with reverb — and you wanted a tweed type sound on one channel and another sound — say a Blackface sound

Conversations for Tone

— on the other one. Let me see if my thinking is correct on this. You want to maybe lower the voltage on the preamp tube of the one channel. That would be raising the value of the power resistor. Right?

Gerald: You might end up having to give it its own resistor and filter cap, because on the Fender Silverface, all of the preamp tubes get their supply from a single point. Therefore, you would have to add another "L" section of filtering. Maybe you could put, uh I don't know, a 47K or a 50K dropping resistor and maybe another 10 mfd filter cap. You don't want to use too big a filter cap because on your preamp stages, the filter cap is in parallel with your coupling cap. You don't want to lose all your tone by having it go through the filter cap instead of the coupling cap.

Johnny: That was another question I had; does having the high voltage on the power tubes matter? I know that the lower voltage is part of the tweed sound — the lower voltage all the way through. That's where tweaking comes in, right?

Gerald: The thing about a tweed amp, you know, is that they have lots of compression. You would have to listen to the particular amp to see if it has enough compression. Let's use a solid state rectifier Bandmaster, for instance. That's going to sound different, power supply-wise, than a Super Reverb. The Super Reverb has the tube rectifier. So you may need more compression to emulate the tweed sound exactly. You may have to settle on a compromise. Just leave the output stage alone and go for getting more compression on the front-end of that preamp side.

Johnny: That's where knowing your tweaking comes in.

Gerald: Yeah, but you might get enough compression just by lowering the voltage of the front end of that preamp side. Again, you'd have to listen and see what you've got.

Johnny: Let's start at the beginning. Say you go through your input and you've got your 1 Meg and your two 68K resistors. What happens if you change those to different values?

Gerald: The 68K's are actually part of a voltage divider circuit that is activated when you use the number two input. When you plug into the number one input, the 68K's are switched in parallel so your circuit only sees 34K resistance. You don't really need that 34K, it doesn't really do anything, but it was a compromise they had to make in order to have a number two input that cut the signal in half.

Johnny: Ok, I will get a little off in left field. I was thinking about finding a Princeton and wiring it up like a tweed Deluxe — to get the interactive volume controls and everything. I'd have two separate channels so I'd just have 1 input per channel on this. So, I'd have to have a 1 Meg on each input jack, but really don't have to have anything from there? I mean I would not need the 68K resistors?

Gerald: Correct, those 68K's are unnecessary in a single input amp. I would say you are on the right track with using just the 1 Meg resistor on each input.

Johnny: That's what I'm going to try to do. Should I use 1 Meg pots in there for both tone controls?

Gerald: You see, the tweed amps had a gain stage before the tone driver circuit. In the Blackface amps, the first stage was the tone driver circuit. The reason they did that was that the tone controls on the earlier tweed amps did not work very well. You can adjust the tone settings on a tweed amp and it will affect it a little, but it really doesn't do a lot. On the Blackface amp, Fender designers eliminated a stage of gain in front of the tone driver circuit, so there is less gain driving the tone circuit. The controls seem to do more because they have less gain to work with. If you are trying to shape tone, you can see that it is easier to shape it if you have less signal to work with.

Johnny: Let's move along the circuit now. You've got your plate resistor and your cathode resistor. Do you have to keep those balanced? By that, I mean, like adjusting a carburetor. Going higher, do you get more gain?

Gerald: Well now, the cathode resistor is going to bias the tube. A typical cathode resistor value for a 12AX7 for example, would be a 1500 ohm. We are talking about a single section of the 12AX7. However, if you tied both cathodes together and only use one cathode resistor for both sides of the tube, you would cut the resistor value in half. Two halves of a tube tied together draws twice as much current as a single section. To maintain bias voltage, if we are drawing twice as much current, we only need half as much resistance to create identical voltage drop. Stated differently, a 1500 ohm cathode resistor on one section of a 12AX7 will obtain the same bias voltage as a 750 ohm resistor connected to both sections. Almost always, the 820 ohm resistor is used because it is a standard value.

The cathode resistor will usually have a bypass capacitor across it.

The purpose of this cap is to bypass A.C. signal voltage around the resistor. The D.C. goes through the resistor, but the A.C. goes through the capacitor. A bypass capacitor will pass A.C. signal but not D.C. voltage. The value of the cap is carefully chosen so that the capacitor's capacitive reactance at the lowest frequency of the circuit equals a tenth of the cathode resistor's resistance. There is actually a formula for the capacitive reactance of a capacitor. I am trying to think of what it is. It's capacitive reactance equals one over 2 pi frequency times capacitance (in farads). For instance, the lowest note on a guitar is 80 hertz. Therefore, you simply plug 80 hertz in the formula. You know what pi is — it is going to be 3.1416 and the capacitance in farads — a microfarad is going to be .000001 farads- so a 25 microfarad would be .000025 farads. Multiply 2 times 3.1416 times 80 hertz times .000025 farads. This comes out to .0125664. Now you divide 1 by .0125664 and get 79.57728 capacitive reactance. So, a 25 microfarad capacitor has a reactance of about 80 ohms when an 80 hertz signal is run through it. This is about a tenth of the D.C. resistance of the 820 ohm resistor. The A.C. signal would prefer the 80 ohm path to the 820 ohm path.

If you were using a 1500 ohm cathode resistor, to get the same frequency response, you would need to cut the capacitor value roughly in half. Doubling the capacitor value will halve the capacitive reactance.

We are talking about keeping the frequency response flat at the lowest guitar frequency, however sometimes we want to voice an amp to get more of certain frequencies. This is where changing to non-standard values can be useful.

The same would hold true on a cathode biased output stage circuit. Let us say you have a 250 ohm cathode resistor. You would need a capacitor whose capacitive reactance at the lowest possible frequency would equal 25 ohms. So if you do the math, you will find a 100 mfd capacitor at 80 hertz has about 20 ohms capacitive reactance.

Of course, in all of these cases, if we are working with a bass amp, the lowest frequency is 40 hertz. This, of course, would double all of the capacitor values in order to end up with the same reactance.

Johnny: Let us say you are going for a California type sound. Are you going to get a hotter sound by getting rid of the 68K resistors on the input?

Gerald: There is no current going through the 68K's. If there is no current going through a resistance, there will be no voltage drop either, and hence, no gain loss. However, anytime signal is passed through a resistance, the first thing to go is high end. Therefore you would have more high-end without those resistors, but it will not make much difference in gain.

Johnny: But if you wanted a darker sound, that wouldn't be the place to tweak it anyway?

Gerald: Well you could tweak it there if you wanted to, but you would have to tweak the number 2 input. What you could do is plug into the number two input. The signal would see two 68K load resistances or 136K. The first 68K that the signal sees will be a dropping resistor and the second will be a load resistor. (When you are plugged into the number two input, the one Meg is shorted and not used). You could easily design this into a filter. If you wanted less high-end, you could put a cap across the load resistor, in other words the junction of the two 68K's to ground. That would take high-end off to give you a darker sound.

However, if you wanted more treble, you could put a cap on the first 68K, which would bypass highs around that resistor. If you wanted a British sound, perhaps a 5000 pf cap.

Actually, if I were going to voice it on the input, I would probably just use the number one input. I would eliminate the one Meg and the two 68K and simply use two 470K's as a voltage divider. The cap could go across either resistor depending on what I wanted. I would use this, because the cap would be more effective across a 470K than a 68K.

When you put a capacitor across a resistor, there are two paths for the signal. If you put the cap across a 470K resistor, the high-end will act like it is seeing much less resistance. So let's say the capacitive reactance is only 50K. Well then, the high-end will go through the capacitor and not the resistor, while the lows will be affected only by the resistors.

Johnny: If you are looking for a high gain sound, would we want to tweak the cathode resistor of the first stage to get higher gain?

Gerald: Maybe, but maybe not. Let us say you cut your bias in half. Normally you would use a 1500 ohm, you want to cut it in half, but there is not a standard value that is exactly in half, so let's say you use an 820 ohm. That will give you a hotter sound, because it will idle that 12AX7 up a little hotter. Sometimes, when you have the thing biased like that and you are cranking the volume, you can hit a note and it may seem the amp wants to hesitate — like it is trying to catch its breath. In this case, it is under-biased. You may have to go to a 1000 ohm or a 1200 ohm.

We tried that circuit on our Black Gold 35 and did not like the 820 ohm as well as the 1500. The reason was that if you had the amp turned up and you jammed a bar chord hard; there would be this hesitation.

Johnny: I think you see where I am going with all this.

Gerald: You are taking it systematically. The next question is going to be about the plate resistor and the coupling cap. You know the coupling cap along with the plate resistor is in parallel with the filter cap. If you want more bottom end, you would use a bigger coupling cap. The 220K plate load resistors are sometimes used and other times the 100K is used. The problem with the 220K is that it will sometimes force a little grid emission. That is not too cool if you are trying to adjust the volume on your guitar and the pot sounds scratchy because of the D.C. leakage current. The 220K sounds good and that is why people sometimes use them. A Vox AC30 for example or Kendrick Climax, both use the 220K plate resistor. The 100K is my overall favorite. For one thing, it more accurately matches the resistance of the tube. The signal transfer is better, because the impedance is matched more closely. I always use the 100K in my designs — and we don't have "scratchy volume pot syndrome" with the 100K.

Johnny: If we went on, we would have the coupling cap.

Gerald: We have to couple it to the next stage with a coupling cap and a load resistance. That load resistance can either be a volume pot, a resistor, a voltage divider, or a tone stack, or it could be a tone filter. At the coupling, we could make a filter that feeds the next stage.

Maybe take two 470K ohm resistors and put them in series to ground, so you have a voltage divider. Take your signal off the middle of that junction. Then, you could tone sculpt by putting a capacitor on the first of those resistors (which would bypass more highs) or you could have it on the second of those resistors which would bypass highs to ground. It all depends on what sound you need and what you need to sculpt.

Johnny: So the coupling between stages is a good spot to sculpt the tone?

Gerald: That would be a damn good spot. Your cathode capacitor would make a big difference too. For example, instead of using a 25 mfd at 25 volts, try a one mfd. or perhaps .68 mfd. Marshall used that quite a bit. To make that capacitor more effective, you can increase the value of your cathode resistor. If you have a real small value cathode resistor, the cathode capacitor does not have a lot of effect. You will hear more difference in having the capacitor as the ohm value of your cathode resistor goes up. That is why Marshall used a 2.7K resistor with the .68 bypass cap. The 2.7K is such a large resistance that the bypass cap made a big difference.

Johnny: Looks like Marshall knew what they were doing. In addition, if you had a Silver Fender you were trying to convert to sound more like a British amp, you could use some of their circuits and see what you could get out of it. I get a lot of information out of the back of your books in the question and answer section. Tell me more about the coupling caps.

Gerald: The bigger the cap value, the easier it is for lower frequencies to get through. You'll notice that usually the coupling caps start out smaller in the front of the amp, but get larger as the signal progresses through the amp. Usually, by the time the signal gets to the last coupling cap (the ones feeding the grids of the output tubes) the value is up to about .1 mfd. On the Fenders, they used a smaller cap on the input of the phase inverter, which scooped enough mids and lows to get that characteristic Fendery scooped mids tone. If you wanted to go more British, the input of the phase inverter would be a good place to put a…

Johnny: A .02 microfarad!

Gerald: Exactly!

Johnny: I like those.

Gerald: Me too.

Johnny: That little Champ I bought at the Dallas Show a few months ago had a 40 mfd capacitor on the main power supply!

Gerald: That's a good way to go. That is what I like to replace them with. Whatever the stock schematic value, I like to pretty much double it. I like a lot of filtering on the mains because when I hit that low "E" on my guitar, I want to hear a note with some substance. I do not want it to compress the front off the note or compress to air! In this case, the only thing you would hear is a cymbal and the drummer laughing at you! If you knew my drummer, you would understand why that is especially important in my case!

Johnny: I've heard a lot about people trying to "age" a circuit, for example, using different value resistors and so forth. That is just tone sculpting, but what about the coupling capacitor values?

Gerald: Bigger value coupling caps give you more bottom-end. Smaller value will give you less bottom-end. If you get it too big, you may have sub-harmonic oscillation problems. The general rule is keep them smaller towards the front of the amp (early preamp stages) and have the values get progressively larger as the signal gets amplified. For example your last coupling cap — on the phase inverter — that feeds the grids of the output tubes — might be a .1 uf whereas the coupling cap after the first gain stage may be only a .01 uf.

On a Blackface Fender, a smaller value was used on the input of the phase inverter to sculpt the tone. The smaller value blocks some mids and bottom. This keeps the signal from distorting and gives that characteristic of scooped mids, the familiar Fender clean sound.

We talked about getting a British tone by modifying a Fender Silverface. The input cap on the phase inverter would be an excellent place to modify. You could change this cap to either a .02 uf or a .047 uf, which would beef up the mids and bottom.

This would give you that "British Bark" that is lacking in Blackface and Silverface Fenders.

Johnny: I've used the .02 uf and it definitely added more "beef" to it. What I would like to know is this: Is there a benefit to leaving the voltages higher on the power tubes, but dropping them on the preamp tubes?

Gerald: The benefit from having higher voltage on the power tubes is in the tone of the bottom-end. Higher voltages are going to sound punchier, and the bottom-end is just going to hold together better. In addition, I like a little kicked-up filtering on the mains power filters. I don't like much filtering on the preamp circuit. Again, the filters are in parallel with the coupling cap and plate resistors, so you are going to rob tone if you use large filtering on the front-end signal path.

Johnny: That Champ has 425 volts on the plate so it's running on up there. Very clean — all the way up!

Gerald: One of our Kendrick amps, the Black Gold 15 stereo, has two output stages, like a Champ doubled. Think two Champs but with one preamp. We use two 100 uf capacitors separated by a 250 ohm resistor as the main filter supply. This is called a "pi" filter (the capacitors are separated by the resistor, thus resembling the Greek letter "pi.") A "pi" filter using two 100 uf capacitors will filter much better than using just two 100 uf capacitors in parallel.

Johnny: That's interesting. I was looking at some of those chassis earlier. Do those output stages share the same preamp section?

Gerald: Same preamp section, same power supply, but two single-ended Class A self biasing output stages — each with its own output transformer and speaker.

Johnny: I took notes at the Tube Amp Seminar you held last year. Maybe you would like to comment on some of this. The closer to the front-end that you sculpt the tone, the more effect it has.

Gerald: Yes, the signal is progressing in strength as it is amplified from stage to stage. If the sculpting happens early on, then that sculpting gets amplified as the signal is amplified. If on the other hand, you try to do your tone sculpting "downstream" so to speak, the signal will be so strong, that it will be difficult to make as much difference.

Johnny: Ok, here's another one: Tubes, Speakers, and Transformers make the most difference in the tone of an amp.

Gerald: The output transformer is probably the most important thing in the tone of the amp. It can make or break an amplifier — of course the speaker is what is actually making the sound and every tube has its own voice as well. These are the critical tonal components.

Johnny: Here's another one: Tube bias makes a big difference in the tone. To bias, the grid is made negative in relation to the cathode. In a preamp tube, a cathode resistor is used for biasing. A 12AX7 idles at about one milliamp (.001 amp). There is about 1.5 volts difference between the grid and the cathode. Put one end of the meter on the cathode and the other end on the grid to measure the bias voltage.

Gerald: That is one way of doing it!

Johnny: Ok, The bigger the cathode resistor value, the less gain and more headroom.

Gerald: Oh yes, let's say, for example, that you knew you were going to be hitting this tube with a big signal and you didn't want it to clip. You could use a big cathode resistor, maybe a 4.7K; and don't use a bypass cap. With this arrangement, the tube can take a large input signal without clipping. As the bigger signal hits the front-end and the tube begins to draw more current, the bias is changed. Since there is no bypass cap, both A.C. signal current and D.C. quiescent current are passing through the cathode resistor. In other words, all of the current that the tube is passing must pass through the cathode resistor. As more current passes, the biasing is increased so that the tube can take an even hotter input signal without clipping.

This type of biasing is sometimes used in the first stage of a bass guitar amplifier. You don't get as much gain out of the tube when running the cathode resistor unbypassed, but it won't clip and it will compress nicely.

Johnny: Also on that same one it says, The cathode resistor alters the biasing of the tube. Double the resistor value to hear changes.

Gerald: Of Course! Let us say you had a 1.5K biasing (cathode) resistor and you wanted to experiment with some A/B sound testing. The next value up, you would probably want to use a standard value such as a 2.7K and then maybe try a 4.7K, then a 10K. It's basically double the value each time to hear a change.

Let us say you went from a 1.5K to a 1.6K. In that case, you would not be able to hear any difference.

Johnny: Here's another one: Capacitors made from different materials have different sounds. The Mallory 150 series polyester film caps sound like a Jensen speaker or a vintage sound. The Sprague Orange drop has more of a full range type sound like a JBL speaker. Do you agree?

Gerald: I agree with that! In fact, I believe I was the one who said that.

Johnny: I believe you were. I just wrote it down.

Both loudly: Ha, Ha, Ha.

Johnny: Coupling cap values affect different frequencies. Try using 50 to 500 pf for the highs, .01 to .047 for mids and .1 uf or more for lows. Coupling caps are usually around .02 uf. Smaller values let a higher ratio of highs through while larger values allow more lows to pass.

Shorting a plate resistor with a small value cap such as a 250 to 500 pf, can remove hiss. You can put a resistor in series with the cap to "tweak it."

Gerald: Yes, this is useful to get rid of some high-end sounds that guitars don't produce. I'm talking about noise.

Johnny: Let's dig deeper. Which gain stage is this used on?

Gerald: You could use it on whichever gain stage is giving you noise. In a high gain amp, you would probably end up putting it on the final gain stage before the phase inverter. This would help filter all unwanted frequencies before the signal leaves the preamp section.

Johnny: You said I can use a voltage divider to sculpt tone and bump down gain. Putting a capacitor across the first resistor in a voltage divider (sometimes called the dropping resistor) improves highs. Putting it across the second resistor (or the load resistor, as it is called) will remove highs. Of course in the latter case, it seems like you have more lows because of the absence of some highs.

Gerald: I used that circuit in an amp one time. We used to build a 6 watt practice amp called a Roughneck. It had a bright and a normal input. Here is how we did it. Each input had a switch on the jack that would ground out the "hot" lead when the jack was not being used. Each "hot" on the jack went to a 470K ohm resistor. These resistors apexed together and went to the grid of the first gain stage preamp. Only one of the resistors had a cap across it, I believe we used a 250 pf value. If you were plugged into the input whose 470K resistor had the cap across it, then you would have much more highs and thus your bright input. In this case the highs would see the capacitor as a "short" around the first 470K dropping resistor. On the other hand, if you plugged into the other input, the highs would short to ground around the same resistor (which would now become the load resistor due to the switching of the ground reference; thus your normal input.

Johnny: You said coupling caps and tone caps should be at least 400 volts and sometimes 600 volt.

Gerald: It depends. The 600 volt cap will be physically larger and I like a larger cap. With caps at least, bigger is better. Therefore, you might want to use a 600 volt cap although you are dealing with a 200 volt circuit.

Johnny: Is there going to be a benefit to it?

Gerald: It's going to be a bigger cap. Everything else being equal, the bigger cap wins tonally. A higher voltage cap will have a thicker dielectric to get the extra voltage rating. Since a thicker dielectric will cause the capacitance to go down, the area of the internal plates of the capacitor must be increased. What you end up with is a larger capacitor with a smoother more consistent sound tonally. I'm sold.

Conversations for Tone

Johnny: You said raising the value of the treble capacitor will also increase the mids coming through the tone circuit. The opposite is true, lowering the value will decrease the midrange. Use a 250 pf as a center value and go up or down from there. Can you give an example?

Gerald: Well for instance, a Vox AC30 Top Boost used a 50 pf for the treble cap and certain Marshalls used a 500 pf value.

Johnny: Let's talk more about filtering.

Gerald: As I said before, the only place I like a lot of filtering is on the mains. Oh, did I say that sometimes more filtering is needed in the preamp section to get rid of motorboating? Let us say you have three stages of preamp gain that were all connected to the same point on your power supply. You may need to isolate those stages with some more "L" sections of filtering. An "L" section is another power resistor and a filter capacitor.

Of course, signal is amplified as it progresses through the amp. By the third stage, it could be very strong. It may be too much for the one filter cap to keep stable. By using multiple "L" sections, the voltage is stabilized so that each tube is getting power that does not have another stage's voltage fluctuation imposed on it.

You can see where if the third stage tube began to pull major current and it was to impose this on the first stage, that this could start a feedback that sometimes manifests itself as motorboating. The "L" section keeps voltage fluctuation from the third tube from being superimposed on the first tube.

Johnny: When you said that, in my mind, I was thinking about good lead dress and not criss-crossing circuitry. In other words no zig-zagging the signal path back and forth.

Gerald: I can tell you have some first hand experience.

Johnny: Yeah, when you got a Silverface Pro and you got that vibrato tube that you are not using, so you decide to use it as an extra gain stage in front of everything. You soon find out that it doesn't work; not unless you move everything over to avoid criss-crossing circuitry.

Gerald: Lord, I could tell you some bad lead dress stories — maybe later.

Q&A

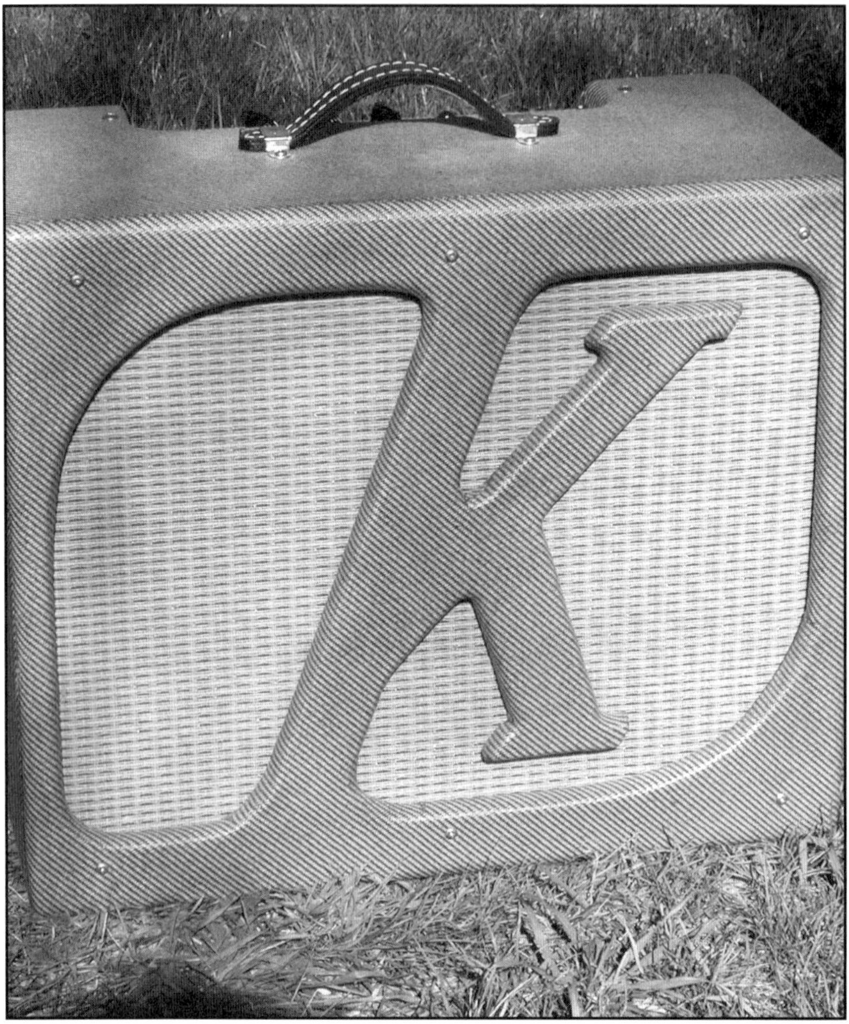

FENDER

On my mid 60s Super Reverb, the speaker baffle is a piece of ½" fiberboard that has some cracks and appears to be a real cheesy material for such an important piece. I would like to replace it. What type of material do you recommend that I replace it with?

I recommend voidless Baltic Birch. It comes in metric sizes. There is one size that is about ½" that is best to use. Make sure and put a ¼" X 1" wide perimeter strip all around the baffleboard perimeter. It is not critical what this perimeter strip is made from. Any ¼" plywood will work. The 1 inch wide perimeter strip is only a spacer that keeps the grill cloth from rattling on the baffleboard. Leave this off and you will hear rattle every time you hit a note.

My Twin is blowing fuses occasionally after playing for about an hour and a half. So I went through your "fuse blowing" paradigm — with removing the output tubes and replacing them one at a time. No problems! No fuse blew! I can leave the amp on for several hours without incident, yet play it for about 30 minutes and the fuse will blow. Got any ideas? It has all new caps!

If you are blowing fuses while using a 2½ Amp Slo Blo fuse, then the amp is drawing too much current. Since you said it had new caps, I am suspicious that one of the filter capacitors is in backwards. I have seen amps behave this way if one of the filter capacitors were installed with the polarity backwards. When you remove the cap pan, the filter capacitors should all face the same way except the one closest to the output transformer and it will face opposite polarity with respect to the others. My crystal ball tells me this is your problem.

If all the filters were installed correctly, the next most probable cause of the fuse blowing would be a tube arcing only when it is under load — thus blowing the fuse. It doesn't arc when idling. To find out which tube, simply turn on the amp while watching the output tubes and play it until the fuse blows. If you see a particular tube arc when the fuse blows, simply replace the tube and you are done. This test is easier to perform with the lights out! The arcing will be obvious.

Is the power transformer rusted? That could also cause this type of malfunction. If the transformer is rusty and there are eddy currents, the power drain on the power transformer could be borderline overload when idling and just over-the-top-too-much when jamming.

I have what used to be an AB 763 Super Reverb. It has been modified to a Twin type circuit by removing the vibrato circuit completely and opening the phase inverter hole to except a power tube. The phase inverter was moved over and reinstalled into the vibrato tube socket next to it. This completely disabled the vibrato circuit. The rectifier was changed to solid state and that socket was used for a power tube. It has Twin power and output transformers and a 15" speaker. It's been my main gigging amp for 20 years. Can I use those two unused vibrato controls to make my reverb sound like my 6G15 Fender Stand-alone Reverb? I have tried your "jumper reverb mod" to my normal channel and liked it, but I play steel and lead guitar, so I need to keep the normal channel open for lead guitar. Can you just aim me in the right direction so I don't cook a bunch of parts?

The prospects for a real 6G15 sound are not good. For one thing, you are limited to using passive circuitry because there is no room for another tube in that amp. To install a tone control and have it work well, you are going to need another gain stage and you don't have another tube available. Here's what you could do — short of adding another tube.

You will need some shielded wire and two 1 Meg pots. On your two vibrato controls, we are going to need to install a 1 Meg pot for each of these. The control closest to the input jacks is going to become your dwell control and the other is going to be your tone control. The dwell control will adjust how much signal is driving the reverb pan. The tone control will roll off high-end on the reverb pan return circuit.

If you look at the reverb driver tube (that's V3, the 12AT7 near the reverb transformer), notice there is a wire connecting pin #2 and pin #7 together and then that wire goes to the board. It goes under the board and connects to the junction of a 1 Meg resistor and a 500 pf cap. Remove the 1 Meg resistor from the amp and remove the wire going from pins #2 and #7 to the board. Pin #2 remains connected to pin #7; you are just removing the wire going from there to the board. In fact, if you heat up the solder connection at the junction of the 1 Meg and the 500 pf, you should be able to give a gentle tug on that wire and completely remove it from the amp.

Next, we need to wire the pot. Mount the 1 Meg pot with the three leads pointing up — just like the other pots. Looking from the back of the pot:
1. The left lead gets grounded.
2. The right lead gets connected to the end of the 500-pf cap that formerly connected to the 1 Meg resistor you removed earlier.
3. The middle lead goes to pins #2 and #7 of the reverb tube.

Use shielded wire for all this and remember to ground the shielding only on one end — to avoid inducing hum. I would ground the shielding from both wires at the pot end and remove all the naked shielding at the other end to avoid causing any short circuits.

Here are some suggestions for a tone control. I will tell you how it is done and then you will have to experiment with capacitor values. The tone control will be a 1 Meg pot. Looking from the back of the pot, the left lead gets grounded and the other two leads are connected together and to a capacitor (the exact value of which is unknown so we will have to experiment.) The other end of the capacitor will go to pin #2 of V4, which is the same point electrically as both the hot lead of the RCA reverb pedal jack and the RCA reverb output jack. You must use shielded wire for this connection and the shielding must be grounded only on one end. Again, be sure and remove any naked shielding from the other end to avoid causing a short circuit somewhere.

Here are some suggestions of which value caps to try. I would begin with a .005 uf cap. Voltage rating is irrelevant because we are talking about less than a volt in this circuit. Listen to the .005 uf capacitor and turn the new reverb tone control. Notice how the tone control works when you turn the knob. If it is giving you what you want, fine. If you need to experiment more, you must either double or half the value to notice any difference in performance. To try a smaller value and roll off less upper mids, try using a .003 uf (this is a standard value). If you aren't rolling enough highs off, try a .01 uf cap. If neither of these values gives you what you want, you would then try the .02 uf or the .001 uf (same as 1,000 pf), depending on which way you need to go from there.

On the Fender vibrato circuit, I am supposed to have 300 volts coming off the plate of the 5th tube. I am getting the correct B+ voltage (from the power transformer), but I get 450 volts on the plate of the 5th tube. I have traded out all the resistors surrounding this circuit as well. Do you have any ideas about that?
There is nothing wrong with the voltages here; I would guess this to be operator error. I'll bet you don't have the tremolo switched on via the footswitch. Almost all Fender's have bias voltage going to the oscillator tube to overbias it into absolute cutoff.

This is the default mode. When the footswitch is plugged in and turned on, it grounds that voltage out and the tube comes on. That means there is zero current flowing in the vibrato tube unless the footswitch is on. With zero current flowing, none of the resistors will drop any voltage and so you end up with the entire B+ voltage on the plate.

I have a late 50s Fender Twin Amp (5F8A), and it seems kind of "dark" in the normal channel and apparently lacking in high end. Is there anything that can be done without altering the vintage value?
The 5F8A Twin design uses the same preamp as the 5F6A Bassman. Both the Bassman and the Twin use a 250 uf bypass capacitor on the first stage. (The plus end connects to the first preamp tube on both pins #3 and #8, while the minus side goes to ground). Using a 250 uf cap for the bypass will improve low end, but when you improve lows, it can sometimes seem boomy and seem to lack high-end, especially on the normal channel.

I have two possible suggestions. First, you could change the bypass capacitor to a smaller value. Perhaps a 50 uf at 25 volt would work for you. In general, the larger the cap, the more bottom-end. A 250 uf cap boosts the bottom end down to about 16 Hertz in this particular circuit, which is just a wee bit overkill. The 50 uf boosts down to 80 Hertz, which would probably work better for you. Of course, you could experiment and perhaps try a 10 uf, 25 uf or 50 uf to replace the 250 uf. Remember, the smaller the value, the less bottom.

Besides using the electrolytic bypass cap across the cathode resistor, add yet another smaller value cap to add some shine on top. This cap would be soldered across the other bypass cap. I like the .68 uf cap. This is very similar to the high-end one would get when they activate a Wah Wah pedal and then use it only as a treble boost and not a Wah Wah. It will add enough sparkle on the front of the note to shine through any mix.

I have a 1958 Deluxe, (5E3 circuit)…and want to use it for blues harp. It's stock, except for a Kendrick replacement power transformer. Can I replace the 12AX7 with a lower gain 12AT7 (or 12AY7) to get more distortion before feedback?

The 12AT7 and 12AY7 have lower amplification factors than the 12AX7. Since there is less gain, one can turn them up and make them work harder and get a more "cranked" kind of tone before the threshold of feedback. Any of the 12-volt tube types mentioned could be used for the 5E3 Deluxe.

There is another advantage of the 12AY7 or 12AT7 for harp. Those draw more current than the 12AX7 and therefore will cause the power supply voltage to drop lower. The lower voltage is helpful for a harp because it causes a loss of headroom (better distortion) and the lower voltage softens the high frequencies. This can be helpful with the voicing of the harp and suppressing feedback. If the amp doesn't want to produce high frequencies above the frequency response range of a harp, then that squealing feedback is actually being suppressed.

Here's is a tip for making any guitar amp better for harp. Place a small value cap across the plate load resistor of the first stage. Usually the first stage is going to be the first preamp tube in the amp. The plate of a 12AX7 style twin triode tube is pin #1 and pin #6. If you look at pin #1 or pin #6, you can follow the wire going to that pin and it will terminate to a resistor — usually a 100K resistor but sometimes other values — perhaps a 220K. You would find that resistor (also called a plate load resistor) and solder a cap across the resistor. I would experiment with different value caps ranging from .001 uf to 500 pf to 250 pf. Use a 400 volt or better rating. This cap will roll off high frequencies that are above a certain frequency. This helps eliminate feedback, but it also allows you to use the controls on the amp.

When a harp player uses a guitar amp, he almost always has to turn the treble control off, the bass control all the way up and the mids turned down. By using the "cap across the plate resistor" trick, one already has that squealy treble handled. This allows you to use the tone controls.

I have a '67 Super Reverb with very low power and high plate voltages on preamp plates. The strange thing, when I replace the original 7025's with new JJ or Sovtek tubes, I get even less power.
I would look for D.C. leakage from a coupling cap. A coupling cap is attached to the plate circuit of every preamp tube so that A.C. signal can pass but D.C. voltage is blocked. If D.C. is leaking from the cap, the bias of the next stage is thrown off.

Desolder the end of the coupling cap not connected to the plate of the preamp tube and check from there to ground with a voltmeter. If there is more than .25 volts D.C. on the non-plate end of the coupling cap, then that cap needs replacing. Remember, if D.C. leaks, it throws off the biasing on the preamp tubes and causes constipated preamp syndrome. I'll bet you have more than one that is leaking. It could even be one of the tone caps, because those were used as coupling caps.

I have a 5A5 Fender TV Front Pro that had a field coil speaker in it. The speaker was pretty shot, so I'm replacing it with an old Jensen P15N. My tech and I have already properly removed the extra electrical leads to the field coil, but I was curious as to whether or not we need to add a choke or extra filter cap now that the field coil speaker has been replaced by a standard speaker. A friend of mine thinks the field coil acted like a choke...but he wasn't sure. Do we need to add anything to the circuit?
Funny, the 5A5 Pro schematic shows a permanent magnet speaker and no field coil type speaker. If it had a field coil speaker in it, the

field coil was obviously used as a choke. It could be replaced with an ordinary Fender choke, or you could use a fixed resistor. The original 5A5 Pro used a 10K 1 watt resistor. The 1 watt rating is borderline too small. If you decide to use the 10K resistor, use a higher wattage than stock. Perhaps a 3 or 5 watt would be best. Or better yet, use a 250 ohm 5 watt in place of the field coil. The 250 ohm will give you a little more screen voltage and preamp voltage, which is what that amp is lacking.

I have a Fender Champ that takes a 5Y3 rectifier tube. What other rectifier tubes could be safely substituted for the 5Y3?

In choosing other rectifier tubes, we need only find those with the same pin out, so they will connect to the circuit properly, and we need a tube that doesn't draw excessive filament current. The 5Y3 stock tube draws 2 amps of 5 volt filament current. The Champ's transformer winding can probably take a little more than the 2 amps, but not much more. Full wave rectifier tubes, with similar pin-outs, that draw 2 Amps of filament current or less would include the indirectly heated cathode types:

5AR4 – 1.9 Amp
5CG4 – 2 Amp
5V4G – 2 Amp
5Z4 GT – 2 Amp
6087 – 2 Amp
6106 – 1.7 Amp

Besides those, there is also the family of directly heated cathode types:

5AZ4 – 2 Amp
5R4G – 2 Amp
5T4 – 2 Amp
5W4G – 1.5 Amp

Stay away from the 5AT4, 5AS4, 5AU4, 5AW4, 5AX4, 5U4, and 5V3 as they all draw excessive filament current.

With a 5F6-A Bassman, the speaker cables are 4 individual cables coming off of individual R.C.A Connectors. Are these each individual 8 ohm taps? Are the four R.C.A jacks simply connected

in parallel to a single 2 ohm output? Specifically, can I disconnect the internal speakers and connect just one of the RCA outputs to a 2 ohm cab?

Yes you may. There is only one two ohm output on a 5F6A Bassman. It does connect in parallel to all four R.C.A output jacks, but there is a reason it is done this way. On an amp with a 2 ohm output, the current is very high and the voltage is low. If you look at Ohm's law (voltage drop equals resistance times current), you can see that when more current is applied to a resistance, there is a larger voltage drop developed across that resistance. The hookup wire that goes from the speaker to the R.C.A jack is itself a resistance. With a large current going through that wire, a sizeable loss could occur due to the large current passing through the resistance. To minimize this resistance, the 5F6A Bassman had four separate sets of wires. Each set connected an individual speaker to the output of the amp. This way, only 25% as much current would have to run down a single pair of wires. If you reduce the current by 75%, then you reduce the voltage drop across that resistance (also called loss) by the same amount.

I have an original 4x10 Fender Bassman. There is a constant annoying hum — even with the volume turned down. I even pulled the output tubes and it still hummed. I unplugged the speaker to see if somehow the power transformer was magnetically coupled to the voice coil of one of the speakers. When I unplugged the speakers, the hum went away, but I noticed that if I ground one of the speaker leads (and the other speaker lead is NOT connected to anything), it still hums. I thought you had to have both wires of a speaker connected for the speaker to make any sound. What gives?

This is an odd problem. You would think that connecting only one speaker lead to ground would not make a complete circuit. The other speaker lead is not connected to anything, so where's the circuit? The magnetic field from the power transformer is being induced into the speaker. There is not much coupling, but just enough to make an annoying hum.

I had a similar problem with an amp in my service department and here's how I fixed it. Remove the power transformer mounting screws and turn the power transformer 180 degrees then bolt it back down. You need not unsolder anything, as the wires are most likely long enough for you to turn the transformer the full 180 degrees. This will change the magnetic field around the speaker and most likely cure your hum problem.

I recently had my tech change the choke on my 1957 Twin 5E8A. Since then, the amp hasn't sounded right. What should I do?
That's a tricky one, as the 5E8 uses a rather unique Fender amp circuit. This is one of the few amps that used a Pi filter BEFORE the output stage. If you look at the schematic of a 5E8 Fender Twin (it's on page 366 of my 1st book, *A Desktop Reference of Hip Vintage Guitar Amplifiers*), notice how ALL of the current from the output transformer AND ALL the other current from the entire amp has to go through the choke on its journey towards the rectifier/power supply. Configured this way, a choke must be able to handle all the current from the entire amp all the time. If it cannot handle this amount of current, it will overheat and perhaps burn up. Is that what happened to your original choke? Did it burn up? Although a choke rated for around 5 Henries at 500 mA would work nicely, it is interesting to note that Fender designs were changed back the following year and have remained the same ever since. Is there a reason why?

Comparing the 5F8 power supply design to the 5E8 design (see page 368 of *A Desktop Reference of Hip Vintage Guitar Amplifiers*), notice that only the preamp current and screen current go through the choke on the 5F8. The output current does NOT go through the choke. Therefore a 5 Henry 50 mA choke would be overkill and you would never have to worry about it burning up.

So Fender experimented one year, did it differently than before and then changed it back. I too have experimented with this design and I like the regular way better. For one thing, the way the 5E8 was hooked up, the screen was at a higher potential than the plate. This is a bad design because we want the electrons to go through the screen to the plate. By having the screen at a higher potential, you are confusing the electrons and will draw excessive screen current. Remember, screen current doesn't make sound in your speaker; only the plate current goes to the output transformer.

We made several amp replica copies of the 5E8A Twin for export to Japan. In that design, I simply used the same choke as for the 5F8A. We simply moved the output transformer center-tap to the other side of the choke so that it was wired like the 5F8, therefore, none of the output transformer current had to pass through the choke. This also put the screen at a lower potential than the plate. I think configuring the choke to be like all other Fenders makes the amp more reliable with a more aggressive quality.

I have several 60s Fender amps that are in regular use, serviced with good tubes and working fine. I've noticed that they tend to get mushier as the night wears on, and was wondering if this was due to excessive heat build-up (my Showman in particular gets hot, plus I like to tilt them back on the legs). Would mounting a small fan help in keeping the amps tight and prolonging tube life?

All 60s Fender amps have the tubes hanging down. One thing for sure — heat rises. When it rises, it meets the metal chassis that absorbs and holds heat. Some of the 60s amps (such as the Princeton and the Deluxe) do not produce that much heat, but others produce enough heat to fry up some eggs for that 2:00 AM after-gig breakfast. The worst heat producer of all is the Showman, partly because it uses four output tubes in a small cabinet, but also because it has almost no ventilation.

Mounting a fan or even bringing a small fan to the gig and pointing it in the direction of the amp will certainly help the heat buildup and prolong tube life, but I'm not sure that heat alone is the source of your problem. The problem you describe seems to be a power supply problem that could be related to filter caps (which are affected by heat).

You mentioned that your amps were serviced with good tubes, but you didn't say anything about serviced with fresh electrolytic caps. I would make sure to replace all electrolytic caps with new, American-made caps. When I say new, I mean for you to check the date code on the capacitor and see that it has not been sitting on a shelf for a year or two before it was sold! When I say American-made, I am talking about one that was made by Americans in America. I am not talking about a cap made in Taiwan and labeled with an American-sounding name. (For example: Illinois brand capacitors are made overseas and even when new, sound absolutely horrible. They are used in new Fender amps and account for the ugly out-of-tune tone associated with those new amps).

Make sure to replace the bias filter caps and the cathode bypass caps. These are electrolytic type capacitors and must be replaced; just as you would replace the power filter caps.

Someone stole my '64 Fender Reverb unit a few years back, and I managed to replace it with an identical one. For some reason, the new one has never sounded as good, despite trying different tubes, reverb pans, etc. They both work fine, are stock and unmolested — it's just that my first one clearly sounded better. Perhaps you can address the larger issue of why amps, particularly Fenders, from the same year and production run with identical components can sound so different?

There are many inconsistencies found in Fender amps from the 60s. For one thing 20% tolerance resistors were used almost exclusively. When a resistor company makes a batch of resistors, the resistors are checked and the ones that are within 10% tolerance are sold as such. The ones that read 5% tolerance are sold as such. You can easily see how one could almost guarantee an 11% margin of error for each resistor used in a Fender amp. If one resistor in one amp reads 11% high and the similar resistor in another amp reads 11% low, then that's a difference of 22%! We have just looked at best case scenario. What if the resistor in one amp read 20% high and the corresponding resistor in another read 20% low? Now we are talking about a difference of 40%! Besides the fact that the resistors were not very consistent to start with, a resistor's value can drift even further in due time.

In addition, there are variances in capacitors. Coupling capacitors offer reactance to the circuitry. Reactance is like a resistance in the signal path except it varies with frequency! As the capacitor's actual value changes from stock, so does the reactance.

These amps were handwired and how much actual wire was used and exactly how the wires were dressed would have made a tonal difference. Think of these amps as variations of a basic recipe.

While converting the bias balance of a Silverface Fender amp to pre-CBS specs, I noted the usual .002 disc caps from the power tube grid to ground. But this time, I found large 10 watt, 150 ohm resistors between pins 8 and ground, almost like cathode bias resistors. What were they doing with that design and can the parts simply be removed?

When CBS bought Fender, they wanted to streamline the amp production so they made a few changes. They thought that if they used a bias circuit that was both cathode biased AND fixed bias, they could eliminate using matched tubes, set the bias balance quickly by ear, and ship the amps quicker. Since the output tubes of a push-pull amp cancel hum induced from the filament circuit, one could simply use any tubes (not necessarily matched) and adjust the bias balance for the least hum. When they are adjusted for the least hum, the tubes would become "matched" as far as idle current. With the cathode bias circuit (or self-bias, as it is sometimes called), the idea was to eliminate having to spend time adjusting the bias setting of production amps.

This theory sounds good on paper, but does not sound good for guitar tone. In fact, this is the circuit that gave the silverface amps a bad name. When this change was made, the amps sounded so bad that sales almost stopped. After a few months of this, Fender realized that guitarist would not buy such a bad sounding amp, and they changed back to pure fixed bias. They left the bias pot as a balance control rather than a true adjustment, thus allowing the use of non-matched tubes and simply adjusting for the least hum before the amp was shipped.

Part of the Blackface conversion is to re-wire the bias balance pot to become a bias adjustment pot. This allows you to actually set the idle current of the output tubes, which is not possible with a silverface amp.

Those 150 ohm resistors should be removed and pin #8 should be grounded. When this is done, sometimes your bias control will not adjust far enough to tame down the tubes. In this case, you may have to change the value of the load resistor that is mounted on the back of the bias pot. This resistor alters the range of the bias circuit. A smaller resistor will drop bias voltage (resulting in higher plate current). A larger value results in higher bias voltage (and less idle current). You will most likely need a higher value resistor.

I recently performed the "Silverface to Blackface" conversion (as outlined in your first book, "A Desktop Reference of Hip Vintage Guitar Amps") on a mid 70s master volume model Super Reverb. The amp has higher output tube plate voltages before and after the conversion than its Blackface counterpart. My question is "How detrimental are these higher plate voltages (505) plate volts versus 460 plate volts portrayed on the Blackface schematics) to the amp's ability to reproduce the Blackface tone and what, if anything, can or should be done to lower these voltages to Blackface specifications? Also, would a reduction in plate voltage change the operating parameters of the now "functional" bias pot, which I can presently, only adjust to a maximum of 30 mA output tube current?

There is more going on here than what meets the eye. In general, when the idle current of the output tubes decreases, the plate voltage increases. This happens because the transformer has an internal resistance. The actual wire that is on the inside of the transformer has a resistance. When current is run through this resistance, a voltage drop appears across the resistance (This is basic Ohm's law in action — resistance times current equals voltage). As more current is drawn, there is more voltage drop. Conversely, if less current is drawn, there is less voltage drop. The voltage drop is subtracted from the applied voltage and the difference is the actual plate voltage. (In transformer lingo, this difference is referred to as "copper loss"). That is to say that if you idled your tubes hotter, then the plate voltage would drop.

The real problem is that your bias parameters are such that you cannot idle the tubes any hotter than 30 mA. Look on the back of your bias adjustment potentiometer. There is a resistor going from one lead of the pot to ground. This resistor value must be reduced in order to increase the idle current parameter of the bias circuit. Usually a 15K resistor will do the trick. If by chance you already have a 15K, you will need a smaller value to get that idle current up.

When you get the output tube current up to 35 mA per tube, your plate voltage will probably go to around 485 volts or so. This is not much difference from an actual Blackface. I know the Blackface schematic shows 465 volts. In real life, the schematic is usually low and by actual measurement. A typical Blackface measures around

475 volts. If you get 485 volts from your amp, when idled up to 35 mA, that is not enough difference to worry about.

If you find, after getting your idle current up to 35 mA, that the plate voltage is still too high, you can get it lower by using a 5U4 or a 5R4 rectifier tube.

The plate voltage does affect the parameters of the bias circuit. Higher plate voltages want to draw more current (assuming the bias voltage does not change.) Therefore, if you change your rectifier tube after biasing, you will want to re-bias using the new rectifier tube.

I have a Silverface Fender Twin (approximately 1968–69 vintage). Did Fender wire some of the 68–69 twins incorrectly? If yes, in what way were they wired incorrectly?

If the Dual Showman is wired correctly, it is pure coincidence. The Fender assemblers were not paying attention to filament polarity and it was a crap shoot if it was wired correctly. Actually, with four sockets there are 16 possibilities of wiring them with random polarity. Only two of those possibilities are correct. That means seven out of eight are wrong (88% wrong!). So there is a 12% chance yours is wired correctly. There are four possibilities that, even though not 100% correct, the hum will still phase cancel. So there is still a 62% chance that your amp will suffer from excessive hum due to incorrect polarity of the filament circuit! A coin toss has better odds.

I play mostly hollow body guitars and don't want the amp to get too "flubby" when I hit an open E. It seems my previous Blackface Deluxe Reverb with a GZ34 and same exact speaker had a stronger bottom end. Would the GZ34 help do that? Or maybe I'm wrong? I have a '73 Deluxe Reverb with a 5U4 rectifier now. Could I wire it so it could run on a 5AR4? I just want the amp to hold a more solid low end.

You want the bottom to "hold together" and have some solid substance. That takes power. True, the GZ34/5AR4 will give you more voltage, but the voltage on your particular amp design is already about 75 volts over the design maximum of the tube. Add another 30 volts and you are asking for tube failure.

I would recommend going a different approach. The 5U4GB can

take the current. I'd beef up the main filter capacitors. I would put a pair of 220 uf at 350 volt caps configured as a "totem pole" stack. This is where the caps are connected in series with each other. The plus end goes to the circuit and the minus end goes to ground. Of course, each cap would have a 220K ohm 1 watt resistor across it to keep the voltages equal on each cap. This would give you a total of 110 uf at 700 volts capacitor rating. When your tubes need a lot of current, the caps will have stored enough to give the tubes what they want. Low notes take a lot of energy and you need to have enough electrical energy stored to satisfy the demands of the low notes.

I have a '66 Super Reverb that I absolutely love (but)... I am a tinkerer at heart so nothing in my world stays stock. I have recently acquired a new baffle (beautiful birch), which holds one 15 inch speaker. I want to put this baffle and an old 60s EV 15" speaker into my rig. The problem is that the EV is a 16 ohm speaker and the output impedance of the Super Reverb is 2 ohms. What do I do? Is there a mod I can do to make the EV look like a 2 ohm load?

Your suggestion will sound awful and lack power if you attempt to run it with the stock 2 ohm transformer. The EV 15" speaker is a wonderful choice for your project, but only if you use a 16 ohm transformer. Since no one makes a 2 ohm 15" speaker, you can't match a 15" speaker to the amp. You will have to match the output transformer to the speaker. Your only option is to replace the output transformer with a good sounding 16 ohm transformer.

I know it's an off-the-wall question, but I'll throw it at you anyway. Is there a particular lacquer suited to apply to tweed ("59 Bassman RI)? Any reply is appreciated.

I'll tell you how I would lacquer the tweed on a RI Bassman. Completely disassemble your amp chassis from the cabinet and remove the baffleboard and speakers. Go to Sherwin Williams, Home Depot or Builder's Square and buy a pint of "Honey Pine" Polyshades by Minwax. It comes in gloss or matte finish. You choose matte.

Apply it generously with a rag to the cabinet and back panels. Before it is dry, inspect it and wipe smooth any drips with a fresh rag.

It has a tendency to form drips after it sets for 20 minutes, so I would recommend going back and checking for those drips.

After one coat, let it dry then sand it with Scotch-brite. Apply a second coat. Let it dry and sand with Scotch-brite. Apply a third coat and look at it. If it feels smooth, you are done.

If it is still rough, sand with Scotch-brite and then apply a fourth coat. This should give it the patina of an original 1959 amp.

If doing a tweed guitar case, be careful. The tweed on your reissue amp is cotton and works great with Polyshades; however there are some tweed guitar cases made with polyester tweed that turns green when Polyshades is applied. I recommend doing a test swatch in an inconspicuous place on your tweed case unless you are absolutely certain it is cotton tweed.

I've been working on amps for 2 years now, so I'm not an expert by any means. I'm working on a very early Silverface Deluxe reverb. I replaced the power transformer (the old one was toast because someone put a 10 amp fuse in the fuseholder to temporarily "correct" a problem in the amp) and replaced the filter caps (I used 20 mfd instead of 16 mfd, and I added an extra cap in parallel with the first power cap).

But the amp still has a loud, annoying hum. The amp doesn't have enough power for a Deluxe, and it breaks up very easily. I checked all of the components...most resistors have drifted a bit, but not severely. I pulled the first and second preamp tubes...no change. I pulled the phase inverter tube, and that stopped the noise. I double checked all the parts in the phase inverter circuit and they all read OK. I performed the "chopstick test" as well.

The only thing I haven't done is replace any parts in the phase inverter. I don't know what else it could be. I suspected that the lack of two 100 ohm resistors connected to the pilot light might have been a probable cause, but I checked the schematic and saw that Fender didn't use them on this amp.

Anyway, the bias is about 37 mA per tube with about 420 volts on the plate. I've played with this, but there is no change in the hum. Any info you could give to point me in the right direction would be greatly appreciated. Usually I try to solve these

things myself, but this one has me stumped. I will continue to troubleshoot the phase inverter until I find out what could cause a loud hum with early breakup. Thanks for your time!

It sounds like you have done some nice work on that amp. Here are my comments:

Regarding the hum,

1. Check to see if the filament winding has a centertap to ground. If it doesn't, add the 2 /100 ohm resistors. You said Fender didn't use them on that model, but you changed transformers and the transformer you used may not have a ground reference for the 6.3 volt filament!
2. Check to see if the filament is wired in correct polarity. This is a common wiring mistake of Fender amps. Specifically, check to see that the filament wire on pin #2 of one output tube goes to pin #2 of the other output tube. Likewise pin #7 of one should go to pin #7 of the other. If this is not correct, the output tubes will induce 60 cycle hum. Don't worry about preamp tubes; they are all wired humbucking.
3. Check to make sure all the filter caps have a ground reference on the minus side. Sometimes the ground is made underneath the board and could be disturbed during the performance of a cap job.
4. Regarding the low volume, I suspect a coupling cap is leaking D.C. voltage onto a latter stage. This will throw the bias of the next stage preamp off so badly that the gain and clean tone goes south. Disconnect each coupling and/or tone cap on the end that has no D.C. voltage. The end that goes to the plate of the preamp tube (pin #6 or pin #1) should be left attached. Turn the amp on and check the cold side of the coupling/tone cap to ground with your meter. If you get .25 volts D.C. or more, change the cap — THAT IS YOUR PROBLEM.

I would like to find out if I can put 5881/6L6 tubes instead of 6V6 tubes in my Tweed Fender Deluxe?

It depends on your particular tweed Deluxe. The power transformers on Tweed Deluxes are very inconsistent. Here's how to see if your particular Tweed Deluxe can handle it: Set your voltmeter for A.C. volts and hook the meter leads to pin #2 and pin #7 of one of the output tubes. Install 6L6 tubes in the amp and turn the power on. If the voltage reads at least 6.1 volts A.C., then it is safe. If the voltage reads 6 volts or less, I would recommend staying with the 6V6's unless you install an auxiliary 6.3 volt filament transformer.

You can always tell when a transformer can't handle a particular load because the output voltage will drop below what is needed.

I read through your book *A Desktop Reference of Hip Vintage Guitar Amps*. You didn't say how to fix the tone on the 1965 Deluxe Reverb Reissue. What are the opportunities to improve the brittle/harsh sound of this classic amp reissue? Speakers? Caps? Circuit mods? Blowtorch?

With my first book, I tried to keep the subject matter about "Hip Vintage" amps rather than modern Mexican-made tube amps.

Here's the scoop on the Fender Deluxe Reissue. It uses the worst sounding filter caps known to man. The brand name is Illinois capacitor and they are made in Taiwan. There are no cheaper capacitors available anywhere on this planet.

So the first thing you need is a complete cap job using American made Sprague filter caps. I mean replace every electrolytic capacitor in the amp, including the bypass caps, filter caps and bias caps.

Next is the speaker. The DRI uses the Eminence speaker, which is the only speaker in the world that does not have a staked magnet structure (it is spot welded to save money). There is no cheaper American-made speaker anywhere, and that was the criteria used to select this one. Replace it. Possible choices: Fane Alnico 12" about $250, Jensen Alnico 12" about $225, Kendrick CerAlNiCo $260, or Kendrick ceramic $150. Any of these speakers will offer a dramatic improvement in tone and response.

And lastly, the tubes in the DRI are again the cheapest available in this solar system. Invest about $80 in a pair of NOS American — perhaps RCA or Tung Sol. This will make a huge difference in your overall tone. People use tube amps to get great tone. It doesn't make sense to buy a tube amp and then use tubes that sound awful. The NOS tubes not only sound better, but they last longer, so over the long run, they may end up costing less!

Fender does not sell to musicians. Their customers are dealers only, so they are forced to keep their designs cheap enough for tremendous dealer profits. Unfortunately, superior quality caps, tubes and speakers cost money and the current owners of the Fender name could save the most money by cutting quality here. Of course, these components are the same components that affect the tone the most, so you would be well advised to replace these shoddy components with quality components.

I read in one of your books where you suggested adding a screen resistor to the Champ circuit because the original design runs the screen voltage at a higher potential than the plate. You go on to say this is poor design that a simple 470 ohm 1 watt resistor could correct. What do you mean by this? Can you send me a circuit diagram or tell me where and how to add it?

I have always thought it bad design to run a screen at higher voltage than a plate. Even though the plate has much more mass, there will be those electrons that get confused and "think" the screen IS the plate. This results in excessive screen current (less tube life) and not as much power output. Some of the electrons that should have gone to the plates go to the screen instead, and that is how some of the power is lost.

There are other amps that have this flaw. The Fender amps that come to mind are the 5E6 Bassman, the 5E7 Bandmaster, the 5E4 Super and the 5F4 Super. The 6G15 Fender standalone Reverb is another device that lacks a screen resistor and runs screen voltage higher than plate voltage.

Here's how to correct the problem on your amp. You will need a 470 ohm 1 watt resistor. Take off the back panel and look at the output tube socket. The wire that goes to pin #4 of the output tube should be unsoldered. Solder one end of the 470 ohm 1 watt resistor to pin #4. Then take the wire that was on pin #4 (before you took it off) and solder it to the other lead from the resistor.

Here's a tip: There is no pin #6 on a 6L6 or 6V6 tube, even though there is a pin #6 on the socket. Sometimes, amp builders use pin #6 (of the socket) as a mounting terminal for other components. If your amp uses a 6V6 or 6L6 tube, look at pin #6 on the socket. If there is nothing mounted there, you may want to mount the screen resistor between pin #4 and pin #6 and simply move the wire that was on pin

#4 to pin #6. This will achieve the same result as stated above, except the resistor will be mounted at both ends.

I am experiencing some problems with my 1994 Deluxe Reverb reissue. After I had bought the amp, I was totally frustrated with higher volume response — the amp sounded mushy, weak, and overly mid-rangy.

I retubed the amp, with no improvement. **The output tubes show a difference in plate current. Right now, one runs at 29 mA, the other at 30.5 mA, both plate voltages are 402v. Can a persistent hum from the amp result from the mismatch on the 6V6 tubes? The amp still appears to lack some power, but maybe I expect too much from 22w? At very low volumes, I hear a strange distortion on the signal, almost like very cheap transistor overdrive, I suspect the speaker or the caps.**

In this specific case, and in general for a '94 amp, is a cap job necessary? Can bad caps result in a very subtle distortion at low volumes (I am talking really low volumes, where the kids could sleep next to it)?

The Deluxe Reverb reissue uses Taiwanese made Illinois capacitors that sound horrible — especially at high volume. You would do well to change those to Sprague. I like to beef up the first stage to about 100 mfd. and use 40 mfd on the screen supply. Use 16 mfd everywhere else.

As far as the distortion at extremely low volumes, that is most probably a voice-coil rub in the speaker.

I would not worry about the slight mismatch on your output tubes. One and a half milliamps difference is a pretty close match. I don't think that slight mismatch could cause a hum problem. I would check the ground reference of the 6.3 volt filament. I don't have a reissue here to look at, but there are probably two 100 ohm resistors that go from each side of the filament heater to ground. This is an artificial center-tap. If either one of those resistors is bad, then the amp will have a louder than normal hum. If you ever blew an output tube in there, chances are the extra current burnt these resistors.

There is a "bright" cap that goes across the volume control on channel 2 of my 1959 5F6A Bassman. Have you ever experi-

mented with its value and had any real success? I know Marshalls and Blackface amps and tweeds all have different values and I know the smaller the brighter and the bigger the more mids. Is that right and can you recommend any other values? What am I after you ask? When I have my Bassman set to clean, I'd like it to be just a little more Blackfaceish like a Pro Reverb. What do you recommend?

You are correct about the smaller values being brighter and the larger values including more mids, but regarding your Blackface tone — you can't get there from here. You don't need a bright cap to accomplish your Blackface tone; you need a midrange scoop filter to emulate the Blackface tone. Basically it is two capacitors in series with a resistor across one of them. Use a .1 uf in series with a 250 pico farad silver mica cap. Next, place a 220K ½ watt resistor in parallel with the 250 pf. Use this assembly in place of the .02 uf first gain stage coupling cap (for the bright channel) and you are there. The .1 uf end goes to the plate, and the 250-pf side terminates on the volume pot.

I've used that midrange scoop filter before with great success. It can be used on any tweed Fender but I like it best on those Fender amps that have two channels that are almost identical. That way, with an A/B switchbox, you can go from tweed to Blackface — two very usable tones.

I recently put together a 5E3 Deluxe and it sounds pretty good. The only problem is the normal channel doesn't work. No Sound! I tried bending the preamp tubes to see if a good connection was being made, still no sound. I checked the wiring and resistors on the input jacks, I even used the chopstick method to push and prod the components and wires—still nothing. Do you think I should take apart the input jack wiring and re-wire? Have you run into this problem before? I can't seem to find it, please help.

This is not a common problem, but easy to find. I assume you substituted another 12AX7 to rule out the possibility of the tube having a bad section? When a tube amp fails, it is usually a bad tube.

The second most likely cause would be with the input jack. It could be that the shorting switch on input jack is not coming unshorted when a ¼" plug is inserted into the jack. This sometimes occurs even on brand new jacks! Or, it could be that you have the wire that leads from the grid of the first tube (pin #2) to the input jack connected to the wrong lead on the jack. If you accidentally connected that wire to ground (instead of hot), then the channel would not work.

If the problem is not with the tube or the jack, look over the circuit really good and check voltages. Check your socket pins for voltage and check various A.C. and D.C. voltages. From this, you should be able to find your problem. If the cathode voltage shows the same as the plate, then you have a bad ground in the cathode circuit. If there is no voltage on the plate, then you have either a miswire or open plate resistor. If you still can't find the problem after all this, try replacing the coupling cap to see if that makes any difference.

I was reading in your book, *A Desktop Reference of Hip Vintage Guitar Amps*, about changing the 5Y3 rectifier tube to a 5V4 in a Fender Tweed Champ amp to tighten low end and give it a punchier attack. Can I do this to my Black face Champ? Also, there are two small tubes in the Vibro Champ. Which one do I change out? The one closest to the power tubes?

Yes, you may use the 5V4 in place of the 5Y3 in your Vibro Champ. When I originally wrote that in my book, no really good 5AR4 (a.k.a. GZ34) rectifier tubes were available and there was ample new old stock of 5V4 tubes available. I am now recommending using the 5AR4 in favor of the 5V4. There are several reasons to use the 5V4 or the 5AR4/GZ34 instead of the stock 5Y3.

A 5Y3 is directly heated, which means the filament IS the cathode. Tubes of this design heat up very quickly. Since the rectifier tube is what is rectifying the wall A.C. to D.C., this means the tube produces high voltage almost immediately. Champs and Vibro Champs do not have standby switches. This means that the preamp tube and output tube get high voltage applied to them when they are still cold. When you apply high voltage to a cold tube, the coating on the cathodes tends to flake off. That is why there are standby switches—to allow the preamp and output tubes to warm up before high voltage from the rectifier tube is applied.

Enter the indirectly heated cathode (controlled warm-up time) rectifier tube such as the 5V4 or the 5AR4/GZ34. These tubes take longer to warm up than the output or preamp tubes. This means the other tubes in the amp are warmed up BEFORE high voltage is applied. The other tubes in the amp will last longer. It is like having a built-in "smart" standby switch!

I prefer the Chinese made, Mullard copy of the 5AR4 (a.k.a. GZ34). I have performed electronic tests and listening tests on these tubes and believe them to be a great choice of rectifier tube. Not only do they sound good, but they last a long time, can take more punishment (in terms of current) than what they are rated for, produce within 2 volts of an original Mullard, and cost a fraction of the price. They put out more voltage than a 5V4.

The two small tubes are 12AX7's. Like all tubes, they wear down, tonally, after a while of usage. The first one is for the channel amplification (preamp) and the other one (closest to the power tube) is for vibrato. I would recommend replacing the first one, which is the preamp tube for the channel. The one nearest the output tube is a vibrato tube; and unless your vibrato is not working, I would suggest you leave that one alone.

I want vibrato in both the normal and reverb channel of my Blackface Fender. I also want to be able to switch the normal channel vibrato on and off from a footswitch, and when off, bypass it completely so I don't have to go through the vibrato driver section when in the normal channel. The reason why I want vibrato in the normal channel and not the reverb channel is that I use an outboard reverb unit. I find that I like the sound of the outboard unit in the normal channel...so I would like to be able to add vibrato.

Getting the vibrato on both channels is easy. There is a yellow wire going from the right leg of the intensity pot to the board. It goes under the board and connects to a 220K resistor. Move the wire from the side (of the 220K resistor) it is on, to the other side of the same resistor. This will give you vibrato in both channels.

To remove the vibrato circuitry from the signal path, simply lift this wire. It doesn't matter which end you lift it, but I would lift it at the pot (on the right lead of the intensity pot). Remember this wire feeds a grid circuit, so you must use shielded wire going to your footswitch. You would need a two wire shielded coax for your footswitch wire, because both wires to your footswitch must be shielded and neither is at ground potential.

I am rebuilding/redesigning a '71 Bassman and was thinking of switching over to cathode bias. I have read both of your books and the recent article in *Vintage Guitar* on the subject. You didn't mention what to do with the bias section of the rectifier. From what I gather, the pair of 220K resistors becomes grounded and pin #8 of both 6L6's get connected together and connected to a cathode resistor, which is grounded. A bypass cap is placed in parallel with the cathode resistor. The polarity of the cap is minus to ground.

Does the bias supply (the trim pot, diode, resistor and cap) just get unhooked? Also, what values would you recommend for the cathode resistor and cap? The Fender AB 371 schematic says the voltage going to the plates of the 6L6's is about 430V. They recommend a bias voltage of -48V and a current range of 27 — 33 ma. I calculate the cathode resistor to be from 730 to 890 ohms (with actual values at 750 and 820). Do these numbers sound right? Another amp designer said 500 ohms would probably be the one I want, but that would push the plate current way up past 33 mA, wouldn't it?

There are many variables here. The voltages listed on the schematic are usually wrong. In fact, the plate voltage will change depending on how much idle current is going on. When you cathode bias an amp, you are in effect lowering the plate voltage and the tube won't draw as much current when plate voltage is lowered. Let's just say you started out with 430 volts as a fixed bias amp with -48 on the grid. The plate to cathode voltage is 430 volts, so the tube performs as a tube running at 430 volts on the plate.

If you cathode bias it to get 48 volts on the cathode, you are no longer running the tube at 430 volts — EVEN THOUGH THERE IS 430 VOLTS ON THE PLATE!!! You are running the tube at 382 volts. Why? Because that's the difference between the cathode and the plate and that is all the tube knows! If you ran a tube at 382 plate voltage, and fixed biased it with -48, it would draw almost no current. That is why you need to experiment with your particular amp and see what works. Forget the math and go for the actual result. If I were guessing, I would guess 500 ohms. Also, when cathode biasing an amp, it is fine to go more idle current because with the tube operating at less voltage (cathode to plate), it can take more plate current without exceeding the plate watt dissipation.

I too was big in math when I first started dealing with tubes. There are so many variables to consider that I found that nothing beats starting with an educated guess and then fine tuning by trial and error. It may not be as scientific, but it has the homely virtue that it works. Just imagine with your cathode bias equation, you would have to consider the impedance of the power supply (including the internal copper winding resistance of the B+ winding), how much current is flowing through the power supply (to tell how that would affect plate voltage), the particular set of output tubes you are using and the difference between the cathode voltage and the plate voltage (so you would know at what voltage the tubes are actually operating). Even if you did all your math correctly, the answer would still be wrong, because there are other factors that you failed to consider. Math is great to an extent, but the Henry Ford/Thomas Edison approach gets the job done.

Remember it is OK to idle those tubes on the hot side (40 - 50 mA) when converting to cathode bias, because since the tube "thinks" it is operating at a much lower voltage (due to the positive voltage on the cathode), you can idle up the current and still not exceed the plate watt dissipation. How do you know if you have exceeded the plate watt dissipation? Forget the math, the plate of the tube will glow cherry red. If the plate doesn't glow cherry red, you have not exceeded the plate watt dissipation. It is that simple.

Unhook the negative voltage bias supply from the two 220K resistors feeding the output tube grid circuit. You don't need to ground the bias supply itself. You can take all the components out or just leave them in and not hooked to the two 220K resistors. (Note: If you are converting to cathode bias on other Fender amps that have vibrato, you will want to leave the negative voltage supply in an operating condition because it is being used to stop the oscillator on the vibrato effect –when the effect is footswitched "off").

You can use anywhere from 500 ohms to 1000 ohms for the cathode resistor, depending on how you want to run it. Just guessing, I would say use a 10 watt value. You are going to need a fairly hefty wattage rating. Here's how to tell exactly what you need.

Measure the voltage across the cathode resistor you end up using. Square the voltage and then divide by the resistance. This will give you the wattage being dissipated. For safety, double that wattage and then round up to the next standard value.

Let's say the voltage is 40 volts using a 600 ohm resistor. You would square the voltage 40 X 40 = 1600. Next divide by the 600 ohm resistance to get 2.66 watts. That is how many watts are being dissipated across that resistor. For safety, double it to 5.32 and then round up to the next larger standard wattage value (probably 7 watts.) It certainly won't hurt to go more on the wattage rating, but the resistor will catch on fire if you go too low.

The 100 uf 100 volt value is about right for the cathode capacitor, but you can always experiment with different values. To fine tune it perfectly to your ear, you could connect (to pin #8) the plus end of several capacitors whose values change by a factor of 2. For example, you could try a 400 uf, 200 uf, 100 uf, 50 uf, 25 uf, 10 uf, 5 uf, etc. Solder the positive lead of each of these to pin #8 on the output tubes. (Pins #8 of each output tube are connected together and connected to the cathode resistor spoken of earlier. The cathode capacitor attaches across the resistor.)

Using a jumper wire, ground the minus end of each bypass cap — one at a time — in some A/B/C/D/E sound testing. From this you should be able to discover the best value cathode capacitor to use.

I have a problem with a 135 watt Fender Twin. I just finished a cap job (power supply caps and electrolytics inside were changed), I re-tubed the amp and it seemed to fire up ok. All the tubes are lit; I even have bias current. But there is no sound. All I get is a hummmmmmmm sound. No response to volume changes or plugging in or out of amp. Here's what's weird; as I work my way from left to right, my high voltage stops at the 5 uf at 50v cap that is connected to pin #8 of V5. Also, there wasn't any high voltage on two 100 uf caps in the filter bank. Where do I start on this one?

Assuming the amp worked before the overhaul, I would recommend intense visual inspection. Something is hooked up wrong or backwards. Perhaps a polarized cap's polarity is backwards. A visual inspection should find the problem. Also, the 5 uf cap will not ever have voltage unless you have the vibrato footswitch plugged in and turned "on."

You need a schematic to double-check your work. Especially double-check the power supply. Pay particular attention to capacitor polarity. If one is in backwards, the amp will hum and not produce proper voltages.

Got a weird new problem with my Fender Reverb Unit clone and my 1968 Bassman 50 watt head. When I put my Reverb Unit on top of my Bassman head, I get a horrendous hum. If I move the reverb unit off the head say 4 or 5 inches or more, the hum goes away. Both units are working perfectly (so long as they are 5 inches away from each other). How can I shield either the reverb unit, or the Bassman, (or both) to get rid of this?

Your Reverb unit has a reverb pan in the bottom. This reverb pan has two transducers — one on each end. If the "return" transducer of the pan is on the same side of the cabinet as the power transformer of the Bassman, then it will pick up the 60 cycle hum that is present around the Bassman's power transformer. Take the back off the Reverb unit, remove the pan, turn it around and reinstall it opposite to the direction it is now. This should cure your problem.

I went into my local music store for some guitar picks and walked out with a used '59 Bassman reissue. When I first plugged it in and cranked it up to a nice medium growl, I was completely blown away with the tone. Unbelievable! But now after a little recording, it has starting to make a scratching/snapping/crackling sound coming from the speakers when the amp sits idle and on. What gives? Also, I see that the rectifier socket has a solid-state replacement instead of a rectifier tube. Would it sound better if I were to put in a GZ34 tube?

For starters, I would slightly rock each preamp tube in its socket (with the amp on) to troubleshoot a dirty socket. If rocking the tube in the socket causes intermittent noise, then you need to clean and retension or replace the socket.

Next, I would check for a noisy preamp tube. Substituting a known good 12AX7 for each preamp tube — one at a time, can easily troubleshoot this.

If neither of these techniques produces results, you could have a noisy plate resistor. The reissue Bassman uses ¼ watt resistors instead of the usual ½ watt resistors that can be found on all vintage Fenders. This is a design flaw. In fact, if you use a 12AY7 for the first gain stage (like an original), the circuit draws .26 watts. That is not enough to burn a ¼ watt resistor up, but it will cook it to a crisp. I would change every plate resistor in the amp and I would use ½ watt resistors. The plate resistors are the ones that connect to pin #1 and pin #6 of the 12AX7 preamp tubes and all are 100K value except an 82K on pin #1 of the phase inverter tube. Changing all the plate resistors would probably cure the noise.

Regarding your rectifier socket: If you add a tube rectifier to the reissue Bassman it will sound colder and more lifeless. That is because there is no bias adjustment. The amp's bias circuit is preset at the factory to work with a solid-state device. When you replace it with a real tube such as the GZ34, the supply voltage goes down slightly which makes the tubes draw less current. With the lesser current, the amp will not break up as quickly. This might work if you are going for a sterile clean tone.

I would recommend performing the "Adjustable Fixed Bias for Reissue Bassman" modification found on page 73 of my second book, "Tube Amp Talk for the Guitarist and Tech." This would allow you to adjust the bias after inserting the rectifier tube. You could heat up the idle current and have the amp sound better than it ever has.

Can I use any 600 volt filter caps to do a cap job on my Fender amp, or do you recommend a specific brand?
The 600 volt caps that are being sold today will not fit in the cap pan. Actually, if you dissect a modern 600 volt electrolytic, you will find there are two 300 volt caps inside a shrink tube. I have seen techs replace the 600 volt caps with modern 500 volt capacitors. The 500 volt caps will fit, but the 500 volt value simply will not hold up for the

main supply. Because the power supply of an amp fluctuates while being played, an amp with a 450 volt idle voltage could easily go over 500 volts while being played. This results in electrolytic cap failure if a 500 volt cap is used. There is a better way that involves changing the main filter supply from parallel to series. This technique is described in full on page 31 of my second book, *Tube Amp Talk for the Guitarist and Tech*. The chapter is titled "Performing a Cap Job on your Amp."

I have owned a model AB 165 Fender Bassman Head for about 6 or 7 years, however a few months after acquiring the amp I noticed the two 6L6GC power tubes would turn cherry red. I bought your book *A Desk Top Reference To Hip Vintage Amps* and I tried biasing the amp and this did not help. I know the bias control was not stock and thought it might be faulty so I bought another pot at the same value as the schematic suggest, still this did not help. I would really like to use the amp but the tubes are running way too hot. I was hoping you could give me a little direction. My electronic skills are limited, and because of my location (southern Kansas), amp technicians aren't plenty. So I don't know what to do. Any help would be appreciated.

Have you tried a different set of tubes? It might be an output tube problem. Perhaps another set would not glow cherry red in that same circuit.

You cannot bias that amp using the bias control because the bias control is only a bias balance and not a bias adjustment. That is why you cannot make the tubes quit glowing cherry red. There is a 15K resistor soldered to the back of the bias pot. Increase the value, and the tubes will run cooler. This can stop the "cherry red plate" problem, though your problems may go much deeper.

That amp probably needs an overhaul, perhaps new tubes, and most likely a cap job. Also, if it were my amp, I would rewire it to AA864 Bassman specs. The AB165 is the least desirable Bassman circuit ever made. It is the only Bassman ever made with negative feedback feeding a high impedance circuit. It is the only one with interstage feedback across the phase inverter. Both of those circuits sound horrible.

If you tried to rewire it to the AA864 circuit, it will oscillate. When you modify the circuit to become like the AA864, the output transformer secondary polarity must be reversed to stop the oscillation. This is a job for experts that have done this many times before. I recommend you send the amp to a competent shop for a complete overhaul and rewire (to AA864 specs). The amp will sound better than it ever did and you will have a million dollar tone for a few hundred dollars.

I have a '62 Bassman head. Before I acquired it, some idiot spray-painted it BLACK!! Do you have any ideas on how to remove the paint without damaging the tolex?

It really depends on what kind of paint is on there. I would bring it to a paint store such as Sherwin Williams, and ask their opinion. They should have an expert or two on hand that can identify if the paint is enamel, lacquer, acrylic, etc. Likewise, they should be able to advise you which of their products can remove the paint. You might even get them to do a test patch in the store.

It is hard to believe how nice some of these "painted" amps look, once the paint has been removed. You may want to clean the tolex after it has been "de-painted." Keep reading.

Many years ago you guys gave me some valuable information about cleaning grill cloth. I'm hoping you can share some "tricks of the trade" where cleaning Fender blonde tolex is concerned. I've used Murphy's soap to clean the surface dirt but I'm sure there must be a way to get to the harder grime. Any info you can share would be greatly appreciated. Thanks.

Here's what we do. Take the amp apart. Remove the baffleboard, speakers, back panels, handle, and hardware. Cover the tube label with plastic film (Glad Wrap) that has been carefully taped to the wood. I use duct tape, but I must warn you to take care not to accidentally get the tape on the tube label. You do not want to destroy the tube label!

Bring the cabinet, baffleboard, and back panels to a high-pressure car wash. Spray some whitewall cleaner on everything first. (Most car washes have whitewall cleaner as one of the options.) Tolex is made from rubber and the whitewall cleaner works great on both the tolex and the grill cloth.

Let everything soak a minute or so, then apply the high-pressure wash, and then rinse. Be careful to avoid getting that high pressure near the tube label. Be careful not to let the water stay on the grill cloth and baffleboard very long as baffle boards are sometimes made from particle board, and we don't want that stuff coming apart. Let everything dry, then put it all back together. I like to "help" the grill dry by spraying it with compressed air. This will blow most of the water out. You may want to apply some "Armor All®" to make the tolex shine. It will look brand new.

I have a few quick questions that I hope you can help me with. I read in your book that if I remove the negative feedback loop on a Fender, it will have more gain and sound more "open." You mention that changing the negative feedback resistor value will do the same.

I'm working on a Fender Bassman (AB165). Which one should I do? What does the third 12AX7 do? I am thinking about using a 5751 to get more of a SRV sound, do I install it there? I'm thinking of changing the 6.8K resistor on the back of the bass pot of channel two so it will have a different midrange response. Do you have any recommendations? And one last question, what is a good value cap to use on the bright switch?

Actually, the AB165 was the worst sounding Fender Bassman ever made. I believe I would start out by rewiring it to the AA864 spec. When you do this, you will need to reverse the polarity of the output transformer to prevent oscillation.

The first two 12AX7's are for the bass channel. The third 12AX7 is for the normal channel and the 12AT7 is the phase inverter. I don't know that the 5751 will get you more "Stevie," but if you were using the normal channel, the third tube would be the one to change. If you were using the Bass channel, it would be the first tube to change. Of course, you MUST experiment. Tone is extremely complex — as everything adds its color.

I do not recommend any particular value for the 6.8K resistor on the back of the bass pot on channel two. Remove the 6.8K and temporarily install a 25K potentiometer (as a variable resistor) in place of the 6.8K. Get out your guitar and start playing/listening. Once you find the best setting for your guitar, speaker, playing style, etc., carefully remove the pot without disturbing its setting. Once the pot has been removed, measure its exact resistance, find a resistor with that value, and solder it into the circuit.

Regarding the bright cap value, it depends. As the volume is turned up, the effect of this cap diminishes. Are you playing loud? Do you need more mids, more jangle, etc? Why not experiment with a few different values. Anywhere from 47 pf to 5000 pf are legitimate values. I like a 100 pf on most of my amps, but again it becomes very complex. The smaller values give more jangle and chime. The bigger values give more cream and bark.

Where can I find out more about the selenium rectifier in a 1959 Fender Bassman? I am building a clone of the model 5F6A. I have a selenium rectifier from a Bogen PA that I think I can use — but am not sure how to know I have the right one. Also, what is the danger with a selenium rectifier?

I would not recommend using a selenium rectifier. In 1959, that was the best component available. In the last forty years, there have been substantial improvements in solid-state rectification. In short, the silicon rectifier is much better. Depending on how much voltage you have coming off your bias tap, you could use a 1N4003 silicon rectifier (less than 200 volts) or perhaps a 1N4007 (for more than 200 volts). Silicon rectifiers are more stable, more dependable, and less heat sensitive than their selenium counterparts. Also, silicon rectifiers are readily available because of their popularity. Remember the solid-state rectifier in a 5F6A Bassman is used only in the negative bias supply circuit, which is NOT in the signal path.

I own a TV and VCR repair shop and from time to time I repair tube guitar amplifiers. I do a lot of solid state, as I am an Authorized Service Center for St. Louis Music and Korg products. I have come across two Fender amp's with the same symptom and I have checked every resistor, filter, cap and diode in the units and replaced all the tubes and still get low volume and if I let it run a few minutes, the plates will start to glow orange. The voltage on the screen grid is a few volts higher than on the plate. The control grid is around -51 volts. One amp is the Fender Blues DeVille, the other is the Fender Hot Rod

DeVille, pretty much the same chassis. Any idea's would be greatly appreciated.

There is only one thing that can cause an output tube to glow orange — the plate watt dissipation has been exceeded. There are many ways this can occur.
1. Loss of bias voltage or too positive setting of bias voltage.
2. Shorted or missing screen resistors.
3. Output transformer problems
   A. Short on the primary
   B. Secondary hooked up wrong (the wrong set of taps being used would change the turns ratio of the transformer and mismatch the impedance). There is a technique (described in detail on my third video, "Advanced Tube Guitar Amplifier Servicing and Overhaul.") to determine which wire goes where. Who knows if the factory-worker mistakenly swapped color codes when the transformer was manufactured?
   C. Short in the secondary
4. Parasitic oscillation (likely at frequencies the amp can produce, but the human can't hear. All the power is used to produce the high-pitch oscillation so the tubes and power supply are loaded down, causing low output of the intended signal and glowing output tubes.)

You need to start looking for which of these is causing the problem and isolate the problem. It could even be a multiple problem.

I am working on a project to build two Fender 5F-1 amps, using a Kendrick chassis kit and 10" speaker. Which gives better tone; a solid ⅝" pine speaker baffle, or ¼" ply with ¼" ply border as original?

With that particular design, I would use the ¼" plywood. I recommend Baltic Birch, MDO (medium density overlay), or Fir. I would not use ¼" on other combo amp designs — particularly ones with multiple speakers. Ordinarily, thinner baffleboard material resonates better, but on the other hand; it must be strong enough to support the speaker. In multiple speaker arrays or when using heavy speakers, the baffleboard must be strong enough not to crack under the stress of the speaker's weight.

So in most cases, I would use ½" Baltic Birch plywood when using twelve inch speakers or heavy ten inch speakers. With lightweight multiple ten inch speakers, I would use the ⅜" Baltic Birch plywood. The only time I would use ¼" ply would be in a single speaker configuration where the speaker does not weight very much.

I am building a Bassman 5F6-A. The layout for the Bassman 5F6-A in your book does not include the filter cap section. Where can I get the drawing of this to build the power section of the amp?
The schematic shows it, the layout shows some of it. The four 20 uf 600 volt filter caps mount in a metal pan and the wires (which connect only to the positive end of the cap) connect to the inside of the amp. The negative end of each cap gets grounded to the cap pan. If you look on page 63 of *A Desktop Reference of Hip Vintage Guitar Amps*, you will notice a hole drawn slightly below the treble pot. There are three wires coming out of the hole. One of the wires is labeled red. The red wire goes to the cap pan and two 20 uf / 600 volt caps are connected. The other two wires, that are not labeled, simply go to the cap pan and each connect to a 20 uf / 600 volt cap. Since each of the non-red wires (they are actually yellow) connect to a cap of the same value, it doesn't matter which one goes where.

I just finished rebuilding a tweed Fender Blues Deville. I stripped it all down and handwired it into a 5F6A Bassman circuit. I cathode biased it using a 660 ohm resistor. I have 483 volts on the plates. The cathode reads 47 volts. I first checked the bias using the current shunt method and it read 50 ma per tube which is quite hot. I then used a WeberVST bias meter and read 33 ma per tube. Why the big difference in readings?
Although some circuits, such as the 5E6 Bassman, will not give a good reading with the shunt method, the 5F6A circuit should work just fine using the shunt method.

Obviously, one of the meters is giving inaccurate readings. When is the last time you had your multi-meter calibrated? I usually get my meters calibrated once a year. How accurate is the WeberVST bias meter?

Fifty mA of idling plate current is fine as long as your output tubes aren't glowing red. The output tubes don't see the full 483 plate volts, they only see the difference between the cathode and plate (436 volts). At 436 volts, 40 to 50 mA should be fine — just make sure the plates of your output tubes aren't glowing.

I have a question about my 1957 Fender Harvard. The amp seems to be in excellent working order. It sounds best for my style of playing with the volume at "9." My only problem is, in certain live situations at this volume level, the pre-amp "hiss" can be a little annoying. The front end of this amp uses a 6AT6. I thought about converting to a low noise 12AX7 or 7025. I would prefer keeping the amp as close to stock as possible. Do you have any ideas or tips??

I would not change the preamp tube to a different type, although I would probably try a few different 6AT6's and choose the one with the least noise. Your problem may also have to do with noisy plate load resistors. Sometimes these can really hiss and changing them to quiet resistors may be the ticket. Here's the "Texas Shotgun Approach" to stopping your hiss: Change both 100K plate load resistors. There is one on the 6AT6 and one on the 12AX7 that needs to be changed.

1. Look on the 6AT6 at pin #7. Trace the wire back to the 100K plate resistor on the board. The 100K color code is: Brown, Black, and Yellow. Replace this resistor.
2. If you look right next to that resistor, you will notice another 100K resistor that goes to the plate (pin #1) of the 12AX7. Replace that one also.
3. You are done.

Use ½ watt or 1 watt 100K carbon composition resistors only. Although the 1 watt resistors are very expensive and fairly difficult to find, the 1 watt value will probably be the quietest one to use.

What's the best way to reduce hum on my tweed Deluxe? I guess the filaments have to "float," right? Does this change the original tone in any significant way? Also, if I increase the main 16 uf at 450 volt filter capacitor to rid power supply hum, it will be even more woofy at high volumes than it is right now...so what's a po' boy to do?

The "twisted pair" filament is a good way to go, but you will have to use two 100 ohm resistors on each end of the transformer winding to ground or it will hum worse. The idea is to phase cancel filament hum. Be careful modifying the filament to twisted pair. The pilot lamp will have to have one of its leads unsoldered from ground.

But you also need a 3 prong cord with the third prong directly connected to the chassis. Perhaps a shielded input wire would help, as would matched output tubes.

All of this will alter the tone for the better because you will lack annoying hum that is currently modulating the guitar signal!

Increasing the main filter does not increase woofiness. Besides smoothing out the ripple current in the power supply, it will tighten the blossoming of the note and provide more sting on the front of the note. You should increase the main filter cap to eliminate the 120 hertz ripple current that is modulating every note you play when you are playing loud. I recommend using a 100 uf at 500 volt.

The woofiness you describe is a function of the large coupling caps on the plates of the first preamp tube. (Stock is either .1 uf or .05 uf. depending on which model you have.) I recommend going to a .02 uf or a .01 uf (which ever sounds best to your ears). When you use the smaller value, the woofiness goes away.

A friend has a '48 TV front Fender Pro, which lacks a standby switch. The power transformer appears to be in good order and is not overheating. The B+ voltage is 434v. Measuring the voltage rise at the main filters, during power up, the voltage was peaking at 524v. I changed the 500v 20 uf parallel caps for two 100 uf 450v caps in series (each were bypassed with 220K resistors). This pushed up the B+ by 10 volts or so. Idle plate current is 50 mA.per side, however, peak voltage at the filters for the screens and driver/preamp still appears to be peaking at 512v on "turn on" before settling back down to 395 volt and 350 volt, respectively. The amp has survived 50 years with this "problem." What should I do?

The problem is the rectifier is heating up before the output tubes. With the output tubes cold, they are not drawing current. When they don't draw current, the entire applied voltage appears on the B+, instead of having some of the applied voltage drop across the internal winding of the power transformer. I would suggest you switch to a 5AR4 for a slower turn on.

I have a 1974 Fender Twin (Silverface) amp that I'm going to have refurbished. The silver faceplate is pretty scratched up and tarnished and I'm looking for a replacement. I called Fender and they don't make them anymore but they suggested "Smart Parts." They don't have any either. Do you know of a source?

Your Fender parts dealer can get you a replacement faceplate for a Blackface Twin reissue. If you have a master volume control on your amp, remove it and the Blackface faceplate can be made to fit your amp. You will have to slightly ream out the potentiometer holes on the reissue faceplate so that the holes are big enough for American made pots. I have done this on several occasions and it works great. The amp will sound better without the master anyway.

I have a 1966 Vibrolux Reverb that I bought from the original owner three years ago, who was a retired minister. The amp is as near to mint as one could think. It was never taken outside his house or church in all of its life. It is as new, with all accessories and cover, and it even has all the original tubes and the chassis has never been apart either. I don't think a finer one could be found. My question is what should I do with it? Should I have it serviced? Should I play it? Or should I just look at it? I don't want to devaluate it in any way, but I also don't want any harm to come to the inside of the amp. I don't use it much besides turning it on in my music room once in a while just to hear what it sounds like. I know that the amp has never been turned up past 3. Would it be hard on the amp in its present condition to turn it up enough to get the sweet sound they are known for? Also what kind of condition would the speakers be in after all that time?

You could sell the amp to a collector, you could build a glass viewing case for it or you could use it to make beautiful music. I would use it to make beautiful music.

Here's what I would do: Get the amp overhauled. This would include a cap job and new output tubes. All electrolytic capacitors should be replaced. Any coupling cap leaking more than ¼ volt should be replaced. You may need preamp tubes and a rectifier, too. Replace any drifted or burnt components and have the output tubes biased so that the quiescent (idle) plate current is 35 mA.

Make sure and remove original speakers. That paper voice coil is 37 years old and you WILL blow the speakers if you crank the amp. Replace the speakers now, before you blow them. I would replace them with ceramic FANE 10" guitar speakers. These have tons of clear bottom-end with a smooth midrange and highs. These will actually have a richer and louder sound than the original speakers. The amp will sound several times bigger than it is. Keep your original speakers, because if you ever want to sell the amp, it will bring several hundred dollars more if you have original, non-blown speakers. You'll get more money for the amp and you'll still have the 10" FANE speakers for later.

Maybe you can give some advice about how to clean an old 50's Fender tweed amp. What is the best cleaner to use? Is lacquering recommended? If so, what is the best product and method? Will lacquering reduce the value of a vintage amp, even if it enhances its appearance? The tweed on this thing is ragged around the edges and there are some bare wood spots.

When cleaning tweed, it is good to remember that the tweed is glued to the cabinet with water-based animal glue. If the tweed gets saturated, water will melt the glue! So you don't want the tweed to get very wet. I have taken ordinary washing machine detergent and put hot water in it to make lots of suds. I then take only the suds off the top and use a soft bristled brush to scrub the tweed. Then, I wipe the suds off with a damp, clean cloth. This works great. Careful not to get that tweed saturated!

Although I haven't tried it, I've heard of people using upholstery spray foam or carpet shampoo foam to clean tweed. Upholstery or carpet shampoo foam would have the advantage of not soaking the tweed. It would dampen only the outermost surface and therefore not melt the water-based animal glue.

If there are long strings hanging around ragged edges, trim those first with scissors. You may use Elmer's glue and glue down the ragged edges.

I do not recommend re-lacquering the entire cabinet, however, if you have some scraped spots that really need it, or on the areas around bare wood, you might want to touch up these spots with lacquer after the cabinet is completely dry. The best type of product for relacquering is tinted polyurethane called Polyshades. It is made by Minwax and sold at Sherwin Williams, Walmart, Home Depot, and Builders Square. It comes in different shades and colors. Choose the "Honey Pine Matte" finish, as it closely resembles the color of aged lacquer. It is best to apply this stuff with a rag. When the Polyshades is still wet, it will be much darker than when it dries. So if you apply some and it looks a little too dark, don't worry about it. It will lighten up when it dries.

I hear of people saying they want to keep their vintage piece original. If the tweed is rotten, ragged or ripped; it is not original. Originally the tweed didn't leave the factory frayed, with strings hanging and dirty. So your tweed is already not original.

If the tweed is really bad, you may want to consider having it professionally retweeded. If it is done right, it will look more original than what you have on it now. I like to use the analogy of a vintage collectible car. Would you rather have a 1959 T-bird with chipped, dead, and rusted original paint and dry-rotted and ripped interior or one that has been completely repainted with the original type and color paint and re-upholstered with the original style upholstery. Which one is more original? I rest my case.

I have a model 5A3 Deluxe. On the tube chart, the 6SC7s have been crossed out and 6SL7s written in (in the same green pen and handwriting as the serial number, which is real cool). Going by the stamp on the speaker, the amp was made in '51 or '52. I compared the wiring with some pinout charts of the 6SL7s and 6SC7s and the amp is clearly wired for the 6SL7s. I would like your opinion on what you expect would be the tonal differences if I were to convert to 6SC7s (since it is a simple and reversible procedure, I think all that is necessary would be to move the instrument coupling cap from pin #1 to pin #3, and ground pin #1). What do you think?

I have seen many Fender amps with tube chart scratchovers from the factory. They didn't waste anything. If something was changed and they had tube charts printed, they simply scratched over the printing and corrected it by hand. Very professional indeed!

It will be easy to change the tube socket over. The 6SC7 and the 6SL7 are basically the same tube except the 6SC7 has a common cathode while the 6SL7 has split cathodes. Both have an amplification factor of 70. You may hear a difference, but not much. Go for it.

A 6SC7 has no internal connection to pin #1. So you would take whatever is currently on pin #3 and add it to pin #6. Move whatever is on pin #1 to pin #3 and you are there. You may now use a 6SC7.

I recently purchased a new Twin Reverb Reissue to replace my original '66 that was stolen. The only resemblance to the '66 is the Tolex and the logo. This new amp sounds terrible! Also, what voltage for bias? The original Blackface schematic has -52 volts and the reissue schematic has -50 volts. What do you recommend to make the reverb sound acceptable?

The minus voltage shown on the schematic is only an approximation. The actual bias would vary depending on the particular set of tubes being used.

The first thing you need is a cap job to get rid of the cheapo Taiwanese capacitors. These capacitors, even when brand new, allow ugly, out-of-tune ripple current to ruin your tone. Get some American made caps. I like Sprague Atom caps.

Those Eminence speakers are the cheapest American speakers money can buy. Almost anything else would be an improvement.

Reverb pans have a huge variance from one to another. Perhaps hand-selecting an above average sounding pan would do the trick. The other circuitry for the reverb is all the same except — a NOS 12AT7. Now that would do the trick. Use a 12AT7 for the Reverb driver tube (just like the original).

Greetings from Holland. Two weeks ago, I purchased a Fender Tonemaster with the 4x12 cabinet. Is it normal for the power transformer to get hot even when the amp is in standby position? The temperature is so high that I can't touch it with bare hands. When I connect an Alesis Nanoverb on the effects loop (Channel A), then I get a hum that is not changing when I turn the knobs from Channel A. On channel B, everything seems ok. Thank you for your help.

The transformer should get warm when the amp is in standby, but not hand-scorching hot. Perhaps a professional should check the power transformer to see if there are any shorted windings.

You have a ground loop, which is causing the hum. This is a perfectly normal but tough problem in Euro-town. It is illegal there to use a ground lift adapter (that's how we solve the hum problem here). So you must use an audio isolation transformer (a 1:1 ratio). I know this is a hassle, but it is the easiest way. The other option is to use an isolation power transformer to isolate the ground from one device from the other.

I built a tweed Deluxe circuit. I am using 6L6's with a 50 watt output transformer. My plate voltage is around 290. Using the transformer shunt method, I measure get 65 ma of plate current per output tube. Is this Class A !
Using the simple definition of the tubes remaining "on" for the entire 360 degrees of the input cycle, then yes, it would qualify as Class A. As long as you don't give it enough preamp signal to drive it into cutoff (not likely), you are in Class A by that definition.

There are those that would argue that Class A is more than the output tubes never going into cutoff. Their definition of Class A is that the signal is amplified using the linear portion of the output tube's operating area. Your design may not actually be operating within that linear portion of the tubes output, in which case it is not really Class A by the latter definition.

I finally had to get into my CBS Silverface Fender Twin Reverb. In comparing the schematic with that of my AB763, I can see the differences. There aren't that many differences. With a little re-arranging, it appears to have all the stuff to be a great amp. I have been wondering the possibility of leaving the bias balance pot in place and creating a bias voltage adjustment. There is a 3.3K resistor between the reverse bias diode and the balance pot. Couldn't an additional overall bias pot, leaving the resistor for the wire going to the vibrato, replace this resistor? Or perhaps running the new pot parallel to the resistor- between the diode and the balance pot?
It's the 15K that goes from the wiper of the bias pot to ground that should be changed to a variable cermet pot — perhaps a 25K at-

tached in series to a 5K resistor. The lowest adjustment parameter would be 5K and the highest 30K. This would give you both an adjustable bias control and a balance control. You would have to go back and forth — adjust one then the other, then the bias, then the balance, etc. until you reached an equilibrium point where the tubes were both balanced and biased.

I asked you if I could have a line out installed in my Vibro Champ and have it go to my '66 Bassman head. You said it would work, but my tech installed a preamp out and said I can't go to my Bassman or it will overload. I'm lost??
Let's get clear on what we are talking about. You asked me about a line out, but your tech installed a preamp out. Which one are we talking about?

The line-out is a voltage divider that comes off the output transformer secondary (or speaker leads, depending on which way you are thinking of it) and the preamp-out comes off the last preamp tube before the output stage. The line-out is the way to go for your application because it would include the entire sound of the amp (including the output transformer). Also, the line-out should be plugged into the #2 input of whichever channel you are using.

Is there a formula that I can use when installing a line out jack on other vintage tube amps of various wattage and configuration or will the line out voltage divider resistor values, that work for the Champ, work with most other amps (Super, Twin Reverb, etc.)? I'm not sure I understand the requirements for a good line out jack!
The line out circuit has two resistors, namely: a dropping resistor and a load resistor. These resistors are configured as a voltage divider. The junction of the two resistors goes to the line out jack. The free end of the dropping resistor goes to the hot of the speaker lead and the free end of the load resistor goes to the ground (or minus of the speaker lead). The proportion of these two resistor values will dictate the amplitude of the output signal. A general rule of thumb would be about a 2.2K ohm for the dropping resistor and anywhere from 270 ohm or less for the load resistor. You don't want the dropping resistor (that's the 2.2K) to get too high or you'll lose high-end. If you

already have too much high-end and you want to deliberately lose some, you could approximately double the dropping resistor to a 4.7K ohm value. The 270 ohm could be replaced with a pot so that the load resistance could be variable from 0 to 250 ohms (or 500 ohms depending on what value pot you choose.) This could give you a volume control for your line out. You could put a capacitor in series with a tone pot to make a tone control. The potentiometer/capacitor combination would go across the load resistor (or volume pot as the case may be). I don't know the exact values of the pot and cap without experimenting, but it would probably be a 1000 ohm pot with a 2 uf cap for the tone control of the line out circuit.

I'd like to try replacing the tube rectifier in my '54 Fender Pro with the plug-in solid-state type that comes in the reissue Bassman. I'm thinking it may give me a little more headroom. I just need to know if I'll be damaging the amp before I flip the switch! Any advice would be appreciated.

It is not supposed to damage the amp, but if you need a cap job anyway and the caps are used to a tube rectifier and then you plug in a solid-state rectifier, you could have a problem. The caps could possibly blow when they get more voltage than they are used to having. If you've had a cap job recently, the plug-in rectifier will be fine. If you haven't had a cap job recently, you need one. Forty-nine years is too long for any electrolytic cap. Also, fresh caps will improve headroom. You said you wanted more headroom. The cap job by itself will give you extra headroom.

When you go from tube rectifier to solid-state rectifier, there will be a considerable increase in B+ voltage. Depending on the particular tube rectifier, you could have as much as 50 volts difference. A 1954 Fender Pro is self-biased and will easily self-correct for this difference. However, when changing from tube to solid-state rectifiers in amps that are not self-biased, you would be well advised to re-bias your output tubes, because plate current is affected by plate voltage.

I'm going to power up my 5E3 copy in a few days. I've read the instruction on powering up the amp. Start at 40 volts, overnight, then up 10 volts every hour until I reach 120 volt. Do I start at

40 volts or slowly turn it up to 40 volts? Also, how long should I leave it on at 120V? I am using a 250 ohm, 5 watt, wire wound resistor as the cathode bias resistor. Is this OK to use or will it affect sound quality?

The 250 ohm wirewound resistor is an excellent choice for a cathode resistor of an output stage.

Although there is no "chiseled in stone" method for bringing up an amp for the first time, starting at 40 volts will work fine. At 40 volts, the filaments to the tube will not be giving off very much heat and therefore there will be little current flow. This is good because it will allow everything in the amp to power up slowly.

I see schematics of Twins and Bandmasters, but I have never seen anything on what type of diode is used for the rectifier or bias supply.

On most Fender amps, a 1N4007 is used for the six diodes in the rectifier circuit. The 1N4007 is a 1 amp 1000 PIV diode. On most Fenders, the diodes are wired with three diodes wired in series on each side of the B+ winding. This is done to get the Peak Inverse Voltage rating up to 3,000 volts. The bias tap winding also uses a diode. This diode is the 1N4003 which is rated for 1 amp and 200 PIV.

I prefer using the RL-157 or the 1N5399 as an upgrade replacement for 1N4007. These diodes can take more current than the 1N4007 and are therefore not as likely to malfunction.

I recently came across an old Fender Bassman 2x12 cabinet without speakers. I would like to make it into an 8 ohm cabinet. I know if I use two 16 ohm speakers, they should be wired in parallel. If I use 4 ohm speakers they should be wired in series. I have not purchased the speakers yet. Is one way of wiring better than the other? Is there any advantages or disadvantages for either situation, tone-wise?

The consideration would be what amp you are using it with. If your amp has a 16 ohm, 8 ohm and 4 ohm tap, the 16 ohm will be best. This is because the highest impedance tap of a transformer is the full secondary winding. All other, smaller taps are only a portion of the secondary winding on the output transformer. The whole secondary of the transformer sounds better than a portion of it!

Also, the higher impedance setting sounds better because the higher impedance secondary winding is the smallest turns ratio (of any of the other impedance taps on the secondary) and the smaller the turns ratio, the more efficient (more sound out per amount of power in.)

I have decided to perform a two to three prong conversion of my 67 Blackface Deluxe Reverb. While I'm in there, I decided to disconnect the vibrato since I don't use it. I was also thinking about disconnecting the 47 pf "brightness" cap across the second channel volume pot. What is your take on this considering I'm no longer in a band and play mostly at home at low levels? Some say it will be an improvement, others say it will rob the amp of that vintage tone.

Do any mods ONE AT A TIME. Spend some time listening to each of them before doing any additional mods. Trust your ears. Does it work for you? You know what sounds good, what inspires you and what doesn't. If it pleases you, who cares if it is vintage or not? You are playing at home and who is the primary listener? HELLO! An amp is supposed to inspire you to play better. If yours does that, it is right FOR YOU.

I have an eighties Rivera Princeton Reverb II. I am interested in installing an effects loop on this amp. I use a wireless (Samson) with a Boss D3 delay to expand my sound. With this setup, I hear a scratchy, distorted sound in the background. I am thinking that an FX loop could get rid of this and get a much cleaner delay sound for both harp and guitar.

I would suggest troubleshooting around a bit to find out where the original noise is coming from before doing any kind of major modification. To do an FX loop and really have it work correctly — without the delay loading down the amp or vice-versa, we are talking about a major modification. The delay is a relatively low impedance device when compared to a tube amp and therefore the "send" of the amp's FX loop must be changed to make it much lower than the "already low" delay pedal. Source impedances should always be lower than destination impedances. Also, the "send" from the amp, must be padded to keep from overdriving the pedal. Because the level would be padded to drive the delay, the output of the pedal would need to be amplified considerably to get the signal back up to the level needed to drive the "return" circuit of the FX loop. This modification is do-able if you want to spend the time and money.

You could put a passive loop in for the price of two ¼" jacks, but the impedances would not allow the devices to work with each other and it would not sound good. Here's a suggestion: Take a line out off the Princeton, run that through the delay and then feed another amp with it. Set the mix on the delay to full wet and you have true stereo delay. You would need an auxiliary amp, but it would kill!

I am currently building an amp based on a 5F4 Super and would like to know how to modify the bias circuit so that it could be fixed adjustable with a potentiometer wired permanently. To monitor tube current (when setting output tube bias), I would like to wire the output tubes as you describe in *A Desktop Reference of Hip Vintage Guitar Amps* **using the cathode resistor method. Thanks for your advice. I'm learning a lot from your books and columns in Vintage Guitar magazine!**

Good choice of circuitry. The 5F4 has always been a circuit close to my heart. You are going to need to do more to the bias circuit than add an adjustment pot!

Locate the 56K load resistor that is in parallel with the electrolytic filter cap for the negative voltage bias supply. Note: On the 5F4 schematic published by Fender, the capacitor is shown, but there is no value marked. In the layout published by Fender, the value appears to be a 100 mfd at 25 volts. DO NOT, UNDER ANY CIRCUMSTANCE, use that value capacitor. It will blow up. The bias voltage is going to be around -40 to -45 volts. To use a 25 volt cap is asking for trouble. Try instead a 100 mfd value at either 75 volt or 100 volts.

Now we are going to remove the 56K load resistor and replace it with a 20K resistor that is wired in series to a 50K cermet element pot. You must use a cermet element pot and not a carbon trace pot. Remember that the bias circuit is dealing with D.C. electricity. A carbon pot will eventually burn up if used for D.C.. A cermet element pot can take D.C. without fear, so use the cermet element pot.

To wire the pot in series with the resistor, start by making a subassembly. Take one lead from the 20K resistor and attach it to both the middle lead of the cermet pot and one end lead. This will be your subassembly. Now we will install the sub-assembly where the 56K resistor was. It doesn't matter which polarity the sub-assembly goes in, as long as the one unused end of the 20K resistor counts as one end and the unused lead for the cermet pot counts as the other. The pot is usually a 20 or 25 turn pot and it can be adjusted from zero ohms to 50K ohms. Since it is in series with the 20K resistor, together they can be adjusted from 20K to 70K. The original non-adjustable circuit was simply 56K so by being able to go from 20K to 70K, you have a wide range of adjustment.

If you are building the 5F4 circuit, you cannot get original transformers for this amp. Therefore, depending on which transformer you use; you may have to modify the other resistor in the bias circuit. You can see it in the schematic and the layout. It is the 6800 ohm (6.8K) resistor that is in series with the bias tap and bias diode. This actual value may need to be altered in order to get the appropriate bias voltage in the rest of the circuit.

Monitoring tube current by placing a 1 ohm resistor in series with the cathode of the output tube is a great way to go. I used this extensively on my Black Gold amps and also the Climax amps. On a fixed bias amp, the cathode of the output tube is grounded and the current coming into the tube gets there by coming from ground. On this design, instead of the cathode being grounded, the cathode of the output tube is attached to a 1 ohm resistor and the other end of the resistor goes to ground. This way, all the current that is going into the output tube must first go through the 1 ohm resistor. When you figure Ohm's law, the voltage drop across the resistor equals the current going through the resistor. This is true only because we are using a 1 ohm resistor. When the voltage is divided by the resistance (resistance = one ohm), it equals the current. I like using a precision wirewound resistor for this because it is so accurate. You can use either a 1 watt or 3 watt and it will never blow, even if the tube completely shorts. There is less than 2 milliwatts of power on this circuit under normal conditions and even if a tube shorted completely there would only be ¼ watt of power through the 1 ohm resistor.

Of course you would do this on each output tube. The cathode is pin #8 on a 6L6, or 6V6 or EL34. The resistor goes between pin #8 and ground. When you connect your meter, one end goes to pin #8 and the other goes to ground. The meter is set for the 1 volt range. Adjust bias voltage until the meter reads the appropriate voltage (usually around .035 volts, which converts via Ohm's law directly to 35 milliamps).

I have a '71 Princeton Reverb that is in overall, good condition. I have a question regarding the volume control. I don't know if my volume pot is a replacement or if my problem is indicative of other difficulties. I don't get any sound from my Princeton until I turn the volume up to 3. From 3 and up is seems to be fairly smooth, no sudden volume changes but below 3, I get nothing. Does the pot need to be replaced?

I don't think there is anything to worry about with your volume control. Volume controls have a taper. Not all of them have the same taper. If yours doesn't come on until you get up to three, you must be playing at a level higher than 3 or you wouldn't be able to hear what you are playing. So here are your options:

1. Play with the volume control set higher than 3 and live with it.
2. Unscrew the mounting screw for the volume knob, rotate the volume knob so that when the sound comes on, the knob is pointing to 1 and not 3.
3. Change the volume pot to a new 1 Meg Audio.

I recently lost the reverb function altogether in my Silverface Fender Twin Reverb amp. This is a practice amp that stays in one place and hasn't been moved in years. The reverb still "crashes" if you bump the pan; but the reverb effect is missing. Where do I start troubleshooting? (I am no whiz in electronics).

When a reverb goes out, it is about a 95% probability the problem exists in the RCA connectors or cable going from the amp to the reverb tank. There are two cables connecting from the reverb pan to the amp, namely the "send" and the "return." If the pan crashes and "makes thunder," then the "return" cable/connectors and recovery circuit are all working properly.

Your problem is probably in the "send" cable. When there is no signal driving the input of the pan, there won't be any reverb. Try adjusting the RCA plugs on their RCA jacks to make sure you have a good "metal on metal" connection. Sometimes the oxidation on the jack is enough to prevent a good connection and stop the reverb from working. Substituting a known good patch cord is another possible cure.

If that doesn't cure the problem, try substituting a known good reverb pan. If a good pan and good cables still don't cure the problem, try substituting a known good Reverb Driver tube (V3 - 12AT7). If that still doesn't work, bring it to a tech and have him trouble shoot it.

I just bought a mid 70's Fender Vibro Champ. I read in your first book, *A Desktop Reference of Hip Vintage Guitar Amps*, that all Champs sound better with 5V4's than they do with 5Y3's. Mine has a 5Y3. Can I have the 5Y3 changed to a 5V4? And what is the difference between a Silverface and a Blackface Vibro Champ? Thanks!
With regards to the tone of the Blackface Fender Champ versus the Silverface Fender Champ: this is the only instance where I prefer the Silverface to the Blackface. Although the Silverface is overall a better amp, there is a 2000 pf cap going from the grid circuit of the output tube to ground, which must be removed. The Silverface has better transformers and better filtering. It is louder with more efficiency.

The advantage to the 5V4 (or 5AR4/GZ34) rectifier tube is twofold. It takes longer for these tubes to warm up than the output and preamp tubes. Since the Champ has no standby switch, the controlled warm-up time rectifier is like an "automatic built-in standby switch." Because they take so long to warm up, the 5V4 or 5AR4/GZ34 rectifier tubes are much easier on the preamp and the output tube. The 5V4 or 5AR4/GZ34 each put out more voltage than a 5Y3. This means you get more headroom, more power, and better bottom-end than using a stock 5Y3.

I'm rebuilding a '65 Vibro Champ. For some reason the voltages across the board read at least 100 volts above the rating. I have a good guess the power transformer is defective. I ran a test,

like pulling out all the tubes and letting the amp run for 2 hours and disconnecting all the wires from the transformer but the blacks ones. It still works and lights up, but the voltages are so high and the amp runs at 60 mA idle current on the output tube and I want it to idle between 30 - 40 mA.

Put all the tubes back in and let it run at 60 mA of output tube idle. You are going to check the 6.3 volt heater winding. It is easiest to check it at the pilot light. You want to have a meter lead on each of the pilot lamp's terminals.

This will tell you if the primary of your power transformer is shorted. If the heater voltage reads 6.2 to 6.6 volts, the transformer is OK. If it reads 6.8 volts to 7 volts or even higher, the primary has some shorted turns.

Champs are supposed to run fairly high plate current because they are Class A and must idle half way between saturation and cutoff. The GE Vacuum Tube Manual has a graph chart of the characteristic curve of a typical GE 6V6. At 400 volts, the tube saturates at 110 mA. To bias in Class A, the idle point is selected half way between cutoff (no current) and saturation (110 mA). So 55 mA would be ideal and 60 mA is fairly close.

If the voltages read high and the primary is NOT shorted, then the rest of the amp circuit is not drawing enough current.

My bandmates were discussing Blackfacing my Silverface Bassman amp. One question was raised concerning total harmonic distortion. Have you noticed any variance good or bad in this area after Blackfacing a Silverface Fender amp? I was told that most tube amps are lucky to get 2 or 3 percent. I realize this isn't audiophile equipment and probably doesn't mean much in the real world but I want to know your thoughts nonetheless.

The audiophile mentality and specifications mean nothing to me. In 1973, I went out and traded in my 45 watt Blackface Pro Reverb amp on an Acoustic 271 head / 201 speaker cabinet, piggy back amp, with two 15's and a horn. The specs on the Acoustic looked better than the Pro. It had bigger speakers, it had more speakers, it had more power, it was bigger, it had more impressive specs and in real life — the Blackface Pro Reverb ate its lunch. Forget the specs —

specs are for spectators. You and I are not spectators; we are players.

When an amp is Blackfaced, it is simply "put back" to the circuitry that made Fender famous. The CBS engineers (mostly MIT grads with no ear for music, but very good at solving mathematical equations and proficient at reading an oscilloscope!) put in some parasitic suppression capacitors that actually bleed signal to ground. Also, they lowered the input impedance of the phase inverter section, which made the amp cold and non-responsive. These modifications almost stopped people from buying Fender amps! By removing those capacitors and putting the input impedance (of the phase inverter) back to Blackface specs, the amplifier gets livelier with more of a "rack and pinion" kind of feel. It responds more to your playing. When your amp responds better, you sound better. You will play better when you sound better and the experience of playing guitar is brought to a higher level.

I have Tweed Champ (5C1). Although the amp has a good clean tone, it just does not have enough gain for a good lead sound. I would like to get a more screaming and funky amp tone — just like Clapton's "Layla" tone. What do you suggest?

Here's some suggestions:

1. Change the 25K (connecting to pin #4 of the 6V6) to a 4.7K. This is the dropping resistor that supplies voltage to the preamp tube. By modifying this resistor to 4.7K, the voltage isn't "dropped" so much and you end up with more voltage on the plates of the preamp section. Higher voltage increases both gain and preamp headroom.

2. Change the rectifier tube to a 5AR4 — this will increase voltage overall because it has less losses than other 5 volt rectifiers. More voltage will allow more power from your output tube, but the preamp voltages increase also and that spells more gain and headroom.

3. Change first two 8 mfd filter capacitors (that go to either side of the 500 ohm resistor) to 40 mfd 500 volt. This is your main filter supply. Bigger and better filtering in this part of the circuit provides extra reserves of power when the output tube "needs" it (especially noticeable in the focus of the bottom-end). Also, on a single-ended amp such as this, the extra filtering helps smooth out 120 Hertz pulsating D.C. ripple current, thus eliminating annoying power supply hum. This is especially a problem with

single-ended output stages, because they are not humbucking like the push-pull output stage design.

NOTE: When you change the filter caps, notice there is a 500 ohm resistor and a filter cap that go to pin #2 of the rectifier tube. Move the 500 ohm resistor and the filter cap from pin #2 to pin #8. This corrects a wiring mistake that was made during manufacture of your particular model. (This mistake was corrected on the 5E1 Champ!) Leave the yellow wire (coming from the power transformer) on pin #2, but nothing else should be on pin #2. Pin #8 should have the plus side of a 40 mfd cap, the 500 ohm resistor and the other yellow wire (coming from the power transformer).

4. Go ahead and change the other filter cap to a new 8 or 10 mfd at 450 volts. We are doing a cap job on this amp and this is the last filter cap that needs changing.
5. Change the 25 uf at 25 volt cap that goes to pin #8 of the output tube to a 50 or 100 uf at 50 or 100 volt. (Use a 50 uf at 50V, 50 uf at 100V, 100 uf at 50V or 100 uf at 100V). The extra voltage from the B+ supply may make this output tube develop more than 25 VDC on the cathode of the power tube. We want to increase the stock voltage rating of this cap. We also want to use a higher microfarad rating, too. The bigger the microfarad rating of the cap, the more stable the cathode bias voltage—and the easier for low frequency signal to get through the cathode circuit.

Now you are almost done.

We still need to change the 6SJ7 from grid leak bias to cathode bias. Here's how:

1. Replace the .02 uf capacitor, that goes to pin #4 of the 6SJ7, with a straight wire.
2. Replace the 5 Meg resistor (that goes from pin #4 to ground) with a 1 Meg resistor.
3. With the stock setup, pins #1, 2, 3 and 5 of the 6SJ7 are grounded.

Only pin #1 and pin #2 should be grounded. pin #3 and pin #5 connect together and a 1K resistor should be installed from those two pins to ground. This is your cathode resistor.

4. A bypass cap should be placed across the 1K cathode resistor. Use about a 10 uf at anywhere from 6 to 25 volts. The minus side of the cap goes to ground and the plus side goes towards pin #3 and pin #5.

That should do it, but remember you'll have to adjust that volume control to get the best "shade" of overdrive.

I have a '55 Bassman that needs a vintage style, speaker wiring harness. My amp, the older style, only has one ¼" speaker jack in the amp chassis. I understand the original harness should be a "Daisy Chained" style, but it's better to go with a later design (like the speaker wiring harness used for a Brown Concert or Super Reverb). I heard the older "Daisy Chain" style might put an extra load on the first speaker in the chain and make the speaker more susceptible to blowing. What are your thoughts on this?

The split style is better but not because of what you heard. Either way is safe for the speakers. With any 2 ohm configuration, there is loads of current. Instead of running all that current through the first wires, then the next then the next, etc. — it is easier for the current to get to the speakers if it splits into fourths and goes to the speakers like that. You end up with a quarter as much current going down each wire instead of ALL the current trying to pass through each wire. In fact, that is why the later Bassman amps (5F6) had four individual outputs. Each speaker had its own leads to the transformers output. Only a quarter as much current had to pass down each pair of wires. This keeps the losses at a minimum. By Ohm's law, the voltage loss equals current times resistance. By cutting the current on each wire by three fourths, the voltage drop across the connecting cables is dramatically decreased.

Fender used this same logic on their other two ohm output amps, such as the Super Reverb. A pair of wires goes to a central distribution point and from there separate pairs of wires are used to feed each of the four speakers (four pairs total).

I have a problem with my 5F1 Champ. If I turn it up more than half way, it starts to produce an intolerable humming noise. My amp tech couldn't find any obvious fault. Any suggestion where to start? It is a tweed amp with a recently replaced output transformer. At first I thought the noise problem had to do with the transformer, but after changing the transformer, the noise persists.

The hum comes from the filter caps not filtering out the 120 Hertz ripple current that is created when rectifying 60 Hertz wall electricity into high voltage D.C.. Actually the rectifier changes the A.C. (goes both directions) wall electricity into pulsating D.C. (goes all the same direction). Then the filter caps are supposed to smooth that pulsating D.C. into smooth, non-pulsating D.C. I believe the D.C. ripple current is not being filtered adequately. That amp is very old and probably needs a cap job anyway. I recommend using a 100 uf at 500 volt for the first cap (the one that goes to pin #8 of the rectifier tube) instead of the 16 uf stock value. The amp is single-ended which means it does not have hum cancellation in the output stage. The bigger filters allow you to turn the amp up and still have the hum (ripple current) filtered out. When your amp was first made, in general, guitar amplifiers were not turned up nearly as much as we like to turn them up today. So what seems like hum today, may not have been noticeable with the volume turned way down — like the amp was played 40 years ago.

GIBSON

I have a '54 Gibson GA-40 Les Paul amp. It doesn't work, so I've never heard any tone out of it — "vintage" or otherwise. In other words, I don't have any benchmark for what a good GA-40 should sound like. For starters, it needs new caps. It has the original Cornell-Dublier caps and some of them show signs of leakage. In my initial enthusiasm, I bought some Solen fast metalized capacitors to replace the large electrolytic caps, some SBE Orange Drops and a few Sprague Atoms. Then I thought, "Whoa. I don't know if using some modern caps like the Solens might completely change the sound of the amp." What do you recommend for caps? The only experience that I have is building one tube amp from a kit. That was fun, once I got the hang of it, and the amp sounds good. Am I over my head in considering trying to re-cap the amp on my own or would you recommend that I get a professional like yourself to do it up right? Any help would be greatly appreciated.

If you have the GA 40 with the 6V6 output tubes and the 5879 pentode preamp tubes, it should sound like an early tweed Deluxe.

Yours has the paraphase style phase inverter, which is impossible to get a clean sound out of. The amp would be great for slide guitar or harmonica. You can recap it yourself. We recommend the Sprague ATOM electrolytics. I wouldn't change the coupling caps unless they are leaking .25 D.C. volt or more.

I am fixing up an old Gibson GA-5T Skylark that I have had since I was 13 years old, and I'm a bit unsure about how to wire up a replacement grounded A.C. cord? Please explain how to connect the three wires of a grounded plug to the current configuration? Changing to the 3-wire A.C. cord is quite simple. Look at your existing 2-wire A.C. cord. Notice that one wire goes to the fuseholder and the other wire goes to the switch.

Now, look at your 3-wire A.C. cord. You will notice that there are three colors: black, white, and green.

You are basically going to substitute the black and white wires (from your 3-wire A.C. cord) for the two black wires of your existing A.C. cord. Then you will ground the green wire to the chassis.

The black goes to the fuse holder, the white goes to the switch and the green connects directly to the chassis.

It is difficult to solder to a chassis. One solution is to drill a small hole in the chassis and fasten the green wire to the chassis with a small nut and bolt. You could solder the green wire to a grounding lug (or washer) and then bolt the lug to the chassis. If you have a high wattage soldering iron, you could solder the green wire directly to the chassis, but you will need a heavy-duty iron. I use a 175 watt soldering iron for soldering chassis grounds.

I recently purchased a late 30s Gibson EH-150, which has amazing tone and great volume on the microphone channel, but only low volume on the instrument channel. By comparison with the instrument channel volume set to high #9, it is equal to the microphone channel volume set to #2½.

I can't believe this is normal but I have checked all the normal troubleshooting items noted in your books to no avail (all tubes voltages ok/all resistors and caps check out / tube switching input and volume pots test ok). This particular vintage is dif-

ferent than noted in your book, and different from the schematic shown in Pittmans book.

#1 6F5- preamp stage 1 for mic
#2 6C5 preamp stage for inst
#3 6C5 preamp stage 2 for mic which blends with tube #2 - inst stage 1
#4 6C5 preamp combination stage 3 for mic and stage for inst
#5 6L6 power tube
#6 6L6 power tube
#7 5U4 rectifier

This amp has a tone control and uses a transformer for the phase inverter. Is this normal or have I missed or need to double-check something?

I think this is normal. There are many different versions of the EH150. On every EH150 I've ever seen, the microphone channel has one extra stage of gain that the instrument channel doesn't have. Evidently, they were not going for overdriven guitar tones in the 1930's.

On your particular version, the microphone channel signal path goes to a 6F5 and then goes everywhere that the instrument channel signal path goes. The amplification factor of the 6F5 is 100. This would translate into about 35 dB of extra gain! Is it any wonder that the microphone channel is fairly loud while the instrument channel is wimpy? This has been the case on all the EH150's I've seen whether they used the tube compliment like yours or if they had the 6SQ7's (these sounded the best because the 6SQ7 has an amplification factor of 100 while the 6C5 only has an amplification factor of 20!)

You could get a little more power by upgrading the 5U4 to the 5AR4/GZ34. This would make the plate voltage go up slightly and give you slightly more power. I checked my tube manual and there is not a substitute tube for the 6C5 that has more gain. I was hoping I could turn you on to a tube that had the same pin-out but with a higher amplification factor than the 6C5. Such an animal doesn't exist.

Why not simply use the microphone channel for guitar? That's the channel that sounds the best anyway.

I have a GA-75 on the bench. It is a two channel, four input, two 6L6 amplifier with a solid state rectifier. All electrolytic ca-

pacitors have been replaced and re-checked. There is a hum in the amp that when one volume control is down and the other is turned up the hum gets quieter but it is still there. The only caps I can't get to are the tone caps. They are behind a brass plate, which is soldered to the back of the controls. The voltage on the preamp cathodes looks good.

You need to find where the hum is coming from. To isolate the hum, use a jumper wire. It can be used in two ways to find the source of hum. You can short across both ends of the plate resistor with the jumper (this will stop any amplification beyond that point in the circuit. If shorting the plate resistor stops the hum, then you know the hum is before that point in the circuit.) Or you can use the jumper wire to short the grid to ground (this will stop any amplification beyond that point in the circuit.) By using the jumper, you should be able to stop amplification at various points in the signal path until you find the point where it stops it and the point where it doesn't stop it. The hum is coming between those two points.

It might be coming from a grid wire not being shielded. That is common. You just have to dig in and look at what's going on.

I found a basket case of a '64 Gibson GA-77RET. The old transformers were in good shape and after replacing the filter caps and re-coning the speakers, the amp came alive and actually sounds great. The reverb unit is a small motor that turns a cylinder inside a drum of oil. The name on the drum is "Adeniko." The unit works, that is I can hear the effect, but it is very subtle, almost non-discernible. Can you tell me anything about this creature that may lead me to determine how to boost the effect? What is the oil in the drum? Can\should it be replaced? What volume of oil should be there? Should I set it on a shelf as an interesting part of history, or should I install a spring system?

Also the preamp section uses 6EU7 and 6FQ7 tubes. Should I rewire these sockets to accept the more abundant 12AX7/12AT7 series?

This is a fairly rare amp. I've always loved amps and effects that had motors in them. Perhaps you are having trouble getting enough reverb because this unit is not wired with the same signal path as other, more familiar, reverb equipped amplifiers. For starters, the reverb is only on Channel II. In addition, the Loudness (volume) control is after the reverb send. This means the "dry" signal works independently from the reverb-echo control. For more "effect" in the overall mix, try this: Plug your guitar into Channel II high gain input. Turn the loudness control on Channel II "off" and the reverb control "up," in order to get all "wet" signal in the mix. Now add just enough of the loudness control to get the "dry" signal back in the mix. This should give you the correct mix you are after, but will limit you to a certain overall volume setting.

The reverb in this unit works like this: The unit "records" the music, with an electronic "pen." The record is made on a film of oil, which also serves to lubricate the revolving disc, which is the platter for the film. The oil film is constantly replaced and can never wear out. Following the electronic "pen" are two sensors, which reproduce the pattern of electrons from the oil recordings. The effect is multiple choice of echo and reverberant sound. The three-way switch chooses between one or the other or both electronic sensors. Position #1 simulates room reverberation with a soft echo. Position #2 provides reverberation with a bold echo with a given repetition rate. Position #3 is similar to position #2 except the echo rate is quicker. To identify these sounds quickly, mute the strings near the nut or bridge and then listen to the string plucked with the three different positions.

The Gibson Service Manual warns: "This unit should only be operated in the horizontal position. The exact angle is not critical, but do not operate upside down, on end, or on its back. The recording medium is oil. The correct amount is placed in the unit at the factory. The unit is sealed at the factory and if not tampered with, no problem will be experienced. Do not open the metal container which surrounds the recording element!"

If you after all this, you still want more reverb-echo, try substituting a 12AT7 for the 12AU7 (V3). You may find that this improves reverb-echo but reduces the vibrato effect. If this is the case, try a 12BH7 in V3. I haven't actually tried these substitutions, but looking at the schematic, this appears to be the logical thing to do. In fact, I'll bet the 12BH7 is just what the doctor ordered. In addition, try changing the 470K resistor marked R57 to a 220K. You could also change R74 from a 4.7K to a 2.2K for more reverb "return."

I would not recommend changing the pin #outs on the 6EU7's and the 6FQ7 to accept 12AX7 and 12AT7 tubes. Though the stock tubes are more difficult to find, they are not impossible and you can still find these tubes as NOS. Unless the reverb is completely useless, I would not recommend changing to a "spring" type. You cannot simply plug in a "spring" type pan and go. The circuitry would have to be re-designed.

I have a problem with a Gibson GA20 RVT Minuteman 1965/66 vintage amp. I bought the amp at a swap meet for $10. The transformer was fried and the diodes were missing. After I got those replaced, I was able to get the amp working by rearranging the tubes. But – this was only after buying some replacements. Not ever seeing a picture of a photo resistor on the schematic and since it was not even listed on the parts list; I removed it in the process and destroyed it. I was able to get the thing working by using a Vactec Vactrol but it stopped working after I did a cap job. Since then, I have tried neon bulbs, incandescent bulbs and even a spare Vactec Vactrol, but nothing really works. What can I do?
Many of the tremolo circuits of the sixties used an opto-isolator device. Although the device itself was usually made "in house" (and each manufacturer had their own idea of what it needed to be for their particular circuit), the workings were basically all the same.

There is a light source and a light dependent resistor (LDR). A tube operates the light source and the light source "modulates" the light dependent resistor. The LDR goes from the signal path to ground. When the light is bright, the resistor becomes less resistive and grounds out the signal — thus making it not as loud. When the light is not bright, the resistive value goes up and does not ground out the signal.

Well, here's a chance to look at a circuit from the designer's point-of-view and see what is needed to make it work. A look at the GA20RVT schematic reveals a 12AU7 driver for the opto-isolator device. A quick look at both my GE and RCA tube manual show the 12AU7 typical characteristic plate current at 11.8 ma. This means the opto-isolator device should be turned "off" and "on" between zero and 10 ma roughly. What we need is a device that is "off" (high resistance) when there is no plate current flowing, but "on" (low resistance) when there is 10ma of plate current. The EG&G Vactec brand Vactrol is a device made with an LED and light dependent resistor, both encapsulated in epoxy. I called Vactec once and they sent me a design book with the different Vactrols they make and performance characteristics of each. They also sent this cool design idea booklet. Some of these Vactrols are made specifically for audio and some are not. You will be surprised at how many of these are available. I would get the one that is normally 100K ohms or so and drops to 200 ohms when 10 ma of current goes through the LED. The actual EG&G Vactec part number is VTL5C4. You might try Newark Electronics at 1 800 NEW ARK-X (1-800-639-2759). Newark's stock number for this part is 43F888.

Also, when installing a Vactrol, there is a polarity on the LED portion of the hookup. The cathode goes to the plate, the anode goes to the power supply.

I recently purchase a 60s Gibson GA5 that sounds great. It saturates above five or six on the volume setting and has excellent swirl and sustain and dynamics at that setting. I do not have (and cannot afford) a tweed Fender Champ, but have a few Blackface Champs and Silverface Vibro Champs. How does the GA5 Skylark differ from the tweed Fender Champ? The sound of the Skylark seems a little dark in the low register when playing the neck/rhythm pickup on a Hammer Archtop with P 90s. The amp excels in the higher registers.

In addition, will your recommendation for converting the Blackface and Silverface Champ/Vibro Champ to tweed specs give me the swirl and response that I found in the Skylark?

The Gibson GA-5 Skylark is very similar to the Fender tweed Champ. The main difference is that the GA-5 uses 220K plate load resistors for the 12AX7 while the Champ uses 100K. The only problem with the 220K plate resistors is that they can sometimes encourage grid emission from the 12AX7. This will make either the volume pot on the amp or the volume pot on the guitar (or both) scratchy. When a little bit of D.C. voltage gets on a pot, it will sound very scratchy — as if it is dirty — yet cleaning doesn't help.

Another minor difference: The Gibson GA-5 Skylark has 2200 ohm cathode resistors for the 12AX7 cathode circuits whereas the Champ uses 1500 ohms. This doesn't amount to much difference when you consider that a 2200 ohm 20% tolerance resistor may measure as low as 1760 ohms and still be within the 20% tolerance and a 1500 ohm resistor could measure as much as 1800 ohms and still be within spec. The output transformer and speaker on the GA-5 are 8 ohms, whereas the Champ is 4 ohms. Because of this, the GA-5 uses a higher value feedback resistor. This must be done to compensate for the fact that the output stage is running at 8 ohms. At 8 ohms, your transformer secondary will have twice the voltage and half the current of the same amp running at 4 ohms. Since negative feedback voltage is taken directly off the secondary of the output transformer, we would need a feedback resistor about twice as big when running 8 ohm. The GA-5 uses a 47K, which is just about twice the Champ's 22K feedback resistor.

Other differences — though minor — the Gibson uses 20 mfd bypass caps while the Fender uses 25 mfd., again very little actual difference.

Yes, converting your Blackface and/or Silverface Champ/Vibro Champ to the classic tweed Champ circuitry would likely give you the swirl and response that you find so appealing with your GA-5 Gibson Skylark.

I recently acquired a 1967 Gibson GA-20 RVT (Minuteman) amp that is all original. I had it serviced (cap job and tremolo calibration). It also got a matched pair of Sovtek EL 84 output tubes. Even after this, the amp sounds compressed and plinky. I don't want to alter/modify the amplifier, so how would I change the voicing of the amplifier? Could I change the 6EU7 pre-amp tubes to another such as 12AX7's (or others) to get a fatter, less choked result?

I do not know how to change the voicing of the amp without modifying it. There is no 6EU7 substitute tube that you could use. To use a 12AX7, the tube sockets would have to be rewired. The bad news is the GA-20 RVT (Gibson Minuteman) amp is not a very good sounding amp in the first place. It has many, many problems. For one thing, the transformer driven phase inverter is not a very good sound. The cabinet for that amp is too thin (front to back) and the cabinet sounds thin and weak. I would say minimize your loses and get rid of the amp. Find another amp. To fix this one to sound good would require so much time and effort that I question if it would be worth it.

Help! I have a 1966 Gibson Explorer amp (RVT 15) and it's so bright it'll peel the chrome off of your car bumper at 100 yards. I got a schematic, and everything is hooked up right and stock values except instead of two dual capacitors 20-20uF, it has 4-80uF at 450V ones in their place (polarity is correct). I've tried different tubes and an external speaker instead of the one inside. No change. Other than the four caps, the amp is dead stock and dead mint. I've other similar Gibson and Epiphone amps that sound great — kind of like a Blackface Deluxe — but not this pup. Any ideas?

For starters, you might want to change the filter caps to stock value. The bigger the capacitance, the easier it is for low end to go through the cap. Since the caps are in parallel with the signal, you can see how the low end would short through the filter caps instead of going through the signal path circuit, thus filtering the bottom out of the signal. This could be a big problem if these filter caps are used in the early preamp stages.

When the filter caps are back to stock, if there is still too much high end, I would suspect a corroded tube socket connector. When a tube is inserted into a socket, the tube pins are supposed to make contact with the connectors inside the socket. If there is corrosion on the socket's internal connector, and no direct connection is made, the amp may still work, but there is no direct connection. Remember two conductors separated by a non-conductor make a capacitor. In this scenario, the value of the capacitor accidentally formed (by no direct connection) will be very small, thus only allowing high-end to pass. This problem is particularly noticeable when it occurs on the grid connector. The equivalent circuit would be the same as inserting a 10-pf capacitor in series with a grid circuit. This constitutes a high pass filter and the amp would sound like what you describe.

SILVERTONE

I acquired an old Silvertone model 1341 amplifier about 26 years ago and decided to see if I could get it going. I replaced the power cord, checked all the solder joints and re-tubed the amp. Voila — it worked! Unfortunately, lately when I turn it on, it makes an electronic whistle sound and doesn't really amplify anything. What did I do? Would you know where I could get a schematic?
You are lucky to have replaced the power cord, checked the solder joints, and re-tubed; and have the amp work for another 26 years. My guess is that it is time for an overhaul. That electronic whistle is an oscillation. It could be a number of things including: bad filter caps, cracked solder joint, broken wire, bad tube, etc.

I would overhaul the amp first and see if the problem clears up. The overhaul would include completely replacing all electrolytic capacitors in the amp, including the small bypass caps and the filter caps. You will also want to clean the sockets, pots and jacks. Do a careful visual inspection specifically looking for charred or burnt resistors and other components. Replace anything that looks amiss.

The overhaul should "accidentally" fix the oscillation problem you are having. If it does not, you will have to troubleshoot the amp to find where the "whistling" is coming from. Locate the phase inverter tube. I don't have access to your particular model, but the phase inverter tube is usually the preamp tube closest to the output tubes. Remove the phase inverter tube and see if the "whistle" persists. If it does, then the oscillation is coming from the output stage. If the "whistling" stops when the phase inverter tube is pulled, then the oscillation is either coming from the phase inverter or from the preamp section. In a like manner, you could pull preamp tubes to see which tube stops the "whistling." I would start at the phase inverter and work backwards toward the input jacks. When you find the earliest stage that stops the oscillation, then you will have isolated the problem to either the tube you just pulled or the circuitry immediately before that tube.

I do not have a schematic of this particular amp, but I'm sure you could find one on the Internet. There are many websites that offer schematics as a free download. Try a search engine or two and either print it or save it to your hardrive.

I have an old Silvertone amp, Model 1481 (which sounds great!) which has a Quam speaker (I think it is a 5" speaker and has a small transformer attached). Can you tell me where I might be able to find a speaker (with attached transformer) like this? Thanks for all your help.

The 5" Quam speaker with attached transformer is no longer in production. There is no market for a 5" guitar speaker and therefore no one makes one. You may find a 5" vintage Alnico speaker (not necessarily a Quam) by checking with a tube radio repairman.

In 1994, my good friend, Carlos Juan, of American Guitar Center in Germany; sent me some antique radios. Almost all of them have 5" alnico vintage speakers. I'll bet you could check around and find an old-timer in your area that repairs old radios and he'd probably have a 5" speaker available.

Many of these old speakers had the transformer mounted directly on the basket, but if you find the speaker and don't have a transformer, there are many substitution transformers available and your radio guy would more than likely have one.

I have an old Silvertone tweed amp, which I think is from the 50s. It has 2x12 speakers, vibrato and two independent channels with volume, treble, bass, and three inputs for each channel. All four 6L6 power tubes have been replaced. The problem is this: It's a little weak to begin with, and as the amp is on and played for 5 minutes, the sound gets progressively lower until no sound can be heard. Could this be resolved by replacing the other tubes (6SJ7, 5U4, 6SN7, two 12AX7) or is it something deeper? Any info would be appreciated.

You might try replacing the other tubes, but my guess is that it is time for an overhaul. I'll bet the caps in that amp are bleeding chemicals. You probably have a few cooked resistors as well. When you changed output tubes, did you have the bias set? Incorrect bias would not cause the problem you describe, but could make a difference in the amp's performance.

Send your amp to a competent tech and have it gone through with a complete overhaul. A 50's Tweed Silvertone with four output tubes is too cool to have sitting up in disrepair.

I am writing to you to ask for your help. You are my last hope. I recently acquired a vintage Sears Silvertone amp with Jensen speakers for free. The amp is in great shape except that one of the output transformers (yes, it has two output transformers — one for push and one for pull) is shot. It seems that almost everyone I know owned one of these as a kid, but no one knows anything about them. The only marking on the transformer is 0-50. I was wondering if you could tell me where (if anywhere) I could obtain schematics or specs for the amp, or better yet an original replacement part. As I have said, the amp is otherwise in great condition and I would like to get it working again.

If you wanted to keep it original as possible, forget about finding an original replacement part. Instead, have the bad transformer rewound to exact spec, using the same core. Of course, the core should be cleaned of all rust and corrosion with a glass bead cleaning and the laminates should be re-lacquered.

Depending on who does this work, you may want to send them both transformers so that a better reverse engineering job can be done. Certain measurements such as primary incremental inductance, copper loss, etc., can be taken off the good transformer that will help rewind the bad one to exact spec.

Another option would be to get rid of both output transformers and replace them with a single push-pull replacement transformer that has the correct primary and secondary impedances. You never did say anything about the speaker configuration or what kind of output tubes.

If you think the amp has not been modified, you could simply draw your own schematic. This is actually a lot easier than it sounds if you start by drawing each tube and then draw the cathode circuit, the grid circuit and the plate circuit for each tube. (You will need to know the pin out of each tube socket.) Think of the power supply as a separate section and draw it last. You should have it drawn in an hour or two. Next, look at the schematic and re-draw it to make it more readable.

I have done this myself when an unusual piece comes in my restoration shop and I need a schematic for my files.

I own an early to mid sixties Silvertone Model 1474 Twin Reverberation Twelve, for which I have enclosed the schematic. I have recently re-tubed it, with the exception of the rectifier, resulting in a markedly improved tone. The treble is somewhat lacking, but almost not worth worrying about. My main concern is with the tremolo. It does not have the range of speed I would like, and at its slowest speed, the intensity of the tremolo is weak. From looking at the schematic, can you suggest any ways to address these issues? Any help you can provide would be greatly appreciated.

This looks like some real fun. First things first. To improve the treble in channel one, we are going to bypass a certain resistor so the highs will go around the resistor and increase your overall top end. The resistor is the 330K resistor that connects to the channel one volume pot wiper. (The wiper is the center lead of the pot.) Locate this resistor. We are going to connect the cap in parallel with the resistor. Here's where the value of the cap comes into consideration. A 100 pf will have a crisp, bright tone. As you try different values, the range of treble will descend. Suggested values: 100 pf, 250 pf, 500 pf, 1000 pf, 2500 pf, and 5000 pf. By the time you get to the 5000 pf, you should be getting plenty of upper mid boost. Let your ears decide which value you like for your style. When selecting caps for this mod, remember that there is no D.C. and very little signal voltage in this part of the circuit, so almost any voltage rating capacitor will do. A 50 volt or better will be fine.

Increasing top end in channel two cannot be achieved in the same way. Instead, locate pin #6 of the reverb driver tube (12 AX7). It is connected to a .01 mfd capacitor, which is connected to a 560K resistor (the other end of this resistor is connected to a 100K balance trim pot). Bypass the 560K ohm resistor in a similar manner that you bypassed the 330K resistor in the previous example. Since this circuit is different than the first channel, you may decide on a different value cap in order to get the appropriate high-end response.

Now let's talk about the tremolo circuit. I will tell you how to increase the range of speed and improve the intensity. The oscillator (6AU6) in this circuit is a phase shift type oscillator. Phase shift oscillators are typically used on tube guitar amps. In all phase shift oscillators, there are a series of capacitors (usually three) that connect the plate of the tube to the grid of the same tube. These caps are called the feedback caps. Increase the value of any one of these and the oscillator will slow down. But wait a minute! There are resistors going to ground in between each of these caps. Increase the resistance of any of these and the oscillator will slow down. In the Silvertone, there is a rheostat (1 Meg pot) in series with one of those resistors (68K). It is called the "speed" knob on your schematic. When the resistance of this pot is set high, the speed slows down. As the pot's resistance is lowered, the speed is increased.

Perhaps changing the "speed" pot to a 2 or 3 Meg will help your range of speed. Use a reverse audio taper pot for smoothest range. When installing the reverse audio taper pot, looking from the back of the pot and with the leads facing up; the left and middle leads get grounded and the right lead goes to the 68K resistor in the circuit. Come to think of it, Fender typically used a 3 meg reverse audio taper pot in their tremolo circuit.

Now let's move on to intensity. To increase the intensity in this amp, you will need a little circuit modification. We are going to replace the "strength" (intensity) pot, change the way the "strength" pot is wired, replace a resistor with a straight wire, and remove a resistor.

You will need a 250K linear taper pot and a short piece of hook-up wire. First, change the 1 Meg tremolo "strength" pot to a 250K linear pot. When you change it, you will reverse two of the connections. On the original 1 Meg pot, one of the three leads is grounded. When you change the pot, you will keep this same lead grounded. Instead of wiring the other two leads as they were wired on the 1 Meg pot, swap the connections. When you are done, one lead on the end will be grounded as stock, but the middle lead (wiper) of the old pot will now be wired to the end lead of the new pot. The end lead of the old pot will be wired to the middle lead (wiper) of the new one.

When you are done, you should have a 330K resistor going to the middle lead. Replace this resistor with a straight wire or if more convenient, solder a wire across it to short it out.

The end lead that is not grounded, now goes to a .02 mfd cap, the footswitch jack, and three 220K resistors. Only one of the three 220K resistors is grounded. Remove this 220K resistor from the circuit. You are done.

Listen to the amp with the tremolo "on." If you find that the modification made the tremolo too intense, you may fine-tune it by changing the straight wire (that replaced the 330K resistor and is now connected to the center lead of the "strength" pot) with a 100K or 220K resistor. Of course the straight wire is the most intense, the 100K is slightly less intense, the 220K is even less, and the 330K would be stock intensity.

OTHER AMERICAN

Several years ago I bought a new Carvin PB200 Bass Combo amp. When I got it home and plugged in, I started to get all kinds of snap, crackle, and pop after playing for about twenty minutes. I changed cords, basses, plugs, and even changed houses, but nothing changed. I took the amp back to the factory and swapped it for another one. Same story, finally I took it back again, and played it in their showroom for about 45 minutes. No noise not even a single pop. I talked to various people at Carvin, at repair shops, etc. No one could give me any idea what was going on; let alone what to do about it. I don't think it was the amp. It must be me. What did I do wrong? I've played other amps under the same conditions without experiencing this problem.

Tube amps are known to behave perfectly and never duplicate their problems when they are in the presence of a service technician; and then they will act up severely when you get them alone.

There are many things that can cause an intermittent problem such as you describe. For example, a bad resistor can cause intermittent popping/crackling noises. Sometimes the resistor's lead will be slightly broken on the inside of the resistor. The resistor will work perfectly most of the time and then make noise when it is not near a service shop. This can occur with a brand new resistor especially if the lead is stressed during assembly of the amp.

A bad solder joint can make similar noises. Sometimes heat can affect a bad solder joints threshold of noise. It can be perfectly fine until the amp heats up and when the heat causes the metal to expand you could end up with noises.

An arcing capacitor can make intermittent popping and/or crackling noises.

I love to troubleshoot amps for intermittent noises. I turn the amp on and poke every component and every solder joint with my trusty wooden chopstick. When the offending component/solder-joint is poked, all hell breaks loose and I know where the problem lies.

I have this old amp that was given to me last week and I wonder if you would know anything about it? It is a Bogen Challenger and has CHB 50 on the front. It also has two 6L6 tubes and the first pre tube is a 6EU7, the second one is an ECC83 (same as 12AX7) and the third is a 6C4.
My band used one of those for a PA in 1965! They make a great guitar amp. You may need to install a ¼" standard input jack. They had those high impedance screw on mike inputs that can be easily changed to ¼" guitar jacks.

Those amps might be considered as the unsung heroes. Bogen amps are point-to-point hand wired and all tube. They may have been the first amps with a master volume!

Terry Kath, of the band Chicago, used Bogen amps and what a sweet tone he had! At first he used the 100 watt version through a Dual Showman cabinet and then later used two 200 watt Bogens. Those amps sound best played loud! Surprised?

I have a Kendrick 2112TC (1994) and found a NOS GE 5R4GYB. Could I swap out the GZ34 for this rectifier tube without any damage to the amp. If so, what would the tone characteristics be?
You could swap it out if you like, but the output voltage of the 5R4 is about 30 to 40 volts less than the 5AR4. This will make it have less power, less overall gain, and less headroom. If that's what you want, go for it, the pin outs on both tubes are identical.

Actually, you will want to rebias the output stage, because when you give it less voltage, the idle current will go down and the amp will be cold.

My cabinet, a Peavey 410E, needs to be wired for 4 ohms. It is rated at 16 ohms mono and 8 ohms stereo via a selector switch from the factory. Can you tell me if it possible for this cabinet to be wired for 4 ohms and if so how I could I do it myself?

If those speakers are each 16 ohm speakers, and I am almost certain they are, then you could wire everything in parallel and have 4 ohms. In parallel, all of the pluses (+) get wired together and go to the hot (tip) of the speaker jack. All of the minuses (-) get wired together and go to the ground (sleeve) of the speaker jack. It is that simple.

To check to see if they are 16 ohm speakers, you can measure one by itself with a ohmmeter. If it measures 12-14 ohms or so, it is a 16 ohm speaker. A 16 ohm speaker will measure lower than 16 ohms because with an ohmmeter you are not measuring impedance, only D.C. resistance. (Impedance = D.C. resistance + inductive reactance + capacitive reactance).

I own several of your Kendrick amps, with a 2x10 Texas Crude 25 watts Rig as my favorite. What is the correct way to bridge the two channels, which input should I use for the guitar?

Plug your guitar into the #1 input on either channel. Use a short patch cord and plug one end into the #2 input of the same channel your guitar is plugged into. Take the other end of the patch cord and plug it into the #1 input of the other channel. The channels are now in parallel. You can now adjust the volume control of each channel. This same procedure is used to bridge the channels on a four-input Marshall. You cannot do this on a Blackface or Silverface Fender, because the channels are out of phase and will phase cancel each other.

The two springs on my reverb unit on my Lab Series L5 are broken. What do I need to order to fix the unit?

When a spring on a reverb tank breaks, it is time to get a new pan. The springs cannot be repaired without great effort. They are mounted with a magnetic, hair-sized wire that is almost impossible to solder. The particular pan you need is different from the Fender style or Ampeg style pan. The difference lies in the impedance of the transducers. You need to have the transducer impedances match the impedances of the design. The Lab series amp uses a 600 ohm input impedance and a 2,250 ohm output impedance. A Fender pan has an 8 ohm input impedance and a 2,250 output impedance. The Ampeg pan on the other hand, has a 1,475 ohm input and 2,250 output impedance.

I have a Peavey Heritage VTX in the shop and noticed that the two large filter capacitors have some hot melt glue (or equivalent) all over them and on the PCB. Is there a reason for this? The only thing I can think of is mechanical vibration during shipment may have prompted Peavey to do this. I've seen it on other amps as well.

This is commonly done on printed circuit board amps for two reasons:

For one thing, all capacitors are microphonic to some degree. The manufacturers don't want the capacitors to rattle against the printed circuit board and have the rattling sound come out of the speakers.

Secondly, they don't want vibrations rattling the pads on the circuit board because it could cause an intermittent connection, and therefore unpredictable static. Actually, I have a Fender Reissue Bassman in my shop right now with this problem. The capacitors came unglued off the board and the pads holding the leads are starting to give way. When you crank it, on certain resonant notes, there is a loud static sound on top of the note. The solution is simply to hard-wire the capacitor to the other components in the circuit.

I have a Carr slant 6V that has some weird ghost notes in the clean channel. I took it down to a local shop and they thought it was a speaker problem. They put in a new Celestion, but the noise is still there. I ran it into an auxiliary cab (bypassing the onboard speaker), heard the noise less but still there. I talked to Steve Carr, he mentioned preamp tubes, switched them out one at a time, and the noise is still there. What could it be that is causing this problem?

Four things usually cause ghost notes. First, you could be suffering from Strat-itis. This is where the pickups are adjusted too close to the strings and the magnet is pulling on the string as it vibrates. It is pulling so hard that it's magnetism slows the vibration of the string when it is closest to the magnet, but not when it is far away from the magnet. This causes a weird out of tune subharmonic.

Second, a speaker with a dragging voice coil sometimes causes ghost notes. When the voice coil is rubbing against the gap, the friction causes the frequency to slow down during the note — slightly causing a weird, out-of-tune subharmonic.

Third, ghost notes are sometimes the result of "cone cry" (aka "edge yell"). This occurs mainly in 12" speakers — especially when they are new. Almost all 12" speakers do this to some degree.

Fourth, D.C. power supply ripple current can causes ghost notes if the ripple current is large enough to modulate the signal. I don't know what brand of capacitors are being used in your amp, but certain caps made overseas will read good on a meter, yet don't filter the ripple current out of the power supply as they are supposed to. Or, some manufacturers use too small a voltage rating and the caps fail prematurely. You can tell how much voltage the main filter capacitors should be rated by a test. Remove the tubes from the amp (except for the rectifier tube, if it has one) and check the voltage on the main filter cap. With the tubes out, you are simulating zero current going through the power transformer and this will give you a good idea of the applied voltage. Your filter caps should be rated more than the applied voltage and I would add another 50 volts or so for a safety margin.

I've checked out a lot of schematics, but to my knowledge only Mesa Boogie uses the zener diode to bias the preamp tubes. Is this some kind of "trick of the ninja"? And why doesn't anyone else, other than Boogie, use this biasing method for the preamp tubes?

I remember seeing on some Boogies a diode going from pin #3 to ground, and could see how this would work, but I didn't know the answer to your question. I contacted Randall Smith, founder of Mesa Boogie and asked. Here's what I found.

Boogie no longer uses the zener diode method of biasing preamp tubes. There are zener diodes being used in some current production Boogies, however the zeners are only used as a power supply for the footswitch functions (light up LED's, and operate voltage controlled switches for channel switching, etc.). During the early 70s, somewhere between the end of the Mark I era and the beginning of the Mark II era, Boogie did use a "constant current" diode from pin #3 to ground. This was used for a special reason. Boogie's are known for their high gain. When high gain is used on a preamp tube, flaws in the tube are actually magnified. I like to think of it like looking at a diamond. Consider the perfect diamond, that is graded "internally flawless" by a gemologist, and really has no visible flaws at 30 times magnification. Take the same stone at 300 times magnification and flaws will become apparent. Boogie needed a way to solve the problem of microphonic preamp tubes. The solution was the Fetron TR1009 device. You may have seen these before. They look exactly like a metal preamp tube, with the 9 pins and everything, except they are not vacuum tubes. Inside this device you will find two high voltage FETs. When Boogie went to this device, they found that the device was not functioning properly unless they used a "constant current diode." This diode would still work with a tube or the Fetron. The resistor would only work with the tube — they chose the diode so someone could use either. The Fetron solved the problem of microphonics, however it did sound different than the tube, most players preferring the tube. The Fetrons are no longer being made and Boogie changed back to the resistor biasing method when they stopped using the Fetron devices.

I have an old Sylvania hi-fi Model 4308M. The record changer in it is shot, however, I noticed that the amp section has two 6V6GT, two 12AX7, and one 5Y3 in it. Is there potential to make a guitar amp from this? What would I need to do? Your reply on this would be greatly appreciated.

You have the makings of a great guitar amp! In fact, the Tweed Deluxe has the exact same tube compliment! You will have to figure out how and where to put an input jack, but the potential is there.

The 5Y3 is the rectifier, the 6V6's are the power tubes, the 12AX7 closest to the power tubes will be the phase inverter and the remaining 12AX7 will be where you will install the input jack. It's either going to be pin #2 or pin #7. The circuit will probably need slight modification to get the best sound for guitar, but it sounds like fun to me.

I own an old premier twin 8 amp serial #412385, ugly brown vinyl and tan covering with leather handle. Is there a way of dating this piece? It has a dry clean sound and is slightly over driven at full volume. Is it best to leave it as it is or is it worthwhile to turn it into a tone monster like Jimmy Page's little magic box? If so, how should it be done?
You can perhaps date the piece by looking for date codes on either the speaker or the pots. There will be some guesswork because the speakers and pots were obviously made before the amp.

I do not recommend modifying this piece, however I would recommend an overhaul that would include replacing any burnt components, components out of tolerance, electrolytic capacitors, rotten insulation, bad wire, etc. Most vintage amps will sound wonderful just by making sure all the components inside are performing correctly.

I have a Mesa Boogie Mark-IIB. The bass response is "floppy." I would like to tighten up, clean up and generally improve the bass response. Can you recommend any mods I can make to tighten up the bass?
Before recommending any mods, there are a few things to check out, so that we are working on the problem and not the symptom. Here are some things to check: New output tubes that have been correctly biased. Filter caps (particularly the two 220 uf 285 volt main filters). New driver tube (12AT7). Speaker and speaker cables.

One more thing to be aware: when you turn the volume control up, turn down the bass control, for clearest bass. If you turn your bass control up while playing at a loud volume, the bass will be overcompensated. This is because bass frequencies are easier to produce at loud volumes and harder at low volumes. The control is there to compensate bass frequencies — depending on the volume. It is the same logic as the "loudness button" on your home stereo. You would push the "loudness button" when turning the volume down — to increase bottom-end. Similarly, the bass control on an amp should be turned down when the volume is up and vice versa. Check everything out and if you still have "floppy" bottom, write back.

I have an old Ampeg B15 bass amp, which has developed a clicking sound. I have taken it to two local shops. The first shop said it was a filter, but could not find the correct value. They replaced it with a used one. This helped for a day and then the clicking came back. The second repair shop said it was a bad transformer, which of course, they could not find either. What do you think could be causing this problem?

It is probably the transformer, but I would replace the used cap with a new one as well! The transformer could be checked with a high pot tester to see if it is the problem. A high pot tester puts a very high A.C. voltage (mine uses 1533 volts A.C.) between the primary and the secondary of a transformer. A.C. is more likely to arc than D.C. and high voltage is more likely to arc than low voltage. Normally the arcing is intermittent, but with a high pot tester, we are causing the transformer to arc if it is prone to arcing anyway. This test is conclusive. If current flows through the high pot tester, the transformer is definitely arcing.

Perhaps the old filter was not filtering the D.C. very well, which made the transformer more likely to arc. When the first shop changed the cap, the problem may have improved, but the arcing got worse as time went on.

I have an Acoustic 140 head and 106 bottom. (I bought it in the early 70s, does that make it vintage?) The speaker cabinet is termite ridden and the city I live in has recently passed a noise ordinance. I want to saw the cabinet in half to reduce the weight (one 15" is more than sufficient for our gigs here). Am I going to have an impedance problem? If I make two cabinets, can I plug the second cabinet in the Aux output jack? Is there a trick to wiring? I've never taken the cabinet apart but over the years I've been told Acoustics have weird ohms, etc. I figure one 15 instead of two 15s would give me better tone at the low volume that the law demands. Please help.

Let's re-think this. If you have a termite-ridden cabinet, do you really want to waste your time and effort rebuilding a cabinet whose structural integrity is questionable? Also, if you are looking to reduce the weight, why not build a cabinet from a lighter wood? There are several speaker cabinet builders, that could build you exactly what you want for a couple of hundred dollars. On the other hand, you might want to try purchasing a used 1x15 cabinet. Either way, these other options would keep you from destroying your 27-year-old Acoustic speaker cabinet. I would say, "YES" your piece is vintage.

On another note regarding impedance mismatches, the rule of thumb is this: Transistor type amps can tolerate an impedance mismatch into a higher load, but not into a smaller load. The power cuts in half (3dB) when the speaker load impedance doubles. Most tube amps can tolerate a 100% mismatch either way, however tube performance and wattage will be affected. The amp will have more clarity and power when the speaker impedance matches the amp. If you have to mismatch, it is much better for the tubes if you use a speaker cabinet whose impedance is more than the amp — but not more than 100%. The reason this is better is that the tubes will see the extra impedance as current limiting circuits that will actually make the tubes last longer. This might even sound hip in a situation where you are wanting to play at low volume because you will have a more compressed sound (generally desirable at low volumes) and the mismatch will cause the amp to lose about 3 dB. You wanted to reduce volume anyway.

Lower powered tube amps can tolerate a 100% mismatch where the speaker is half of what is required by the amp. When you use a speaker whose impedance is half of what the amp requires, the tubes see the primary transformer impedance as half way between "what the tubes want to see" and a short circuit. On amps with high plate voltage or otherwise high-powered amps, you will wear out your tubes in a few hours and eventually a tube will overheat and short.

Although I am not familiar with the model 140 Acoustic head, I am familiar with Acoustic amps in general. Acoustic tube amps have an 8 ohm transformer with a 4 ohm tap. I would check the speakers with a multimeter to determine the individual speaker impedance and if the speakers are wired in parallel or series.

If the speakers are wired in parallel, removing one of them will double the impedance of the speaker load. This could work very well for you because of the current limiting effect we talked about earlier. In addition, the Aux. speaker jack could be used to hook up the other 15" speaker.

If the speakers are wired in series, removing one of them will half the speaker load, in which case the output stage could be adversely affected.

The other option would be to use a power attenuator.

I need a schematic for a Mesa Boogie Single Rectifier Recto-Verb 50 combo (single 12"). This unit has bad hum and "Ocean" hiss like you wouldn't believe on all channels. I really need to study the schematic to work on this one. (If I could figure out how to oscillate the hiss, I could close my eyes and be on the shores of Maui, poppin' a cold Corona).

If I sent you the schematic, it will not help you find a hum problem. Unless someone has modified the amp, or recently overhauled the amp, a schematic is of no use. To find noise and hum, you will need to troubleshoot.

I would simply remove tubes, one at a time, until the hum stops. This will allow you to isolate where the hum is coming from.

Sometimes a preamp tube will hum.

Start at the input and start removing preamp tubes one at a time. You are working your way towards the output.

If you remove all the preamp tubes and the hum is still there, you have eliminated the preamp as the source.

When you remove a tube and the hum stops, either the tube is bad or there is something associated with that circuit (immediately before the tube in the circuit) that is humming.

Sometimes hiss is caused by a noisy plate load resistor. Here's a technique to troubleshoot the plate resistors. With the amp on, and working your way from the input towards the output, take a jumper wire and short out each plate resistor on every preamp tube one at a time until you find out which one is making the hiss. When I say "short" the plate resistor, I mean to bypass the resistor with a jumper wire (so as to make the amp think that the plate resistor is not there by allowing all the voltage to flow through the jumper wire). When you short the offending plate resistor, the hiss will go away. The plate is pin #1 and pin

#6 on a 12AX7. So you would look at the pin #1, for example, and follow it to the 100K plate resistor associated with it. Take a jumper and short the resistor. If it is the "hisser," the hiss will go away.

When you find a resistor that when shorted makes the hiss goes away; you change the plate resistor and see if that fixes the problem. If it does not, then the hiss is coming "before" that tube in the circuit.

When you short the plate resistor, amplification cannot occur on that stage. If the plate resistor was making noise, then shorting it will stop the noise. This is a great troubleshooting technique. It is faster than removing tubes and you can pinpoint the actual circuit that the noise is coming from.

I own a used Mesa Boogie Dual rectifier Trem-o-Verb combo, I've had it for a while and I think the tubes need to be replaced. Can I substitute two 5U4GBs instead of the 5U4Gs in it now? Why does the tube chart only say "5U4" instead of "5U4G" or "5U4GB"?
The tube chart lists the basic tube type. Don't sweat the small stuff.

The "G" suffix simply means it is a glass tube with an octal base. "A," "B," "C," "D," "E," and "F" suffixes, assigned in that order, signify a later and modified version which can be substituted for any previous version but not vice-versa. The assignment of a suffix in this series does not convey any information as to the nature of the modifications incorporated.

In the case of the 5U4G: the 5U4G is rated for 225 mA output, the 5U4GA is rated for 250 mA and the 5U4GB is rated for 275 mA. So the "A" and the "B" are just heavier duty versions of the 5U4. Any of these will work.

I have a 1960s Ampeg Reverberocket I would like to find out specifics about the reverb circuit design, original speakers, etc. I also have an old National amp that I would like to know more about.
The Ampeg Reverberocket came in three designs and several versions of each. The first design was the Model No. R-12-R, which was the original Reverberocket. There were perhaps four or five versions of this design. This had two 6SL7's, two 6SN7's and two 6V6's as well as a 5Y3 rectifier tube. The reverb was capacitor coupled and used one of a 6SN7's two triode sections to drive the reverb pan. The

6SN7's other triode section provided the reverb recovery circuit.

The second and third designs were the Reverberocket II and the Reverberocket III which both used 7591 output tubes. They produced two or three versions of each of these designs. Both of the later designs used miniature preamp tubes rather than the octal tubes of the original design. The reverb circuits on all designs were capacitor coupled. The Reverberocket II used a 6U10 for Reverb drive and recovery.

As with all Ampeg amps, Jensen or CTS speakers were usually stock; however, Ampeg also sometimes used Quam, Oxford, or Utah speakers as equivalent speakers. JBL and Altec Lansing speakers were an option at additional charge.

The National amps, Supro, and Gretsch amps were all made by National and share similar designs, but with different logos. I've always appreciated the tidy layout, point-to-point wiring and craftsmanship of these amps. Most of them used a dual chassis with the power supply and output stage in a separate chassis mounted in the bottom of the amp. The preamp and controls were in a separate chassis in the top of the amp. This design, though more expensive because of the additional cost of having two chassis' instead of one, was cool because it kept the 120 volt line A.C. out of the preamp section (less hum).

The circuit was laid out using terminal strips. Many of the grounds in the amp were made through the mounting leg of the terminal strip. It probably seemed like a great idea at the time; however, many of these grounds are not what they appear to be. For instance, if you check the integrity of the grounds with a meter you will likely find an unwanted resistance between the terminal mounting leg and ground. I once had a National amp with malfunctioning reverb brought to my shop that several other shops had looked at, but no one had been able to fix. Upon inspection, everything seemed correct. The ground for the reverb driver transformer was made through one of the terminal strips. The terminal was very shiny and clean and looked like a nice connection. When I measured resistance from the terminal ground to the chassis, there was an unbelievable resistance of 65 ohms! This ground was in series with the 8 ohm reverb transformer which turned the reverb drive circuit into a voltage divider — losing almost 90% of the reverb drive!

This same problem could cause problems with cathode resistor grounds in the preamp section — causing the bias of the preamp tubes to be too high. Tone and gain would suffer.

By comparison to other tube amplifiers, most of these amps used very low voltage on the output tubes. This makes the amps much less powerful than other amps with similar output tube configurations.

I play dinner clubs with small vintage amps. I like to use 1950s Fender and Gibson amps with an L-5 on the neck pickup to play jump blues. I like a lightly distorted, compressed tone. These amps have some qualities I would like to alter, if possible.

1. **Tweed Fenders with only a tone control (pro, Deluxe, Super, etc.) need more treble and/or less bass. Ideas?**
2. **My Gibson GA 40 with 5879 preamp tube has "way" too much gain. It goes from crunch to wail. How can I reduce the gain and clean it up? Changing the phase inverter tube to 12AU7 sounds worse!**
3. **Would it hurt a '57 Bassman to play through one upgraded 10" speaker to reduce the overall output? I have already converted it to cathode bias.**
4. **I had a tech do your "Save that Princeton" mod and also converted it to cathode bias. I use 6L6's and an upgraded 12" speaker. This amp is really a beau, however it has so much gain that I have to use 12AU7's or it feeds back on itself. Ideas?**
5. **My '54 Deluxe only appears to run on one output tube. It is very quiet with bad tone. My tech could not figure it out. Ideas?**

I have done considerable experimentation with Tweed Fenders that only use a single tone control. In fact, two of the Kendrick Texas Crude amps and the entire Black Gold series of Kendrick amps use the "single tone control" circuit. Here are three ideas to reduce bassiness and improve treble. I would do one modification and listen before doing the next one. Each will improve the treble and remove some boominess.

1. Change the first stage coupling cap to a smaller value. A cap comes from each plate of the first tube to each volume control. Stock value is .1 mfd. I would recommend changing to either a .02 or a .01 mfd. This will filter some of the bass out and help remove the boominess.

If this modification leaves you with too much bass for your ear, the second step would be to reduce the value of the bypass capacitor. This is the cap mounted on the board and connects to pin #3 and pin #8 of the first preamp tube. Stock value is 25 mfd at 25 volts. I would suggest experimenting with a 10 mfd, 5 mfd, 1 mfd., or even a .68 mfd. The smaller the microfarad value, the less bass. Whichever cap gives you the tone you seek is correct. The voltage rating needs to be anywhere from 6 to 25 volts.

There is one more modification to try if these first two mods are not dramatic enough. Looking on pin #1 of the second preamp tube, you will find a wire that leads to the board and is connected to a .02 mfd coupling cap. Experiment with smaller values. I would recommend trying a .01 mfd or a 5000 pf (same as .005 mfd).

2. The Gibson GA 40 used a paraphase style inverter, so changing the 12AX7 phase inverter tube to a 12AU7 would not be recommended. The 5879 preamp tube is a pentode with no substitute. If you are looking to get a clean sound out of that amp, forget it. With the paraphase style phase inverter, it is always going to be crunchy sounding. With the paraphase style circuitry, some of the signal driving one output tube is injected through a triode in order to reverse phase. The output of that triode drives the other output tube. Voila, phase inversion achieved. However and on the other hand, any distortion that is introduced by the extra triode section is amplified by one output tube only. This gives a non-symmetrical waveform which will sound distorted.

Here are a few suggestions: Turn the volume down on your guitar. This will avoid hitting the amp with too much signal and is always my first recommendation for getting a good clean tone.

Second, play both channels and listen. Choose the channel with the lessor gain. This will lose another 3 dB or so.

There are two input jacks for each channel. The number two jack has 3 dB less gain. Use the number two input jack.

3. When you run your Bassman with one 8 ohm speaker, you are running a 2 ohm amp with an 8 ohm speaker. This will reduce power because of the impedance mismatch. It will not hurt your amp, however the amps will not sound its best with such a mismatch. What you really need is a power attenuator. The power attenuator hooks up between your amp's output and your speaker. With the power attenuator, you can reduce the power feeding the speakers without mismatching the impedance of your amp. The amp

will have much better tone AND you will be moving much more air using the stock four-speaker setup.

4. The "Save That Princeton" modification which was printed on page 103 of my second book, *Tube Amp Talk for the Guitarist and Tech*, dramatically improves the gain of the Princeton. Using 12AU7's to reduce some of this is perfectly legitimate.

If you would prefer to use 12AX7's, you can drop the gain by the following technique. The first preamp has a connecting wire from pin #1 to both a 100K plate resistor and a 100K slope resistor on the board. (The slope resistor is the one that connects to a .047 mfd and .1 mfd tone cap on one end.) Ignore the slope resistor and change the plate resistor to a 10K ½ watt value. Next, substitute a resistor (either 90K or 100K ½ watt) for the wire that goes from the plate resistor to pin #1 of the first preamp tube. Technically, you should use a 90K, but the 100K may be more convenient and with no audible difference. Plug a 12AX7 into the first preamp socket and wail.

5. Your '54 Tweed Deluxe probably is running on one tube. A blown output transformer on a Tweed Deluxe is very common. Those amps use a 15 watt output transformer and put out about 22 watts at full clip. (Fender did not think anyone would ever crank it up to full clip.) They actually sound their best, minutes before they blow.

I've got an Ampeg Gemini II. I'd like a midrange control, especially for maxing out the midrange. How can I wire that in? Also, are the gases in tubes toxic? If so, what should I do if I break a tube?

The Gemini II and most other Ampeg amplifiers used a passive tone control. The circuit was fed from a .1 mfd coupling cap coming from the second gain stage. The output of this circuit was the wiper of the treble pot. To make a midrange control, you will need a 3 Meg audio taper pot and a .01 mfd 400 volt capacitor. Looking at the back of the 3 Meg pot, the right lead connects to the wiper of the treble pot. The middle and left lead both connect to one lead of a .01 mfd capacitor. The other end of the .01 mfd capacitor goes to the .1 mfd coupling capacitor (which is connected to the plate of the second gain stage.) This will bypass mids around the tone circuit, turning it "off" would return the circuit to almost dead stock.

Although I have never seen any warnings in either the GE or the RCA tube manual, I would not recommend deliberately ingesting (or otherwise contacting mucous membrane including the eyes) any chemical or metal found inside a vacuum tube. If you break one, I would not worry about the gas inside. What little gas that is inside a vacuum tube is mostly inert gases. Inert gases by definition do not react with anything.

Different tube manufacturers would not necessarily use the same chemical coatings, plating, or alloys in the manufacture of their particular company's tubes. As I was researching this question, I came across a list of materials used to manufacture RCA vacuum tubes. It includes: acetic acid, acetone, acetylene gas, alumina, aluminum, aluminum nitrate, ammonium chloride, ammonium hydroxide, amyl acetate, antimony, antimony trichloride, argon, Bakelite, barium, barium carbonate, barium nitrate, barium strontium titanate, barium sulfate, bentonite, benzene, beryllium, beryllium oxide, bismuth, boric acid, boron, butyl acetate, butyl alcohol, butyl carbitol, butyl carbitol acetate, cadmium, cesium, cesium chromate, calcium carbonate, calcium nitrate, calcium oxide, camphor, carbon, carbon black, carbon dioxide, carbon tetrachloride, castor oil, chlorine, chromic acid, chromium, clay, cobalt, copper, diacetone alcohol, diatol, diethyl oxalate, distilled water, ether, ethyl alcohol, ferric oxide ferro titanium, glass, glycerin, gold, graphite, helium gas, hydrochloric acid, hydrofluoric acid, hydrogen gas, hydrogen peroxide, illuminating gas, iridium, iron, isolantite, isopropanol, lava, lead, lead borate, lead oxide, magnesia, magnesium, magnesium nitrate, malachite green, manganese, marble dust, mercury, methanol, mica, misch metal, molybdenum, monel, natural gas, neon, nickel, nickel chloride, nickel oxide, nickel sulphate, nitric acid, nitrocellulose, nitrogen, oxalic acid, oxygen, palladium, palmitic acid, petroleum jelly, phosphoric acid, phosphorus, platinum, potassium, potassium carbonate, potassium feldspar, potassium nitrate, porcelain, radium, rare earths, resin, rosin, rubidium, rubidium dichromate, shellac, silica, silicon, silver, silver oxide, sodium, sodium carbonate, stannic oxide, steel, strontium, strontium carbonate, strontium nitrate, sulphur, sulfuric acid, talc, tantalum, thallium, thorium, thorium nitrate, tin, titanium, titanium dioxide trichlorethylene, tungsten wax, wheat flour, wood fiber, xenon, zinc, and zirconium hydride.

MARSHALL

I own a Marshall 4203 Artist combo, hybrid solid-state preamp and tube output section. The other day the volume cut out and went low, after the amp had been on for a while. It sounded like when the pots get dirty on your guitar, and the signal goes. Anyway the volume would come back up, the amp would behave, and then it would cut out again. I run it with an extension cabinet, with the impedance selector at 4 ohms. Any suggestions were to start looking to solve the problem? I doubt it's the tubes because I recently retubed with NOS Mullard/Amperex tubes.

The amp needs to be troubleshot by a competent technician. There are many things that could be responsible for your malady. This problem could be related to the input jack, the output jack, the output transformer, the filter caps, grounding integrity, the impedance selector, a tube socket, a potentiometer, etc. When it is troubleshot, the technician will isolate which stage it is coming from and focus in on it from there. This will not be an easy troubleshoot for a novice. Bring it to a technician.

My old Marshall has always sounded tight and solid but the other day I cranked it up and when I hit low notes, it sounded like my speakers had a razor blade put to them. I ran another head to the cab and the speakers sound fine; so I know it's coming from my old amp head. Can filter caps make your speakers sound blown on the bass notes?

Yes, bad filter caps can make an amp sound like the speakers are gone. The filter caps are supposed to take out the 120 Hertz ripple current that occurs when the wall A.C. (current alternating and going both directions) is rectified into D.C. (current all goes the same direction). This ugly, almost ring-modulator-like, out-of-tune sound occurs when the ripple current is modulating the signal. What's even worse is that certain brands of filter caps will measure correctly on a capacitance meter, but in actual circuit application, they will fail to filter out the 120 Hertz ripple current. I would never put a British made

LCR cap in a guitar amplifier, yet that brand is almost always used with Marshall amplifiers because of its country of origin. The German made F&T brand multi-section can caps are the best way to go.

I have an open-back Marshall JCM 800 combo, model 4104, with two G12 65 speakers. I had it professionally rebiased for Svetlana EL34s a while back. As much as I like this amp's features (master volume control, portability, very usable tone controls, as well as it's sheer volume control), I can't quite escape a certain displeasing quality in the overall tone. Try as I might, I can't seem to evade what my ears perceive to be a bit of brittleness in the high-end. Put simply, I'd like to get a warmer, creamier, softer, "chewier" tone out of this amp. I suppose I'd like it to sound a bit more "vintage." The high-end seems too cold, spiky, harsh, depending on the song, various amounts of pre-amp gain. Over the years, I've read all kinds of stuff on "tweaking" various components of an amp for different tonal effects, but frankly, I'm not sure where to start. Easier to distort Chinese output tubes? Different pre-amp tubes? (I tried both 12AU7s and 12AT7s in the first tube socket, which made a difference, but not for the better. They just seemed to "neuter" the sound too much). Different, lower watt, "rounder"-sounding speakers? Are there any simple mods I can have a tech do to the actual circuit, which will warm up, or soften, the treble frequencies of this amp? As I said, I mostly like what this amp has to offer. I'm just not quite finding what I want, tone-wise. Any suggestions?

There are many things you can do to rid yourself of high-end brittleness and hardness of attack.

For example, a trick to smoothing out the top-end is to put a small value cap across the plate load resistor (This is the 100K resistor that connects to pin #1 or pin #6 of a 12AX7). This modification will cause high-end to be bypassed around the plate load resistor, thus removing it from the signal path. This can be done on a single stage or on several stages — depending on what it takes to do the job. Typical values would range anywhere from a 100 pf to a 500 pf — depending on how high the frequencies are that you want to smooth.

Changing the value of the coupling caps to a larger value will also let more mids and bottom through the circuit, thus giving the appearance of less highs. In particular, you may want to change the coupling caps that couple the phase inverter to the grids of the output tubes. I would recommend using a .1 uf 600 volt orange drop capacitor for this modification.

Changing cathode bypass caps to a larger value will re-voice the amp to apparently have less highs and more bottom. Your tech will know where the bypass caps are physically located (typically pin #3 and pin #8 on a 12AX7). Start with the first gain stage cathode bypass cap and try doubling or quadrupling its value. If you get too much "boom" in the bottom end, reduce the value slightly (to the point where the boominess leaves) and try something else. To get the amp sounding the way you want will require patience.

I would recommend you being physically present when this experimentation is done because you will want to hear the difference of each modification before trying another one.

A friend of mine owns a Marshall JCM 800 100 watt head. I performed the usual 6550 to EL34 conversion. The amp has two inputs, a high and a low gain. He wants to use the high gain as the main input and using the low gain input as a dedicated foot switch jack for switching between the two gain levels. Despite the amp only having one channel, is this "channel switching" mod possible? Another project I'm attempting is the conversion of a Silverface Bassman head from 50 watts to 100 watts (or thereabouts). I plan on using transformers from a twin reverb, while replacing the 6L6's with 6550s. Do you recommend this mod? And if so, are there any other stock parts I should replace? Regarding the Marshall, your friend cannot channel switch the Marshall JCM 800. It only has one channel. The high gain input is simply a stage in front of the low gain input. The problem is that the low gain input jack has a switch on it that disconnects the high gain circuit when a ¼" plug is inserted to the low gain input jack.

Regarding your Bassman, you can make a really great sounding bass amp doing the modification you describe. I would begin by first rewiring the Bassman to Blackface AA864 specs. In particular, the phase inverter and output stage and biasing circuit could be made to match the AA864.

Use the 6550's with a Twin output transformer, just make sure and run it with an 8 ohm speaker load. This will be correct for use with a pair of 6550 output tubes – given the turns ratio of the Twin output transformer. You should have no problem with the mod, just be sure that if the amp starts squealing that you reverse the brown wire with the blue wire on the primary of the output transformer (blue wire and brown wire each terminate on pin #3 of opposing output tubes).

You may also need to experiment with the negative feedback resistor. Since the Bassman circuit is already 4 ohm and you will be running the new modified version at 8 ohm, you will probably want to use a feedback resistor that is larger than stock. Here's why: An 8 ohm output will have 1.412 times the voltage and .707 times the current of a 4 ohm output. Since negative feedback is figured from voltage, to keep the stock feedback amount, you will need a feedback resistor that is 1.412 times stock value. The AA864 Bassman uses an 820 ohm resistor, so ideally an 1,159 ohm resistor would keep it sounding like an original circuit. A standard value would be a 1200 ohm. Get several and check them with a meter. Pick one that measures low and you are there. Or you could check a few 1000 ohm resistors and find one that measures high to get there.

Generally speaking, using a larger value feedback resistor will make the tone more raw with more distortion. Conversely a smaller value feedback resistor will make the tone cleaner and more even with less distortion.

One last suggestion, beef up the main filter caps and the screen supply filter. I would use two 220 uf/ 350 volt caps in a totem pole arrangement for the main filters (series). This would give you a rating of 110 uf at 700 volt when the two caps are arranged as a totem pole. Make sure and use the 1 watt 220K balancing resistors across each 220 uf cap. Also, I would use a 40 uf / 500 volt electrolytic capacitor for the screen supply filter.

How can I get more treble or highs out of a Marshall JTM 45 Reissue and keep the great fat tone?
You like the overall tone of the JTM 45 Reissue, but you need more highs. That must be the same thing that Marshall thought about the JTM 45 because when they evolved the design in the late 60s, they re-voiced the amp to have more highs.

There are a few things you could do to achieve this. You could change the value of the bypass capacitor on the first preamp tube (pin #3 and 8). Stock value is 320 uf. You could change this to a much lower value, perhaps as low as .68 uf (which is what Marshall chose later). Actually a 1 uf, 5 uf, 10 uf, and 25 uf would be some good values to listen to. The smaller the value, the less bottom-end you will hear. This sounds like more highs. After listening, choose the value with the best tone for your ears.

You could also bypass the volume pot and/or the merger resistors (470K connected to the wiper of each pot) with a compensating capacitor. That is what Marshall did later. Perhaps a 250 pf or a 500 pf capacitor would give you the results you need.

Here is how you bypass the volume pot with a compensating cap. Choose a channel to modify. Look at the back of the volume pot for that channel and notice there are three leads. The lead on the left is going to ground. The capacitor goes to the other two leads. To bypass a merger resistor, locate the two 470K resistors on the board which go to the wiper of each pot. Choose the 470K for the channel you are modifying and simply install the capacitor in parallel to the resistor. The 250 pf will have a slightly crisper tone than the 500 pf, but you should try both to see which one you prefer.

When you bypass the merger resistor on one channel, it will give you more highs on that particular channel, but it will make the other channel darker. When you bypass the volume control, it will give more highs when the volume is set to less than full up. When you turn the volume full up, the compensating capacitor will not make any difference.

I have an old Marshall 2203 amp. I bought it new in 1983 and it had 6550s in it. I changed it over to EL34s, which made the amp sound more like a Marshall. The modification directions said to move the feed back wire from the 4 ohm pin to the 8 ohm pin. Why did this wire have to be moved?

The voltage on the 8 ohm pin is more than on the 4 ohm pin. Moving the feedback wire to the 8 ohm pin allows for more negative feedback, which is needed with EL34's because it doesn't take as much gain to drive them. The 6550 requires more drive signal and is a cleaner sounding tube in general, so giving it less negative feedback sounds better.

Will replacing the electrolytics in my 1976 Marshall 50 watt JMP MK II help me lower my output tube bias? I can't get my bias current below 80 mA. and sometimes it almost reaches 150 mA. I've checked everything obvious from the impedance selector to the tube sockets to the bias adjuster to loose or corroded connections. I'm measuring the bias by measuring the current from pin #8 on the 6550's to ground with a meter. I've also got a nice hum, and all electrolytic caps are original. (27-year-old DALY R50/Y50 uf, 500v) The amp does play but I have brand new output tubes (GT 6550Cs) and I don't want to blow them up or damage the amp. Any help would be appreciated.

It looks like you've got multiple problems. The caps need changing, but that won't help your bias problem. And when you change the electrolytic filter caps, don't use LCR brand caps. Use F&T brand (German made). They sound the best.

Your negative bias voltage needs to be increased in order to suppress some of that idle current. You mentioned 6550 output tubes. I wonder if that amp had been converted to EL34's at one time. If so, the bias voltage range would be lower. Lower negative bias voltage would make 6550's draw excessive current. In fact, if someone were going to mod that amp to take EL34 tubes, they would modify the bias supply to have less negative voltage. If I were a gambling man, I would wager the amp had been converted to EL34's and then someone went ahead and put 6550's in later.

If the amp has not been modified to take EL34's, then there are other problems that could cause the negative bias supply to have a lower range.

It could be that one of the 10 uf caps in the negative bias supply is leaking current. That could drag down the voltage. Changing to fresh 10 uf caps would solve that problem, if that were the case.

There is also a 47K resistor in the bias circuit. If this resistor has drifted to a smaller value (or if someone has changed it to a smaller value to convert the amp to take EL34's), the negative bias voltage produced will be too low.

There is also a 150K resistor between the bias tap on the transformer and the diode in the bias circuit. If this resistor is drifted high, then the voltage will be low — thus causing too much plate current.

My advice to you is to double-check the schematic to see that it is wired right. If everything is wired right and the voltage is still too low, then you may have to make the 150K smaller or make the 47K larger to bring bias voltage up to where it can tame those output tubes.

A couple of years ago, my '72 Marshall blew during a sound-check, so I grabbed my Les Paul and headed out to find something before the show. I ended up with a Fender Tone-Master. At the time, it suited me well, as I used humbucking pickups exclusively. Since then, I have become fond of single-coils, but my amp doesn't agree. I find the tone extremely harsh and brittle, with "ice-pick in the eardrum" highs even with the treble turned to 0. I use the Tone-Master 2x12 cab with 80W Celestions. What can I do to tame the high-end? I am concerned about keeping this amp original. Would different speakers help (I've tried vintage 30s and 25W Greenbacks — both sounded even thinner and more trebly.) I have tried many different 6L6 tubes, played with the impedance switch and fat switches — nothing makes the highs any more bearable. Any recommendations or mods would be greatly appreciated.

You are in a dilemma. On one hand, you want the amp kept original, but on the other hand, you cannot stand the way the amp sounds. If you want the amp kept original, you will need the either change guitars, pickups, or speakers.

There are some speakers on the market that will "brown-out" your sound, but Celestion does not make them. You could also try some overwound pickups such as the Seymour Duncan APS 1. These pickups have a mellow tone and I have used them on high-endy, maple fretboard Strats with excellent results.

Now, if you were willing to have a minor modification done to your amp (this one is easily reversible) here's the simple thing to do: Have your tech place a small capacitor across the plate load resistor of your first gain stage tube. The plate load resistor will come from pin #1 of the tube and is probably a 100K ohm resistor. You simply put the capacitor in parallel with the resistor. Try some different values and listen. Typical values to try: 100pf, 250 pf, or 500 pf. As you increase the value of the cap, you will cut more high-end. If the 500 pf does not cut enough, you could go to a 1000 pf (same as .001 mfd.) If this still is not enough, shunt the second gain stage plate resistor (terminates at pin # 6) also, again experimenting with different values. The cap is easily soldered directly across the plate resistor and could just as easily be removed to bring the amp back to stock. A side benefit is that the amp will "hiss" less with the cap mod installed.

The other options are to go back to humbuckers or get a different amp.

I recently purchased a 4x10 Marshall combo Model 4145. I have improved the bass response from one of your earlier articles but I find that the reverb sounds poor. Is there anything that can be done to give the reverb sparkle? I have tried the regular tube replacement and tank, but the reverb still sounds dull and faint.
Something like this might take a little time to tweak just right. I would normally use a trial and error guerrilla approach combined with critical listening tests. I do not have your particular amp to work with, however I could give you some ideas of what to try and then you will be on your own to do your own critical listening tests to decide what is working.

Between C10 and C11 there is a one Meg dropping resistor that feeds both the grid of V2a and R15 (a 1 Meg). I would change this one Meg dropping resistor to a 470K or a 220K. This will increase the gain of the signal driving the grid of V2a. In addition, the reverb pan returns to a 10K grid return resistor. Try increasing the value of this to 100K or 220K. This should give more reverb and wetter reverb. The cathode resistor of that same reverb return tube uses an 820 ohm unbypassed cathode resistor (R17). You might try changing to a 1500 ohm and bypass it with a 10 mfd. 25volt electrolytic capacitor. Make sure the minus side of the cap goes to ground and the plus side goes to the cathode. This would increase the gain of the reverb return circuit.

What is the life expectancy of an output transformer when there is no load hooked up to it. I have a '67 Plexi Marshall 100 watt PA head with the original output transformer. One time the amp was on for about 5 minutes before I stupidly realized that the speaker cable was not hooked up at 16 ohms. The head

sounds okay, but I would like to know what possible damage could have been done (primary or secondary). Thanks a million!
This is a tough question, because there is no set time. You do not want the transformer to arc. If it arcs, there will be carbon in the arced area. This will promote more arcing. An output transformer with no load thinks it is an ignition coil. When a current is alternating within the primary, it's self inductance can cause very high voltages (much higher than your D.C. power supply) as the magnetic field around the transformer expands and collapses. Higher voltages are subject to arcing. If you did not put signal through the amp, it is not likely damaged.

If your amp was turned up, it will be more likely to become damaged if the speaker load is not hooked up.

What do you do if you notice you have flipped the standby switch to "play" with no speaker load attached? Do not try to put the amp in the "Standby" mode and do not cut the power "off." Remember its the expanding and collapsing magnetic field that causes the problem, therefore, it is better to simply plug a speaker into the speaker output without turning off the power or standby switch. In other words, the act of turning off the standby switch could promote arcing in this case.

I have a '72 Marshall Super Lead that needs a cap job, but before I change caps, I would like to convert the amp to '67 Plexi specs. Can you give me some insight on what needs to be done?
I advise against converting your amp to Plexi specs just yet. If your amp needs caps, it probable also needs tubes and a general tune-up. I would recommend performing the service first, on the amp as it is, before evaluating whether or not it should be changed.

Here's the truth: if your amp is in disrepair, changing to a different circuit will not help. In other words, changing the transmission does not help the engine that is running on two cylinders.

In addition, you cannot make your amp into a '67 Plexi without considerable expense. For one thing, the transformers are different, produce different voltages/impedances, and will not give identical results.

I have heard some '72 Marshal Super Leads that were set up correctly that sounded excellent. One of the best ones used 6550's!

I have heard many differing opinions about the use of variacs and attenuators with amps to get a better distortion sound at lower volume levels. I would like one more opinion. Will the use of a variac or an attenuator damage my Marshall amp in any way? What about using both at the same time? I use the variac to lower the mains voltage to about 90 VAC. Will there be any harmful effects with long term use?

You cannot harm your Marshall amp (or any other amp) by running it at lower than normal voltage. I think the adverse opinions you may have heard concerns running the variac at higher than normal levels. Obviously, the power supply for the amp was designed figuring on a particular wall voltage. If you exceed that wall voltage, then all of the secondaries for the power transformer will put out more than normal voltage. Some damage could occur because there is only so much the components can take — considering the design. If you run it at lower voltage, then all the voltages coming out of the power transformer will be low by comparison, but that will not hurt anything except your tone.

Your tone suffers when you use the variac in the manner you describe. The tubes have to be hot to work properly and that is why there is a 6.3 volt filament heater in each tube. When you run the variac and set it for lower than normal wall voltage, the filament voltage goes down too low and the tubes lose their liveliness.

Here is my suggestion for using a variac. Install a 6.3 volt 8 amp filament transformer with its own separate 120 VAC line cord. Disconnect the filament circuit from the power transformer and instead connect the filaments to the auxiliary filament transformer. The filament transformer plugs directly into the wall and the old power cord from the amp goes into the variac. This way, you can lower the D.C. voltages in the amp without altering the 6.3 volt filament supply.

My good friend and master luthier, Tony Nobles, used a Laney amp that was far too harsh. I suggested this same setup to him years ago. He has run it for approximately six years with no problem. I would recommend double-checking the bias of the output tubes once you have established what voltage you are going to run.

Some well-designed attenuators out there do not damage the amp, however, when a player has an attenuator, he is more likely to "crank it up to the max." Running a tube amp louder will wear out the tubes faster, attenuator or no attenuator! Also, if there is any weakness in the output transformer, running the amp "cranked" can cause these deficiencies to surface sooner rather than later.

I have had good luck with the THD Hotplate and the Kendrick Powerglide. I would not recommend using a transformer driven designed attenuator. A transformer driven design steps down the power, but it also steps down the impedance. This is not good for the tubes, and in extreme cases can cause output transformer damage.

I have a question concerning the Marshall 25/50 Jubilee series amplifiers introduced in 1987. In the preamp section, Marshall uses a series of diodes and LED's to distort the signal to emulate the "big Marshall on 10" sound. I feel that this is the best sounding Marshall to date. Can you explain what goes on with these diode and LED's?

The basic principle of diode clipping lies in the fact that it will limit or clip the amplitude of an A.C. waveform to its characteristic barrier voltage. These type circuits are sometimes used for audio compression and limiter circuits. With silicon diodes such as the 1N914, the A.C. voltage across the diode will not exceed .7 volts. For example, if you run .7 volts or less of A.C. signal voltage through this diode, the waveform will pass through unscathed. However, if you run .8 volts through it, the .1 volt on the top of the waveform will be clipped off. This would change the waveform to be shaped more like a square wave. If the input signal were amplified to .9 volts, then .2 volts would be clipped off the top of the waveform, thus making it even squarer than the previous example. In other words, the bigger the signal going into the diode, the more the signal will be clipped and the more square the wave becomes.

If you used a different type of diode, let's say a Germanium diode such as the 1N34A or similar, the barrier voltage will limit at roughly .3 volts instead of the .7 volts mentioned for the silicon diode in the previous example.

Sometime diodes or LED's are connected back to back (in parallel but different directions of polarity) for the purpose of clipping and/or limiting the negative and the positive wave peaks in an audio amplifier. An example of this would be the phase inverter input of an Ampeg SVT.

Sometimes diodes are stacked in series so that they will clip at a higher voltage. For example two 1N914's in series would clip at 1.4 volts instead of the .7 volts (clipping voltage of one diode). Similarly, four diodes in series will clip at 2.8 volts.

Diode clipping is not a new idea. It has been used for years to improve intelligibility of speech for HAM Radio operators.

Jim Kelly used diode clipping quite successfully in the classic, "Jim Kelley" amplifiers.

After the first gain stage, a pair of 1N914's were wired in series to ground (anodes facing ground). When the volume was turned down, the signal was clean. Turn it up, and the waveform began to get squarer, but the volume stayed the same. This allowed for many degrees of distortion, but without really increasing the volume.

I used diode clipping when I designed the Kendrick Buffalo Pfuz Overdrive pedal. Two 1N4001's were used back to back and connected to a switch. The switch could then toggle between clean boost and overdrive.

If any of you Fender guys out there would like to try a little diode clipping. Here's a simple mod. Take two 1N914's or two 1N4001's or two 1N4003's. Put the two diodes in series, that is to say: connect the anode of one to the cathode of the other one.

Next, decide which channel you want the mod on. Perhaps doing it on the normal channel would be cool, because then you could use an A/B Box and channel switch between clean (with reverb) and overdrive (without reverb).

Looking from the back of the volume control on the channel you want the mod on, connect the cathode end of the two diodes to the middle terminal on the volume pot (This is the wiper). Connect the anode side of the diodes to the left lead of the volume pot (This is ground). You are ready to rock. As you turn the volume up, you'll reach a point where the volume won't get any louder, but the waveform will get squarer and squarer.

Try out the mod, if you don't like it, simply clip it out.

OTHER BRITISH

I have a 1961 British amp its is supposed to be about 15 watts, although I have no confirmation. The transformer has a pin on top to change voltages. The choices are 205, 225, 245. The power cord has a British plug with the three fat flat prongs (two horizontal, one vertical). It looks a lot like our 220 volt plugs. On the amp side of the cord, there is a round, three-pin plug. The transformer is currently (no pun intended) set on the 245 setting and was operational in the UK before I got it. How can I convert it to 110? I saw one 110-220 step-up transformer, but I'm not sure what size (watt) converter I need. The Jameco is a two-prong setup, no dedicated ground? I don't think I will be able to work with the British plug, I will just have to make a new power cord, but I still need to find a converter.

I wouldn't sweat the end plug. You can always whack the end off and put the appropriate style connector to match your step-up transformer. You definitely need a step-up transformer, available at Mouser (1-800-34MOUSE). A 15 watt amp would not use more than a 3-amp fuse. Three amps at 120 volts equal 360 watts. A 400 watt or better rating will work nicely. Mouser part # 553-N1000MG will work very well for your application.

I have a Vox AC15 (reissue) amp that is blowing the one amp fuse that is in line BEFORE the primaries of the power transformer. I have done the following: Tested with ALL secondaries disconnected and all tubes out — still blows the one amp fuse; Replaced the 47 nf 250 VAC cap — same result; Checked wiring from the wall to the primaries — they are correct; Tested each primary winding separately — blows fuse on each winding; Removed ALL connections to the Transformer — no blown fuse; Plugged in the unit to my variac — blows fuse at anywhere from 20 VAC to 40 VAC; Tested the "On" switch and the readings show the switch is function properly. Any suggestions?

If your transformer is blowing fuses with all secondaries disconnected, then either the switch has a short (not likely or should I say nearly impossible) or the 250 VAC cap is bad (not likely either) or the power transformer is bad. Clip the cap out and jumper the switch with the secondaries ALL disconnected from the circuit. If it still blows a fuse, the power transformer is bad.

I have an old AC30 and was wondering if there is any way to get my Vox to distort at lower volumes? There is a guy in England that switched his GZ34 tube to something lower that gave him less headroom and a little less wattage so it's not as loud and distorts faster. He said you can change the GZ34 to a GZ32 or a 5U4 and it will lower the voltage a bit?

Although changing to a GZ32 will lower the voltage, it will not be roadworthy. The Vox AC30 draws around 200 mA of current in an idle condition. Remember it is Class A and a true Class A push-pull circuit draws the most current at idle. The GZ32 has a maximum output current of 175 mA. Although it would probably work for a day or two, it would not be dependable. Instead, I would try the GZ31 (aka 5U4 GB). This tube will lower the voltage considerably, and it can handle up to 275 mA continuously. In fact, the 5U4G, or 5U4GA will also work perfectly. Another choice would be the 5AS4, which is also a directly heated cathode (like the 5U4 style tubes) design with 275 mA current capability. Another possibility could be the 5R4G, 5R4GY, 5R4GYA or 5R4GYB. The 5R4 style tube will give even less voltage than the 5U4 style tubes and the 5R4 tubes can easily take 250 mA of constant current.

I have a question about JMI VOX AC30 with four EL84 tubes. If I remove two of four EL84 tubes inside the chassis, what will become of the sound of the amp? Besides, will the ohms of output change?

Although that trick is used on four output tube Fenders and Marshalls (which are fixed bias output tubes), you cannot do that on the Vox AC30 because it is a cathode biased design, which depends on the tube current of all four tubes to develop output tube bias voltage. When you remove two tubes, then half as much current goes through the cathode resistor and therefore only half the bias voltage is developed.

If you wanted to run two output tubes (instead of four) on a permanent basis, here's the modification: Locate the 50 ohm cathode resistor that connects to pin #3 of each output tube. Replace it with a 100 ohm / 5 watt resistor. Now to keep the reflected impedance correct, you must use a speaker load that is twice the amp's output impedance.

I am not sure if your particular amp has an 8 ohm tap on the output transformer. Many of the vintage Vox AC30 amps had this tap. Stock setup for the Vox is 16 ohms, which is two 8 ohm speakers in series. If your amp has an 8 ohm tap, leave the speakers wired for 16 ohms, but use the 8 ohm tap instead of the stock 16 ohm tap.

If the amp has no 8 ohm tap, you could replace the speakers with the 16 ohm type and run them in series to get 32 ohms. In this case, you would still use the 16 ohm output from the amp, but the speakers would be wired in series to get 32 ohms total speaker load.

I have a 1978 Orange OD 120. I like the tone overall but would like a little more head room as well as staying cleaner at higher volumes. I've just had it biased and re-tubed. Also, what can be done to make the effects loop more useable? Do you have any suggestions? I run at 4 ohms thru a 4x12 loaded with Celestion vintage 30s.

For starters, forget about the FX loop. It is a passive loop without any buffering and it is high impedance. There might be an effect or two that would work with it, but basically it is useless. Anyway, effects sound better through the front of an amp.

That amp has a solid-state rectifier and no standby switch. This is a bad design because your tubes will have high voltage placed on them before they have a chance to get hot. The tubes will wear out prematurely. I would advise adding a standby switch to this amp to prevent tube damage.

Since it is a vintage amp, you don't want to be adding holes to that chassis. You could replace the power switch with an ON/OFF/ON double-pole double-throw toggle switch. (Remember to keep the old switch in case you ever want to sell the amp). You could wire one pole of the switch where ON is either the "up" or "down" position (the center is OFF). The other pole of this switch could be wired as a standby switch with "up" as ON and the "center" and "down" as OFF. To warm up your amp, the toggle is switched "down." After the amp warms up, the toggle is switched "up," which will put the amp in the play mode. Of course to turn off the amp, the toggle is placed in the center position. This would save your tubes. If you don't know how to do this, any competent tech could do this for very little dineros and you would save big-time on tube replacements. Have the standby circuit lift the power going to the output transformer and choke. Leave the main filters connected to the rectifier so the mains get charged as soon as the amp is turned on.

After that, you only need to do three things to get your amp sounding great. You need to increase the filtering on your main and screen supply, cool down the idle current (bias colder), and change the output impedance of the amp. Let me explain.

Increase the filtering on your main and screen supply. Your main filters are the two 100 uf 450 volt caps that are in series from your rectifier to ground. On your particular amp, the center-tap of the power transformer attaches to the junction of those two capacitors. (Technically, this is called an economy power supply and it is a take-off of the full wave bridge rectifier.) Replace both of these capacitors with 220 uf 350 volt capacitors. Take note of the proper polarity, if you get it wrong there will be a small explosion!

The screen supply filters are the two 32 uf 450 volt capacitors that are in series with each other and attached to the choke, screen resistors and a 33K power resistor on one side. The minus end of the other one goes to ground. (Each capacitor has a 100K 2 watt resistor across it.) Replace these with 100 uf 350 volt capacitors. Again, be careful to observe correct polarity.

All of these filter capacitors provide power to the output tubes. When you hit a low note and need a burst of power, the bigger values will perform better and keep the notes powerful and focused with minimal washout.

Cool down the idle current (bias colder). When an amp is biased, the idle current is adjusted to a point between saturation (maximum current) and cutoff (no current). If you want a cleaner sound, the bias should be adjusted closer to cutoff. This gives you a lot of headroom before the tubes saturate. Conversely, if one wants the tubes to break up early, the bias should be set closer to saturation. You want a cleaner sound; therefore the output tubes should be idled down. This amp is fixed bias but has no bias adjustment pot. That does not mean it cannot be adjusted. Any competent tech can figure this out.

Change the output impedance that you are running the amp. If you are running your 4X12 cabinet at 4 ohms, you are missing a lot of what the amp has to offer. Consider this: Your transformer has a 16 ohm, 8 ohm and 4 ohm tap. When the transformer is made, the 16 ohm tap is the entire secondary, the 8 ohm tap is 70.7% of the secondary and the 4 ohm tap is 50% of the secondary. This means when you use the 4 ohm tap, only half of your transformer is being used!

Rewire your speakers to parallel/series. This will get your cabinet to 16 ohms. Next, run the output transformer at 16 ohms and you will be using the entire transformer. There is yet another benefit. When running 16 ohms, the turns ratio of the transformer is at its lowest which means there is less coupling loss. Less loss translates into more dynamics, better tone, improved touch sensitivity and a little more volume.

SPEAKER

I've noticed that you frequently mention matching amp to speaker impedance. I'm a little puzzled about Fender amps. As far as I can tell, BF and SF Fenders have a single output tap off the output transformer. If you add an extension speaker, that should cut the impedance in half.

Apparently, the transformer is happy with a 50% reduction in impedance (for example from 8 to 4 ohms for a Deluxe Reverb).

Is it important to have exact matching only on amps that have highly stressed OT (Marshall, tweed Fender)?

Matching the speaker to the amp is a mathematical thing. An output transformer consists of an iron core with two coils of wire wound around it. It is a step down transformer. There is a primary (goes to the tubes) and a secondary (goes to the speaker) on an output transformer. The output transformer is wound for a particular turns ratio and that is what dictates the impedances. If the winding going to the speaker (secondary) is connected to too small of impedance, then it will still work, except the tubes will "see" a smaller than normal impedance. Conversely, if the speaker impedance is too large, then the tubes will "see" larger impedance.

This doesn't damage your amplifier to hook something up wrong; but it may shorten tube life.

For example, let's say you have a Fender Pro Reverb amp that is normally 4 ohms. The transformer is wound so that under normal conditions, the tubes are operating into a 4,200 ohm primary. If you hook up a 2 ohm ohm load, the primary becomes 2,100 ohms. Why? The turns ratio of the transformer remains constant, so if the secondary impedance is cut in half, so will be the primary. The tubes are normally operating into 4,200 ohms, but with the extra speaker, the "reflected impedance" on the tubes becomes 2,100 ohms.

Consider this: A direct short is zero ohms, so at 2,100 ohms, the tubes are exactly halfway between the 4,200 ohms (where they were designed to operate) and a direct short. This can be hard on the tubes, especially if the amp has lots of gain.

However, let's say we went the other way. Suppose you had a Bandmaster head (4 ohm output) and you plugged it into an 8 ohm speaker cabinet. Since no one changed the turns ratio of the transformer, the reflected impedance becomes twice what is normal. If 4,200 ohms is normal for a Bandmaster, then when plugged into an 8 ohm load, the "reflected impedance" (that the tubes "see") is 8,400 ohms. This is actually easier on the tubes, because of the current limiting effect of having a larger impedance. The tone will be more compressed and spongy. This might be very useful when doing some Ry Cooder slide guitar licks or any other application where you may want more compression.

How does wiring in series or parallel effect the tone of speakers in a multi speaker enclosure? For example two 16 ohm speakers in parallel versus two 8 ohm in series from the same manufacturer?
When wiring speakers, impedance and inductance become a factor. I once experimented with a 9x10 speaker cabinet and learned a lot. With the nine-speaker array, I wired three sets of three ten inch speakers. Three speakers were wired in parallel to get 2⅔ ohms. This was done with all three sets of three. I then wired the three sets

in series with each other to get 8 ohms ($2^{2}/_{3} + 2^{2}/_{3} + 2^{2}/_{3}$ = 8 ohms). I thought this would sound great because I would be moving a huge wavefront of air (707 square inches of air!). This speaker configuration sounded awful. The highs were muted and there was zero cut. I had too much branch inductance!

In general, there is less branch inductance when wiring speakers in parallel. Less inductance gives a cleaner; more defined, clearer, brighter overall tone. For example, Fender always wired their multi-speaker amps in parallel. This gave them the least branch inductance and the clearer tone — brighter and more jangley.

On the other hand, British designs almost always used series or series/parallel speaker wiring. For example, the Vox AC30 had its two twelve inch speakers wired in series. The Marshall amps used series/parallel with their four 12" speaker cabinets. Two speakers were wired in series to make one set of two. The other set of two was wired in series. Then each set (of two) were wired in parallel with each other. If you started out with four 16 ohm speakers, by the time you wired four of them in series/parallel, you ended up with a 16 ohm load.

Series wiring, in general, has a duller top-end, with less definition. Think bark not bite.

Of course, if I were designing a speaker cabinet for a particular amp, I would find out what the most ohms the output transformer is designed for and I would use that as the target impedance. When a transformer is made, it is wound for the largest impedance output and all the other taps are simply portions of the transformers secondary. If a transformer is wound for 16 ohms with an 8 ohm tap and a 4 ohm tap, the full winding is 16 ohms. To get 8 ohms, the transformer is tapped at around 70% of the winding and to get 4 ohms, it is tapped in half. Using the largest impedance output allows you to use the entire secondary of the transformer rather than using 70% or 50%. There is a noticeable difference when using the entire transformer.

Should phase shifting be considered in choosing series vs. parallel speaker wiring arrangements? Since in a series circuit, the audio signal must travel through one speaker before it gets to the next speaker, is the phasing effect compounded to "sound bad" as in an Ampeg V9 enclosure with nine 5.3 ohm speakers in a par-

allel/ series configuration. Or, does it "enhance" the sound as in the mystique of the Vox AC30? Or, is it downright insignificant?

I love to "see" people that are really thinking about this kind of thing! This is the kind of minutia that makes for an anal, obsessive, compulsive tone freak that has a hard time sleeping at night because he can't stop thinking about it. I once had a German design engineer fax me your same question!

Let's think about this a little. Light and electricity travel at about the same speed 186,000 miles per second. When you consider that a mile is 5,280 feet or 63,360 inches, you can quickly surmise that electricity travels 1,178,496,000,000 inches per second. If you have a speaker cable that is 10 inches long between the speakers in question, the second speaker will get the signal 1/117,849,600,000 of a second later. I don't think a trillionth of a second time delay could be heard or even measured.

The Ampeg V9 used custom-made 5.3 ohm CTS speakers. These were made in Paducah, Kentucky. When wired in parallel/series, the nominal impedance was actually 5.3 ohms. Their literature calls the cabinet 4 ohms nominal impedance because it was intended that they be used as 4 ohm cabinets. Of course, the output impedance for the V9 amplifier was 4 ohms and 2 ohms, the V9 being the exact same amplifier as the SVT. The SVT used eight 32 ohm CTS speakers wired in parallel to get 4 ohms per cabinet.

I have never seen an Ampeg V9. My friend, that worked for Ampeg, claims that he has only seen a few of these and they were built for the Rolling Stones. I did some experimenting once with a nine speaker configuration and came up with the conclusion that nine speakers in a series/parallel or a parallel/series configuration simply had too much branch inductance to get an outstanding tone. The highs were garbled as was note definition/separation.

I have a 4 ohm 45 watt tube guitar amp head. What are my speaker options?

With a 4 ohm head you could run two 8 ohm speakers in parallel to get 4 ohms. These could be 10", 12", or even 15" — as long as they were 8 ohms each. When wiring them in parallel, you would simply hook the pluses together and the minuses together.

Use four 16 ohm speakers. They could be wired in parallel to get 4 ohms. Again, all the pluses would connect together and go to the hot lead. All the minuses would connect together and go to the ground lead.

Use four 4 ohm speakers. They could be wired in series/parallel or parallel/series. The difference between series/parallel and parallel/series is this: With series/parallel you would wire a pair in series, wire the other pair in series and then wire these two sets in parallel with each other. With parallel series, you would wire a pair in parallel, wire the other pair in parallel, and then wire these two sets in series with each other. The series parallel may have slightly less high-end clarity than the parallel series (less branch inductance).

I have an 8 ohm output amplifier with two output jacks and I wish to run two 8 ohm speakers. Should I install a load resistor either in series or parallel to maintain an 8 ohm load?
Absolutely not! Putting a resistor in the circuit will rob power from the speaker and give it to the resistor. Most output transformers will tolerate a 100% mismatch. If you are going to always run it with an extra speaker, you might want to go to a 4 ohm transformer, but if you are only going to use it with the extra speaker some of the time, the 8 ohm is the way.

I have two 8 ohm speakers wired in parallel to get 4 ohms. Will the amp sound differently if I wired them in series or some other combination? If I have the option of 2, 4 or 8 ohms (selector switch), which ohm option would work best with two speakers? Can a 16 ohm selection be added?
You cannot add a 16 ohm tap to your present transformer. With your situation, the ultimate setup would be to use two 16 ohm speakers in parallel. That way, you could use the 8 ohm tap. When a tapped transformer is being made, it is first wound for the largest impedance (8 ohms in this case) and the other taps are at 70.72% of the secondary winding (that would be the 4 ohm tap in your case) and at 50% of the secondary winding (2 ohm).

When you use the largest setting (8 ohm in your case), then the entire transformer is being used and that will get your best sound. If you use the 4 ohm tap, only 70.72% of the transformers secondary is being used. The best way to match two speakers to 8 ohms is if they are 16 ohm speakers wired in parallel. Though 4 ohm speakers are rare, if you had two 4 ohm speakers, you could wire them in series and get the 8 ohm nominal impedance.

My question is about ohm settings on tube amps. I am running two cabinets, one is 16 ohms and the other is 8 ohms. My amp has settings for 4,8, and 16 ohms. What setting do I set it on?
When you run a 16 ohm and an 8 ohm cabinet, the 8 ohm cab is getting 2/3 the power and the 16 ohm cabinet is getting the other third. The total nominal impedance is 5.3 ohms. (16X8 / 16+8) or 128 / 24 = 5.3. So you have a choice, either 4 or 8. Even though the 4 is the closest, you are using 22% more of the transformer on 8, therefore I would recommend you listen to 4 and listen to 8 and whichever one sounds the best is the one to use.

I would like to run a single 12" speaker amp (Kendrick Black Gold 35 with 8 ohm output but with using a 16 ohm 12" speaker) with a 2x12 extra speaker cabinet. The extra speaker 12's are each 8 ohms. What would be the best way to hook these up? Am I going to loose any punch and tone using the 8 ohm speakers instead of using two 16 ohm speakers in the extension cabinet?
I recommend using a 16 ohm speaker in the amplifier cabinet and two 8 ohm speakers (wired in series to get 16 ohms) in the extension speaker cabinet. This would give you a total nominal impedance of 8 ohms. Exactly half the power would come out of your amp cabinet's speaker and the other half out of the extension speaker.

   To wire the extension cabinet speakers in series, simply connect a jumper wire from the plus terminal of one speaker to the minus terminal of the other one. That will leave an unused terminal on each speaker. Those remaining two leads connect to the speaker jack. Get the polarity right when hooking the remaining two leads to the speaker. The minus lead (on the speaker whose plus lead is connected to the other speaker) goes to ground and the plus lead (on the speaker whose minus lead goes to the other speaker) goes to hot.

   You want to check the speaker polarity for the 16 ohm 12" that is in the main cabinet. The minus should go to ground (the sleeve of your jack) and the plus to hot (the tip of your jack). This will assure you of having all speakers move in the same direction at the same time. Remember to point the speakers in the same general direction to avoid phase problems.

I was wondering why amp makers don't use different size speakers in their amps anymore? Why not an amp with a 10" speaker, 12" speaker, and a 15" speaker. I know some companies such as Gibson (in the fifties) used different size speakers in their design. It seems like a good way to get a multi-dimensional, rich tone. So what gives?

You are right. A multi-speaker set-up will provide a multi-dimensional tone. I used to make an amp with two 10" and one 15" speakers. It sounded fabulous and the cabinet was huge. (Most gigging guitarists would have had to pre-qualify their girlfriends: Do they own a truck?)

However, to answer your question, I would think impedance matching with respect to efficiency matching would be a major turn-off for a manufacturer. If you are using a 2x12, a 2x10, a 4x10, or a 2x15 configuration; then you can use identical speakers and know that one will not overpower the other. It is a built-in balance.

Besides that, there is the consideration of time-alignment. Time alignment of identical speakers will be identical. Time alignment relates to the acoustic origin of a particular speaker, which is determined by the position of the voice coil and the net phase shift. For most drivers and purposes, the acoustic origin is typically located at the back edge of the magnet systems back plate. (Translation: the rear of the magnet structure.) You can see how a 15" speaker whose acoustic origin is far from the baffleboard will not be in time alignment with a 10" speaker that is not nearly as deep. In real life guitar tone, I don't think this hurts guitar tone, but many designers would disagree with me.

I did a design once that used a 15" and two 10" speakers. If you are wondering how I did it, here is the Kendrick design. I mounted them on the same baffleboard and ignored time alignment. I used two Kendrick Blackframe 10" 8 ohm speakers and a JBL D130 15" 16 ohm speaker. I wired the two 10" speakers in series to get 16 ohms; then I connected that 16 ohm load in parallel with the 16 ohm JBL. This brought the total speaker load to 8 ohms. Of course, I used an 8 ohm output amplifier design.

With this type of connection, half of the power went through the JBL, a quarter of the power went through one 10" and the other 10" also got a quarter power. To over simplify, on a 50 watt amp, the JBL got 25 watts and each 10" got 12 ½ watts. Considering the efficiency of the speakers vs. wattage distribution, I have found this to be a pleasing balance — especially when the amp is pushed, forcing the 10s" to go creamy while the JBL is still hanging tight bottom. Time alignment didn't present any problems. Everyone agreed that this amp rocked, but again the size was prohibitive for most people.

If we could expand the multi-speaker concept, the next level up would be the multi-amp concept. This way one could use dissimilar amps (in terms of personality) with dissimilar speakers — all simultaneously! I call this the Texas Tone Del Maximo. I wrote of it extensively a few years ago and even devoted a section of my second book, *Tube Amp Talk for the Guitarist and Tech*, to it.

Is there a way to determine the ohm rating of a cabinet if the individual speaker impedance is unknown. I purchased a 1968 SUNN cabinet advertised as a 4x10, 8 ohm cabinet. It turns out to be a 4x12 cabinet with CTS speakers marked 67-6935 and wired in series.

If it really were an 8 ohm cabinet, wouldn't the speakers need to be 2 ohm each? Or do I have this backwards?

You are correct. If it really were an 8 ohm cabinet, the speakers would have to be 2 ohms each. I have never seen a 2 ohm guitar speaker. My guess is that your cabinet is wired wrong.

The easiest method to get speaker cabinet impedance would be to check the cabinet with a D.C. ohmmeter. Remember the D.C. resistance in ohms will be a little less than the actual impedance. For instance, an 8 ohm cabinet will probably read around 6 ohms D.C. resistance. Similarly, the 2 ohm cabinet will read 1 ohm or so and the 4 ohm cabinet will measure around 2.5 to 3 ohms of D.C. resistance.

A four-speaker combination can only be wired four ways, namely: parallel, series, series/parallel, and parallel/series. Assuming you are using speakers that are all the same impedance, both series/parallel and parallel/series will end up with the same impedance as a single speaker. For instance, four 8 ohm speakers wired in series/parallel or parallel/series would still end up as 8 ohms. You will probably never see anyone hook four speakers in series, but if they did, four 8 ohm speakers would be 32 ohms. If you hooked all four in parallel, you would end up with 2 ohms.

When thinking of four speakers in parallel, I like to think of it like this: If you had one 8 ohm speaker and you added another (in parallel), then the current would have two pathways of 8 ohms each instead of one pathway of 8 ohms. This would always impede the flow of current less because there are two pathways now instead of one. However hard it was for the current to go through one pathway of 8 ohms; it is now twice as easy because of the additional pathway. In the case of two 8 ohm speakers wired in parallel, one could visualize how two pathways could halve the impedance of one and therefore the circuit would see 4 ohms.

If you had a third 8 ohm speaker, you would then have three 8 ohm pathways. The current sees this as 3 times easier to pass through this than a single 8 ohm pathway. In this case, the circuit would see 2 $\frac{2}{3}$ ohms. (Think of it this as 8 ohms divided by 3 speakers).

Add one more 8 ohm speaker and you now have four 8 ohm pathways and the impedance is now a fourth because it is four times easier for the current to pass. The circuit sees 2 ohms in this case.

In the case of series, you will be adding the ohms. Why? Because in series, there is always just one pathway and when another 8 ohm speaker is added, it is just that much harder for current to pass. One could say that the current is impeded more. Two 8 ohm speakers in series will make the circuit see 16 ohms. Add another 8 ohm speaker and the circuit sees 24 ohms. Add another and the circuit sees 32 ohms.

In a series/parallel or parallel/series configuration, the four speakers are arranged with two in series and two in parallel. Whether you double and half or half then double, you will still come out with the same impedance as a single speaker (assuming all four speakers are the same impedance.)

I have a 1960's Vox Essex Bass Amplifier. I am getting a vibration in the cabinet — a buzz when playing a certain 2 or 3 notes on

my bass guitar. This increases with volume. **The cabinet back screws are tight with one or two screws missing or stripped-out near the bottom. Could I eliminate the cabinet back vibration by porting the cabinet? If so, would it be better ported in the front or the back, and what size should they be?**

Let's focus on the problem and how to cure it rather than focusing on the symptom of the problem. I would not recommend redesigning the cabinet to eliminate the symptom. The symptom of the problem is the buzzing sound. I have chased down this symptom many times and found that a variety of problems could cause this symptom. Here are some possible cures to the problem.

First, check the baffleboard. I cannot remember how the baffleboard attaches in an Essex amp. If it screws in, you must remove the screws, and reseat the baffleboard where it is completely flush against the battens and then rescrew, taking care that there is no air gap between the baffleboard and the battenboard. The slightest air space will cause rattle on certain notes and this buzz will seem elusive. If it is glued in, and it seems to me now that it is glued, check to make sure that it is glued 100% around the perimeter. There cannot be any air gaps or it will buzz on certain notes.

Another possibility is a crack in the baffleboard itself. I have seen baffleboards with a hairline crack that was hardly noticeable, yet buzzing on certain notes would occur. In this case, replacing the baffleboard is the only option to cure the problem.

The missing or stripped-out screws are another source of buzzing. Remove the back panel and fill the stripped-out holes with a small wooden dowel. Glue the dowel in the holes with wood glue and after it is dry, cut the dowel flush with the batten. (Hint — I use a chopstick for this. You may have to whittle the chopstick down a little with a utility knife to get it to fit perfectly in the hole.)

When all stripped holes are filled, check the back panel to make sure there is a perfectly flush fit against the rear battenboards. Does the covering material have bare spots that could cause air gaps? The slightest air gap will cause buzzing. When reinstalling the back panel, make sure you use all good screws and double check there is no air gap between the back panel and the battens.

Would a Marshall style 4x12 cab made of finger-jointed pine instead of plywood have any advantages sonically, and would your Kendrick Black frame speakers be a good choice to use in it? Can these be wired for 16 ohm?

I would not say that one sounds better than the other. I would say they sound different from each other. Each has its advantage and disadvantage, depending on what type of tone you are going for. The multi-ply voidless birch cabinet of the Marshall gives it a distinct sound — much different than pine. The Birch has more high-end, more presence and is much more focused — a tighter sound. The pine would sound warmer, and more vintage-like. The notes would have blurred edges when compared to the crisper and more focussed birch.

Of course, the Kendrick Blackframe speakers would work fine in such a cabinet, however they only come in 8 ohm. This means that four of them can be wired in either 2 ohm or 8 ohm. 16 ohm hookup is not a possibility when wiring four 8 ohm speakers.

TRANSFORMERS

I'm working on an amp that has a Hammond transformer with a 6.3V center tapped filament supply rated at 5 A. When I measure the voltage (no load) it is 7+ volts (green-green). Will it come down under load to 6.3 volts? How critical is this voltage? What can be done if it is (still) over voltage? Could you please explain?

There is a problem with Hammond transformers. Most Hammond transformers are wound for a 115 volt primary. Your wall puts out between 120 and 135 volts. This makes the voltages all read high on the Hammond. It is bad news for the 6.3 volt filament. The tubes will sound awful running them at 7+ volts. You could put a couple of very small value, high wattage resistors in series with each side of the 6.3 volt winding.

To determine the correct value resistor to use, you figure it out by Ohm's law. Figure how much too much it is; lets say .8 volts too much. Then you want to drop an equal amount of voltage on each side of the winding, say .4 volt on each side. Let's say the amp is drawing 6 amps of filament current. So .8 volts divided by 6 amps equals .13 ohms; Divide that in half, and you need .065 ohms on each side of the winding. You may have to take a couple of .1 ohm resistors in parallel to get this value, but that will do the trick. The resistors need to be around 5 watts total per side. Drop .4 volts on each side and you're operating at 6.3 volts.

Now you need to drop the 5 volt rectifier winding too. I would drop it on pin #2 of the rectifier tube socket. You probably need to drop about .6 volts, which means you will need a .3 ohm resistor. It needs to be around 3 watts. The .3 ohm resistor gets soldered in series with the 5 volt winding and pin #2 of the rectifier socket.

I have a problem with my amp blowing fuses. I was told to remove the tubes and if the amp still blows fuses, the power transformer is bad. Can you help?

If your amp is blowing fuses, it could be many different possibilities. What you were told about removing the tubes to check for a bad power transformer is only about 25% true. There are other possibilities that could cause a fuse to blow.

Besides a shorted output tube, a common cause of fuse blowing is a bad rectifier tube or a bad solid-state rectifier. If you replace the rectifier and the output tubes and the fuse is still blowing, there are other possible causes other than a power transformer problem. For example, it could be a malfunction in the bias supply, a shorted filter cap, a shorted tube socket or just an internal short somewhere.

After everything else has been ruled out, if you believe the power transformer is bad, here is the test for the power transformer:

Disconnect all the leads on the secondary of the transformer. This includes the heater wires, heater center-tap (if applicable), the B+ wires, the 5 volt rectifier heater (if applicable), the bias tap, the B+ center-tap, and any other wire that is a secondary of the power transformer. At this point, the only wires from the transformer that connect to anything will be the primary, which is hooked up to the A.C. supply via a switch, a fuse, and perhaps a ground switch.

Turn the amp "on." If the fuse blows at this point, the power transformer is probably bad. If the power switch is a DPDT, there is a very unlikely possibility that the switch is shorted internally. There is also the unlikely possibility that the ground switch is shorted internally.

I just got done building my first complete amp. It's built and I'm double-checking to see if everything is connected correctly. All of my "hot" wires I've been checking to ground to make sure there's no grounding mistakes. I came upon something weird. The high voltage (red) leads from the power tranny were reading to ground!!! UH OH, I thought. I disconnected them from the circuit and they show continuity to ground. What's the deal? Could the leads have been severed in mounting? Where do I check next?
You are OK. The center-tap of the transformer B+ winding goes to ground. When you measure the end of the wire, it will have continuity to ground as long as the center-tap is grounded.

You cannot measure resistance with a component "in circuit." Sometimes there are multiple paths across a resistance and this will give you a false reading. I remember years ago, building an amp circuit and checking components "in circuit." When I would read the feedback resistor (in circuit), I would get a really small reading. This was because the feedback resistor is in parallel with the output transformer secondary (fraction on an ohm) and negative feedback load resistance. (In this particular case, the load resistance was the presence control.) Every time I measured the resistor in the circuit, it looked completely out of tolerance. I would change it and then the new one looked bad too.

I recommend using a current limiter when bringing up a newly built amp. That way, if there is a problem, you will know about it quickly and nothing will burn up. The directions on how to build a current limiter for under $20, is in my first book, *A Desktop Reference of Hip Vintage Guitar Amps*.

I've just completed my first hand-built, one channel amp. Up until now, I've just been modifying Fenders and what not. I used a 60 watt Hammond output transformer. The power transformer is a Hammond, rated at 350-0-350 Maybe you can "decipher" any problems or weirdness. High Voltage red wires on power tranny read 377 VAC both sides. This was with the EL34's idling at 31 mA idle plate current per tube. The heaters read 6.7 volt A.C.

I have had several amplifiers come into my shop with Hammond transformers and I have yet to hear one that I like. The 700 volt B+ winding on your power transformer should read 350 volts on each side of the centertap, and not 377 volts. Also, the heater should read 6.3 volts instead of 6.7 volts. My guess is that the transformer primary is rated for less than the 120 volt wall voltage you are using. Perhaps your transformer has a 110 volt or a 115 volt primary. That is common for that brand.

There are other possibilities. Perhaps your meter needs to be recalibrated. If the meter is not the problem, since the heater voltage is high, that tells me either the B+ is rated for several times the current you are actually using, or the primary of the tranny has a couple of shorted turns on the winding. If a few turns are shorted, the volts-per-turn on the primary will increase. This, in turn, will make the volts-per-turn go up on every winding.

Also, your wall may be high. For example, if your wall were 130 volts, everything on the power tranny would read high. (At press time, this reader emailed me and the Hammond transformer had a 115 volt primary. When used in a normal wall outlet, all the output windings read high.)

I would like to share with you my method to determine the primary impedance of a tube-type audio output transformer. Apply 120 VAC to the primary leads of the transformer (usually blue to brown). Don't use the center-tap if the primary is center-tapped. Next measure the A.C. voltage at the secondary (let's say it's 4.8 volts) and divide the 120 volts on the primary by 4.8 volts on the secondary. This gives you your turn's ratio of 25. (Technically it would be 25 to 1) Square the turns ratio (and get 625) and then multiply by the intended speaker impedance (let's say 8 ohms). We get 5,000 ohms.

At first glance, this may seem brutal, but the 2,000 plus turns of wire on a primary and the lack of secondary load keep the power draw next to nothing. In short, the transformer receives far less punishment here than when installed in an amplifier. Of course, it is very important that none of the secondary leads touch one another. If they touch, then there will be damage!

It is also a good idea to wire a 25 watt light bulb in series with

the primary as a current limiter. This could save a tripped circuit breaker if the transformer is shorted. Of course, if the light bulb lights, the transformer should be discarded or rewound.

I have a shoe box full of transformers with labels depicting the value thanks to this procedure. This procedure will aid in identifying correct secondary leads (which lead is the 16 ohm or 8 ohm, etc.)

All in all, this procedure will tell everything you want to know about a transformer, including any change in impedance that may have occurred, such as if a 10,000 ohm transformer has dropped to 5,000 ohms. I hope this helps in one way or another.

Your technique seems sound. Pun intended. I use a similar technique except I feed the primary with a smaller voltage using a variac. When the secondary voltage is divided into the primary voltage, the quotient is a ratio. This ratio is constant so if the primary voltage goes up, the secondary voltage goes up but in the same ratio. Therefore it doesn't really matter if you use 120 volts or 10 volts, the result will be constant.

I received another letter from a reader claiming he uses this same procedure, but with a 10 volt A.C. wall wart.

Regardless of what voltage source is used for the primary, I would measure both the primary and secondary voltages accurately with a good A.C. voltmeter. This would improve the accuracy of your calculations by giving you the most accurate turn's ratio. If you get the turn's ratio accurate, the rest will be much more accurate.

Also, when doing the math, we simply get the ratio of primary voltage to secondary voltage and then square it. This number is then multiplied by the intended speaker impedance, which gives us the primary impedance.

Important Note: you do not hook up a speaker when using this procedure. How do you know what speaker impedance to use in your calculations? You don't! You simply assume load impedance and do the math. In the preceding example we assumed an 8 ohms speaker load to get the 5,000 ohm primary. Had we assumed the secondary to be connected to a 16 ohm speaker, we would have ended up with 10,000 ohms as primary impedance.

I would like to learn a good method for specifying power transformer B+ current. Heater current at 5 volt or 6.3 volt seems fairly easy. Tube specs plus a safety margin. I don't know what tube specs to use for B+ current. My G.E. *Essential Characteristics* tube book lists plate current and screen current, but I think that these are Class "A" values. I'm guessing these aren't the numbers to use for a type AB amp. My RCA *Receiving Tube Manual* lists zero-signal and maximum-signal currents. I'm guessing that maximum signal is the way to go, but these are not listed for triodes, and only a few voltages for pentodes.

My subject amp is an Ampeg B-42X, which I want to wire for 6CA7 (or EL34) tubes at about 400 volts B+. Depending on rectifier tube, here are my calculations:

	B+ mA	6.3 volt heater
6CA7	66 plate + 7 screen	1.5
6CA7	66 plate + 7 screen	1.5
7199	12.5 + 9.0	0.45
12AX7	1.2 + 1.2	0.3
12AX7	1.2+1.2	0.3
6CG7	9 + 9	0.6
12AX7	1.2 + 1.2	0.3
12AX7	1.2 + 1.2	0.3
	195.1 mA	1.9A
Totals		5.25A

I have a catalog that lists a 250 ma, 600 volt center-tapped, power transformer that will also do the heaters. This is a big safety factor; I'm wondering if the secondary voltage might run too high if run a 250 mA transformer at 195 mA. Any insights appreciated.

With Class AB (push-pull), there is a difference between what a tube idles at and how much current it draws when the amp is cranked. With Class A (push-pull), the tubes draw their most current at idle (zero signal), which is how most tubes are listed in the G.E. manual. Your power transformer needs to have enough current rating to handle whatever the output tubes need. If the rating is too low, the transformer can overheat and/or the notes can wash out or oversag — depending on how severe the transformer is underrated.

Besides what the transformer must do to make the circuit work, there is the issue of how it sounds. In actual listening tests with the Kendrick Climax amp (which uses a 400 volt B+ and two E34L output tubes), I found the larger (350 mA) B+ secondary to perform the best it terms of dynamics and punch. In order to get 400 volts D.C., I had to use a 570 volt center-tapped B+ winding. That's 285 volts each side of the center-tap. The Climax, uses a solid-state rectifier. To get the same 400 volts D.C. with a tube rectifier, one would need about 620 volts center-tapped (310 volts each side of the center-tap). The exact voltage will vary depending on what kind of rectifier tube, and the microfarad value of your first filter cap (coming off the rectifier), and the idle current of the circuit.

You could try the 250mA transformer and see how you like it and what kind of voltages it will produce in your particular application. I'm sure it will work; I am not sure how it will sound tonally and how it will feel — performancewise. It may exhibit a fairly spongy response. Sponginess may good a good thing.

I am considering building a Vox AC15 type circuit — Two EL84's in Class "A." Could I use a replacement output transformer for a Deluxe, Deluxe Reverb, Tremolux, Vibroverb, or Vibrolux? What is the primary impedance for the Fender Transformers? Also, should I use separate cathode resistors/bypass caps for each EL84? What do you think?

Using a stock Fender transformer could be done if you used a little savvy. The AC15 needs about 8K primary impedance. Most Fender transformers that use two 6L6's run about 4200 ohms on the primary. If you deliberately used a speaker load twice of what the transformer was designed for, then the reflected impedance would put you at 8400 ohms. This should work very well. Here is an example: You could use a 60s Bassman output transformer that normally would be run at 4 ohms, but hook it up to an 8 ohm speaker. With the turns ratio being what it is, the tubes would "see" 8400 ohms!

If you wanted to run a 16 ohm speaker, use either a brownface Pro or a brownface Vibrolux which normally would be run 8 ohms.

If you decided to use four EL84's, you could run these transformers with the designed speaker load. For example use a Bandmaster output transformer for four EL84's running into 4 ohms!

I would recommend using only one cathode resistor and bypass cap for the AC15 circuit. This is the stock setup and for good reason: when one tube draws less current, the other is drawing a little more so the cathode voltage stays a little more stable.

MISCELLANEOUS

Recently I was reading somewhere, perhaps in one of your books, that when an amplifier manufacturer has both 12AX7 and 7025 tubes listed on the tube chart, he wants to see a higher grade or better tube at the 7025 positions than in the 12AX7 position. Alternatively, some other readings seem to indicate that the two tubes are direct replacements. What's up? I have a 1966 Fender Super Reverb and it calls for both tubes. I have a couple of old, but test good 7025's, but I feel like I should probably look for some NOS backups. What do you think?

Back in the old days, when 12AX7's were made, the military would require the ones with lowest microphonics and best gain. The military number for the 12AX7 is 7025.

Designers loved to have these in the first gain stages of a guitar amp, because even when the imperfections of the tube were amplified 10,000 times (as any tube-noise was amplified from the first stage to the next), the amp's output would still be quiet with no squealing or excessive noise.

Nowadays, the 12AX7's being made are sometimes simply labeled both ways: 12AX7/7025.

The idea is to use quiet and non-microphonic tubes in the first gain stages of the channel. That would be the first two tubes in your case. Both the GE JAN 7025 and the RCA 7025 are the crème de la crème first gain stage 12AX7 style tubes, but any 12AX7 would work fine in that socket so long as it wasn't noisy or microphonic and you liked the tone of it.

I serviced a Selmer Treble and Bass 50 S.V. by replacing the caps and obvious out-of-tolerance resistors. My problem is hum. Though not excessively bad, I've thought that it would have been greatly reduced by the new caps and in-tolerant resistors. It seems worse. There is a grounding buss, a large piece of heavy wire, with everything tied to that. Any ideas?

It is not that the grounds are bad, but they were perhaps not done right. When you overhauled it, it probably came back to life and amplified the hum more than it did before. You could also be getting some hum from an unshielded grid wire. I would recommend shortening all the grid wires. For the first two gain stages, change the grid wires to shielded. With a shielded grid wire, you only ground the shielding at one end, lest it make even more hum.

To get the grounds quiet, I would put the power tube cathode grounds, the main filter ground, the screen filter ground and the B+ center-tap ground all in one place and as far from the input as is feasible. The other filter caps should be grounded near the cathode ground of the preamp tube they are associated with.

I've seen it suggested that you could increase distortion on fairly high headroom amps by using a less effective rectifier (for example, using a 5Y3 instead of a 5U4 on a Super or Bassman). It certainly should cause more sag, but will it improve compression/distortion on prolonged notes? Is it going to hurt anything?

Changing rectifier tubes will certainly alter the tone. If the rectifier is underrated for the circuit it is in, it may improve compression so much that the front of the note is compressed off, so you can't play fast. Different results can be gotten with different amps. My advice is to try it and let your ears decide.

A WORD OF CAUTION: some rectifier tubes produce more voltage than others. If you are changing to a rectifier tube that produces less voltage, then your output tubes will be overbiased and they will be idling cold. On the other hand, if you use a rectifier tube that puts out more voltage, like a 5AR4 for example, the output tubes will want to draw more current and the output stage will be underbiased and running on the hot side. You can try it and let your ears decide but you may want to rebias the output tubes so they will be adjusted in relationship to the voltage produced by the actual rectifier you choose.

I purchased a used amp and had some preamp tube buzz. I tried to put in a Mullard preamp tube, but couldn't get it to hold. Do I need a new socket?

Evidently, someone used a tube with extra large pins and sprung the female part of the connectors in the socket. This can easily be re-tensioned with a safety pin or dental pick. You will need to drain the amp of voltage first so you don't shock yourself. (Unplug the amp, take the back off and put a jumper wire from pin #1 of the preamp tube to the chassis. After 20 seconds, the amp will be drained of power.) After the amp is drained, simply take the dental pick and carefully re-tension each pin of the tube socket so that the female part of the connector is tighter. (Don't all musicians prefer tighter female connections?) If for some reason this doesn't do it, a simple socket replacement will work.

I am working on a Univox that I believe to be a U202R. It looks similar to a late 50's Magnatone. Do you know where I can find a schematic? Is there a substitute for a 6AV6? I believe it is used as a reverb driver in this amp.

There are schematics and other good amplifier information on the Internet. Go to www.dogpile.com, type in the name of the amp, and do a "Fetch." Dogpile will access other search engines and you will find your schematic on some website somewhere. Sometimes the schematics are available and sold for a nominal fee. Typical fees may range from $3 to $5 for a downloadable schematic. This is a deal, because websites that offer this type of service have to maintain their sites and equipment and if they don't, we will not be seeing those services in the future. So if you like being able to find a schematic you don't own, support the people that offer it.

Checking the GE Essential Characteristics Tube Manual, there are a few versions of the 6AV6:

6BK6 – This one is almost identical in gain (similar in gain to the 12AX7) and other characteristics.

6BT6 – This one is less gain (similar in gain to the 12AT7) and useable as a substitute.

6BU6 – This one is the low gain version (similar in gain to the 12AU7A).

6BF6 – This one is the lowest gain version (similar in gain to the 12AU7).

I play harp and want to reduce all the preamp tube voltages. When you talk about increasing the value of the dropping resistor in an amp's power supply to reduce plate voltages, do you mean to add another resistor in series with one of the 100K ohm plate resistors?

No. A plate resistor goes to the plate and is important so the signal can have a place to develop. You should never change values of a plate resistor to change plate voltage.

The dropping resistor is the resistor that feeds the plate resistor. At the point where it feeds the plate resistor, there is a filter cap. The filter cap prevents the dropping resistor from turning into a plate resistor.

The dropping resistor will drop the voltage feeding the plate resistor (and the associated filter cap).

You may need to simply increase the value of the dropping resistor that is already in there. The best dropping resistor to change to reduce all preamp voltages, is the one that is between the choke and the phase inverter plate resistors. If you increase this one, all the preamp plate voltages will go down.

I charged the caps in the amp I built (5F6-A circuit) per your variac technique, starting at 40 volts for 12 hours and raising 10 volts per hour until reaching 120 volts. I now know that I do not particularly care for the putrid odor of melting dielectrics! I had some caps explode!

The caps that exploded were put in backwards. That will make them explode. Before you start an amp for the first time, do a visual inspection of all electrolytic capacitors and make certain the polarities are correct. All electrolytic capacitors go minus to ground except the caps in the negative bias supply, which go plus to ground.

Before actually starting an amp for the first time, you should always put it in the standby mode with the rectifier tube removed and hook a meter to the grid of an output tube socket (pin #5 for

6L6). Adjust the bias voltage until you see approximately -50 volts. This will assure you that the output tubes will be tame enough to set later. You don't want to turn the amp on and have the output tubes draw saturation current! Also, when you are adjusting the bias pot, note which way makes the negative voltage go less negative as you will need to turn it that direction to bring the idle plate current up later (when you actually set the bias).

Then, I would set the variac for 40 volts and start bringing it up. You must bring it up with the standby switch in the "play" mode. This will assure D.C. voltage on all the electrolytic caps in the amp.

I have a 6V6 style tube amp without a standby switch. Would I need to add a standby switch to change to 6L6 operation? I am under the impression that with the 6V6, a warm-up circuit is not essential. Would the amp be better off with a standby switch, even when using a 6V6?

Whether you use a 6V6 or a 6L6 makes no difference with regards to a standby circuit. The standby is to keep D.C. high voltage off the tubes (preamp tubes, and output tubes) when they are cold. If high voltage gets on a tube while it is cold, the tube gets shocked and the coating on the tube's cathode begins to come off. This looks like dandruff inside the tube.

You have two options to solve this problem: Either install a standby switch, or switch the rectifier to a "controlled warm-up time" rectifier such as a 5AR4 or a 5V4. With a "controlled warm-up time" rectifier tube, it takes longer for the rectifier tube to warm up than for the preamp or output tubes. By the time the rectifier tube is warm enough to start putting out D.C. voltage, the other tubes are already hot! It's like having an automatic standby switch.

I have a small number of very nice preamp tubes (Telefunken, Amperex and Mullard) pulled from amps and purchased NOS whenever I could find them. They sound great in my classic amps (Fender/Marshall/Vox/Kendrick, etc) but tend to be too noisy for my more modern amps (Wizard, Roccaforte, Fuchs, etc). Are there some of the magic, non-microphonic Telefunkens still out there or are they truly gone?

All tubes are microphonic — some worse than others. When a 12AX7 is put in an earlier gain stage of an amp, all the imperfections of the tube get amplified as it goes from one stage to the next. It is just like taking a flawless diamond and looking at it under a 300-power microscope. You can see flaws that otherwise would go unnoticed. Vintage amps do not have the high gain of modern amps and that may account for the extra noise in the modern amps.

Another point to consider is that since NOS preamp tubes haven't been made in years, whoever owned them originally probably removed the quietest and least microphonic ones and sold the remainder to someone else. That person removed the best ones and sold the rest to the guy you bought them from. Need I say more?

I just came across a pair of RCA metal-bodied 6L6's. They have one more pin than the glass ones. Can I use them in place of the regular glass 6L6's in my fender amp?

Probably not. The 6L6 (metal) can only take 19 watts plate dissipation per tube. Most Fender amps run them much hotter than that and you should therefore use 6L6GC tubes that are glass envelope and rated at 30 watts per tube dissipation. In other words, you can substitute the 6L6GC (30 watts plate dissipation) for a 6L6 (19 watts plate dissipation) but you can't substitute the 6L6 for the 6L6GC.

Note: The extra pin on the 6L6 (metal) doesn't connect to anything. It is strictly cosmetic.

My amp recently blew a fuse. Now, every time I replace the fuse, the new one blows up as soon as I power up the amp. I wasted a few fuses figuring this pattern out, but I'm now convinced there's something else wrong. What do I need to do? Is it an obvious problem?

Anytime an amp blows a fuse, the problem is NEVER the fuse. The fuse blows because something else is wrong. That's why they put fuses in amps. When something is amiss and draws too much current, the $1 fuse blows instead of the $200 transformer. In an amp, when a fuse blows, 95% of the time, the problem is a bad rectifier tube or a bad output tube. (I suggest you make a copy of this and put it in the back of your amp because eventually the fuse will blow and you need to know the correct procedure.)

Here's what to do:
1. Take out the rectifier tube and the output tubes.
2. Put in a good fuse
3. Turn on the amp

If the fuse blows, you probably have a blown power transformer. (Or if the amp is solid state rectification, it could be one or more of the diodes that is blown.) If the fuse doesn't blow:

1. Put the rectifier tube back in the amp and turn the amp on but leave it in standby mode.

If the tube blows, the rectifier is bad. If the fuse doesn't blow:

2. Switch the standby to play.

If the fuse blows, you probably have a blown filter cap, if it doesn't blow:

3. Install one of the output tubes

If the fuse blows, that output tube is bad. If it doesn't blow:

4. Install the other output tube.

If the fuse blows, that tube is bad.

This troubleshooting sequence is the same for any tube amp.

What are the advantages or disadvantages to using a D.C. supply for tube heaters. Wouldn't D.C. filament supply be quieter?

There are advantages and disadvantages to D.C. heater supply. I once used D.C. heaters when I first started building the Kendrick 2410 amp and I found there were more disadvantages than advantages. If you are using humbucking filament circuits, like a 12AX7 wired for 6.3 volts humbucking for example, or push-pull output tubes, hum is not really a problem. Plug a single-coil pickup guitar; such as a vintage Strat, into the amp and the pickup hum far overshadows any filament hum.

D.C. filament heater supply could be an improvement for amp designs with either a single-ended output stage (which doesn't cancel hum like a push-pull design) or when using non-humbucking filament preamp tubes such as the 6EU7.

The problem with the D.C. heaters is that the filaments themselves draw about 5 to 10 times as much current when they are cold and first turned on. The rectifier for the D.C. filament supply would have to be 25 to 50 amps to handle this because if the amp is hot and the player turns it off during a break, the filament rectifier is still hot yet the filaments cool off. Heating any semiconductor device negatively affects its wattage handling capability. When the switch is turned on, a blast of current goes through the rectifier, which blows the rectifier — unless it is of very high wattage (25 to 50 amps). Also you have to have massive filtering (figure 5000 uf per amp of current) – otherwise there will be excessive ripple current (pulsating D.C.). Pulsating D.C. sounds the same as hum!

Regulation is also a problem. No one makes a simple high current voltage regulator. When I made a D.C. filament supply amp back in 1989, I had to take some .1 ohm resistors (5 watt) and add or subtract these from the finished filament circuit to dial in 6.3 volts. With that much current, even the least resistance difference from one amp to another made a huge difference in voltage.

I want to build an amp with a switchable rectifier. I would like to switch between a GZ34 rectifier tube and a solid-state bridge rectifier. Would it be better switched between the transformer and the rectifiers, or run the B+ windings to both and switch between the outputs to the filter caps?

Neither. I assume you are talking about a full-wave bridge rectifier. If that is the case, then you will have to run your rectifier tube as a full-wave bridge also. To do so, you would hook up your rectifier tube as though it was configured as a regular full-wave design, and then add four diodes. (I would suggest using 1N4007 diodes). You would have two diodes in series going from pin #4 of the rectifier tube to ground. The cathode end of these series diodes would face the tube socket. You would have two more diodes in series going from pin #6 of the rectifier tube to ground, again with the cathode end of the diodes facing the tube. This would complete your bridge. In this case, the diodes will not affect the tube tone, as all of the current must pass through the rectifier tube first and any sag imparted by the tube rectifier's impedance will still be there.

The way I would design the switchable rectifier is to configure the switching so that the tube rectifier is always on. When the switch is activated, the diodes would short the rectifier tube and since the impedance is lower through the diodes, the current goes through them instead. This way, you won't hear a bunch of loud popping when switching and since the solid-state diodes are much lower impedance, the higher impedance tube rectifier won't affect the sound of the solid-state rectifiers when switched into the solid-state mode.

To wire this switching, you would need a double-pole single-throw switch (DPST) and four more 1N4007 diodes. Take a pair of diodes and wire them in series and then wire the other pair in series (cathode to anode). Take the cathode end of one pair and the cathode end of the other pair and wire both cathode ends to pin #8 of your tube rectifier socket. You will now have two anode ends of the series diodes left. These ends are each wired to one side (each with their own pole) of the DPST switch. The other side of the switch gets wired to pins #4 and pin #6 respectively (each pin gets its own pole too). When the switch is turned on, you have a solid-state full wave bridge rectifier in parallel with the tube.

Why did I always use two diodes in series? Because even though the 1N4007 is rated for 1000 volts PIV, after it gets hot from being near the rectifier tube, the PIV rating comes down. Also, a typical tube amp can exceed the 1000 volt PIV rating at times while a semi-conductor device can not operate outside its parameters without blowing (unlike a tube).

I built the Power Attenuator featured in this book. I love it. It was easy to build and all the parts cost less than $20 dollars. I doubled the wattage rating suggested, because I was using this for a 50 watt amp instead of the 25 watt amp described in your article. I need to attenuate more than 6 dB. Suggestions?

(My wife also thanks you in advance if I can get this to work!!!!)
Why not build another attenuator exactly like the first one and put them in series? You could mount them in the same enclosure if you like. Connect P1 of the first attenuator to the output of the amp. Connect J1 of the first attenuator to P1 of the second attenuator. J1 of the second one goes to the speaker. That way, you would have two switches. With both switches off, you would have full power and true bypass. Turn on one switch (either one, it doesn't matter) and you have 6 dB attenuation. Turn on BOTH switches and you have 12 dB attenuation. This would give you some versatility for when you play bigger places and need less than 12 dB attenuation; and it would get you pretty

close to the most attenuation you can get (15 dB) before screwing up your tone. You've already built one unit; just build another exactly like it. This would bring you from 50 watts attenuated down to either 12.5 watts (-6 dB) or down to about 3 watts (-12 dB).

You recommended four ways to bias an amp in your book, *A Desktop Reference of Hip Vintage Guitar Amps*. I'm going to bias my first amp and I was wondering if the "meter in series with the plate" method was as accurate as the others. It sounds like the easiest and safest. Also, from what I have read, is the current more important than the voltage when setting the bias? I'll answer your last question first. When you set bias, you are adjusting the negative voltage supply that feeds the grids of the output tubes. When the negative grid voltage is made more negative, less current flows through the tube. Conversely, when the grid voltage is adjusted less negative, then more current flows. So you are adjusting bias voltage, but only as a means to set the idle current.

All four ways of biasing described in my first book, *A Desktop Reference of Hip Vintage Guitar Amps*, are accurate. The safest method is the cathode resistor method.

With the cathode resistor method, you solder a 1 ohm resistor in series with the cathode and leave it. Next time you want to bias your amp, it is already there. Using the cathode resistor method, I use a 3 watt 1 ohm precision wirewound resistor. You don't need the 3 watt rating except 3 watts is such overkill that you never have to worry about the resistor drifting and it will not be affected by heat.

With the cathode resistor method, you would set your meter for voltage as you are measuring a small fraction of a volt that develops across the 1 ohm resistor. What is cool about this method is that you can adjust the bias, play your amp, and listen to it at the same time! You cannot do this with the "shunt method" and it is not recommended with the "meter in series with the plate" method. The problem with the "meter in series with the plate" method is that you have to unsolder the plate and then resolder. It is not good to play it with the meter hooked up, as you will be running the power of that amp into your meter. If you want to listen to it, you have to unsolder and resolder.

How hot you bias your output tubes is like how many jalapenos you like in your fajitas. It is a matter of personal taste. With the cathode resistor method, you could start by adjusting the bias voltage until your meter read .035 volts. Whether your meter reads .035 volts or 35 millivolts, either would convert directly to .035 amps, which is also expressed as 35 milliamps. When you use Ohms's law, (current equals voltage divided by resistance), the voltage converts directly to current because any time something is divided by one, the quotient is the same number. In the cathode resistor method, you are using a 1 ohm resistor. When you divide the .035 volts by 1 ohm to calculate current, you get .035 amps, which is 35 milliamps.

After you set it, play your guitar and listen to that for a while. Do you want it to break up at a lower volume or stay clean even at higher volume? If you want breakup to occur at lower volume, adjust the bias until your meter reads .04 volts, which converts directly to 40 milliamps of current going through the tube. On the other hand, if you wanted it to stay cleaner at higher volume, you might try adjusting to .03 volts (converts to 30 milliamps). With the cathode resistor method, you can listen / adjust / listen / adjust / etc. and get your amp where it feels right. Once you have documented how you like that amp, it will be a simple matter to bias it in the future.

I want to put a light in a footswitch that will be powered by a 9 volt battery (so I don't have to run any power down from the amp.) I tried it with a 13 volt bulb and the battery, a brand new Duracell, only lasted 1 hour. I am using a vintage style jeweled bezel fixture and bayonet-base incandescent lamp.

Using a 9 volt battery to power an incandescent bulb with the notion that it will be left on for long periods of time doesn't work well. Remember what happens to your flashlight if you leave it on for a long period of time.

The light bulb probably draws around 100 to 250 mA of current. Your battery cannot take this for a long time without running down. Why not try using a high-output LED? I know you have already designed your footswitch with the vintage Pilot assembly and bezel, but wait; you could retrofit a high-output white LED in series with a resistor and mount it so that the light from the LED illuminates the jeweled bezel. It would look cool and last a long time. This could easily be done.

To figure the resistor value:

The LED needs about 20 mA of current with 2 volts across it. That means the resistor has to drop 7 volts at 20 mA of current. If the resistor drops 7 volts from the applied voltage (9 volt battery), then that leaves 2 volts at 20mA to power the LED.

Ohm's law is R = E/I, where R is resistance, E is voltage, and I is current. Substituting our 20 mA (same as .020 amps) and our 7 volt voltage drop we get:

R = 7/ .02

Divide 7 by .02 and get: R= 350 ohms

Now lets look at the wattage needed.

W= E X I, where W is wattage, E is voltage and I is current. Substituting known values we get:

W= 7 X .02

W= .14

So this circuit is drawing .14 watts.

It is good design to multiply by two to get a 100% safety factor.

Times two for safety = .28 watts. A ¼ watt resistor would work, but I would probably use a ½ watt, which is the minimum wattage rating for resistors I will use in an amp.

There are also available low-current, super-brite LEDs that do well with only 10 mA of current. This would require a 700 ohm resistor because as the current is cut in half, the resistance required to drop those 7 extra volts would double from the 350 ohms we talked about earlier. You can do the equation if you like, but it will work out that when you half the current you end up doubling the resistance if the voltage is kept constant.

In a situation where Slo Blo fuses are blowing right away, have you ever used circuit breakers instead of using up all your "blow them once and throw them away" fuses?
If a Slo Blo fuse is blowing, there is a problem with the amp that should be addressed. It is not normal for an amp to blow fuses, especially Slo Blo fuses! A Slo Blo fuse can take a quick surge without blowing. That is why they are called Slo Blo fuses; they don't blow

unless they are continuously given more current than their rating.

With a tube amp, there are surges at times in the power supply that are only temporary. A Slo Blo fuse is perfect in this application. A circuit breaker on the other hand blows all at once as soon as the current rating is surpassed.

What do you recommend using to remove the old solder that is in heavy concentrations? For example: the grounding leads on a can type filter cap that are soldered to the chassis. In my experience, 30+ year-old solder can take some serious temperatures to melt. In addition to this, when it is spread across a large area, and is bonded to the chassis (a giant heat sink), it can be even more troublesome to melt. I do not have a desoldering station, only a typical Weller soldering station with a 40 Watt tip and a couple of solder suckers. I just figured I'd ask for your suggestion about how to get that old solder up when replacing can capacitors.

It's not the age of the solder that makes it hard to melt. It is the fact that the chassis acts as a heat sink when you are trying to melt the solder. I use a 175 watt soldering iron like the ones plumbers use for soldering copper pipe. It works great. A 40 watt iron will not work at all.

When using the 175 watt iron, be sure and let the iron heat up to full temperature before applying the iron to the solder to be melted.

I am having a tough time finding a certain metal tube. A (silicon) rectifier with part number S5207/1N2490. Any information you can shed on this little guy is welcome. It is supposed to be a substitute for the 6X4 rectifier tube. I have some great NOS 6X4's but I like the sound of this solid-state one.

The part you are describing looks like a vacuum tube, but fits into the socket for the 6X4 and replaces the tube. You do not have to have this format in order to use a solid-state rectifier. You could wire some 1N4007 silicon diodes across the 6X4 socket to replace the 6X4 with silicone rectifiers. This would give you the solid-state silicone diode sound.

Here's how to do it. The 6X4 is a seven-pin socket. Looking from the underside of your socket, pin #1 and pin #6 are the plates, while pin #7 is the cathode. Get a pair of 1N4007 silicon diodes and notice the banded side on them. That is the cathode of the diode. Take the banded side of each diode and have them go to pin #7. Take the other side of one diode (the side that is not the cathode is the anode) and have it go to pin #1. Have the anode side of the other diode go to pin #6. Make sure there is no 6X4 tube in the socket. You are ready to play!

I just had my amp overhauled and it sounds great. I am concerned that my amp is much louder as far as overall noise. Is there any particular reason? If I were playing loudly it would be a non-issue, but I play mostly alone and I can really hear it. Any thoughts as to why noise would increase?
You could have a noisy preamp tube, but maybe the amp is normal. Noise is relative. What would not be noticeable in a loud traffic jam may seem like an explosion at 2:00 AM in your bedroom. When you play alone, there is nothing else going on. The noise seems louder. Perhaps that same noise level would be unnoticeable in a gig situation. Perhaps the amp has more power and more gain now that it has been overhauled.

You mentioned a first-stage filtering scheme you had called a "totem pole," but I am not sure of what it was exactly. Could you take the time to explain it to me or point me in the right direction to a description?
The totem pole filter is when you use two filter caps in series and then put a 220K 1 watt resistor across each capacitor. The plus of one filter goes to your B+ voltage (pin #8 of a 5AR4 or 5U4 rectifier), and the minus end of the other one goes to ground.

This was done on the AB763 Super reverb and is usually done only on the FIRST filtering from the rectifier. It is used to get the voltage rating high enough for safety (700 volts rating when using two 350 volt caps in series). When you put the two identical caps in series, you double the voltage, but half the capacitance. For example, if you use two 100 mfd at 350 volt caps in series to make a totem pole; then the circuit "sees" 50 mfd at 700 volts.

I'm aware that the Fender/Vox article in the April VG was intended as a historical, rather than a technical overview, but in

the spirit of truth, I would like to point out the technical misinformation:
1. **The Fender Champ is the Class "A" circuit, the Vox AC30 is in fact a push/pull circuit**
2. **Class "A" means that the tube does not shut down for a half cycle as in class AB. It does not mean the "amp runs full up even with the volume turned down."**

With the volume turned down, the tubes in class A run an idle D.C. current, just like all other amps

My intent is not to nitpick, but let us not waste paper. Besides can't you guys just "Ask Gerald"?

You are correct, the Fender/Vox article was intended as a historical rather than technical overview. To clarify your question, both the Champ and the Vox AC30 run in Class A operation. The Champ is Single-ended, Cathode biased, Class "A" and the Vox is Push-Pull, Cathode biased, Class "A." Push-pull or single-ended has nothing to do with class of operation. Neither does the type of bias (cathode versus fixed). In a Class A amp, the output tube/tubes are not driven into cutoff during any part of the input cycle.

Not to be be nitpicky either, but your definition of Class AB in your question above is actually the definition for Class "B." Class "AB" is when the tube shuts down for LESS than a half cycle. Class "B" is when the tube shuts down for a half cycle. Class "B" is never used for audio.

When the writer said, "(the) amp runs full up even with the volume turned down," I believe he was referring to this: With a push-pull Class A circuit such as the Vox AC30, the total current drawn by the output stage is maximum current at idle. That is to say, the operating point for a Class "A," push-pull amp is chosen to permit power supply current to flow over the entire 360 degrees of the input signal cycle. Therefore, the average supply current does not vary with the signal level. In other words, with the Vox AC30, there will never be any more current drawn than the current the output tubes draw at idle. A non-technical, "easily understood by the layman" way to communicate this is to say, "the amp runs full up even when the volume is turned down."

Perhaps a more technically correct way to communicate this would be to say, "the output tubes draw maximum current, even when there is no signal."

Q & A

In your VG column "NOS and Current Tube Review," you mentioned that your Kendrick Black Gold 35 test amp's plate voltage runs about 470 volts. I recently acquired a '66 Super Reverb that's running about 480 volts on the plate and just a little less on the screen. Is it safe to use Tungsol 5881's at that voltage? How about Sylvania 5932's (cool tubes and odd looking)? The manuals have them both rated much less than 470 volts. Will using them wear them out quickly? Maybe I should save them for a lower voltage 6L6-type amp? Also, will the extra heater current of KT66's and EL37's burn my power transformer up? Does the Groove Tube KT66 run the same heater current as N.O.S. G.E.C (Genelex)? Is it 1.5 amps vs. .9 amps for 6L6GC?

Funny as it may seem, most tube guitar amplifier designs run voltages in excess of the manufacturers highest specified ratings. For instance, the G.E. Vacuum Tube Manual shows a 6V6 G.T.A. as having maximum plate voltage of 350 volts with a maximum of 315 volts on the screen. How many Blackface Deluxe Reverbs run between 420 and 450 volts? All of them! On an original 5F6A Bassman, plate voltages typically run 445 to 475 as a range. The Tungsol 5881 was the stock tube in that amplifier.

What wears tubes out quickly? Driving them hard; so certainly running higher voltages would wear them more quickly than running them at lower voltages. For that matter, you could save your tubes and use them only on special occasions, but you will always wear them out faster when you drive them harder.

To answer your heater current questions about the KT66's and EL37's and so forth, let me say this: I am a practical kind of guy. Being an amp designer myself, I look at things from a practical design standpoint. If your heater voltage is stable with a particular tube, then the transformer in that power supply can handle the heater current of those tubes. Most designs are over built by a factor of 100%. In other words, if we were planning to run a circuit that needed 5 amps of current; we would overbuild to, let us say, a 10-amp circuit. If you are running this circuit at five amps, this actually leaves quite a bit of leeway for using higher current tubes. In my opinion, the ultimate test would be to check the voltage when the tubes are in circuit. If the filament voltage is stable at 6.3 volts or better, then the power supply is handling the requirements of those tubes satisfactorily and I see no harm in using them in that particular circuit.

If the power transformer had a hard time with the current requirements, the filament voltage would drop, and this would be your tip-off that the transformer could not handle the heater requirements of that particular tube.

Your column has inspired me on a new project. My father bought a Westinghouse Radio/Phonograph back in 1958. I've held on to it over the years, since it had a nice mahogany cabinet. Would it be feasible to mount a ¼" jack to the wires from the tonearm and convert it to an amplifier input? The only schematic I have is the one mounted on the cabinet. The tube configuration is 12BE6, 12BA6, 12AX7 and two 35C5's. It is a Model HR 112 AN and states: 105-120 VAC 60 cycles 65 watts. It has one 6 inch and two 3½ inch speakers. I would be playing harp through this amp. Any help would be greatly appreciated.

Although I am not familiar with the Westinghouse Model HR 112 AN, I am familiar with tube configurations in amplifiers. This circuit is most likely a power transformerless design. How do I know? I know because the sum of the filament voltages is 107.8 volts and all of the tubes mentioned use .15 amps of filament current. In an American tube, the first number is the filament voltage. The 12BE6, 12BA6, and 12AX7 are all 12.6 volt filament heaters at .15 amps (or 150 ma). The 35C5 is of course a 35 volt filament at 150 ma. The only time this tube complement is ever used, is when the design runs all of the filaments in series — so that the design could be power transformerless. Why go power transformerless? Two reasons: First, power transformers cost money — perhaps the most expensive single component on an amp; and second, power transformerless amps can run on D.C. as well as A.C. current.

I would not recommend going ahead with your project. Here is why. In a power transformerless design, there is no B+ winding and you are using your A.C. mains as the B+ supply. This means one side of your A.C. line is connected directly to the chassis of your amplifier (as a chassis ground.) I can think of no greater shock hazard (except perhaps playing an electric guitar through a pair of ungrounded SVT heads while hanging out in the jacuzzi spa.) If you just cannot stand it and must proceed with the project anyway, here is how to do it. Don't misunderstand, I do not recommend pursuing this project any further, but if you choose to do so anyway, here are some pointers.

Isolate the input jack somehow. One way would be to use an input isolation transformer; perhaps a 1:1 ratio would do nicely. A Jensen input transformer would work well. These are the type of small transformers that are sometimes used on a tube mic preamp. You may have also used a similar transformer on a low-impedance mike cable when plugging into a high impedance device.

As a matter of fact, you could probably use a low to high impedance transformer (such as the one used on a mike cable adapter). These generally cost around $30. A low to high impedance transformer is not going to have a 1:1 ratio. Perhaps a 1:7 ratio would be realistic. This can still work anyway, just hook up the low impedance side to the input jack and the high impedance side to the circuit. You will actually get some gain out of a transformer hooked up this way.

Oftentimes, the phono input will have too much gain. If you find that the case with this project, try using a potentiometer between the secondary of the input transformer and the amp circuit — to control the gain — sort of like a pre-gain control. Perhaps a 1 megohm would be a good value to try. Remember, one end of the pot goes to the secondary of the input transformer, the other end goes to ground (as well as the other end of the secondary), and the wiper (center lead) goes to the circuit/amplifier.

Another possibility is to install a power transformer, simply using a 1:1 ratio A.C. Main Power transformer. (Use one rated at 300 voltamps or better). This would protect you from being "attached" to one side of the A.C. Mains. This type of transformer would be between the wall A.C. and the amplifier. Since it is a 1:1 power transformer, it will only have four wires. Two will go to the wall A.C. and two will go to the amplifier.

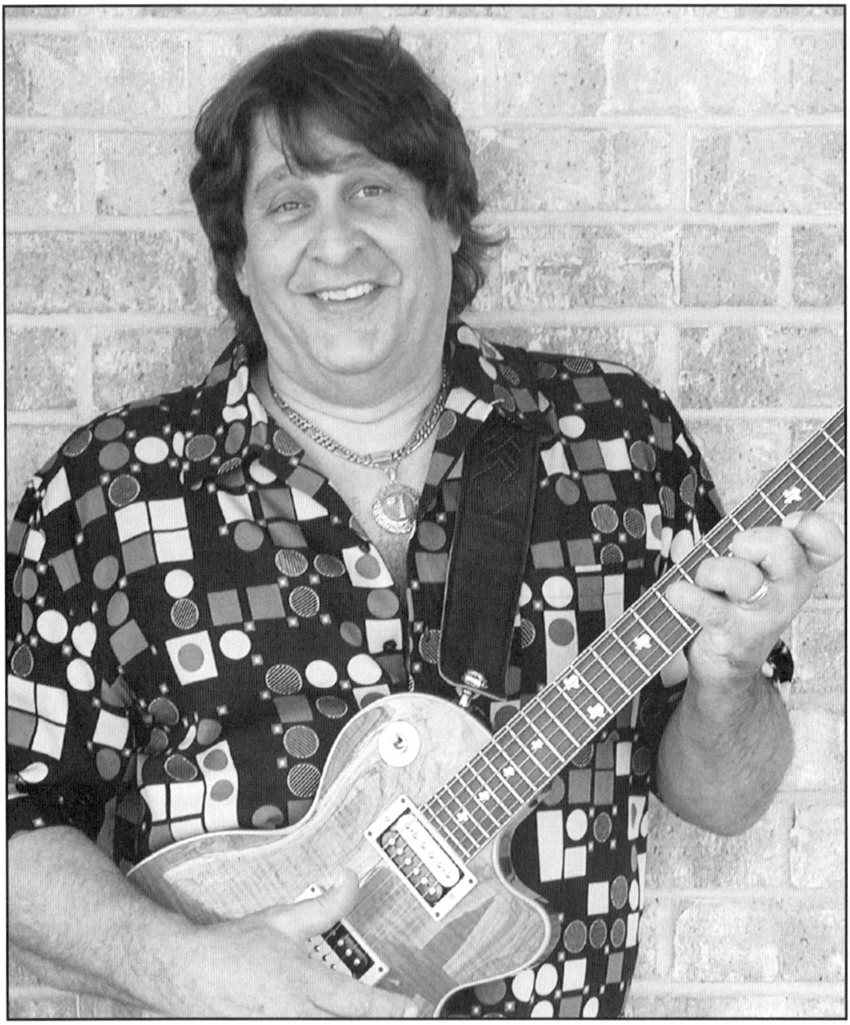

GERALD WEBER'S NEXT PHASE

VINTAGE GUITAR, 2004: BY WARD MEEKER

In the fall of 2003, Gerald Weber announced that his company, Kendrick Amplifiers, was winding down its efforts as a boutique amp builder. One of the first companies to get into the game, Weber started Kendrick by building vintage Fender-style amps before Fender started building reissues. But changing times and a changed focus brought Weber to the conclusion that his time and that of his employees, would be better spent in other areas.

In 2004, part of Weber's new focus will involve taking his much-discussed tube amp seminars on the road, perhaps to a city near you. We recently sat with the amp guru to check on his plans.

Vintage Guitar: What prompted the decision to stop building amplifiers?

It's kind of an evolution, really. When I started building tube amps in the 1980s, it was a hobby. I just wanted to sound great and no amplifiers in the music stores satisfied me. I started just building amps for myself, my son, and a few close friends. As people found out about what I was doing, I was drafted into the business. People sought me out.

Eventually, I went from part-time to full-time; I remember the day I went full-time — July 3, 1990. That was the day I decided to sell my meat companies and start building amps.

When I made the change, there were certain milestones and goals I wanted to achieve. Well, here I am 14 years later and I've already accomplished everything I set out to accomplish. So it's time to set some new goals and face new challenges.

Also, I want to expand my line of kit amps such that someone can buy one and have the fulfillment of "rolling their own." We'll offer different versions of each, depending on how much assembly the customer wants to do. In other words, a customer could purchase a kit to build just a chassis, the speaker cabinet to go with the chassis, and the actual speaker. We call this the "Kit and the Kaboodle." The cabinet can be covered with a baffleboard and grillcloth, and the speaker can be installed.

On the other hand, the customer may have cabinetmaking experience and may only want the chassis kit and the speaker. Whatever combination it takes to satisfy the customer is the combination we'll sell.

In the 13 years I've been writing amp articles and the "Ask Gerald" advice column for VG, I notice players are a lot hipper about their tube amps. With both of my books in the fifth printing and the 15 tube amp seminars I'll be hosting this year, it is only natural for me to start selling kits for those who are interested in building an amp of their own. The obvious advantage of building a kit is the fact that it's my design, and when it's built, there will be a predictable result.

We know how to design a terrific set of transformers. Our circuit designs and layout have been tweaked to the max. The customer will have fun building it and the amp won't just sound good; it will be exceptional.

And you'll be fulfilling all existing orders, right?
Lord o' mercy, yes! The entire second floor of the factory has amp chassis lined up in rows, in sequence of the oldest to the newest order.

I am blessed with great employees. My people are well-trained, and they're real good humans, as well. I am talking about the kind of people you would want with you if you were going to climb Everest. Some of them have been with me for 10 years.

These guys know what to do and they do it. And they're players, too. Working with a bunch of guitar slingers has huge advantages. Besides the obvious advantage of copping some OPLs (Ed. Note: that's Other People's Licks), we get into some groovin' impromptu jams when we're "testing" amps.

Will you altogether stop building amps? Or are you planning to continue to build on a limited basis?
I do not intend to take as many retail orders. To do so involves a huge percentage of my time, and I want to spend my time promoting my seminars and kits. My crew will continue building the Kendrick Jazz amp, the K-Spot 35 watt combo amp and a few other models. I

also have a distributor in Japan that has been with me for over a decade, and I'll continue to supply him. This is enough business to keep my regular people working and me not have to devote much time to Kendrick factory.

After my orders are filled, I promised to design a special amp for my good friend and Texas guitar hero, Mark Pollock. Besides producing the Dallas Guitar Show, Mark is Michael Stevens' business manager. Mark will be selling Mike's hand-made guitars, I'll design the Mark Pollock signature amplifier, and my talented staff will build them for Mark to sell along with the guitars.

In recent years, you've been diversifying, expanding your amp kit line, selling the German-made Klotz line of instrument cables, and doing more of your amp seminars. Talk about the reasons for each.

It's so funny... If someone had told me 10 years ago that I would be selling cable, I would've called them a quack!

Over a decade ago, a business aquaintance gave me a Klotz cable as a gift. Of course, it blew my mind. To get to use it, I had to arm wrestle the 17 guitar players who worked for me at the time. Everyone wanted it because of the obvious tonal difference.

So I contacted my German distributor for Kendrick and was able to locate the company. I bought a couple of 100-meter spools and used it to wire my ADAT studio. Plus, employees used some for themselves. As time went on, eight of our employees eventually had 16-track home studios, so we'd order cable from time to time.

About a year ago, I called to order more, and Klotz asked if I wanted to be their American distributor. I thought it was a miracle they didn't have one in the U.S. — they have distribution in 42 countries. Besides guitar cable, they make about 100 other types; cabling for television broadcast, digital stuff, and much more.

I really couldn't see myself selling cable, but I could see this as an opportunity because I knew it was superior. And my customers ate it up. I sold tens of thousands of dollars worth of if and, "poof!," I was drafted into the cable business.

And the seminars?

I got the idea to do the amp seminars because my phone rang all day with people wanting information about their amps. For the first four or five years I was in business, I'd take every call and help every person, even if it meant having to stay late to do my own work.

Well, that got old after a few years because I would stay on the phone all day helping people, and then when everyone at the factory went home, I'd stay and work until midnight.

So I began hosting the Tube Amp Seminar, where people of all experience levels could come to my factory in Texas and have their concerns addressed in a very interactive format. We've done seminars now for seven years, but only a couple of times a year, and only in Texas. In 2004, I am going to be hosting seminars in 15 major cities across the U.S. This will give people a chance to do the seminar in their area — no having to fly to Texas, rent a car, get a hotel, etc.

What can we expect if we attend one?
Each is different, depending on who's in the room and what they want to get from it. In fact, when you enroll, you send me an e-mail or letter with a description of your experience level, and what you intend to get from the seminar. Then I can make it a point to unfold the seminar in your direction. Everyone gets what they came for.

One thing is certain: you can expect to meet some other very cool people who are "into" tube guitar amps. You can count on having more than one "Aha!" moment. And you can count on exchanging contact information for networking with some of these hardcore tone addicts.

Whenever possible, the seminars are scheduled to coincide with a major guitar show in the same city. That way, a participant can do the seminar on Saturday and go to the guitar show on Sunday. It's what us addicts call a "double fix!" And who knows? Maybe you'll find an amp or two that needs some love.

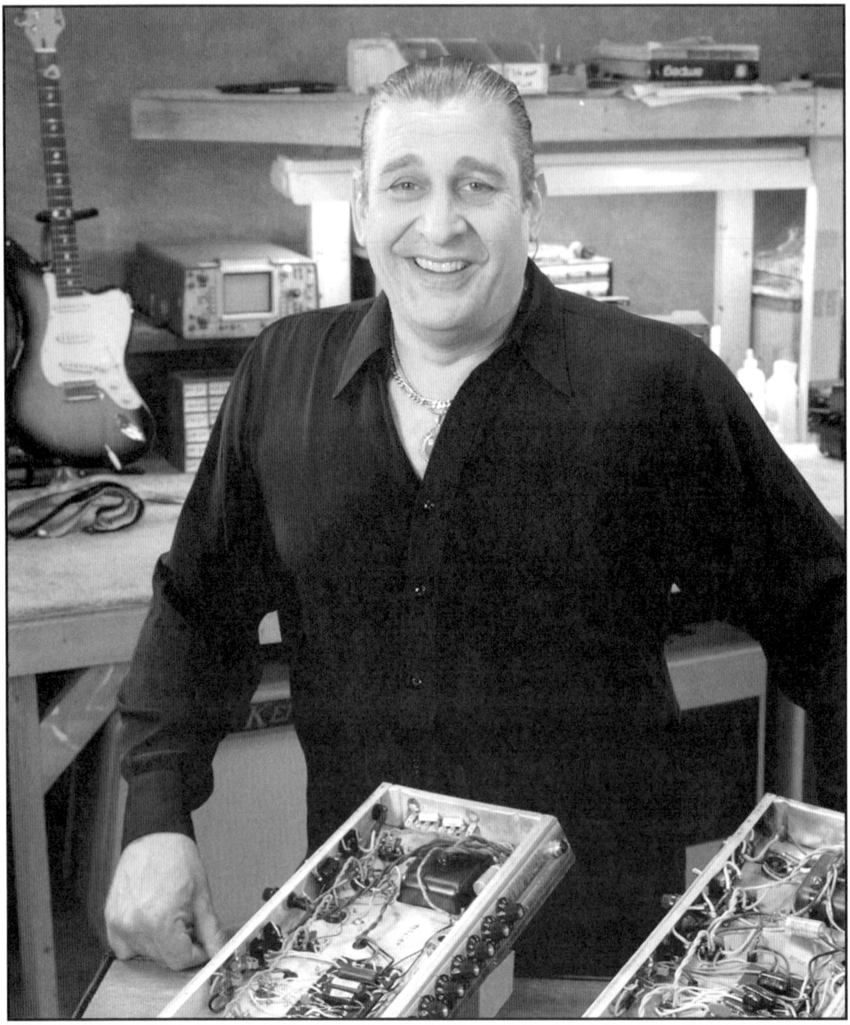

A FINAL WORD FROM THE AUTHOR

Dear Friend,

   Although we may have never met, we have a unique relationship. If you got this far in the book, you must be a person that loves great guitar tone and I can relate to that. I started playing electric guitar over 40 years ago and my life has been consumed with tube guitar tone. I invite you to visit my website www.kendrick-amplifiers.com. If you would like to further your tube amp knowledge, I have written several books and produced numerous instructional videos about Tube Guitar Amplifiers. I produce several Amp Camps per year at my ranch in Texas and I host Tube Guitar Amplifier Seminars all over the US and some cities in Canada. Whenever I am not doing that, I am almost always at my shop restoring vintage amps and helping people with their tone. If you are near the beautiful hill country in Texas, I invite you to visit me at my shop. Also, I would love to meet you in a seminar or Amp Camp soon. I invite you to communicate with me.

Gerald J. Weber Jr.
El Presidente,
Kendrick Amplifiers
(512) 932-3130

INDEX

A

AA864, 407, 408, 409, 464, 465
AB, 77, 113, 114, 116, 136, 313, 279, 300, 380, 402, 407, 493, 509
AB165, 407, 409
AB763, 339, 419, 508
AC100, 319
AC15, 474, 494, 495
AC30, 21, 77, 80, 114, 116, 135, 141, 293, 297, 349, 368, 374, 475, 476, 480, 481, 509
Allen Bradley, 255
Alnico, 127, 214, 219, 396, 442
Altec Lansing, 457
Alternating Current, 66, 115, 335
Ampeg, 19, 80, 318, 257, 258, 449, 453, 456, 457, 460, 473, 480, 481, 493
Amperex, 462, 499
Astatic, 285

B

B15, 453
Bakelite, 461
Bandmaster, 246, 292, 297, 344, 364, 397, 479, 495
Bandmaster Reverb, 297
Beatles, 252
Bias, 22, 28, 29, 40, 57, 59, 65, 69, 70, 73, 74, 77, 89, 99, 101, 107, 113, 115, 116, 122, 133, 134, 135, 136, 137, 139, 140, 141, 142, 143, 154, 175, 187, 188, 229, 232, 253, 254, 255, 309, 310, 311, 312, 313, 315, 316, 317, 318, 319, 258, 259, 279, 288, 336, 351, 353, 357, 358, 361, 365, 367, 371, 372, 382, 384, 389, 390, 391, 392, 394, 395, 396, 402, 403, 404, 406, 407, 410, 411, 412, 418, 419, 420, 422, 424, 425, 426, 428, 430, 442, 450, 457, 458, 467, 468, 471, 475, 477, 478, 489, 498, 499, 504, 505, 509
Bias Adjustment Circuit, 316
Bias Supply Circuit, 315, 410
Biasing, 28, 29, 37, 39, 54, 59, 70, 89, 97, 109, 115, 116, 117, 1, 133, 134, 135, 140, 141, 142, 184, 255, 309, 268, 292, 353, 357, 371, 372, 384, 392, 403, 407, 450, 451, 464, 504
Black Gold, 187, 188, 368, 370, 425, 458, 483, 510
Blackface, 27, 32, 33, 34, 48, 55, 58, 72, 73, 79, 81, 88, 93, 114, 135, 136, 140, 154, 184, 214, 217, 239, 242, 253, 303, 305, 306, 257, 259, 261, 262, 263, 264, 273, 275, 277, 279, 286, 293, 297, 326, 332, 333, 343, 348, 361, 363, 365, 370, 390, 391, 392, 399, 401, 415, 418, 423, 427, 428, 429, 438, 439, 440, 448, 464, 510
Blackframe, 188, 484, 488
Bobbin, 23, 199, 254
Bogen, 410, 447
Boogie, 450, 451, 452, 455, 456
Bypass Capacitor, 79, 108, 110, 115, 141, 143, 149, 174, 175, 311, 269, 365, 366, 382, 458, 466

C

Cathode, 39, 59, 69, 70, 74, 75, 77, 79, 87, 108, 109, 110, 115, 116, 120, 121, 122, 133, 134, 135, 136, 137, 139, 140, 141, 142, 143, 149, 154, 168, 169, 173, 174, 175, 229, 233, 245, 304, 305, 309, 310, 311, 312, 258, 268, 269, 270, 279, 287, 288, 298, 299, 324, 325, 326, 331, 335, 336, 338, 351, 352, 353, 355, 357, 365, 366, 367, 368, 369, 371, 372, 383, 385, 389, 390, 400, 402, 403, 404, 412, 413, 418, 422, 424, 425, 426, 430, 438, 439, 443, 457, 458, 464, 469, 473, 475, 476, 494, 495, 496, 499, 502, 503, 504, 505, 507, 508, 509
Celestion, 449, 468, 476

Index 523

Champ, 87, 116, 309, 310, 311, 287, 357, 369, 370, 385, 397, 400, 420, 427, 429, 430, 431, 438, 439, 509
Class A, 73, 74, 75, 77, 113, 114, 116, 136, 313, 285, 287, 288, 292, 371, 419, 428, 475, 493, 494, 509
Class AB, 77, 113, 114, 116, 136, 313, 493, 509
Climax, 183, 184, 242, 368, 425, 494
Clip, 101, 175, 235, 259, 351, 371, 372, 460, 472, 473, 475
Coupling Capacitor, 79, 108, 110, 149, 150, 153, 154, 174, 240, 263, 264, 348, 370, 460
Current, 20, 22, 29, 40, 54, 65, 66, 67, 69, 70, 71, 74, 75, 76, 77, 85, 86, 88, 89, 98, 99, 102, 107, 109, 113, 115, 116, 117, 119, 121, 122, 126, 127, 133, 134, 135, 137, 139, 140, 141, 142, 147, 148, 149, 153, 155, 161, 163, 164, 167, 168, 174, 175, 179, 180, 181, 183, 184, 187, 188, 189, 191, 192, 197, 200, 206, 207, 208, 209, 211, 212, 213, 214, 227, 231, 232, 234, 235, 239, 240, 242, 252, 253, 304, 310, 313, 318, 286, 288, 292, 294, 324, 331, 335, 336, 338, 343, 344, 345, 350, 351, 352, 356, 357, 358, 365, 366, 367, 368, 372, 374, 379, 382, 383, 385, 386, 387, 388, 390, 391, 392, 393, 397, 398, 401, 402, 403, 404, 406, 412, 414, 415, 418, 419, 421, 422, 424, 425, 428, 429, 431, 432, 433, 437, 438, 439, 448, 450, 451, 453, 454, 455, 462, 465, 467, 470, 475, 477, 479, 486, 489, 490, 491, 492, 493, 494, 495, 496, 499, 500, 501, 502, 504, 505, 506, 507, 509, 510, 511

D

Daisy Chain, 431
Deluxe, 27, 33, 80, 116, 135, 236, 240, 241, 303, 305, 306, 259, 279, 280, 281, 282, 287, 292, 297, 342, 357, 363, 365, 383, 388, 392, 394, 395, 396, 398, 399, 413, 417, 419, 423, 432, 440, 451, 458, 460, 478, 494, 510
Deluxe Reverb, 303, 279, 280, 292, 297, 392, 394, 396, 398, 423, 478, 494
DeVille, 410, 411, 412
Diode, 91, 92, 120, 121, 122, 137, 140, 141, 163, 235, 254, 310, 311, 315, 316, 318, 319, 336, 338, 402, 410, 419, 422, 425, 450, 451, 467, 472, 473, 507, 508
Direct Current, 66, 335
Dremel, 258
Dual Showman, 88, 241, 392, 447

E

E34L, 183, 184, 356, 494
EH-150, 433
EL37, 28, 181, 189, 192, 292, 355, 356, 510
EL84, 141, 355, 356, 362, 475, 494, 495
Electro-Harmonix LPB1, 303
Epiphone, 440
Explorer, 440

F

Fabulous Thunderbirds, 213, 285
FANE, 362, 396, 416
Fender Reverb, 73, 162, 389, 405
Filter Capacitor, 73, 316, 259, 276, 293, 294, 325, 331, 343, 374, 413
Fluke, 99, 231, 243
Full-Wave Bridge Rectifier, 121, 337, 339, 502
Full-Wave Bridge Rectifier Power Supply, 337
Full-Wave Center-Tap Rectifier Power, 336, 337
Full-Wave Center-Tap Rectifier Power Supply, 336, 337
Full-Wave Economy Power Supply, 338, 339

G

GA20 RVT, 439
GA30RV, 344, 345
GA40, 432
GA5, 433 ,438, 439
GA70, 344
GA75, 434
GA77RET, 435
GA88, 344
GE Vacuum Tube Manual, 428
Gemini II, 460
Genelex, 188, 189, 190, 191, 292, 355, 510
Germanium, 472
Gibson, 19, 77, 135, 257, 258, 344, 345, 432, 433, 435, 436, 437, 438, 439, 440, 458, 459, 484

Goodman Alnico Magnet, 219
Grid, 69, 70, 74, 77, 79, 99, 108, 113, 115, 133, 134, 135, 136, 137, 139, 140, 141, 154, 155, 173, 174, 175, 184, 188, 233, 234, 236, 239, 240, 241, 242, 243, 244, 245, 246, 247, 255, 305, 310, 311, 312, 257, 258, 270, 274, 275, 276, 279, 282, 324, 325, 326, 330, 331, 332, 333, 341, 342, 347, 353, 354, 355, 368, 371, 373, 390, 400, 401, 402, 403, 410, 427, 430, 435, 438, 440, 443, 445, 469, 496, 498, 504
Grid Resistor, 79, 174, 258, 270, 305, 325
Ground, 22, 39, 46, 47, 59, 72, 73, 80, 98, 110, 111, 115, 121, 122, 134, 135, 140, 141, 143, 149, 150, 151, 154, 162, 163, 164, 169, 207, 223, 233, 234, 236, 242, 243, 245, 246, 254, 257, 258, 270, 273, 276, 277, 287, 292, 305, 306, 310, 311, 312, 316, 318, 324, 325, 326, 331, 333, 335, 336, 338, 339, 343, 349, 354, 363, 367, 368, 373, 381, 382, 384, 386, 390, 391, 393, 395, 398, 400, 402, 403, 404, 414, 417, 419, 420, 425, 426, 427, 429, 430, 433, 435, 437, 445, 448, 450, 451, 457, 466, 467, 469, 473, 474, 477, 482, 483, 484, 489, 490, 496, 498, 502, 508, 512
GZ34, 87, 162, 167, 168, 169, 181, 253, 288, 392, 400, 401, 405, 406, 427, 434, 447, 475, 502

H

Half-Wave, 120, 121, 122, 335, 336
Half-Wave Rectifier Power Supply, 335
Hammond, 329, 330, 488, 490, 491
Harvard, 413
Heater, 65, 108, 168, 173, 234, 259, 298, 331, 343, 355, 356, 398, 428, 471, 489, 491, 493, 501, 510, 511
Henry, 387, 403
Hertz, 22, 51, 330, 337, 350, 366, 382, 383, 414, 429, 431, 462
Hot Rod, 410
Hum, 25, 46, 47, 58, 59, 69, 76, 85, 86, 126, 127, 140, 155, 156, 161, 173, 174, 224, 232, 233, 234, 235, 316, 257, 258, 259, 285, 324, 329, 330, 331, 332, 343, 344, 353, 381, 386, 387, 390, 392, 394, 395, 398, 405, 413, 414, 418, 419, 429, 431, 432, 435, 455, 457, 467, 496, 501, 502
Hz, 199, 233, 234, 316

I

Impedance, 19, 40, 71, 75, 79, 86, 127, 128, 134, 141, 174, 197, 198, 199, 200, 205, 206, 207, 208, 209, 210, 211, 212, 213, 214, 231, 234, 241, 305, 280, 291, 295, 368, 393, 403, 407, 411, 422, 423, 429, 447, 448, 449, 453, 454, 459, 462, 467, 468, 472, 476, 477, 478, 479, 480, 481, 482, 483, 484, 485, 486, 491, 492, 494, 502, 503, 512

J

JBL, 33, 291, 348, 372, 457, 484, 485
Jensen, 188, 372, 384, 396, 443, 457, 512
Jim Marshall, 167, 168, 341, 342
Jimmie Vaughan, 285
Joe Barden, 291
Jumper Wire, 99, 231, 233, 234, 312, 299, 356, 404, 435, 455, 483, 497

K

Kendrick Buffalo Pfuz Overdrive, 473
Kilohertz, 239
Kinkless Tetrode, 292, 355
Korg, 410
KT66, 28, 139, 188, 189, 190, 191, 192, 292, 355, 356, 510
KT77, 292
KT88, 292
KT90, 292

L

Lab Series L5, 448
Laney, 471
Les Paul, 432, 468

M

Magnatone, 267, 268, 269, 270, 271, 497
Mark I, 451
Mark II, 451
MARSHALL, 21, 38, 75, 76, 81, 109, 110, 121, 128, 137, 140, 167, 168, ,

211, 213, 257, 261, 263, 269, 297, 341, 342, 344, 345, 349, 355, 361, 369, 448, 462, 463, 464, 465, 466, 467, 468, 469, 470, 471, 472, 478, 480, 488, 499
Mallory, 149, 150, 262, 277, 348, 372
Mesa Boogie, 315, 450, 452, 455, 456

N

NOS, 55, 184, 188, 189, 190, 191, 344, 354, 355

O

Ohm, 25, 40, 67, 70, 71, 72, 86, 87, 102, 128, 143, 168, 169, 175, 197, 198, 199, 200, 205, 206, 207, 208, 209, 210, 211, 212, 213, 214, 227, 229, 239, 245, 252, 304, 268, 269, 276, 281, 287, 291, 297, 298, 331, 343, 345, 352, 353, 356, 365, 366, 367, 368, 369, 371, 373, 385, 386, 390, 391, 393, 394, 395, 396, 397, 398, 404, 412, 413, 418, 420, 421, 422, 425, 426, 429, 430, 431, 437, 439, 444, 447, 448, 449, 454, 457, 459, 462, 465, 466, 468, 469, 476, 478, 479, 480, 481, 482, 483, 484, 485, 486, 488, 489, 490, 492, 494, 495, 498, 499, 500, 502, 504, 505, 506, 507, 510
Output, 19, 20, 21, 25, 26, 27, 28, 29, 34, 37, 40, 48, 54, 57, 58, 59, 67, 70, 73, 74, 75, 76, 77, 78, 79, 80, 81, 86, 88, 89, 91, 92, 93, 94, 97, 99, 101, 107, 110, 111, 113, 114, 115, 116, 117, 119, 120, 125, 133, 134, 135, 136, 137, 139, 140, 141, 142, 143, 154, 163, 167, 168, 174, 181, 183, 184, 187, 188, 197, 198, 199, 206, 210, 211, 213, 224, 225, 232, 233, 234, 235, 236, 240, 242, 247, 253, 255, 258, 259, 273, 276, 277, 280, 281, 287, 288, 291, 292, 293, 294, 303, 304, 309, 310, 311, 312, 313, 315, 316, 317, 318, 325, 330, 331, 333, 336, 338, 341, 342, 343, 344, 345, 348, 349, 350, 351, 354, 355, 357, 358, 359, 363, 364, 366, 369, 370, 371, 379, 380, 381, 386, 387, 388, 390, 391, 393, 395, 396, 397, 398, 400, 401, 403, 404, 407, 409, 411, 412, 413, 414, 415, 419, 420, 421, 422, 424, 425, 426, 427, 428, 429, 430, 431, 432, 439, 441, 442, 443, 447, 448, 449, 452, 453, 455, 456, 457, 458, 459, 460, 462, 463, 464, 465, 467, 468, 469, 470, 471, 472, 475, 476, 477, 478, 479, 480, 481, 482, 483, 485, 489, 490, 491, 493, 494, 495, 496, 498, 499, 500, 501, 503, 504, 505, 509
Oxford, 457

P

Parasitic, 34, 233, 235, 236, 239, 240, 241, 242, 243, 244, 245, 247, 257, 273, 325, 326, 330, 332, 333, 342, 343, 411, 429
Peak Inverse Voltage, 92, 164, 336, 422
Perfboard, 311
Phase Inverter, 25, 40, 58, 77, 79, 113, 114, 122, 150, 175, 233, 234, 235, 242, 247, 268, 276, 279, 280, 281, 287, 294, 298, 299, 303, 304, 305, 306, 309, 341, 342, 343, 348, 350, 352, 369, 370, 373, 380, 394, 395, 406, 407, 409, 429, 433, 434, 439, 441, 451, 458, 459, 464, 473, 498
Philips, 355
Plexi, 110, 140, 469, 470
Power Attenuator, 27, 455, 459, 503
Preamp, 19, 25, 28, 37, 38, 39, 40, 48, 52, 55, 58, 59, 69, 73, 74, 75, 77, 88, 93, 94, 97, 98, 107, 108, 109, 110, 111, 113, 114, 119, 121, 122, 125, 134, 149, 154, 161, 173, 174, 175, 176, 179, 188, 225, 229, 233, 235, 240, 243, 245, 246, 253, 257, 258, 262, 263, 264, 267, 268, 269, 270, 276, 279, 281, 282, 286, 287, 292, 293, 294, 298, 299, 303, 305, 309, 310, 324, 325, 326, 331, 336, 343, 344, 350, 351, 353, 354, 357, 358, 363, 364, 370, 371, 373, 374, 382, 383, 384, 385, 387, 394, 395, 399, 400, 401, 405, 406, 413, 414, 415, 419, 420, 427, 429, 432, 434, 435, 440, 441, 449, 450, 451, 455, 457, 458, 459, 460, 462, 466, 472, 496, 497, 498, 499, 500, 501, 508, 512
Preamp Cathode Resistor, 268
Preamp Tubes, 25, 28, 38, 39, 40, 58, 59, 69, 73, 74, 88, 93, 94, 97, 121, 122, 134, 149, 174, 179, 225, 235, 245, 268, 270, 276, 286, 292, 294, 351, 354, 357, 364, 370, 384, 394, 395, 399, 401, 406, 415, 427, 432, 441,

449, 450, 451, 455, 457, 499, 500, 501
Princeton, 114, 318, 287, 365, 388, 423, 424, 426, 458, 460
Princeton Reverb, 114, 423, 426
Powerglide, 472
Pro, 246, 297, 363, 374, 384, 385, 399, 414, 421, 428, 458, 479, 494
Pro Reverb, 297, 363, 399, 428, 479
Proper Grounding, 45, 46, 273, 276

R

RCA, 19, 55, 184, 189, 190, 210, 381, 386, 396, 426, 427, 437, 461, 493, 495, 500
RCA Receiving Tube Manual, 493
Rectifier, 21, 25, 28, 37, 38, 54, 59, 66, 87, 91, 92, 94, 107, 116, 120, 121, 122, 148, 161, 162, 163, 164, 167, 168, 169, 180, 225, 251, 252, 253, 267, 276, 288, 293, 294, 309, 310, 311, 313, 315, 316, 317, 318, 331, 335, 336, 337, 338, 339, 344, 350, 364, 380, 385, 387, 392, 400, 401, 402, 405, 406, 410, 414, 415, 421, 422, 427, 429, 430, 432, 434, 444, 447, 450, 451, 455, 456, 476, 477, 489, 493, 494, 496, 497, 498, 499, 500, 501, 502, 503, 507, 508
Resistance, 65, 66, 67, 70, 71, 72, 80, 102, 116, 149, 175, 197, 198, 199, 205, 206, 207, 208, 210, 211, 214, 227, 229, 236, 242, 243, 245, 254, 304, 305, 306, 316, 317, 318, 300, 324, 331, 343, 349, 352, 353, 364, 365, 366, 367, 368, 369, 386, 389, 391, 403, 404, 410, 421, 425, 431, 438, 445, 448, 457, 485, 490, 502, 505, 506
Resistor, 25, 28, 66, 67, 69, 71, 72, 73, 75, 78, 79, 98, 99, 108, 109, 110, 111, 115, 116, 122, 134, 135, 137, 140, 141, 142, 143, 149, 169, 174, 175, 227, 229, 232, 233, 244, 245, 252, 254, 258, 262, 263, 264, 267, 268, 269, 270, 274, 275, 276, 280, 281, 282, 286, 287, 288, 293, 294, 297, 298, 299, 300, 303, 304, 305, 306, 310, 311, 312, 315, 316, 317, 318, 324, 325, 331, 333, 339, 342, 343, 344, 345, 348, 349, 350, 351, 352, 353, 354, 357, 358, 359, 362, 363, 364, 365, 366, 367, 368, 369, 371, 372, 373, 374, 381, 383, 384,

385, 389, 390, 391, 393, 397, 398, 399, 400, 401, 402, 404, 406, 407, 409, 410, 412, 413, 419, 420, 421, 422, 424, 425, 426, 429, 430, 435, 437, 438, 439, 444, 445, 446, 447, 451, 455, 456, 457, 460, 463, 465, 466, 467, 468, 469, 475, 476, 477, 482, 488, 489, 490, 495, 498, 504, 505, 506, 508
Reverb, 21, 46, 48, 55, 58, 73, 75, 81, 108, 114, 135, 140, 161, 162, 208, 213, 223, 224, 229, 239, 246, 262, 273, 275, 279, 280, 288, 292, 297, 303, 309, 329, 330, 336, 339, 344, 353, 363, 364, 379, 380, 381, 384, 389, 391, 392, 393, 394, 396, 397, 398, 399, 401, 405, 415, 418, 419, 420, 423, 426, 427, 428, 431, 435, 436, 437, 444, 448, 456, 457, 464, 469, 473, 478, 479, 494, 495, 497, 508, 510
Reverb Unit, 75, 336, 344, 389, 401, 405, 435, 448
Reverberocket, 456, 457
Reverberocket II, 457
Reverberocket III, 457
RMS, 199, 336, 337, 338, 339

S

Screen Supply Voltage, 344
Secondary, 76, 77, 78, 119, 120, 121, 122, 162, 163, 408, 411, 420, 422, 423, 439, 443, 453, 470, 478, 479, 480, 482, 483, 489, 490, 491, 492, 493, 494, 512
Showman, 88, 197, 198, 211, 212, 213, 235, 241, 297, 335, 336, 337, 338, 339, 388, 392, 447
SILVERTONE, 25, 27, 441, 442, 443, 444, 445
Single-ended, 73, 74, 75, 76, 77, 88, 114, 116, 313, 292, 371, 429, 430, 432, 501, 509
Skylark, 433, 438, 439
Sovtek, 39, 183, 184, 189, 190, 191, 192, 354, 355, 384, 439
Speaker, 26, 27, 33, 37, 40, 41, 42, 45, 48, 49, 52, 53, 70, 71, 85, 86, 92, 93, 107, 125, 126, 127, 128, 147, 149, 187, 188, 192, 198, 199, 200, 205, 206, 207, 208, 209, 210, 211, 212, 213, 214, 217, 218, 219, 224, 233, 234, 236, 239, 240, 242, 254, 255, 257, 285, 288, 291, 294, 295, 304,

306, 309, 324, 348, 356, 357, 358, 359, 362, 371, 372, 379, 380, 384, 385, 386, 387, 392, 393, 396, 398, 409, 411, 412, 417, 420, 428, 431, 439, 440, 442, 443, 448, 449, 450, 452, 453, 454, 455, 458, 459, 465, 469, 470, 476, 478, 479, 480, 481, 482, 483, 484, 485, 486, 491, 492, 494, 495, 503
Sprague Atom, 255, 418, 433
Sprague Orange Drops, 277
Substitution, 94, 140, 224, 231, 294, 315, 442
Sunn, 345, 485
Super, 81, 135, 140, 208, 239, 240, 246, 262, 288, 297, 329, 348, 364, 379, 380, 384, 391, 393, 397, 420, 424, 431, 458, 470, 495, 496, 508, 510
Super Lead, 470
Super Reverb, 81, 135, 140, 208, 239, 246, 288, 297, 329, 364, 379, 380, 384, 391, 393, 431, 495, 508, 510
Super Reverb Twin, 329
SUNN, 345, 485
Supro, 19, 457
SVT, 79, 473, 481, 512
Sylvania, 189, 190, 191, 451, 510

T

Telefunken, 499
Texas Crude, 109, 142, 213, 448, 458
Tolex, 408, 409, 418
Tone-Master, 468
Transformer, 19, 20, 22, 37, 38, 40, 66, 75, 76, 77, 78, 86, 92, 107, 108, 113, 114, 116, 119, 122, 136, 141, 148, 153, 161, 162, 163, 168, 169, 180, 187, 188, 190, 197, 198, 199, 210, 211, 212, 213, 225, 232, 233, 235, 240, 242, 253, 310, 318, 258, 276, 288, 291, 292, 293, 294, 324, 325, 329, 330, 331, 335, 336, 337, 338, 339, 344, 350, 371, 379, 380, 382, 383, 385, 386, 387, 388, 391, 393, 394, 395, 396, 405, 408, 409, 411, 413, 414, 418, 419, 420, 422, 423, 425, 427, 428, 430, 431, 434, 437, 439, 442, 443, 450, 453, 454, 457, 460, 462, 465, 467, 469, 470, 471, 472, 474, 475, 476, 477, 478, 479, 480, 482, 483, 488, 489, 490, 491, 492, 493, 494, 495, 500, 501, 502, 510, 511, 512
Transistor, 20, 22, 224, 398, 454

Tremolux, 494
Tung Sol, 103, 189, 190, 355, 396
Tweed, 20, 27, 75, 78, 79, 80, 87, 88, 116, 135, 140, 149, 167, 208, 236, 240, 241, 242, 251, 252, 253, 257, 261, 262, 263, 279, 280, 281, 282, 287, 293, 309, 325, 342, 348, 357, 363, 364, 365, 393, 394, 395, 399, 400, 412, 413, 416, 417, 419, 429, 431, 432, 438, 439, 442, 443, 451, 458, 460, 478
Tweed Bassman, 208
Tweed Deluxe, 27, 80, 116, 135, 236, 240, 241, 279, 280, 281, 287, 342, 357, 363, 365, 395, 413, 419, 432, 451, 460
Tweed Twin, 167, 242, 293, 325
Twin, 21, 33, 45, 48, 55, 116, 135, 140, 161, 167, 168, 173, 199, 213, 229, 242, 273, 291, 293, 297, 325, 329, 339, 341, 348, 379, 380, 382, 383, 387, 388, 392, 404, 415, 418, 419, 420, 426, 444, 452, 464, 465
Twin Reverb, 48, 161, 213, 229, 273, 297, 339, 418, 419, 420, 426, 464

U

Univox, 497

V

Vactrol, 437, 438
Vibrato, 19, 39, 48, 58, 77, 236, 241, 275, 279, 281, 286, 297, 298, 299, 303, 305, 374, 380, 382, 401, 403, 405, 419, 423, 436, 442
Vibro Champ, 400, 420, 427, 438, 439
Vibrolux, 297, 415, 494
Vibrolux Reverb, 297, 415
Vibroverb, 318, 291, 494
Voltage, 25, 39, 46, 59, 65, 66, 67, 68, 69, 70, 71, 72, 73, 74, 75, 77, 78, 79, 81, 87, 92, 98, 102, 107, 108, 109, 110, 111, 113, 114, 115, 116, 119, 120, 121, 122, 134, 135, 136, 137, 139, 140, 141, 142, 147, 148, 149, 150, 154, 155, 161, 162, 163, 164, 169, 173, 175, 176, 188, 190, 197, 198, 199, 200, 207, 209, 211, 212, 227, 229, 233, 235, 244, 246, 251, 252, 254, 255, 259, 267, 268, 270, 279, 280, 282, 286, 287, 288, 292, 293, 294, 299, 304, 305, 310, 311, 312, 313, 315, 316, 317, 319, 324,

326, 336, 337, 338, 339, 344, 345, 353, 354, 355, 356, 357, 358, 362, 363, 364, 365, 366, 367, 368, 370, 371, 373, 374, 381, 382, 383, 384, 385, 386, 390, 391, 392, 395, 396, 397, 400, 401, 402, 403, 404, 405, 406, 407, 410, 411, 414, 418, 419, 420, 421, 422, 424, 425, 426, 427, 428, 429, 430, 431, 432, 434, 435, 438, 439, 444, 447, 448, 450, 451, 453, 454, 455, 457, 458, 459, 465, 466, 467, 468, 471, 472, 473, 475, 476, 488, 490, 491, 492, 493, 494, 495, 496, 497, 498, 499, 502, 504, 505, 506, 508, 510, 511
Vox, 77, 79, 80, 81, 114, 116, 128, 135, 141, 211, 219, 258, 293, 297, 319, 329, 349, 362, 368, 374, 474, 475, 476, 480, 481, 486, 494, 499, 508, 509

W

Wattage, 27, 28, 65, 66, 125, 141, 167, 168, 197, 199, 200, 207, 209, 213, 227, 229, 324, 385, 404, 420, 433, 454, 475, 485, 488, 502, 503, 506
Weller, 100, 507